Arnold O. Beckman
One Hundred Years of Excellence

Arnold O. Beckman
One Hundred Years of Excellence

Arnold Thackray
and Minor Myers, jr.

Foreword by
James D. Watson

Chemical Heritage Foundation
Philadelphia

Special folio volume in the Chemical Heritage Foundation Series in Innovation and Entrepreneurship. The series records, analyzes, and makes known the human story of chemical achievement. Other volumes in this series:

Everybody Wins! A Life in Free Enterprise
by Gordon Cain

Pharmaceutical Innovation: Revolutionizing Human Health
edited by Ralph Landau, Basil Achilladelis, and Alexander Scriabine

For information about CHF publications write
Chemical Heritage Foundation
315 Chestnut Street
Philadelphia, PA 19106-2702, USA
Fax: (215) 925-1954
www.chemheritage.org

Printed in the United States of America.

Book designed by Mark Willie, Willie•Fetchko Graphic Design
Printed by Alcom Printing Group

A CIP catalog record for this book is available from the Library of Congress

ISBN 0-941901-23-8

This book is printed on acid-free paper.

In memory of Mabel Beckman

and for the children, grandchildren,

and great grandchildren

of Arnold O. Beckman, and

for the Beckman family worldwide.

Contents

Foreword   ix

Preface   xiii

Acknowledgments   xv

1   The Blacksmith's Son   2

2   A Scientist in the Making   30

3   Professor Beckman   70

4   Ink and Lemon Juice   112

5   Battles on Many Fronts   146

6   Dr. Beckman in Control   190

7   Visions of Technology   236

8   Citizen and Leader   278

9   Philanthropist and Statesman   312

Selected Honors and Awards of Arnold O. Beckman   368

The Patents of Arnold O. Beckman   369

Selected Scientific Publications of Arnold O. Beckman   370

Note on Sources and Suggestions for Further Reading   371

Note on the CD-ROM   373

Index   374

Foreword

The now one hundred years of Arnold Beckman's life and his multiple accomplishments, which we celebrate through this volume, mirror well the American twentieth century that his distinguished career so neatly encompasses. Arnold Orville Beckman was born in 1900, when agriculture was the dominant form of life for most Americans, and his youth in a small rural town was the norm, not the exception. At that time the constantly accelerating growth of industry was seen as the main force for national progress. Industry gave our citizens the life-enhancing tools and products that could ameliorate the inherent hardness of lives still far too dependent on the vagaries of rains and blizzards. At the heart of this industrial progress was the generation of new techniques and technologies by American inventors. These inventors in turn relied increasingly upon scientists and their expanding mastery of the laws of nature.

In the nineteenth century it was the physicists who so propelled us forward. Through their understanding of electromagnetism, Alexander Graham Bell gave us the telephone and Thomas Alva Edison invented the electric light bulb. Even so, with most major scientific advances coming from Europe, America's forte in the nineteenth century was still its self-taught inventors—Eli Whitney with his cotton gin, say, or Cyrus McCormick with his reaper. Chemists only became a truly serious force in American industry as the twentieth century began to unfold.

By 1919 the blossoming of American chemical science and enterprise held out both promise and opportunity for the future. That very year the young chemical enthusiast Arnold O. Beckman entered the University of Illinois. With excitement he saw ahead of him multiple opportunities for the chemical engineer and the chemical scientist. He might very likely have gone straight into industry after graduation were it not for the exceptional quality of his teachers. The Urbana department was soon to be regarded as the nation's best collection of chemists. As he studied under this group, he settled on physical chemistry. It was as an assistant in an electrochemistry course that he first saw the need for accurate measurements of acidity and alkalinity, the problem that he returned to in just over a decade when he invented his famous pH meter.

Sensing that his chemical education was still incomplete even after he earned a master's degree at Illinois, Arnold enrolled at the newly founded California Institute of Technology. Here he found himself at an institution with immediate world-class aspirations, both in education and in research. From the start it became the

American outpost of the new European quantum mechanics, as creators of the new physics like Arnold Sommerfeld and Niels Bohr began to make regular visits to Caltech. Very soon quantum thinking began to jump from physics to chemistry, and Arnold Beckman sensed the need for new instrumentation to measure events at the quantum level. Here his education was much enriched by the two years that he spent within his graduate career at the newly formed Bell Labs. In no way dissatisfied with Caltech, he nevertheless left because he could no longer bear the separation from his fiancée, Mabel, in New York. His time at Bell Labs proved an unexpectedly advantageous career diversion. It gave him a firsthand look at electronics, most notably the vacuum tube. Arnold Beckman foresaw that electronics could revolutionize the measuring devices of the chemist.

Returning to Caltech after Bell Labs and his marriage to Mabel, Arnold found his extraordinary ability to create innovative chemical instruments—to invent new tools for asking new questions—was quickly appreciated. He was appointed to Caltech's chemistry faculty upon completion of his Ph.D. requirements. A year later, he for the first time combined advanced physics and sophisticated chemistry in a single invention—a device to measure the quantum yield of a photochemical reaction. In so moving forward, Arnold had his feet on the ground of established knowledge and technique. Never for a moment did he see himself as a grand miracle maker. He was the creative solver of direct scientific and technological challenges. Here he was the temperamental opposite of his fellow young faculty member at Caltech, Linus Pauling, who wanted not only to bring chemistry and physics together but also to use them to give a rational basis to biology and medicine.

It was Pauling's highly articulate message that to understand biology you must understand the molecules of life that first motivated me to find the double helix. Chemical instrumentation at that time held no special fascination for me. My hope was that enough chemistry had already been done on DNA for Pauling-like modeling to have a reasonable chance for success. Happily for Francis Crick and me, that was indeed the case. Several years later, however, while pursuing the genetic code as a young Harvard professor, I sensed that my career would go nowhere unless I generated new facts at the chemical level. Measurements with pH meter and spectrophotometer soon became integral to my life. My first two purchases for my Harvard lab were these Beckman instruments, whose accuracy and reliability I never had to question.

Now, forty years later, I can see even more clearly that our pursuit of the chemical underpinnings of biology has depended as much on the invention of new instrumentation and experimental procedures as on the generation of new experimental results and new ideas. Arnold Beckman's contribution to science and to society came, in part, from his rare talent for creating these new instruments and his decision to make them available to industry and science alike. It has been amplified by his unique philanthropic support of the same forward-looking research that his innovations furthered. Were Caltech to have given us Linus Pauling without Arnold Beckman, or vice versa, the worlds of chemistry, biology, and medicine would not be so enveloped in today's extraordinary rush of discovery and development. And if Caltech had not come so gloriously into existence—welcoming and nourishing our homegrown American genius—we might still be looking to Europe for the ideas and skills that move our industries forward, that continue the story of American progress.

James D. Watson
Cold Spring Harbor Laboratory

Preface

Arnold Beckman's life is at once a personal story of creative scientific genius and a tale with far wider meanings. His odyssey from the Midwest to the California coast epitomizes a major American migration, as does his journey from the craft and agricultural world of the blacksmith to the service-oriented professions. It is given to few undergraduate chemistry majors to be invited to graduate study at Caltech, and rare indeed is the Caltech student who is invited onto its fabled faculty. But it is truly without precedent for that same student to become first a member of the board of trustees and then its chair, then to assume the role of Caltech's greatest benefactor, and overall to be a constant, shaping presence for more than seventy-five years.

America in the twentieth century has been blessed in the vigor and preeminence of its academic institutions. And in the growth of its science-based industries. And in the emergence of California as one of the leading states. And in the vitality of its voluntary organizations. And in the burgeoning of its generous traditions of philanthropy. And in the resilience with which its civic and political structures have responded to challenges as varied as atomic fission, automobile-induced smog, and Cold War hostilities. How striking, then, to find Arnold Beckman playing crucial roles not in one but in all these areas—and many more.

Arnold O. Beckman's biographers have a triple privilege. First is the pleasure of knowing and learning from this remarkable, inventive, acute, humorous, knowledgeable, and fundamentally modest man. Second comes the opportunity to chronicle his life and achievements and lay out the "Beckman story" for family, friends, colleagues, students, admirers, and beneficiaries of his talents and philanthropies. It has been a rare gift to review the chapters of this volume with Dr. Beckman and to watch him return to memories freshly brought to life. Third is the challenge of showing how Dr. Beckman was molded by America, even as he, in turn, has molded and fashioned major elements in our heritage and in our culture. His life exemplifies central themes in much that is best in our national achievement in the twentieth century. To understand his life is to be humbled, encouraged, and inspired to believe anew in the promise of America.

Arnold Thackray
Minor Myers, jr.

Acknowledgments

This biography has, in every sense, been a collaborative project. The hard work and genuine enthusiasm of a wide array of individuals made this book possible.

As authors, we owe an especial debt of thanks to David C. Brock of Historical Services of the Chemical Heritage Foundation (CHF), our principal collaborator and a tower of strength in every aspect of this project. His very considerable historical skills, writing talent, and diplomatic ability were invaluable to us. His sense of priorities and his quiet persistence united to make a daunting endeavor into a manageable task.

We would extend our sincere appreciation as well to James D. Watson for the foreword to this volume; his words confirm Arnold O. Beckman's hope that his life as a creative toolmaker for science has contributed to the growth and expansion of the scientific enterprise.

Without the support, council, materials, and resources made available to us by Arnold Beckman's family and the Arnold and Mabel Beckman Foundation, we would not have been able to understand or convey Dr. Beckman's story in anything like its present form. Our foremost thanks go to Pat Beckman for her thoughtful encouragement and criticism and for collecting and discovering materials from which to tell and illustrate her father's story. We are similarly grateful to Arnold Stone Beckman, Arnold William (Arne) Beckman, Kurt Beckman, Cambria Beckman, and Ellyn Seaquist for giving so graciously of their memories, thoughts, and time.

Jacqueline Dorrance, executive director of the Arnold and Mabel Beckman Foundation, has been a skilled and unwavering supporter of this project through all of its phases. Through her we gained access to many critical documents and key contacts, among them members of the Beckman Foundation's board of directors. To these last—individuals of accomplishment with long-standing relationships with Dr. Beckman—we owe a considerable debt for their time, conversation, considered opinions, and recollections. We thank George Argyros, Ted Brown, Jerry Gallwas, Harry Gray, Gary Hunt, Donald Shields, and Gavin Herbert.

From Beckman Coulter, past and present, came a variety of generous individuals who provided us with their advice, their expertise, their experiences, and an abundance of documents and images. We thank Craig Adams, William Ballhaus, Jack Bishop, Jeannie Herbert, Joe Lewis, William May, Richard Nesbit, Tor Pederson, Clayton Rasmussen, Louis Rosso, Robert Steinmeyer, James Sternberg, and John

Wareham. Clayton Rasmussen shared his unpublished reminiscences of his career at Beckman with us. And we owe a particular debt to Harrison Stephens, the author of *Golden Past, Golden Future*, who shared with us an unpublished manuscript and many hours of audiotaped interviews. We also extend our special thanks to Pat Ashton, Jean Miller, and the "Archives Angels" for creating, maintaining, and giving us unfettered access to the archives at Beckman Coulter's Heritage Center.

David Baltimore, Harold Brown, Peter Dervan, and Carver Mead all took time out from their busy lives to enrich our understanding of Dr. Beckman's seventy-five year relationship with the California Institute of Technology. Joshua Lederberg, president emeritus of Rockefeller University, provided us with his keen insights about Dr. Beckman's impact on and relationship with Rockefeller University as well as the larger impacts of his innovations on the world of science. Paul Berg of Stanford helped deepen our sense of Dr. Beckman's personality. Jiri Jonas, director of the Beckman Institute at the University of Illinois, and Stanley Ikenberry, president of the American Council on Education and president of the University of Illinois at the founding of its Beckman Institute, helped us understand Dr. Beckman's impact on science and intellectual life at that university. John Stephen Kovach, director of the Beckman Research Institute of the City of Hope, and Joseph Holden, of its Division of Neuroscience, guided us to important information. Michael Berns, director of the Beckman Laser Institute, contributed to our understanding of Dr. Beckman as an individual and as a philanthropist. Harry Gray of Caltech's Beckman Institute was constant in his aid and encouragement.

To bring our words about Dr. Beckman to life, we have looked to illustrations. The CD-ROM incorporated with this biography was the brainchild of Jeffrey I. Seeman, Senior Fellow in Chemical Education at CHF's Beckman Center, who oversaw its development with tact, determination, and creative flair. Amy Beth Crow of CHF's Historical Services collected and coordinated visual materials for both the CD-ROM and the book. Moreover, she provided valued research and production support for our efforts. We convey our special thanks to her for her Herculean efforts. Judith Goodstein and her colleagues Shelley Erwin and Bonnie Ludt in the Caltech Archives courteously provided us with access to their wealth of knowledge on Dr. Beckman and his life—both pictorial and documentary.

The creation and production of this work relied heavily on several talented individuals at the Arnold and Mabel Beckman Center for the History of Chemistry and the Donald F. and Mildred Topp Othmer Library of Chemical History, which together constitute CHF in Philadelphia. From Historical Services, we thank the director, Leo B. Slater, and researcher Christina Dunbar-Hester. Paul Giblin of Library Services provided valued resources as well, and Marthenia Perrin of Support Services provided assistance in all phases of the project. The book itself would not have appeared without the efforts of CHF's Publications group. Besides the input from Kerry O'Connor, Megan Susnis, and our consultant Patricia Wieland, we are especially indebted to the tireless efforts and excellent taste of the director, Frances Coulborn Kohler, who edited the text while keeping an eye on the entire project, and of the manager, Shelley Wilks Geehr, who oversaw all stages of production and kept its component parts on schedule against great odds. They were assisted by the detailed attention given the project by the designer, Mark Willie of Willie-Fetchko Graphic Design. We thank them all.

Staff, faculty, and close associates of Illinois Wesleyan University also lent their hard work and thoughtful consultation to our efforts. Robert E. Davis, president of R. E. Davis Chemical Corporation and a trustee and alumnus of Illinois Wesleyan, shared his deep knowledge of analytical chemistry and instrumentation. David Bailey and Wendy Wolbach, professors in IWU's chemistry department, were valued resources, as were Lew Detweiler, Ray Wilson, and Narendra Jaggi, professors in the physics department. Robert de Levie, professor of chemistry at Bowdoin College, was particularly generous with his knowledge of electrochemistry and its history. Susan Bassi, assistant to the president at IWU, provided valued assistance and support as well.

Arnold O. Beckman's
Rules for Success

There is no satisfactory substitute for excellence.

Absolute integrity . . . in everything.

Everything in moderation . . . including moderation itself.

Hire the best people and then get out of their way.

Don't take yourself too seriously.

Courtesy Beckman Coulter, Inc.

Arnold Beckman in the George Washington costume sewed for him by his mother for a school pageant. *Courtesy Beckman family.*

1 | The Blacksmith's Son

In Cullom we were forced to improvise. I think it was a very good thing.

Origins

Arnold in 1901. *Courtesy Beckman family.*

In cities young people of ambition lead lives of relative anonymity. Incipient talent is a thing unseen, or at least unrecognized, until its full blossoming. Small towns and villages are different. There, inhabitants know the strengths and foibles of the young long before those young achieve or accomplish anything significant. In a village, potential is easily marked. Thus the five hundred residents of Cullom, Illinois, knew early on that Arnold Beckman would do something significant in science, or music, or industry—he was definitely someone to watch.

Arnold Orville Beckman was born on 10 April 1900 in Cullom, a small farming community, remote from the forces of change that were giving rise to modern America. Indeed, as late as 1899, there was but one train a day between the mighty city of Chicago and Bloomington, Cullom's larger neighbor some fifty-three miles away. American science is the richer for that, because Arnold Beckman's education was at heart an education in invention. Simply put, young Arnold had to make his own toys and find his own interests in the world that Cullom presented. The creative habits of hand, eye, and mind that he developed in this rural setting became the resources through which he has contributed so much to the science and technology that continue to shape our new millennium.

Arnold himself would learn German only in school, but his grandparents were German, having emigrated to America in 1857, a tumultuous year in the European heartlands. Many sought a new life in the United States at that time, and Rolf C. Beckmann and Agte Wildte Beckmann were among them. Rolf was from Morsdorf, near Jena in Saxe Weimar, while Agte was from nearby Viktorburg. They set out for a land of new hopes, together with their infant child and Agte's mother. The crossing, a difficult one, lasted nine weeks. Cholera broke out on the ship, and neither child nor grandmother survived to see America.

The Beckmans, who as Arnold recalls, lost an *n* by the end of their transatlantic voyage, were among some 250,000 immigrants who arrived in the United States that year. Many Germans had already settled in Illinois and, in doing so, had transplanted much of their native culture to American soil. Upon arrival in their new

3

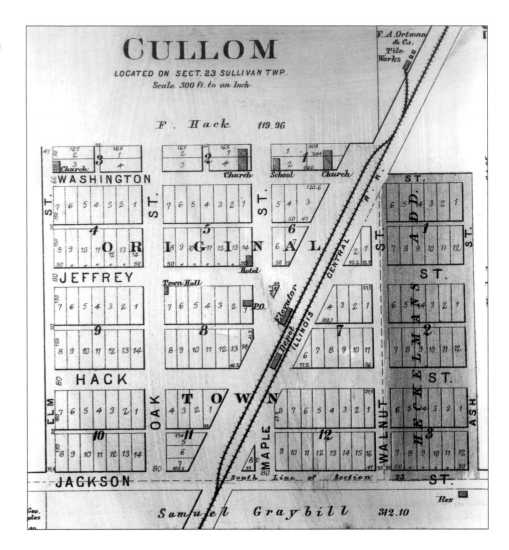

Street map of Cullom, Illinois, at the turn of the century. At the upper right: Cullom's school-house and Tile Works.
Courtesy Illinois State Historical Library.

country, the Beckmans, too, made their way westward. The fertile and still sparsely settled land may have drawn the couple. Railroad promotions of the area and a buoyant economy had helped boost Illinois's German-born population to 200,000 by 1870. Whatever the draw, the Beckmans ended up as farmers outside Fairbury, a town near Bloomington, situated on both the Wabash & Toledo and the Peoria & Western railway lines. Bloomington was by no means unusual in supporting two weekly German newspapers. One survived, with a patriotic intermission in English during World War I, as late as the 1930s.

George W. Beckman, Arnold's father, was born in Fairbury in 1861. After receiving an elementary school education, he was apprenticed to a blacksmith to learn the trade. Displaying the same taste for adventure that Arnold would later show, George as a youth journeyed widely through Texas and the still primitive Southwest, to such sites as that of the Custer massacre in South Dakota and "the home of the James boys, the notorious bank robbers." He married in his early thirties. His bride was Frederica Stevens, a schoolteacher also of German descent. For

The Beckman children. From left: Wilma, Frederick, Roland, and Arnold. *Courtesy Institute Archives, California Institute of Technology.*

reasons now unknown, the young couple headed southwest to Clinton, a small town in Henry County, Missouri. There they had two sons, Roland, born in 1895, and Frederick, born in 1896. Death was a familiar companion in that era, and Frederica died shortly after the birth of her second son, leaving George with two little boys. By 1898 he was back in Illinois, some fifteen miles from his native Fairbury, in the newer, smaller settlement of Cullom. There he set up a blacksmith's shop, with his house just across the street.

Many others made the same choice of where to settle, and Cullom grew rapidly as a village. It had not even existed before 1875, save as the fertile fields of Sullivan Township, and only then did the village begin to form around new grain mills on the tracks of the Illinois Central. A post office opened in 1878, and Cullom was incorporated in 1882. By the end of the century it was a real village of about five hundred people. Laid out in ordered blocks, there were two hotels, grain mills that could fill five hundred railroad cars a year, a bank, a drugstore, a doctor, a printer, two bakeries, two restaurants, a billiard parlor, two barbers, and four saloons. A photographer and a jeweler added refinement, but surely the confectionery was a child's favorite. Blacksmiths were vitally important in a farming community, and George Beckman had no monopoly, for there were other blacksmith shops and two hardware dealers.

In the late 1890s both Jewkes and Kingdon were common names in Cullom. Four of the Jewkes were brothers who had moved from Peoria to farm there, and their sister Elizabeth was a regular visitor. The brothers and sister were the children of English emigrants. Their father and mother, John Jewkes from Dudley in Staffordshire and Mary Kingdon from North Molton in Devon, had come to America in 1858, one year after the Beckmans. John and Mary separately found their way to Peoria, Illinois, then an emerging center of commercial activity in the

From left to right: A wedding portrait of George Beckman and Elizabeth Ellen Jewkes, 1898; the maternal grandparents, John and Mary Jewkes; Arnold's mother, Elizabeth Ellen Beckman. *All courtesy Beckman family.*

Left: The Beckman brothers, Arnold (center), Frederick, and Roland.

Right: George Beckman's blacksmith shop in Cullom, Illinois. *Both courtesy Beckman family.*

river-based commerce of the West, and were married there in 1863. John ran a nearby coal mine, while Mary raised their eight children, of whom Elizabeth was the fifth.

In 1898, shortly after he arrived in Cullom, George Beckman married Elizabeth Ellen Jewkes, who joined her new husband in the house across from the shop. Roland and Frederick were soon to have a new brother, for just a few months into the new century, Arnold Orville Beckman was born on 10 April 1900. He was simultaneously the first-born, positioned to be the favorite of his mother, and the youngest of three brothers. When a sister, Wilma Blanche, was born three years later, Arnold was no longer "the baby," and the family circle was complete.

Childhood Days

On cold evenings George closed the shop across the street and returned home early. Awaiting him were his wife and children, his evening meal, moments of relaxation, and paperwork to be done at the table in the main room of the house. "If it was wintertime," Arnold Beckman remembers, "we'd sit around a large table in our combination living and dining room, which was the only place that had heat outside of the kitchen. We'd gather around the stove, either working at the table or lying on the floor and playing with blocks or toys—whatever we might have. That was the family life; we were all together in this one room."

Arnold's father and mother were available, instructive figures. His father provided an example of dedication to material craftsmanship. His mother embodied comfort and discipline, in an environment of close domesticity. The shop went well, and there was always enough to eat and fuel for the stove. Though there were several dry-goods stores in the village, Elizabeth sewed most of their clothes, and the children are elegant in their pictures. But extras make memories. She prepared special dried cherry jam with fruit baked in the sun, and Arnold still recalls the George Washington costume she made for him to wear in a historical pageant at school.

Elizabeth taught her children habits of discipline, and chores were a regular part of household life. Dishwashing was all right, but Arnold despised one of his jobs, even though it was arguably his first experience with the mysteries of chemicals. The main room of the Beckman house was heated by the stove and lighted by a single, large kerosene lamp. Each Saturday he had to clean the soot-covered glass chimney, dipping pieces of newspaper into kerosene to dissolve away the tarry residues and restore the lamp to its full brightness. If soot cleaning, dishwashing, and brushing the flies off the noses of the horses in his father's smithy were not enough, there was also piano practice.

Piano felt like a chore in winter. When Arnold was six, he was given a few lessons in Cullom, just four or five as he recalls, from a Lutheran minister named Lutz. Those few lessons were to be followed by years of practice, as Elizabeth kept him to a strict regimen at the bench of the family's golden oak Feuhr & Stemmer upright. The piano was in the unheated parlor just off the main room of the house, but Elizabeth would hear nothing of a winter vacation from the musical drills. Whether it was cold or not, she made Arnold retire to the parlor. Music—especially proficiency at the keyboard—came to play an important role in his life as both a passion and a means of earning a living. His mother's insistence on diligent practice, however uncomfortable, conveyed a lesson to him about the importance of disciplined effort in achieving success. The lesson became even more important when, before Arnold had reached his tenth birthday, his mother became seriously ill with diabetes.

An early-twentieth-century view of Cullom, Illinois. *Courtesy Cullom Memorial Library.*

Once chores and piano scales were through, there was time for fun. Arnold and his brothers and sister were a gregarious lot, and their days in Cullom were filled with activities as idyllic and as distinctly American as anything in a Mark Twain novel. Together with other boys, Arnold walked and ran around barefoot, caught catfish in the Vermillion River, and played hide-and-go-seek until sundown. The pond by Cullom's tile factory offered brisk swimming in summer and excellent ice-skating in winter. As the three Beckman brothers got older, they set out on camping and fishing expeditions along the Mackinaw River. Sometimes the excursions extended for days.

The Beckman home in Cullom. In front, left to right, are Frederick, Roland, Arnold, Elizabeth, and Wilma Beckman.
Courtesy Beckman family.

Together, the children of Cullom organized games and mischief. They competed in wrestling, tag, and teasing. They played baseball barefooted and only occasionally overturned outhouses at Halloween. Many of the boys, including Arnold, were nocturnal. The Boy Scouts of America program had begun in 1910 and had members in every state by 1912. Cullom did not have its own troop; nevertheless, Arnold and his friends formed an unofficial Boy Scout troop of their own, known as the Owl Patrol. The name was doubly fitting, for they kept owls' hours and perfected hooting sounds that they made outside each others' bedroom windows as secret signals that it was time to sneak out for unsupervised fun. Arnold himself was soon known by the nickname "Hoot," both to the members of the patrol and to every other kid in school.

Each year brought high points. In August a small traveling troupe would arrive, complete with sideshows. The circus and country fair were "the highlight of my life" (much later in life he would still think of coordinating his visits home for circus time). Then in the winter there were Mrs. Thompson's barn dances, for which one of his uncles played fiddle. Arnold and the other boys would walk across the fields in winter to find a crowd, music, fun, Mrs. Thompson's wondrous oyster stew, and her teenaged daughters.

Train spotting was a perennial sport, especially after the traffic increased to four trains a day, two each way. When Arnold was six or seven years old, his curiosity about the loud rumbling machines got the better of whatever youthful discretion he may have had. The railroad crossed a creek near the Beckmans' house on its way into Cullom, and he climbed out onto the trestle to get a closer look at an approaching engine. He could not have been more than four or five feet from the massive wheels as the train steamed past. While he was unhurt and certainly satisfied with the view, his stunt did not go unwitnessed. The Beckmans' neighbor Mr. Weber had watched the whole thing, and he promptly told Arnold's father. Reacting with fear and horror at his son's brush with death, George gave him the only spanking he ever received. Arnold's fascination with technology, however, was undiminished.

His growing fascination with devices, and with building them, shows in his early efforts at toy making. His imagination filled his free hours, and as he developed skills of hand and mind, his toys became ever more elaborate. Parts became whole creations in his hands. He once built a four-wheeled handcart, an Irish mail, from iron that he salvaged from the demolition of an old windmill tower. His father's craftsmanship as a blacksmith was a constant example and ready resource, giving Arnold additional motivation, skills, and habits of mind for his boyhood efforts at mechanical invention.

Winters were for reading. On cold days he and his siblings were confined to the reach of the family stove, where they "learned to read because we had plenty of time . . . with little else to do. We had books, Horatio Alger and things like that. Particularly, I recall *Peck's Bad Boy*. That was a big, fat, red book I liked." Perhaps Arnold grew temporarily weary of the well-worn copies of Alger and Peck by the time he was nine years old. Whether intentionally searching for something new to read or just following his inquisitive streak, he went searching one day through a storage area next to his room on the attic floor of the Cullom house. There he found a copy of a book that had once belonged to an aunt. It was J. Dorman Steele's *Fourteen Weeks in Chemistry*. He began to read it and fell quickly under its spell. His fascination with chemistry lasted not just fourteen weeks, but more than a full nine decades.

Illustration by True Williams from *Peck's Bad Boy and His Pa*, 1883.

With the inspiration of Steele's book, Arnold Beckman was ready to go. He certainly did not expect his parents to provide an expensive chemistry set. He thought it more fun to search his mother's pantry and shop carefully at Cullom's druggist; in his hands ammonia, lime, vinegar, carbonate of potash, and sal soda soon revealed many of their secrets. George Beckman recognized his youngest son's exceptional drive and curiosity. As encouragement, and as consolation for the stresses and sorrows that came with the continuing illness and decline of Arnold's mother, George gave him a small "shop" of his own for his tenth birthday. The shop was one of four 8-by-10-foot structures that stood behind the Beckman house: One was the privy, another the coal shed, and a third housed corncobs. The fourth, although little more than a simple shed, was a glorious space for a young inventor.

The building itself inspired, even necessitated, one of his earliest inventions. It made a perfect clubhouse for the Owl Patrol, and a clubhouse demanded security. Arnold devised an ingenious combination lock whose three strings had to be pulled in just the right order before a bar holding the door closed would release.

Arnold made the shed into a combination "chemical laboratory" and woodworking shop, for his father had given him his own set of woodworking tools as well. His woodworking occupied one side; on the opposite side, another shelf became his makeshift laboratory bench. Among the first pieces of apparatus was one that imperiled the whole wooden structure. First he made an alcohol lamp from an old inkwell and a piece of cotton cord. Once he improvised a lamp, he needed flasks to go along with it. No kid who sees an elegant Florence flask feels satisfied without one, and there they were in Steele's book—glass spheres with long, thin necks. Arnold thought one of his mother's thick-glass pickle jars might come close. All went well until he tried to boil some water in the jar, atop his alcohol lamp. The "flask" quickly broke. Later in life he would quip that this was his "first experience with the coefficient of thermal expansion." But he got his beautiful flask not long after. His older brother Roland, known familiarly as "Doc," was working in Chicago quite near E. H. Sargent, a major chemical supplies dealer. Suitably impressed by Arnold's labors at improvising equipment and performing experiments, Doc brought home glassware, test tubes, and a mortar and pestle. Nothing would stop Arnold now.

Arnold also undertook electrical and electrochemical investigations. The tile factory with the pond for swimming and skating had a steam engine used for production during the day, but at night it switched over to powering an electric dynamo that provided current for the very few arc lamps that hung above Cullom's street crossings. Here was a great source of supply. Arnold searched out the spent carbon electrodes from the arc lights, and once back in his chemical laboratory, he tried to combine these bits of carbon with scraps of zinc and copper to make batteries. The revised edition of Steele's *Fourteen Weeks in Chemistry* contains a

Joel Dorman Steele (1836–1886) was born in upstate New York and attended Genesee Wesleyan College, now Syracuse University, part time while teaching school to support himself. After college he became principal of the town academy in Mexico, New York.

He loved the study and the teaching of science, and he developed new lectures and experiments. Steele designed his chemistry lessons to foster a spirit of inquisitiveness and the habit of testing concepts by experiment and measurement. He took great pains to relate his lessons to such common objects and materials as matches, ceramics, glass, and mirrors.

Steele, energetic and entrepreneurial, was soon ready to reach a wider audience. Somehow the publisher A. S. Barnes (1817–1888) learned of Steele's plans and contacted him about a book for the home and the high school market. In 1867 *A Fourteen Weeks Course in Chemistry* appeared. Sales exceeded their wildest hopes. Demand continued through many printings, with the title shortened to *Fourteen Weeks in Chemistry*. This and other science books did so well that in 1872 Barnes persuaded Steele to give up his school for textbook writing.

Fourteen Weeks in Chemistry never had a more enthusiastic reader than nine-year-old Arnold Beckman. It transformed his life and thereby modern science.

Several editions of *Chemistry* were published. Since Arnold Beckman's copy has disappeared, it is uncertain which one he had. Each edition had four sections: an introduction; inorganic chemistry, covering metals and nonmetals alike; organic chemistry; and an appendix of experiments, questions, and a guide to qualitative analysis. Particularly engaging for a nine-year-old were the book's illustrations of industrial processes and, even better, laboratory experiments under way. Later editions had directions for 230 experiments in the back and a section on qualitative analysis for beginners, together with a colored frontispiece of spectral lines from a spectroscope. Young chemists, however, were encouraged to learn the full sequence of qualitative analysis to identify compounds.

The first edition claimed that its experiments were within the means of any reader, though Steele surely thought readers were curious adults or high school students, not nine-year-olds. In "any village," Steele asserted, there were sources for the vitriol, acqua fortis, muriatic acid, copper, scraps of tin, corks, wire, iron, zinc, and junk bottles necessary to conduct the experiments. For those who wanted better supplies, Barnes Publishing offered a twenty-dollar set of test tubes, chemicals, flasks, and other apparatus. After 1873 new editions stopped encouraging students to salvage materials around town. Instead they were urged to choose between the bargain fifteen-dollar set and a more comprehensive thirty-dollar set of chemical apparatus "adequate for the performance of all the experiments in any ordinary textbook." ∿

The cover to *Fourteen Weeks in Chemistry*, the book that began Dr. Beckman's lifelong passion for chemistry. *Courtesy Beckman Coulter, Inc.*

passing comment in a footnote: "The electrical character of an element is relative." Whether he even noticed Steele's comment or not, Arnold would later make that "electrical character" the basis of a major corporation.

Schoolboy, Musician, and Jack-of-All-Trades

Arnold approached music in much the same spirit as he pursued his science: He started with significant help from others but took on a lot of independent activity once his interest had been engaged. As in many other villages and small towns, the people of Cullom debated whether dances were moral, asking also the question, "If dances are immoral, what about playing for them?" Arnold Beckman left such questions to those interested in them. He was available. By the time he was ten, he spent his Sunday afternoons as "practice pianist" with Guy Morisette, a barber who played violin, cornet, or drums. Morisette had organized a band, which usually drew Erve Kingdon, an implement dealer who played trombone; George Kingdon, schoolteacher, wallpaper hanger, and drummer; and Johnnie Amacher, carpenter, on clarinet. Beckman was lucky here, because Gertrude Kingdon (all the Kingdons were relatives through his grandmother) was the regular pianist for the band. But she had trained professionally at a nearby music school and did not want to waste her Sundays in unnecessary practice with such amateurs. Young Arnold did, especially when practice might yield income. At age twelve he wore his first pair of long trousers to play for a dance in Cabery just up the Illinois Central Railroad. It was his first overnight, and he earned a whole dollar. Effort paid! By age fourteen he was in the dance band business in his own right.

Other changes were far less benign. In 1912 Elizabeth Ellen Beckman died, her struggles with diabetes over. It is tempting to speculate how much this devastating loss must have affected young Arnold. Perhaps it drove him to a deeper commitment to the more stable and predictable world of science. Perhaps it contributed to the sense of inwardness and hidden depth that forms one attractive facet of the public character that "Dr. Beckman" later assumed. Such speculation is in the end idle, for surprisingly little is known of the personal details of Beckman family life in Illinois. We do know that George Beckman married again, for a third time, but not to whom or when. We also know that more immediately a new female presence entered the household, Hattie Lange. Hattie was the housekeeper charged to care for, and maintain discipline among, the Beckman children.

Restless and unsettled, and with fresh responsibilities and expenses, George Beckman sold his shop to another blacksmith, Frank White. George himself became a traveling salesman and supplier of blacksmith's tools and materials, representing the Cumming and Emerson Company, while Hattie cared for the children. In these new circumstances the twelve-year-old Arnold took on additional duties. He would help earn the family's way. Music was one possibility. He discovered that routine science might pay, too—and also be strenuous fun.

The Leiserwitzes' general store was a center of commerce and community in Cullom, and Arnold soon became its grocery clerk and resident chemist. "This was in the cracker-barrel era. We had a big box of crackers and a cheese covered with a screen to keep the flies off. There was a huge knife—a guillotine. People would come into the store, go over and cut a thick slice of cheese, pick up a few crackers, sit down, and put their feet up on the rail around the potbellied stove and discuss politics and how bad the weather was."

The store sold everyday goods: milk, fresh food, dry goods, tools, cloth, and hardware. But the Leiserwitzes also ran a two-way commerce, for they bought milk and cream directly from farmers who brought it to the store. Price depended on cream content. Arnold relished his job as official cream tester for the store. At age twelve his biggest problem was lifting the five-gallon cans of milk. As tester he put a small sample in a long, thin bottle, added a few drops of sulfuric acid, swirled the sample gently, and as the cream started to rise to the top, put the long bottle in the hand-cranked centrifuge. After spinning the bottle around and around, Arnold pronounced on the amount of cream in the milk, judged by how far the cream had run up the side of the bottle. Years later, the boy who turned the crank would manage a company that made some of the fastest centrifuges in the world.

Even though Arnold lamented not seeing his father as often as he had when shop and father were both across the street, George's new role enhanced his youngest son's appreciation of tools and equipment. He had ample opportunity to learn firsthand the importance of the tools his father now sold, for he, too, had another new job: He started working for Frank White in his father's old shop. He

A Jewkes family farm. Arnold Beckman's maternal uncles all farmed near Cullom.
Courtesy Beckman family.

13

disliked his first job, which was to hold and soothe horses while Frank worked on their shoes. Eventually, Frank had him assist with the blacksmithing itself. Arnold rotated long barn rods—metal bars that attached facing barn walls to one another to keep them from bowing—as Frank hammered on the weld seams. When Frank put iron tires on tall, wooden wagon wheels, it was Arnold who poured water on the hot metal, cooling and shrinking the tires to a tight fit.

Summers and harvest brought still other jobs as Arnold helped his family in the fields with distinctly mechanical tasks. His uncle Charles Jewkes was a prosperous farmer who had started a bank in Cullom. Among other entrepreneurial ventures, Uncle Charlie owned a threshing machine moved and powered by a steam tractor. Charlie and Arnold took the machine from farm to farm, converting wagonloads of hay into bales. Arnold's job was to keep the tractor's engine fed with water. Two large horses drew the water wagon, which he filled using a hand pump. His other task was even less appealing: greasing the threshing machine. There were many other chores that Uncle Charlie could have assigned Arnold that would have put a premium on his strength above anything else. Instead, Charlie saw and utilized his nephew's obvious love for machines.

And then, among all these enterprises, there was school. In his recollections Arnold never categorized his studies with chores or work, for he approached them with an uncommon fervor. He simply remembers that "learning was pleasant in those days."

Cullom student body, taken on 18 April 1913. Arnold Beckman stands in the back row, just right of center, in the doorway.
Courtesy Institute Archives, California Institute of Technology.

An early lesson in moderation, self-control, and political skills came from one of his teachers, Lewis Appel, an Ichabod Crane–type. On one occasion Arnold threw a snowball at Appel, who caught him and took him back to the schoolhouse. He expected to be paddled. Instead, Appel told him that children had fun throwing snowballs, but adults did not like snowball fights and cold, wet collars. Arnold had expected anger and a paddle; instead he got kindness and logic. For decades he would stop to see Appel when on his regular trips to Cullom.

Miss Hart, his fifth-grade teacher, also made a lasting impression. She drew out the competitive spirit of her pupils, instructing them in spelling and in mathematics through contests between teams in the classroom. In addition, she taught all the students, boys and girls alike, an unusual skill: tatting, or making lace. Owing to his unusual manual dexterity, Arnold was good at it. The Cullom years offered many experiences through which his hands learned to make what his mind imagined: in his chemistry laboratory, at his woodworking bench, with his cream testing and his blacksmith work, in his construction of toys from odd parts—and in his operation of machines and his mastery of the intricacies of tatting. All these lessons combined to give Arnold Beckman the power of a bold, creative confidence that if he could envision something, he could build it. That power never left him.

Cullom gained technological amenities as Arnold grew up. By the time he was fourteen, there was a regular electric supply and running water for houses and businesses in town. His Uncle Charlie even had a telephone and a Cadillac. Silent movies arrived, too. The Cullom theater was small by any standard, an old store front rigged up for movies. But it was there. Arnold became its resident, and resilient, pianist. At first the theater depended on its own generator, since the town unit was devoted solely to street lighting. One night the theater's generator simply stopped. Arnold had to improvise for what seemed an age, as he and the audience sat in darkness while his colleagues struggled in the basement to repair the belts on the machine.

Portrait of a Young Chemist

As Arnold and Frederick approached high school age, George Beckman took stock. He saw that both his younger sons had academic gifts. Arnold with his developing

Street map of Normal, Illinois, from the 1910s. Illinois State Normal University, the site of University High, is at the center of the map.
Courtesy Illinois State Historical Library.

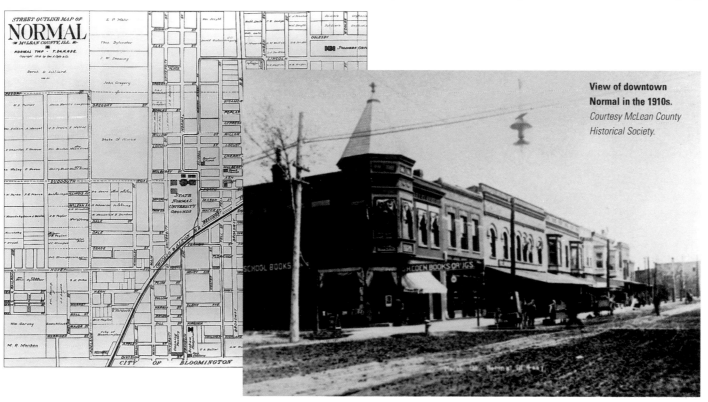

View of downtown Normal in the 1910s.
Courtesy McLean County Historical Society.

talent and drive learned that scholarships were available for University High School in Normal, a suburb of distant Bloomington. He went to Pontiac for the competitive entrance tests and won his spot at University High. That goal achieved, in summer 1914 George Beckman organized a move down the rail line to Bloomington and Normal. The Cullom years had come to an end, even though Arnold continued to visit family and friends there regularly, as he still does.

Most Cullom kids had read the Horatio Alger stories, and whether he was conscious of it or not, Arnold had made himself into a Horatio Alger figure by the time he left Cullom. Alger repeated the same character over and over in his many novels. A young boy is surrounded by poverty, virtuous but unlucky parents, evil grasping relatives, and deceptive, exploitive employers. The hero is popular, strong, courageous, unfailingly honest, and relentlessly optimistic. Through imagination, hard work, and sheer perseverance, with several rounds of luck, he prospers economically, usually rising from train boy to railroad president. Hard work always triumphs, as does character. As the years went on, Cullom would find significant differences between those nineteenth-century Alger heroes and that tall Beckman boy: Arnold Beckman, as a new type of twentieth-century pioneer, would go far beyond the Alger stereotype. He would invent for himself a life in which education and research would be the new motors of success. Perseverance and hard work when combined with extraordinary talent, advanced education, and keen entrepreneurial skill would yield a distinctly modern outcome: sophisticated scientific instruments that themselves would offer the basis for a whole array of new industries. Public service and novel, systematic philanthropy would further enrich his creative transmutation of the Horatio Alger story.

In Normal the Beckman family found better schools for Fred, Arnold, and Wilma, while George had the rail connections he needed for his travels. Their brother, Roland, had already switched from Chicago to Bloomington, where he now had a job in the McLean County Bank and so could help his family find a house at 16 Hollis Street in Normal.

The move brought the family firmly into the twentieth century. Arnold's imagination soared in a town with trolleys, two universities, and theaters, and in a house with running water, indoor plumbing, and an attic and a basement. He appropriated both these spaces, making the basement his electrical laboratory and the attic his new chemical laboratory. Whether from above or below, his private studies on occasion imperiled the whole house with the threat of fire. He surely had a secret life about which the family knew little, for beginning with the incident with the pickle jar, reactions kept getting out of control: "I was heating some yellow phosphorus in a test tube. The test tube broke, and the phosphorus caught fire. Fortunately, I had on a rubber apron and I was able to smother the blaze with it. I burned my hand, but mainly I was scared my father would find out and do something to me for carrying out experiments like that in the house." He also risked life, limb, and home by tapping into the electrical supply in the damp basement: "If I wasn't careful, I'd get a shock when I put my hand on some electrical circuits."

A year after settling in at Hollis Street, George was restless and the Beckmans moved again. This time the destination was Bloomington itself. First they were at

Arnold Beckman in his basement electrical laboratory. *Courtesy Beckman family.*

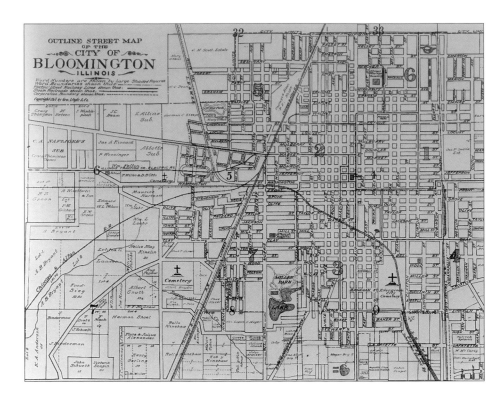

1016 East Olive and then at 802 East Grove, the house Arnold still thinks of as his old home in Bloomington. George's job had its difficulties, and living in Bloomington made his sales calls easier, with the town's immediate access to the Chicago & Alton, Lake Erie & Western, and Illinois Central railroads. Arnold and Fred could still go to University High, commuting together on the streetcar.

Arnold's experience at University High in a real, if modest, chemistry laboratory made a great impression; he could no longer be content with a private laboratory at home that simply provided him with a space to conduct his experiments and to house his equipment and supplies. It must look like a genuine chemistry laboratory as well. The house on East Grove Street, however, lacked the relatively generous appointments of the attic and basement in Normal. Undeterred, Arnold commandeered the small northeast corner room—almost a closet—and called it his laboratory. Laboratories were supposed to be white, so Arnold painted his small room white. He did not know the first thing about paint or painting. He was innocent of the existence and the importance of primer and became increasingly deflated as he applied layer upon layer of white enamel only to see his laboratory remain a dingy, not a brilliant, white. Only the fourth coat brought success. There is something touching in the image of a fifteen-year-old, frustrated and covered in paint, struggling and eventually succeeding in making his closet resemble his ideal.

If motivated, most kids will do a little at home of a favorite assignment at school. With Arnold and chemistry it was the other way around. He now got to do at school what he had done privately for five years, school being an appendage to his private pursuit. University High also presented its own paradox. It was, and is, the laboratory school for the teacher-training program of Illinois State Normal University, now Illinois State University. In that role the school had separate tracks: agricultural science, home economics, manual training, and commercial studies, in addition to the Latin-German curriculum, which was also the basic college preparatory track. Arnold Beckman was there, of course, to prepare for college, but therein lay his problem. Students of agriculture, commercial courses, and home economics all took a whole year of chemistry in their junior year. Latin-German students took botany and zoology as freshmen, physiology as sophomores, math as juniors, and physics as seniors—no chemistry at all, in any year. Here was a grand conundrum indeed.

Arnold took it upon himself to have a constructive chat with Ralph Pringle, the principal (such chats would play critical roles throughout his life). College-bound freshmen took Latin; indeed the language was required of them in all four years at the school. Arnold informed the principal that he was planning on attending college to become a chemist, and therefore he saw no need to study Latin. If he could start chemistry as a freshman, he could begin immediately on the long trail to a college degree in that field. His enthusiasm was persuasive, and the principal agreed to the exception. Perhaps as a conciliatory gesture after begging off Latin, Arnold enrolled in German. As fate had it, his German teacher loved to sing and gave Arnold an "A" for accompanying him on the piano while he belted out German songs. This gave Arnold an impressive transcript and freed up more time for him to work on chemistry, but as he later recalled, "I didn't learn very much German."

Science instruction at University High School was in the hands of Thomas Barger. Arnold was duly enrolled in his chemistry class, along with the vocationally oriented juniors who were taking it in their regular curricular sequence. His imagination was active as always. Late in his freshman year he needed some glass tubing for an experiment he was designing. Mr. Barger could not help, so the entrepreneurial Arnold made his way to the college labs, where he asked Professor Howard Adams for four pieces of glass tubing for "something I'm making." Adams not only gave him the tubes he wanted but showed him how to cut them. He would later remember—perhaps incorrectly, for he did not know of all the Cullom efforts—"Thus I was the first to see Beckman making Beckman instruments."

Young Arnold found more than glass tubing that day. He found a mentor who helped to shape his future course. Howard Adams, who had a bachelor's degree from Iowa State and the title of professor of chemistry, was the only chemist on the Illinois State faculty. He now had suddenly found his most eager student not in the university but in the high school program. Adams was very impressed with the young man's passion for chemistry and his determination to pursue it, and he, too, spoke with University High's principal to ensure that Arnold would be allowed to

The Beckman family in 1915. Arnold and Frederick stand to the left of their father, George (seated). Wilma and Roland stand to the right. *Courtesy Beckman family.*

take advantage of all the chemistry taught at Illinois State. In the end, when he graduated from University High, Arnold had two-and-one-half years of college chemistry under his belt.

The chemistry curriculum at Illinois State Normal University consisted of seven courses. Each was a term long, and Chemistry 1, 2, and 3 made up the first year. The first term explored hydrogen, oxygen, nitrogen, and carbon and their compounds, while the following two terms reviewed metals and nonmetals, with considerable attention given to industrial applications and household chemistry. Chemistry 4 was organic chemistry, Chemistry 5 was qualitative analysis, and Chemistry 6 was quantitative analysis. Chemistry 7 was a practicum for those who wanted to study teaching chemistry in schools, and it was probably not a course Arnold took.

Adams was the entire chemistry department at Illinois State, and though still in high school, Arnold was soon the second most knowledgeable chemist on campus. Adams accordingly offered him an unusual experience. Confident in his protégé's abilities, he asked Arnold—still a high school student—to teach his college-level classes for a week when he had to be away. Arnold supposed that this flattering request came because he was the only student who had taken both inorganic and analytical chemistry. Nonetheless, Fred Beckman must have had a shock when he walked into the chemistry lecture room that day to find his younger brother at the podium.

Few people are fortunate enough to have a mentor like Howard Adams. Beckman, lucky at many crucial junctures in his life, remembers that Adams was "very sympathetic and helpful. He encouraged me to do some of the things I wanted to do. . . . [H]e was a great teacher." Perhaps the greatest thing that Adams offered was treatment as a peer, a colleague, and a fellow enthusiast of science and chemistry. One striking way in which he expressed this esteem was to embark on study *with* Arnold. He proposed that the two of them enroll for a correspondence course in the science of metallography. Metallography is the study of the crystalline structure, or "grain," of metals and alloys. Metallographic studies involve polishing metal surfaces, etching these surfaces with different chemicals, and examining the revealed structures through specialized microscopes and photographic equipment; these procedures produce clues about chemical composition and about the history of the samples' formation or production. At that time metallography was an important new field industrially, as it allowed metals manufacturers and foundries to assess the quality of their products as well as to produce results important for metallurgy more generally.

The chemistry department had neither the expertise nor the equipment for Adams and Arnold to pursue their interest in metallography. Hence the correspondence course. That would suffice for the theory. But what of the practice? For that, Adams made an arrangement with his fellow chemists at the University of

Illinois. Each Saturday, Adams drove himself and Arnold to Urbana, fifty miles away, to use the microscopes and other equipment at the university. Adams's real motivation for the long Saturday trips was to foster his student's enthusiasm for chemistry. Adams "really had no deep interest in metallography," as Arnold put it, adding, in gratitude to his early mentor, "How many teachers do you know who'd take Saturdays to drive a student fifty miles to encourage him to go on with chemistry?"

Chemical analysis was making rapid progress early in the twentieth century, and analytical chemists were in demand. Arnold surely realized that metallography was a form of chemical analysis. His earlier job in chemistry, in Cullom, was also as an analytical chemist—though gauging cream samples in the general store had been a far different sort of analytical chemistry. A vision began to take shape in his mind—one remote from the blacksmith's forge and the farming life, and one that put a new twist on the usual dreams of ambitious youth at the time. Arnold dreamed of becoming a roving analytical chemist for hire. "I visualized having a trunk with apparatus—test tubes and chemicals—that I could take anywhere and analyze anything, just using the things in this trunk."

To further Arnold's experience with the career that interested him, Adams gave him the best lesson possible. He got Arnold a client. If he wanted to be a consulting analytical chemist, why wait? Arnold took the hint and embraced the trappings of a scientific professional. He had business cards printed, and his closetlike home laboratory became the "Bloomington Research Laboratories" in which he was "Chief Scientist." The client that Adams secured for this chief scientist was

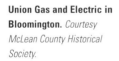

Union Gas and Electric in Bloomington. *Courtesy McLean County Historical Society.*

the local gas company, and the Bloomington Research Labs got an order for regular work.

Union Gas and Electric, as might be guessed from its name, transformed coal into electricity and gas. Arnold's business depended on a distinct drawback of gas made from Illinois coal: High in both sulfur and hydrogen sulfide, it was distinctly acid and smelled of rotten eggs. But industrial chemists had developed a remedy. If the gas could be reacted with ferric chloride, it would oxidize, losing its noxious character. The gas company accomplished this reaction by running the gas through chambers filled with wooden shavings soaked in ferric chloride. Over time the ferric chloride in the wood chips was lost to the reaction, and the company had to replace each batch of chips with a freshly soaked batch. Bloomington Research Laboratories got the job of running periodic analyses to determine the concentration of ferric chloride in the wood chips and thus when they needed replacing.

Working alone in his tiny laboratory at home, Arnold was quite successful, save for the time when the house almost burned down because the chips caught on fire. Luckily, the damage was minor and confined to his laboratory: He put out the chips before the rest of the house went up in flames. (Another time Arnold was forced to toss an out-of-control experiment right out the window of his lab room into the street below.)

Arnold busied himself with analyses for the gas company, experiments driven by his curiosity, and electrical tinkering. Like the house in Normal, his home in Bloomington had electrical service, and Arnold was fascinated by electricity almost as much as he was by chemistry. In just a few years he would combine these fascinations by carrying out experiments in physical chemistry and electrochemistry as an undergraduate at the University of Illinois. In his University High days, however, he was just familiarizing himself with the behavior of electricity, electrical circuits, and electrical devices. He simply could not resist tapping into something so convenient as the household's steady supply of electrical power. As he recalls, "The lab had a switchboard with various voltages. I had a little water-driven dynamo that produced direct current. I was just horsing around for the most part. I don't recall any particular experiments."

Chemist, Musician, and Entrepreneur

The *Index*, the yearbook at Illinois State Normal University, included University High students, and its issues depict Fred and Arnold during their years there. If anything, these pictures show them both as consistently more elegant and even more austere than their generally austere classmates. Fred was on the debate team and in the chorus. Few of Arnold's activities were noted in the yearbook, but the ones that were hint at an extraordinary figure. The tallest in his freshman year, he becomes sophomore class president and "some student star." Junior year he is leader of the school debate team and an officer in the science club as well, and the girls vote him

The Irvin Theatre in downtown Bloomington, Illinois. *Courtesy McLean County Historical Society.*

Arnold Beckman and his associates at the Irvin Theatre. *Courtesy Beckman family.*

"greatest thinker." Senior year he is president of Kappa Rho, a debate and literary society, and the yearbook labels him not "greatest thinker" but—in elegant variation—"worst bone head" and "physics shark."

All these yearbooks missed one major aspect of Arnold Beckman—he was becoming a veritable money-making machine. We do not know the exact mixture of necessity, opportunity, energy, and talent that drove him forward. We do know that the gas company work for Bloomington Research Labs brought income; that he continued his woodworking skills, making money there as well; and that his other great source of income was music.

The Beckman Orchestra. Arnold Beckman is seated at the piano. *Courtesy Institute Archives, California Institute of Technology.*

Compared with Cullom, Bloomington was a wonderland of opportunity. The Irvin Theatre opened a year after the Beckmans moved to Bloomington. Following his apprenticeship in the tiny Cullom theater, Arnold was ready to be a regular movie-house pianist, complete with union membership. He played at the Irvin Theatre almost every night for two years. Some nights it was organ solo for the silent films; on other nights he played piano in the six-piece orchestra. Arnold shared musical duties with the manager's wife. Between them they covered the Irvin's regular shows at 2:15, 3:45, 7:15, and 8:45 P.M.

In early-twentieth-century theaters, the pianist or organist usually improvised as the plot unfolded. Occasionally a theater musician had the luxury of seeing a movie first, giving advance warning of what to expect. The experienced performer could, though, shift music as the scenes changed, whether or not he or she had seen the film previously. Laughter, suspense, and sorrow were all emotional moods to be translated into music through standard selections. For many years after his days at the Irvin Theatre, Arnold could play the *Poet and Peasant* Overture or the *William Tell* Overture on demand.

A show with a formal score demanded more careful coordination. D. W. Griffith's overwhelmingly popular *Birth of a Nation* had Arnold playing almost constantly from 10:00 A.M. to 10:00 P.M. One of the first films of epic scale, with battle scenes and assorted film techniques that no American audience had seen before, it had a full score to accompany the scenes. It was also the longest film made to that point, twelve reels, or two-and-one-half hours, and when it was in town, it ran continuously. Arnold wound up with two very sore bandaged thumbs and a steady income.

His friend Eugene D. Funk, Jr., later president of Funk's Seeds, remembers the great attraction that Arnold held for the other University High students. Funk often led groups of students to the Irvin to hear Arnold play and, quite incidentally, see a movie. They sat near the pit and counted it a major victory when they could get him to repeat a thunderclap or any other sound effect. Years later Funk wrote Beckman recalling the many Saturday afternoons spent in that spirit, "eating peanuts and throwing the hulls at you, sometimes a complete peanut with the hull still on it . . . [and] you thumping the keys real hard when the picture had Indians and cowboys in it."

There was more music besides that for the movies. Sometimes when the Irvin Theatre program finished for the day, Arnold made his way to Hills Hotel, where he joined the Burkes in playing dinner music in the cafe. Paul and Harry Burke were professional musicians who took an interest in the eager and talented pianist. The three played until the patrons went home, then began serious practice. While the waiters finished closing up for the night, the trio ran through a piece in B flat. Then the Burkes would say, "Now, let's do it again in G." Arnold took to such challenges readily, and thus a pianist became a musician.

One wonders how Arnold Beckman found time to study. When he was not playing at the Irvin or with Paul and Harry Burke, he was playing with George Goforth's dance band, or with Arthur Dornaus's band, or, as one might expect, with his own band of students from University High. These jobs made him familiar with most of the people in Bloomington music. Arnold remembers that the Dornaus sound emphasized strings, while the Goforth tended toward drums and brass: If Dornaus played *Poor Butterfly* and Carrie Jacobs Bond, the Goforth band swung with early jazz.

Arnold Beckman's own dance band consisted of Lucky Westoff (drums), Lou Thomas (clarinet), Trent Millikin (cornet and trumpet), Joel Bryant (violin), and Dwight Ramsay (bass). Arnold on piano was as entrepreneurial as he was with his chemistry laboratory: He produced both business cards and publicity photographs of the ensemble at work. The Beckman Orchestra played for parties and dances, often at the Elks and Knights of Columbus clubs. Sometimes Arnold occupied center stage alone, accompanied only by his drummer. Either way, the band's staples were the popular songs of the period. Characteristically, the leader had great fun while at the same time making money: Arnold's talent for harnessing his passionate interests to entrepreneurial opportunity showed very early in life.

His fame was spreading in Bloomington, but friends were still watching from Cullom. Toby Van Alstyne, at that time editor of the school newspaper in Cullom, the *Big Noise*, carried the following news in January 1916: "Arnold Beckman informs the editor that he has gone into business in Normal with another young man. They have a laboratory and a wood-working shop. Many doubtless remember how 'Hoot' was always experimenting with something in his spare time, and now he can put his knowledge to some good use." Arnold's talents were developing along lines that Cullom knew well.

His senior year at University High began in 1917, the year the United States entered the European "Great War." A frenzy of mobilization soon gripped the country: Campuses, offices, and factories emptied; recruiting stations were overwhelmed; cantonments were thrown up around the country to handle new inductees; war bonds were offered; scrap material drives began; and schoolchildren were encouraged to plan gardens and raise livestock to feed to the boys "over there." Industrial enterprises, particularly heavy industry, had demands for their products that far surpassed anything seen or imagined previously. One such firm was the Keystone Steel and Iron Company in Pekin, Illinois. The war, it seemed, had an insatiable appetite for steel.

Arnold was among those of his classmates who were, on account of their excellent academic records, allowed to leave University High two months early to contribute to the war effort. Always Arnold's mentor, Professor Adams found him a position as a chemist with Keystone Steel and Iron in the spring of 1918, where his job was to analyze steel samples during the manufacturing process and to determine the content of carbon and other substances in the melt. The importance of this kind of chemical analysis is hard to overstate, for the varieties and qualities of steel depend upon the carbon content of the iron and the presence of other trace elements. The precise timing of steps in the manufacturing process and subsequent procedures for shaping and handling the steel all hinge on this same measure of the steel's components. Simply put, the value of a batch of steel rests on its chemical composition. The ability of Arnold to carry out his chemical analyses quickly and accurately was of paramount importance to Keystone. He rose to the challenge. Keystone had its own "regular analytical laboratory, with the Alberene stone table tops and the analytical balances." Arnold and the only other analytical chemist working at the plant alternated ten- and fourteen-hour shifts—two weeks on the first shift, two weeks on the second. Even though he was only eighteen, when he was on duty, he was the sole chemist in charge.

Arnold Beckman later painted the scene at Keystone:

This was an open-hearth plant. A hundred tons of glowing hot, molten steel in each furnace. When they're about ready to pour the melt, it is essential to know whether four elements of impurity are within acceptable limits. I'd reach into the open-hearth furnace with a long-handled ladle, get a sample of the molten iron, and pour it into a mold about two inches square and six inches high. As soon as the test sample was solid—although still red hot—I'd pick it up with tongs and run to the laboratory. After cooling it with water, I'd drill chips and weigh out four samples: one each for carbon, sulfur, manganese, and phosphorus analysis. On that they'd decide if they would pour that melt or refine it more. With a hundred tons of molten steel tied up, every minute costs a great many dollars; that's why it was so important to get the results back in a hurry. I'd race against the clock. I could run all four of these analyses in less than thirty minutes. I set a record for the lab, I remember.

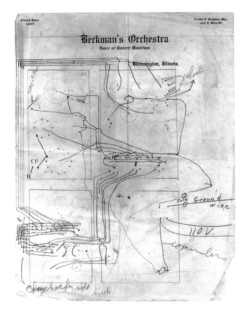

A sheet of the promotional stationery for the Beckman Orchestra. (Beckman's sketch of an electrical circuit was made at a later date.) *Courtesy Institute Archives, California Institute of Technology.*

There was plenty of downtime on the long night shifts when a chemist simply was not needed. Arnold took long naps, stretched out atop those cool, stone bench tops in the analytical laboratory—but more than this, he enjoyed the experience at Keystone because it was a rare opportunity and because, in setting the laboratory record for the fastest analysis, he made it a success. He set one other record that year. At his high school graduation he was valedictorian. His overall average of 89.41 was the highest in University High history. Although these records might leave the impression that he was a grind, Arnold was still an exuberant young man; his class of 1918 spent graduation day playing in the park, and at the ceremonies that night the valedictorian had a bright red, sunburned face as he stood up to give his speech.

The Valedictorian

Although George Beckman had not attended high school, he had a real respect for learning. He encouraged his children to pursue their individual interests and urged them to excel and to take advantage of whatever educational opportunities were within their grasp. All his children pursued formal education past the normal end point for their contemporaries. Roland became a salesman after graduating from business school. Fred became a lawyer after graduating from Illinois Wesleyan. Wilma graduated from Illinois Wesleyan also, before heading to Cornell for a degree in home economics. Arnold pursued his formal education even farther. Beckman still puzzles about the dedication to education in his family. "Looking back," he recalls, "I realize how utterly naive I was. . . . I had no connection of any kind with higher education at that time. My father I don't think even went to high school. . . . On the other hand, for some reason he had four children, [and] every one of them went through college."

As he graduated from high school, Arnold Beckman somewhat resembled the heroes in the Horatio Alger novels he read as a child, but he was much more. Certainly the "pluck and luck" that made Alger's boyish heroes fabulously successful played a role in his life, but luck alone did not make Arnold the person he was to become. Rather, it was a combination of natural talent and remarkable instinct for opportunity. At the age of eighteen he already exemplified Louis Pasteur's maxim "Chance favors the prepared mind."

By 1918 the manual and mental skills, the entrepreneurial spirit, and the creative curiosity that shaped his later careers were already well developed in Arnold Beckman. Discipline and drive were facets of his personality at a very early age, as was a fine sense of humor. He could have fun with the most vigorous of his peers, while his love of adventure would, over a lifetime, outdistance that of anyone else in town. He led his school in academics, and he used his imagination and his manual skills to make things. He was already dexterous in chemistry, music, and woodworking, and he had a youthful but strong sense of industriousness, confidence, and excellence. As he grew mentally, he also grew in physical stature. In his prime he would be just over six feet, and even as a child he stood taller than others. But those who noticed his height could not overlook his mental growth. Toby Van Alstyne remembers him as "the biggest kid in school." He was good at everything, and "good to everybody. . . . The town wasn't big enough to have anyone else like him. I think we all had the idea that he was really going to amount to something, that he was two steps ahead of us."

Arnold Beckman has blended these elements into a unique and extraordinary story. His powers of mind, his skills of hand, his evenness of temperament, and his commanding presence—these talents would enable him to succeed in many contexts. His luck would serve him well on numerous occasions. But great talent and great luck alone are not sufficient to explain the course of his careers or the impact of his life. Time and again throughout his life, Arnold Beckman has displayed an attribute that was already evident in the blacksmith's son. As Cullom and Bloomington yielded him novel opportunities in musicianship, industrial employment, and advanced education that others simply did not see, so in the days ahead Arnold Beckman revealed an uncanny instinct for significant new currents in twentieth-century life, coupled with the ability to demonstrate their importance.

ARNOLD BECKMAN IS BEST STUDENT

NORMAL GRADUATING CLASS

Three of University Teachers are Detained at Home— Other Normal News

Scholastic honors for the class of 1918 at University High go to Arnold Beckman of Bloomington. Statistics compiled by the faculty today show that his average for the four years work is 89.41, the highest average ever attained by a University High graduate. Wayne Moore of the class of 1915 has the honor of having been the next best student ever produced at the Normal preparatory school, his average being slightly better than 87 for his four years work. Mr. Beckman will be the valedictorian for the graduating class and Edward Stein of Gibson City will be the saluatorian. His average was 88. Those who averaged above 85 for the four years besides the two receiving the highest honor were Miss Helen Cade, Robert McCormick, George Davis, Louis Fahnleslow and George Coffey. The latter was captain of this year's football team at University High. The senior class named Paul Packard and Miss Hazel Bechenheimer as class speakers and the faculty will select their two representatives in the near future.

Arnold and Mabel at the beach. *Courtesy Beckman family.*

2 | *A Scientist in the Making*

Luck has played a big role in my life—finding a chemistry textbook and meeting my wife through lucky circumstance.

The Marines and Mabel

After graduating from University High School, Arnold Beckman joined the U.S. Marines. It was August 1918, and the war in Europe ground on. Beckman had every intention of going on to college—that he would enroll at a university was taken for granted—so why he enlisted is not clear. He was not conscripted, and he did not harbor special enmity toward the Germans. His own family was German, and he had grown up in a community heavily populated by German immigrants. Idealistic patriotism was ascendant in the United States, however, and Beckman joined vast legions of young American men in casting aside study for the challenge and uncertainties of World War I.

Machine guns, gas, tanks, submarines, and new explosives showed the horrific, central role that science and technology could play on the fields of war. In fact military commanders, university administrators, and faculty grew concerned as student patriotism emptied campuses and thus diminished the supply of technically trained personnel, vital to the war effort. Both generals and deans tried to increase the number of newly enlisted men who would finish university studies before joining regiments in the field.

Arnold would have nothing of being detailed to a campus. He had signed on for combat and the likelihood of travel far beyond the world he had known in Illinois. His decision displays the spirit of risk and adventure that breaks out at many points in his life. He had already served the cause in the steel plant, but his youthful wanderlust prompted him to follow his brothers into active service. Roland was in the navy, and Fred was serving with the cavalry. Prefiguring his later credo that "there is no satisfactory substitute for excellence," Arnold, at eighteen the youngest of the Beckman brothers, packed up his gear and headed off for three months of marine boot camp at Parris Island, South Carolina.

"I certainly learned the meaning of the word discipline; in boot camp they enforced that to the nth degree," Beckman recalls. The long hours of uncompromising drill, training, and arduous chores gave him a new appreciation of his

Frederick Beckman in his cavalry uniform, 1917.
Courtesy Beckman family.

Top: Arnold Beckman at marine boot camp, Parris Island, South Carolina, 1918.

Bottom: Private Beckman sweeping out the barracks at Parris Island, 1918.
Both courtesy Beckman family.

mother's earlier insistence on piano practice. She had enforced long hours of an often chilly discipline, but it was practice at an art that would train his hands, his eyes, and his will and grant him and his audience pleasure. At Parris Island he learned a swift and brutal lesson in discipline for discipline's sake and for the survival and success of his combat unit.

Boot camp complete, buck Private Beckman and some of his campmates were roused from their bunks one night at 10:00 P.M. The thirty hastily assembled young marines were ordered to make their way, with gear, to the train depot. They were to report to the Brooklyn Navy Yard, a major embarkation point for American soldiers headed to the European front. There they were to board a troopship and head to sea—and to war.

The trip was one of many events in Beckman's life where small changes made great differences. The need to coordinate the war effort had put the government in charge of America's railroads. As his troop train headed north, it moved into a system responsible for moving millions of troops, equipment, and supplies in addition to the raw materials needed by a nation at war, in response to ever-changing priorities, crises, and unexpected shortages. In this system of engines, cars, and conflicting schedules, Beckman's train from Parris Island was delayed. That short delay changed the fate of his unit. When the thirty marines finally reached the navy yard, they learned that another contingent had already sailed in their place. Private Beckman's unit was sent to the yard's barracks to await new orders.

Fate was not done. As the thirty reported in with other troops, they were counted off into groups, ostensibly to determine the floor in the barracks on which they could find their bunks. Later it became clear to the marines that the sleeping arrangements carried a far greater significance. Barrack floors corresponded to deck assignments on future troop-transport ships. Private Beckman's place in line gave him the last bunk on the second floor. The soldier behind him was the first to go to the third floor. Arnold and the second floor would remain in Brooklyn, while the third floor, including the fellow behind him in line, were in the barracks barely long enough to unpack before heading out for two years of combat in Russia against the revolutionary Red Army led by Leon Trotsky.

His late arrival in Brooklyn and his place in line are among the handful of events that have given Arnold Beckman a sense of fate and luck in his life. As with Horatio Alger characters, "pluck and luck" seemed to guide his success. One place in line meant two years in Russia. Yet Beckman himself would never leave the United States as a marine, for within a matter of days after his arrival at the navy yard, the armistice of 11 November 1918 was signed, and the slaughter of World War I was over.

The country did require one more service of Beckman and his fellows. Thanksgiving Day 1918 began like any other day under military command, most notable for the especially heavy dinner the soldiers enjoyed in the mess hall. After that they were ready to relax. It was not to be. Instead, the commander of the "second deck" called his men together to hear a surprising order. The marines were to proceed to the nearby Greenpoint YMCA to eat another Thanksgiving dinner.

The enthusiastic local Red Cross and YMCA women volunteers had organized a celebratory dinner to honor marines returning from France and the struggles at Belleau Woods and Chateau Thierry. Sadly, many had been killed during those last fierce encounters on the western front, and not enough had returned to fill the tables. Healthy marines from the barracks were needed to fill in for their fallen comrades. When the men told their commander they had just finished a hearty meal, he reassured them. They were young, with good appetites, and he had confidence that they would obey their marching orders. They owed respect to the memory of their fallen comrades, no less to the International Committee of the Red Cross, which had just won the Nobel Peace Prize for its relief efforts on behalf of civilians and combatants on both sides of the Great War. Moreover, no slight could be risked toward the local volunteer women of the Red Cross. The dinner that they had prepared could not go unappreciated. The course of true patriotism that afternoon was clear, and as usual, Arnold Beckman gave the assignment his full effort in every way.

Life changed for Arnold that afternoon, immeasurably for the better. There, in the Greenpoint center, serving up plates of food with her mother, was Mabel Meinzer of Brooklyn, then not quite eighteen years old. The young marine from Cullom was transfixed. Whether he realized it or not, he had found his life partner. Later that night, after dinner, Mabel and her mother consented to Private Beckman's offer to serve as their escort home, at least after Mabel showed him how

The Greenpoint, Brooklyn, division of the Red Cross. Mabel Meinzer is seated in the first row, third from the right. *Courtesy Institute Archives, California Institute of Technology.*

Mabel in her Red Cross uniform, 1918. *Courtesy Beckman family.*

to navigate the subways. Mabel also quickly taught him how to navigate in matters of the heart; that much is apparent from a letter he wrote some three weeks later. Arnold Orville Beckman and Mabel Stone Meinzer would not marry until he was far better established, a full six-and-one-half years later. Until that day the post office profited greatly from that fateful dinner. Although they were rarely together, they were certain of each other. They wrote often, each saving every letter from the other.

A Romance Blooms

Miss Mabel S. Meinzer

33 Oakland St.

Brooklyn, N.Y.

   Dec. 16, 1918

My dear friend:

   I wish to thank you for the invitation which I received this morning. So far as I know now, I will not be on duty Saturday, and I shall be very glad to accept this opportunity to be with you.

   I hope that you will forgive me for not writing. By some act of carelessness I had mislaid your address, so I couldn't write, and I was a little afraid to come out without writing for fear that you had forgotten about me. But your note has disproved this, and it is with my sincerest thanks that I accept your kind invitation.

Cordially yours,

Arnold O. Beckman

Marine B[arrac]ks.

Navy Yard, N.Y. 60th co[mpany].

Mabel was the daughter of the director of maintenance at Bellevue Hospital, one of the largest medical centers of the booming metropolis. Mabel had an older brother, Walter, and a younger brother, Charlie. The Meinzer family was much more urbane than the families Arnold Beckman had known in central Illinois, but there were nonetheless similarities. Both Arnold's and Mabel's families were composed of recent immigrants to the United States. Her father's parents had come from Germany, as had the parents of Arnold's father. Mabel's mother was herself an

Mabel with her local YWCA group. She is seated at bottom left. *Courtesy Beckman family.*

**Arnold Beckman and
Mabel Meinzer, outside
the Meinzer home.**
Courtesy Beckman family.

immigrant; Alice Stone and her sister, Katie, had come over as young women from Castlecomer in County Kilkenny, Ireland. Arnold's mother was born in the United States, but her parents came from nearby England. While Mabel and Arnold had led very different lives to this point, the similarities in their family backgrounds offered ground on which their relationship could grow. The pair had seven dates while Arnold was stationed in Brooklyn. Often he would call on Mabel at her parents' house, where her mother would serve them tea and baking powder biscuits.

When Arnold and Mabel first met, he could assure her that he did not plan a future with the marines, for just days earlier, on 22 November 1918, he had applied for a discharge. Military life had given him a chance to serve his country, to travel, and to meet a wonderful young woman; now he intended to return to chemistry. As he wrote in his application, he hoped to return to Illinois State Normal University for the second semester. With the armistice the military had legions of men in its ranks that it could no longer use, and discharges were not hard to get. His came through at the end of January 1919. He took a lingering leave from Mabel and returned to Bloomington. His return was not fast enough, however, to allow him to enter the second semester at either Illinois State Normal or the University of Illinois. Improvisations came easily to Arnold Beckman, and good pianist that he was, he now improvised a wonderful summer.

A Summer Interlude

Music had provided Arnold with a steady, enjoyable source of income in Bloomington, and in late spring 1919 this talent and his sense of adventure together gave him the confidence, and the brashness, to strike out for new places. His stint in the U.S. Marines had taken him to the East Coast. Before returning to the classroom and the laboratory, he filled his free summer months with new wanderings to the West. In a day in which every movie theater—from the grand urban palace to the small-town movie house—needed a living, breathing, and more or less competent piano player, Arnold "Hoot" Beckman and his Bloomington friend Wakefield "Fat" Boyer hopped a freight train with only four dollars in their pockets. If a town had a theater, they could earn their daily bread.

Hoot and Fat rode the rails westward, carefree and virtually cash-free. Luck favored them when a policeman discovered the pair in a railroad yard near Des Moines, Iowa. Instead of arresting them, the officer gave some advice. "He said we looked clean, not like ordinary bums. We told him we wanted to see the West. He said, 'Okay, that's fine. Take some advice from me: Keep clean, keep shaved and washed up, and always be polite. You'll get along all right.'" They did. Beckman and Boyer soon learned that their willingness to do the dishes in a restaurant for a few days—to "pearl dive" in the jargon of railroad tramps—was another reliable source of income. A day or two of washing dishes gave the pair a small amount of cash and a stock of food to be carried on toward the next stop.

Two views of Main Street, Ashton, Idaho, early 1900s.
Courtesy Institute Archives, California Institute of Technology.

All went well until Laramie, Wyoming. That afternoon Hoot would sell programs at a rodeo and then meet Fat at night in the rail yard to hop a particular freight. At train time each waited separately as long as possible for the other before taking the dangerous swing up into a passing freight car, confident that the other was already on the train. Only after several hours did they realize they were on different trains. Fat was on his way to San Francisco. There he joined the army and sailed to Vladivostock for combat against the Red Army. Hoot's train took him toward Yellowstone. He got off at Ashton, Idaho. He had no friend and no plan, and he spent his first night under the stars—worrying about bears.

As he walked into Ashton the next morning, the future brightened. There was the Star Theatre. Finding its owner, Fred Swanstrum, Beckman offered his numerous services. He could sell tickets or run the projector or, best of all, play the piano. "Could the Star use him for tonight's show?" he asked. "Indeed it could," said

Swanstrum, because the fellow then playing for him had trouble with "Come to Jesus" in the key of C. Arnold Beckman played that evening. To his surprise he was offered the position for the entire summer, with congenial lodging thrown in. Proving that chance favors the prepared mind, he had spent one night sleeping in the open and the next night in the guest room of the wealthiest man in Ashton, for Swanstrum owned the bank as well.

When autumn came, Arnold Beckman bade a reluctant farewell to Ashton and headed to the University of Illinois, making the transition from hopping trains and scrounging work to disciplined studying in the classroom and laboratory. He had known since the age of nine that he wanted to be a chemist, and the university's department of chemistry was already familiar to him from his Saturday trips at University High.

Arnold Beckman knew that chemistry and chemical engineering offered lucrative jobs, but such concerns were not uppermost in his mind. He simply had no worries about making his way. His summer became the model for his life and for an unshakable faith in his future: "I learned I could take care of myself no matter what. So what my future life was going to be really never was of great concern to me." Free from self-doubt, he could follow where his curiosity and judgment led him, certain that he would find his way. With great confidence he headed to a chemistry department that was doing important things.

A chemistry laboratory at the University of Illinois, Urbana-Champaign, 1920s.
Courtesy University of Illinois Library.

World War I was a watershed period in American history, leaving no corner of American social, economic, political, and intellectual life unchanged. Many even called the postwar era "a new world," and few were more conscious of this novel environment than American chemists in industry and academe.

The University of Illinois chemistry faculty members, like most academic chemists, had been mobilized for total war. Before it was the "First World War," the conflict was simply the "Great War," while still others with accuracy called it the "Chemists' War." The Chemists' War is a label that conveys the strong international outrage at production, stockpiling, and use of chemical weapons. Gas warfare shocked civilians and combatants alike. The gas masks that infantry were compelled to carry at all times—often on their backs to lessen the chance of puncture by bullets—were a constant reminder that any smoke could hide a silent, burning, indiscriminate killer. Newspaper readers in the belligerent countries reacted to each gas attack as an atrocity committed by the opposing side.

The role of chemists in the chemical warfare services of the nations at war was the most visible and controversial part of chemistry's military role. Chemistry and chemists also found quieter but no less vital roles in the production of explosives, dyes, glass, metal, medicines, oils, and foodstuffs. In the United States chemists were mobilized not only into the Chemical Warfare Service but also into another effort that rivaled it in scale and scope. This was the effort (at which the Germans had already succeeded) to create fixed nitrogen by synthetic means, for fixed nitrogen was the basic building block of fertilizers and explosives alike. If armies were to continue a dreary war of attrition, they needed ample supplies of both food and ammunition. Natural resources were insufficient, and the nation looked to its chemists.

Of necessity, the U.S. chemical industry saw tremendous growth during the war years, and postwar strategic planning cast chemistry in a new light. The nation's leaders now saw that economic health and military security depended on a stable, thriving chemical industry that could make domestically the many specialty products that had previously been imported. Blockades and shortages revealed to decision makers just how dependent the United States had become on European, especially German, chemical firms and on foreign natural deposits of raw materials. Only government-funded research programs, military procurement, and the seizure of alien plants and patents had provided the nation with wartime chemical strength.

The harsh and heady experience of American chemists in the war led to much planning and discussion after the war, as university, military, government, and industry leaders all agreed that still further expansion of the chemical industry was in the national interest. At the University of Illinois chemists and chemical engineers were rightly confident that they would be leaders in that expansion and would develop a great cadre of chemists to staff America's new industries. ∾

The Education of a Chemist

Arnold Beckman had no immediate concern for career prospects or for contributing to the growth of a vital industry. He was simply following the interests sparked by *Fourteen Weeks in Chemistry* and confirmed in his backyard lab, at University High, and in the gas works and the steel mill. "I thought at that time I was going to be an organic chemist. . . . I was intrigued by thoughts of making all these fancy dyes and things of that sort." He would later add: "Keep in mind, I was a young lad in 1919, coming from a small rural community. . . . I wasn't worried about the future of the chemical industry at that time. I was interested in making some interesting chemicals—dyes or things that smelled good."

Because he had taken university-level courses while in high school, he was allowed to begin with advanced chemistry courses at Illinois. Once again he was an extraordinary freshman making it his own special way, and once more he found a superb mentor—this time in Carl Marvel. "Speed," as he was uniformly known to colleagues and students, became one of America's best-known, most respected organic chemists. He was a central actor in the emergence of Illinois as the leading power in national chemistry in the interwar years. He mentored generations of students during his long tenure there, served as president of the American Chemical Society, made pathbreaking contributions to polymer science, and played a crucial role in the synthetic rubber industry during World War II. But when Beckman first encountered Marvel, he was but a recent Ph.D. graduate of Illinois serving as an instructor in the department. Just six years older than Beckman, Marvel provided the freshman with a living, immediate example of how someone could make his way in the world of academic chemistry.

Arnold found Speed to be "a very likeable person, friendly. He commanded the respect of everybody, from first his knowledge and competence and then his general behavior. He was a great fellow." The respect was mutual: Marvel was impressed with his new student. Because of Beckman's thorough preparation in chemistry, Marvel assigned him an individual research project of his very own—not on beer but on mercury compounds. He was to start out on a program of synthesizing dialkyl mercury compounds, namely dipropyl and isopropyl mercury. Through their work together on these compounds, Marvel was both a mentor and a guiding model for Beckman as a chemist.

Marvel himself had synthesized many organic mercury compounds previously. In 1920, as Arnold Beckman began his own mercury syntheses in the organic chemistry laboratory, he worked in a way that would cause shock in our risk-conscious era. Mercury is one of the most hazardous and toxic of the elements, ranking just behind lead and arsenic. A relatively small exposure can cause poisoning and even death. Organic mercury compounds are more dangerous still than the elemental form itself. They can be absorbed into the human bloodstream by almost any route, even through the skin. Working with organic mercury

Arnold Beckman met a kindred spirit in Speed Marvel. Both were sons of Illinois farmers and inhabitants of Bloomington in the early 1910s. Marvel was born on his father's farm in Waynesville, Illinois. As with the Beckmans, neither of Marvel's parents had an education beyond grade school, but they, too, placed a premium on their children's educations.

Speed enrolled at Illinois Wesleyan University in 1911, expecting to be a farmer after graduation. An uncle suggested that studying the sciences could make his future in agriculture more profitable. He heeded the advice, taking all the science courses he could, especially chemistry. Eventually Speed's thoughts about applying science to agriculture faded. He had discovered a love for chemistry itself.

Even though Illinois Wesleyan was small, it had a new science building, new scientific equipment, and Alfred W. Homberger as professor of chemistry. Homberger was as encouraging to Marvel as he, in turn, would be to Arnold Beckman. Homberger was himself a Ph.D. from the University of Illinois—a personable man and a good teacher. There were only 230 students at Illinois Wesleyan, but 14 of them were chemistry majors, and Homberger organized them into a chemistry club. Marvel quickly joined their ranks. His work with Homberger at Illinois Wesleyan provides an early example of student–faculty research, one that Arnold Beckman has long delighted in recalling. Under Homberger's tutelage Marvel spent his senior year (1914–1915) on a study of beer—"Rate of Turbidity in Beverages Containing Maltose, Glucose, or Maltose and Glucose." Published in the *Journal of the American Chemical Society* in 1917, Speed's senior research project explored why some batches of beer turn cloudy. Earlier guesses were that the turbidity was a protein precipitate, but Marvel and Homberger showed that muddy beer came from the mold *Penicillium glaucum*, which had not been killed by sterilization. Maltose solutions, however, somehow prevented penicillin growth. The article said nothing about tasting the liquids under study, as another trustworthy test of their varied states.

Alfred W. Homberger, Speed Marvel's mentor. *Courtesy University of Illinois Library.*

One day during Marvel's senior year, Homberger asked him, "How'd you like to go to graduate school?" Marvel replied, "What's that?" Homberger explained the basic concept and the more immediate practicality that such further education would be free: Homberger had old university connections, Marvel had excellent marks, and the top Illinois Wesleyan student was guaranteed a fellowship at the University of Illinois. Marvel talked the matter over with his father, who was encouraging: "Well, if somebody's going to pay you to go to school, maybe you'd better go. You might accidentally get a good job." Four years later Marvel earned his Ph.D. Even as he began his graduate studies, Marvel had only vague notions about what it would mean for him to become a chemist. While he had hazy thoughts that he might teach after his graduate work, his focus was on the chemistry itself. As Marvel remembered years later: "While I didn't know what a chemist did, I knew that I liked chemistry. It was fun." ◆

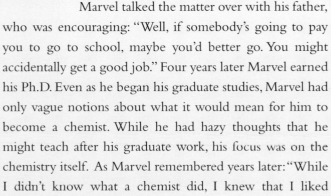

Wallace Carothers and Speed Marvel with the trophy of their 1935 fishing trip at Squaw Lake, Wisconsin. *Marvel Papers, Chemical Heritage Foundation.*

compounds is especially dangerous because of their high vapor pressure. In conditions not at all uncommon in a laboratory of the 1910s and 1920s, these compounds could quickly vaporize into a highly toxic cloud that laboratory researchers ran the risk of inhaling. One can hardly imagine a more direct route of exposure than through the lungs into the bloodstream. Yet while Beckman and Marvel were aware of the dangers of mercury poisoning, they had good reason to be interested in mercury compounds. These compounds had an agricultural usefulness to match their dangers, being familiar as fungicides, preservatives, and as key ingredients in manufacturing.

Marvel had a lifelong interest in chemical puzzles that held the promise of practical use. Given his early fascination with the application of chemistry to agriculture, the fungicidal properties of the organic mercury compounds were simply too enticing for him to resist. Beckman joined in the quest and almost immediately began to suffer from mercury poisoning. Because his work progressed, he stuck doggedly to his bench, despite losing some of his hair. By the time he left to return to his father's house for Christmas, the exposure was more than his body could bear. At home he enjoyed visiting with his family and feeling the symptoms lessen. The holidays lasted nearly a month, but when he returned to his experiments, the mercury symptoms returned with a vengeance. Speed, too, had been afflicted by repeated mercury exposures, and he, like his student, developed an extreme sensitivity to the organic mercury compounds, causing him ultimately to abandon this line of research. Marvel later remembered: "If somebody opened a bottle of mercury compound two doors down the hall, I'd get a headache." Mercury killed the glamour of organic chemistry for Arnold Beckman, and he sought a new beginning with a switch to physical chemistry and a whole new realm of chemical questions and puzzles.

The interaction with Marvel would not end when Beckman switched to a new mentor in physical chemistry. Speed was a department favorite for another role he played, which also set an example for Beckman. The chemical faculty at Illinois did more than preach about cooperating with industry. They also sponsored a regular summer-long operation that ran on commercial lines and made money for the department by using its well-equipped labs as a significant source of industrial supply. In a day before large graduate stipends, summer chemical production provided jobs for the brightest students at what the department called "organic manufactures," the synthesis for sale of rare and expensive fine chemicals in limited quantities. Fine chemicals are those of greater than 99-percent purity, used in small-scale reactions in both industrial and academic laboratories. Naturally they command a considerable premium. Illinois's efforts at synthesis and manufacture served multiple purposes: Students learned the concepts and craftsmanship of chemistry by making dozens and dozens of compounds; the department obtained compounds for its own use; and selling them to others financed the purchase of needed supplies. That the department's reputation went up because of such enterprise was another plus.

Academic and industrial chemists alike had a growing thirst for these exotic, pure organic compounds, the raw materials with which chemists pushed the bounds of chemical knowledge and invented new industrial products and processes. With German supplies cut off during the war and out of favor afterward, sources of fine chemicals were few, while demand was increasing as chemistry grew more ubiquitous and complex. The supplier naturally had to command the respect and confidence of buyers that their limited funds would indeed purchase pure samples of the exact compound required. The chemistry department at Illinois was just such a respected supplier, a designation earned on the basis of the skill and reputation of its members.

Marvel had begun working at these organic manufactures in 1917, during his second summer as a graduate student at Illinois. He continued in subsequent summers. This work, a combination of the educational and the practical, allowed him to earn a student's living and truly become a chemist: "That's how I learned my chemistry." By 1920 Marvel was on the Illinois faculty—and a natural choice for the summer role of director of organic manufactures, making the decisions about which Illinois students would get one of the much-sought-after positions in the manufactures during the summer recess. Starting in the 1921 summer break, he gave Beckman a job on the basis of his precocious grasp of chemical concepts and his skills of hand, eye, and wit at experimental manipulation. As Arnold recalls:

There were fume hoods, but we did not have the concern over toxic substances that we have now. See, this was when Eastman Kodak [the major commercial distributor of reagents on a national basis] encouraged the university to make the fine chemicals and research reagent chemicals which they would then distribute. So we would have summer employment. As I look back on those days, the laboratories were just so full of benzene and toluene fumes, we weren't worried about the carcinogenic effect. We were worried whether we were too close to the explosive limit! We'd blow up!

Despite an introduction to mercury poisoning and the hazard of a laboratory filled with explosive and noxious fumes, Speed Marvel provided Arnold Beckman with a powerful model. Here was an academic chemist much like himself, one who possessed rural Illinois roots, ties to Bloomington, and a delight in the fascinations and challenges of chemistry. Furthermore, Marvel, in partnership with a leading distributor of scientific products, was making money and providing livelihoods by producing the basic tools with which fellow chemists could advance science and technology. Consciously or not, Arnold followed Speed's example closely years later as an assistant professor of chemistry at Caltech.

Halcyon Days in Idaho

In 1920, at the end of Arnold Beckman's freshman year, even a sympathetic Marvel was not yet ready to give the raw recruit a coveted spot with the "organic manufactures." While surely disappointing, the news was by no means devastating, for Arnold had received a telegram from his old employer at the Star Theatre in Ashton, Idaho. The job of playing the piano was his again, if he wanted it. If he could not make his way that summer by working in chemistry, here was another chance to experience the western wilderness. At the close of the semester, he hopped another westbound freight. The memories of that summer linger as some of his very fondest. Then and for years afterward he silently thanked his mother for teaching him more than music. She had shown him the discipline required for mastery, whatever the subject. Her lessons gave him the boldness to take on opportunities that luck brought in his direction.

When he arrived in Ashton, Arnold discovered that throughout the spring the theater had shown slides heralding the impending return of "Professor Beckman" as a summer attraction. He played afternoons and evenings, and since a pianist of his experience needed no time for practice, the rest of his day was free. He quickly teamed up with a trio of colorful characters. One was "Hacksaw Tom" Christensen, a former prizefighter from Chicago. Hacksaw cut his boxing career short, fleeing Chicago to escape what he would only describe as "a little female trouble." He got his nickname from his use of a favored technique for leaving jail unannounced. Also in the group were the brothers Togo and Jerry Manning. Arnold knew Jerry from the Star Theatre and from their shared interest in chemical reactions. Jerry's day job was in photography. At night he ran the Star's projector. Togo Manning had his own shop as Ashton's leather craftsman.

Arnold at the typewriter, perhaps writing to Mabel from Ashton. *Courtesy Beckman family.*

Two photos of Togo Manning. *Courtesy Beckman family.*

During his free hours the pianist lounged around the leather shop soaking up Togo and Hacksaw's stories of adventure and misadventure, from rambles in the Old West to rumbles in Chicago. When Jerry and Arnold finished with the theater in the evenings, they and Togo piled into a Ford Model T dubbed the "Horsefly." Arnold sat in back, atop the fishing box, rifles, and tent, for a drive into the hills for early-morning fishing. His friends taught him not only how to fly-fish for trout but also how to make his own rod and tie his own flies. Togo even made him a pair of fishing shoes out of an elk hide. Impressed with Togo's shooting as well as his fishing and craftsmanship, Arnold boasted back East that Togo shot a grouse down "from the top of a tree about sixty feet high with his six-shooter."

While they were sitting around the campfire on one of their fishing jaunts, Hacksaw described a brush with death in the Arizona desert. The summer before, Hacksaw had tried to persuade Arnold to leave behind his plans for college and go off with him to Mesa, Arizona, to explore the cliff dwellings by descending from the top on ropes rather than by climbing up from the base. Arnold opted for chemistry, but Hacksaw went on undeterred. On his way through the desert his car broke down. The chance passing of some surveyors was all that had saved Hacksaw from dying of thirst.

Once more the summer was idyllic and remunerative. Arnold saved some money from the theater. He made good friends, enjoyed the wilderness, and had hours of entertaining banter with his three unique companions. "Had the life of Riley out there for two summers," He later wistfully recalled. "I wouldn't trade that experience for anything." But much as he loved his summers in Ashton, he never seriously considered abandoning chemistry in favor of music and the outdoors:

"From the time I was nine years old, I was convinced I wanted to be a chemist." With a stock of vivid memories he returned to Illinois and the great laboratories of the university.

A Chemical Education Continues

Arnold Beckman came of age as a chemist within the University of Illinois's Department of Chemistry, gaining both a bachelor's and a master's degree in four years. His education and his visions of the possibilities for a life in chemistry were shaped not only by Speed Marvel but also by three senior chemists who guided the department as a whole: Samuel W. Parr, William Albert Noyes, and Roger Adams. These four worked consciously to create a department in active pursuit of chemical knowledge of the greatest intellectual challenge, while never forgetting that the chemical sciences are charged with great human significance. In short form, what theoretical questions best interacted with issues and practical skills of greatest economic application? Those were the questions pursued first. Linking novel chemistry to industrial innovation was the signature activity at Illinois, one that secured its position as the leading chemistry department in America in the years following World War I. Beckman did not miss the connection.

Still an active presence in Arnold Beckman's time, Samuel Parr was one of the founders of chemistry at Illinois. Beckman knew of him by his reputation for creating an instrument that advanced both scientific knowledge and practical, industrial endeavor. Parr's calorimeter had become the standard in the coal industry for determining calorific value. Beckman could not avoid using Parr's "bomb"; chemists needed to know the calorific values or thermodynamics of chemical reactions, and Parr's device gave laboratory results quickly, simply, and accurately—three noble traits in an instrument. At Illinois, as elsewhere, chemistry students, including Beckman, took short courses on standard instruments and equipment: "I recall going through the standard course on using the Parr calorimeter. There wasn't really any competing method." Within two decades much the same thing would be said of Beckman's pH meter.

William Albert Noyes was head of the department and director of the chemical laboratories at Illinois during Beckman's years there. Born in Independence, Iowa, in 1857, Noyes spent his undergraduate years at Grinnell and then earned a Ph.D. under Ira Remsen at Johns Hopkins University in 1882. Remsen was a towering figure in American chemistry at the end of the nineteenth century, and association with him helped Noyes rise to prominence rapidly. Noyes left Baltimore for a year of study in Munich, then returned to professorships and research positions in rapid succession at the University of Tennessee, Rose Polytechnic, the National Bureau of Standards, and finally the University of Illinois.

Noyes had broad research interests in organic chemistry. He published over forty papers on the complex structure of camphor derivatives and performed many

Samuel W. Parr (1857–1931) owed his renown to the Parr calorimeter. A calorimeter is an instrument for measuring the amount of heat generated by chemical reactions. The design of Samuel Parr's instrument—devised sometime before 1899—was a simple variation of the general type of "bomb" calorimeter.

A chemical reaction is initiated within a thick-walled, sealed metal container, or "bomb." The bomb is then placed in an insulated water bath, and the heat generated by the reaction raises the temperature of the bomb. The bomb, in turn, raises the temperature of the water bath. Thus a measure of the rise in water temperature is an indirect but precise way of measuring the effects of a chemical reaction.

Professors were happy to have the Parr calorimeter to probe the nature of reactions, but its use in the wider world had more immediate effect on daily life. The calorimeter could measure the heat of a very special reaction—combustion—of a very particular substance—coal. Coal fired the industrial development of the United States throughout the nineteenth century and well into the twentieth. Coal powered the steam engines of America's railroads and factories, coal fed the furnaces of America's power plants, and coal heated America's homes, schools, businesses, and churches. Just as Beckman's hand-cranked centrifuge determined the price of milk in Cullom, the Parr calorimeter priced batches of coal. Coal varied from deposit to deposit in its caloric value—the amount of heat it would provide when burned. This is precisely what Parr's calorimeter was built to measure.

Parr's business expanded as the technologies requiring his instrument evolved and increased. So strong was the demand from chemists and the coal industry that Parr formed a company in 1899 to manufacture and distribute the calorimeter. Demand grew, and he moved his com-

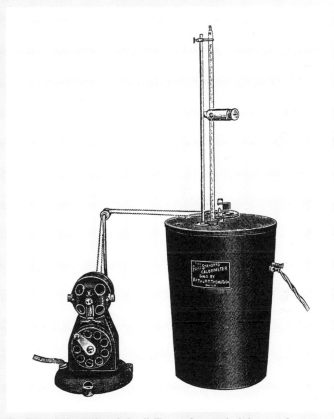

The Parr calorimeter from Arthur H. Thomas Company's *Laboratory Apparatus and Reagents* catalog, 1921.

pany from Champaign to a larger factory in East Moline. World War I increased demand still further, and Parr moved again to a larger combination foundry and manufacturing plant in Moline proper. He then started his own foundry to produce the new acid-resistant, stainless-steel alloys that he had devised to improve the "bombs." Professor Parr and his Standard Calorimeter Company provided a vivid demonstration of how good science could lead to good business. ∿

Left: William Albert Noyes. *Courtesy University of Illinois Library.*

Center: Roger Adams. *Chemical Heritage Foundation.*

Right: Worth Huff Rodebush. *Courtesy University of Illinois Library.*

syntheses, but he was also interested in the atomic weight of oxygen and theories of valence. He was not only a scholar but also an organizer of the national chemical community. In 1920, as Beckman was finding his footing in the department, Noyes was president of the American Chemical Society. Over the years he was the editor of three ACS publications: the *Journal of the American Chemical Society,* *Chemical Abstracts,* and *Chemical Monographs.* These journals disseminated discoveries by American chemists and fostered a growing sense of self-confidence in the chemical community in the United States.

Noyes taught the basic course on organic chemistry. Organic chemistry deals with the transformation, creation, and precise characterization of carbon compounds, the stuff of the living world. It involves making compounds from scratch, puzzling over their essential structure, teasing out mixes to get pure samples, and discovering what materials could be made with and from others. As such, organic chemistry has a long and intimate relationship with the industrial realm—its knowledge can become knowledge of the products and processes of chemical manufactures.

Beckman certainly gained much technical knowledge from the lectures Noyes gave, but it was the nontechnical aspects of the course that most impressed him. Noyes showed how a highly accomplished scientist could tie his knowledge and experience to the broadest aspects of the human condition, not just to the world of atoms and molecules.

> The world war had a great effect on him, and I appreciated his lectures, because he would bring in something more than organic chemistry. He would bring in philosophy. He was very much affected by the war with the Germans because he had many friends in Germany, and he would wander off into philosophical discussions. He'd lecture us about unfortunate aspects of human character that permit them to generate hatred and fight each other, things of that sort. I got a lot out of his lectures other than just some knowledge of organic chemistry.

Noyes, who directed chemistry as a whole at Illinois, had his counterpoint in Roger Adams, who headed the organic side of the department. The organic chemist par excellence, Adams was a Harvard Ph.D. of considerable accomplishment who, after Noyes's retirement, ran the whole department—and much of the national chemical community as well. He was familiarly and correctly known as "The Chief," who, through his own feats of structural analysis and synthesis and by supervising over a hundred Ph.D. dissertations, became the leading American organic chemist of his generation.

Adams's research programs fit well with the signature theme of the department, combining the intellectual challenges of "pure chemistry" with the potential for great practical results. He and his students synthesized hosts of new organic compounds that were not only intricate chemical puzzles but also potentially powerful medicines. (Adams's first doctoral student, Ernest Volwiler, went on to become CEO of Abbott Laboratories, a major pharmaceutical firm. Another student, Wallace Carothers, later invented nylon.) Adams also led important work on catalysts. (Catalysts are substances that increase the rates of chemical reactions but are essentially unaltered at the end of the reactions, allowing use of lower temperatures and pressures.) His development of platinum oxide as a catalyst helped organic chemists create new compounds at the same time that it helped industry manufacture them.

Parr, Noyes, and Adams created a department committed to research and friendly to industry. Organic chemistry was its greatest strength, but Arnold Beckman switched his allegiance from organic chemistry to physical chemistry after just one term—in order to escape from using mercury. The switch brought him to Worth Huff Rodebush, a young professor known as "Thermodynamics" Rodebush. This simple shift in fields from organic to physical chemistry, from Marvel to Rodebush, gave Beckman a different look at how chemistry fits industry and deepened his familiarity with chemical engineering.

Beckman started his new direction with a course on chemical thermodynamics. Rodebush struck him as "a little aloof," befitting his reputation as a tough, demanding professor: "You really had to come up with good, solid, well-reasoned answers if you were going to get favorable reports from him." Beckman was familiar with the habits of disciplined study, however. He took all Rodebush had to offer, which was quite a lot. Rodebush came to Illinois from his own education at the cutting edge of research in physical chemistry and chemical thermodynamics: He had earned a Ph.D. under G. N. Lewis at the University of California, Berkeley. Rodebush's demanding teaching style may have reflected his firsthand appreciation that physical chemistry was a rapidly expanding and fast-changing field. He was equally convinced of the importance of physical chemistry to industrial advancement, for he was working for the U.S. Industrial Alcohol Company when a very generous fellowship, which Lewis arranged, lured him back to the university.

G. Frederick Smith.
Courtesy University of Illinois Library.

Arnold Beckman learned major lessons from each of the chemistry professors with whom he came in contact. A professor of analytical chemistry, G. Frederick Smith, showed him some of the perils that an academic chemist faced when getting involved with inventions and patents. "Perchlorate" Smith, as Beckman and his peers dubbed him (for his expertise as a producer of perchloric acid and perchlorates), was also the founder of a successful chemical business. Smith had invented an aerosol dispenser for whipped cream, and he had taken out a patent on using nitrous oxide as the propellant. While Beckman remembers Smith as a "jovial person, full of jokes," his otherwise sunny disposition must have been clouded, as "he was involved in quite a bit of patent litigation." From him Beckman learned that simply having a patent did not protect a chemist-inventor, except as a basis for stopping imitators in the courts.

Beckman's Illinois education fully covered the facts and concepts of chemistry and provided career models and life lessons through the faculty itself. There is another aspect not to be missed. Through careful observation and repeated practice, he developed the craftsmanship, the skills of the experimental chemist. These skills cannot be easily written down or taught to neophytes through lists and recipes; they are feats of the artisan that can only be acquired by doing. Here Beckman could draw upon his hours with Frank White in the blacksmith's shop, his boyhood practices at his own woodworking and chemistry benches, and his lessons in tatting. Most important was his inner conviction that he could make whatever he needed from materials close at hand, a conviction that began with his earliest efforts at toy- and experiment-making in Cullom. At Illinois he also became a master of what is today the most underappreciated art of chemists of that era: glassblowing. In this craft he worked closely with Paul Anders, the department's resident glassblower.

Just as with Speed Marvel, Beckman's preferred strategy for learning was to join a faculty member at the research frontier, and after Rodebush's class on thermodynamics he became research assistant to another physical chemist, T. A. White. White, whose experimental research delved into the thermodynamic properties of aqueous ammonia solutions, offered new ways to keep Beckman's hands active and his mind exercised at the laboratory bench. Thermodynamics is based on the idea that heat is the energy of molecules in motion. The dynamics of these motions, these kinetic energies, vary from substance to substance and from mixture to mixture, and they have important effects on the physical properties of substances and the way they behave in chemical reactions. White and Beckman were interested in solutions of ammonia in water because they form electrolytic solutions—solutions that can conduct electricity. One of the most pressing questions in physical chemistry at the time was how to bring electrochemistry—the study of the relationship between the electrical and chemical properties of matter—and thermodynamics into a coherent whole. Ionic theory began to create that coherence.

Whatever the specialty—organic, inorganic, analytical, or physical chemistry—the chemist relied on apparatus made of glass. Only in glass containers, tubes, bulbs, coils, chambers, stopcocks, and flasks could chemists isolate the materials that make up the world and make them perform their marvels.

Making and using glass apparatus was a craft tradition that connected chemists of the early twentieth century to alchemists in antiquity.

As Arnold Beckman began his apprenticeship with blowing chemical glassware, McGraw-Hill published the *Laboratory Manual of Glass Blowing*, which became extremely popular. Its author was Francis C. Frary, a Ph.D., onetime professor of chemistry at the University of Minnesota and in the early 1920s director of research for Alcoa—the Aluminum Company of America. Alcoa's research laboratory was a leading chemical center, producing as many new techniques and instruments as it did new alloys. The book itself shows the importance of glass; a leading professor who had gone on to direct research for one of America's leading metal producers took the time to write and then update a practical manual in glass craftwork.

Chemists could buy glass apparatus from national supply houses and from local skilled artisans rather than create their own, but as Frary explained in the revised edition of his manual, glassblowing remained a vital art. "Many laboratories in this country, especially in the West," Frary noted, "are located a long way from any professional glassblower, and the time and money spent in shipping broken apparatus several hundred miles to be mended could often be saved if some of the laboratory force could seal on a new stop cock, replace a broken tube, or make some temporary repairs." Moreover, glassblowing was crucial for work at the research frontier: "Many men in physical or chemical

Glass laboratory apparatus. *Courtesy Beckman family.*

laboratories have occasion to modify some piece of apparatus, designed, perhaps, for other uses, or to design new apparatus. To such, the ability to perform some of the operations herein described [in his manual] may also be very valuable." Beckman proved the truth of this observation, for his mastery of laboratory glassblowing would prove crucial when he made equipment for his academic research. Still later, his skills at the gas jet were vital to producing the oxygen meter that saved the lives of sailors and infants alike. ⌇

51

As Beckman conducted his experiments with White, he learned the physical chemist's new definition of acid or alkali according to the ionic theory. Using a laboratory bench full of apparatus—standard electrochemical cells, tubes filled with liquid conductors, batteries, and galvanometers—he could measure the concentration of ions in a solution and assign precise numbers to the solution's degree of acidity and alkalinity. He little knew how important this new electrochemical definition of acids and alkalis would be for his future career.

Part of a laboratory workspace, one of Beckman's many chemical benches.
Courtesy Beckman family.

Beckman did not remain White's research assistant for long, as he was approached by yet another physical chemist on the faculty, Gerhard Dietrichson, who was looking for a bright student to assist in his course on electrochemistry. He chose Beckman. Beckman accepted, happy for the chance to make and use electrochemical apparatus. He loved equipment, and he would get virtually unrestricted access to the electrochemical apparatus in the laboratory, plus individual attention from Dietrichson. He knew well that to be a useful assistant he would have to master the concepts and content of this important field and the experimental side of electrochemistry.

Working for Dietrichson, Beckman gained both conceptual tools and the skills of hand, eye, and feel needed in making and using appropriate apparatus. Later he would call his assistantship with Dietrichson "a factor in guiding my career because I did gain some firsthand experience with making standard cells and calomel half cells, hydrogen electrodes, and things of that sort." He saw that the importance of these experimental skills lay in their relation to the then-most-modern experimental determinations of the acidity or alkalinity—the pH—of a chemical substance. Just over ten years later, he would come back to these skills to create his pH meter.

While Beckman delved further into the ideas and the experimental skills of physical chemistry, his career ideas evolved. He knew of gasworks and steelworking firsthand before his freshman year, but at Illinois his vision of the contributions

Physical chemists believed that thermodynamics could resolve outstanding experimental and theoretical conflicts in their explanations of electrochemistry.

As Beckman and White explored aqueous ammonia solutions with thermometers and electrical equipment, they were peering into the very heart of physical chemists' ideas of the electrical nature of matter: ionic theory. Ionic theory had been developed at the beginning of the century to explain some very basic questions: Why and how could electrolytes (solutions of acids, alkalis, and salts in water) conduct electricity? How did electrolysis work? The most familiar example of electrolysis is the decomposition of water by an electrical current. If two electrodes are placed at the opposite sides of a water bath, hydrogen bubbles up from one side, and oxygen bubbles up from the other. What is the current doing? Why do the two gases form exclusively at these distinct locations? The electrolysis of water is one of the most elementary experiments in electrochemistry and one of its most fascinating. It was performed from 1800 onward, and needs little apparatus, requiring only water, an electrical current, and two metal wires. Beckman surely performed the experiment himself as a boy, in his combination chemical and electrical laboratory in his house in Bloomington.

The answer that physical chemists devised to explain both electrolytes and electrolysis was the ionic theory. This theory holds that when an electrolyte (an acid, alkali, or salt) is put into solution with water, it divides, or dissociates into ions, both positive and negative. An ion is a portion of

Arnold Beckman's early electrochemical apparatus. *Courtesy Beckman family.*

an ordinary molecule of the electrolyte, one that has an electrical charge. Thus electrolytes carry an electrical current through the motion of ions—negatively charged ions migrate to the positive electrode, while positively charged ions migrate to the negative electrode. This also explains the riddle of electrolysis: Ions of one gas travel to one electrode, collect, and bubble up; ions of the other gas have the opposite charge, and so they collect at the opposite electrode. Ionic theory entails viewing chemical substances in a wholly different way: Any single chemical substance is really composed of positive and negative ions.

Physical chemists began to redefine familiar chemical classifications according to the ionic theory. Acids were first identified by their sour taste, alkalis by their soapy feel when mixed in water. They form an opposing pair, because when mixed they cancel the distinctive properties of one another. Moreover, they have "opposite" effects on the color of litmus paper, acids turning it red, alkalis turning it blue. When redefining the distinction between acids and alkalis in terms of ionic theory, the physical chemist sees an acid as an electrolyte that produces positively charged hydrogen ions, that is, atoms of hydrogen with a positive charge. An alkali is an electrolyte that produces negatively charged hydroxyl ions, an oxygen-hydrogen atom group carrying a negative charge. This change in definition meant that rather than the earlier, more qualitative analysis of acidity or alkalinity, the physical chemist could use the ionic definition to produce quantitative, numerical measurements of pH. ∼

that a chemist could make to science or industry broadened. He also had new feeling for the national chemical lesson of World War I: The United States should have its own independent and powerful chemical industry. That lesson had ignited interest in things industrial inside the chemical community, "and that's why chemical engineering suddenly became the popular field, that chemical engineers received the top starting salaries when they left [college] . . . there was a lot of drive to get people to go into chemical engineering." Beckman's lifelong fascination with making things—from wood, metal, or chemicals—helped sweep him up in this drive for chemical engineers. His boyhood experiments displayed his interest in the "practical side and the engineering side of chemistry," and chemical engineering offered interesting possibilities for making a living. Beckman changed his major to chemical engineering.

The Illinois Chemist—*and Beyond*

Echoes of Arnold Beckman's maturing vision are found in the pages of the *Illinois Chemist*. In his senior year he was editor of this publication, put out by department students. No mere newsletter, the *Illinois Chemist* was a thirty-two-page, quarto-sized magazine with numerous advertisements, charming graphics, and a staff of thirteen. Beckman revitalized the magazine and made it a lively forum for the discussion of interactions: physical chemistry in industry, spectroscopy, chemistry and medicine, and electrochemistry. There were staff and alumni notes, college humor, and social news, too. The advertising manager and news editor at various times was Glen Joseph, who would later go on for a Ph.D. in chemistry at Wisconsin and a career in California. His later request for help in that career would change the course of Beckman's life, but in the early 1920s Joseph's job was to keep the *Illinois Chemist* in the black, recruiting advertisements from Parr's Standard Calorimeter Company, from the local men's clothing store ("Chem coats in stock"), and from such Chicago equipment supply houses as Central Scientific or E. H. Sargent ("Sargent's Sulphur Rack").

In his editorials Beckman showed a serious concern for the lack of prestige given chemical engineering and chemists with industrial interests. His editorials lamented the relative status of chemists and chemical engineers at Illinois, especially in their eligibility for honorary fraternities. He later explained: "We were very much concerned about whether we [chemical engineering students] could be honored by being elected into the Phi Beta Kappa or Tau Beta Pi, and we were excluded from both by being in between. And chemical engineering was actually part of the College of Liberal Arts. But the Phi Betas wouldn't accept chemical engineers as being suitable material, and the engineering school wouldn't accept us, as being, oh, not really engineers—they thought of us as chemists. A chemical engineer was just a chemist with a pipe wrench. That was the attitude. . . . Of course, at that time, whether or not you had a pin to wear was a very important

Courtesy University of Illinois Library.

part of a person's life." In one editorial he compared the prestige associated with chemical engineering at the Massachusetts Institute of Technology (MIT) to the situation at Illinois. In still another, "The Chemist and the Business World," he argued that chemistry students should develop a background in the fundamentals of business, because business savvy was just as essential to the successful chemist as was chemical knowledge. As his editorials attest, he was proud of the faculty's involvement in industrial work and chemical problems of a wide, practical nature.

Honorary fraternities were not the only brotherhoods. Many of Arnold Beckman's fellow students lived in the Alpha Chi Sigma house, the chemistry fraternity. Not Beckman. Almost immediately on arrival at Illinois he was recruited for the Delta Upsilon fraternity and became a "DU," as its members were known. Seeley Johnson was his great friend in DU and ever since, and together they had many adventures. Johnson's mother enjoyed Beckman's piano playing, and his father used to invite him and the other DU brothers to their home for Sunday breakfasts of pancakes and sausages. On occasion Johnson's father would play a practical joke on one of the fraternity brothers new to the breakfast table. The joke was known to all but its victim. Everyone watched in suspense as Seeley's father battered and cooked a hand warmer as a very special initiation "pancake" for his new guest. Beckman is still laughing about this welcome.

From left: Arnold (far right) and a few of his DU brothers; the DU house; Arnold dressed as a clown for a DU party. *Courtesy Beckman family.*

Arnold Beckman graduated from Illinois in 1922 with a B.S. in chemical engineering. The head start he had made in high school allowed him to finish in three years and to recapture the time spent in the marines. A fourth year in the Illinois department earned him a master's degree in physical chemistry. For his master's research he returned to the experimental investigation of the thermodynamics of aqueous ammonia solutions that he had started with T. A. White. As he pursued his master's, he wrote a friend about the decision to stay on at Illinois and how he had weighed his entrepreneurial prospects against the value of graduate work. "I graduated all right in August, but the world had a too cold and forbidding front when I was thinking of starting into business, so I decided to linger here at the schoolhouse. This graduate business is the real essence of education."

The Chemical Club of the University of Illinois, 1922. Beckman is in the third row, second from left.

Courtesy University of Illinois Archives.

Chemical talent at Illinois was not limited to the faculty. Beckman's graduating class of 1922 included two future presidents of the American Chemical Society, Wallace Reed Brode and Clifford N. Rassweiler. A third ACS president, Albert Elder, was a member of the class behind him, as was the Nobel laureate in chemistry for 1955, Vincent du Vigneaud. As noted earlier, Wallace Carothers was a graduate student at Illinois while Beckman was there. Carothers must have picked up something of the Illinois attitude toward industrial challenges, for he went via Harvard to DuPont, where he invented nylon and neoprene.

Meanwhile, the postal romance continued between Bayside, Long Island, and Urbana, Illinois, as Arnold Beckman grew closer and closer to Mabel Meinzer, even though he had seen her only once after he left New York. That was when he arranged for Mabel's mother to escort her to Urbana so that the young couple could be with one another at a big fraternity dance. Mabel saved photos of that trip as carefully as she did of every New York parade in which the young marine had marched. By now, Arnold and Mabel were forming a vision of a shared life together; that is, a life together starting at some point in the relatively near future, when Arnold was more settled and established. Despite the distance between them, they decided to make their heartfelt plans public: Among the alumni notes in the April 1923 *Illinois Chemist* was the news that Arnold Beckman and Mabel Meinzer were engaged.

As he finished research for his master's degree, Arnold formulated a plan that would gratify his passion for chemistry, open career possibilities, and speed the time when he would be settled enough to have Mabel join him as his wife. He would go on for a Ph.D. in physical chemistry, but not at Illinois: "There was a feeling often expressed that a student should change schools—not have all of his training in one school." He heeded this common wisdom and applied to MIT, the University of Chicago, and the California Institute of Technology (Caltech) on the basis of their reputations and his confidence in his talents. He later recalled that MIT and the University of Chicago at the time were "the recognized top schools in the field of chemistry and chemical engineering." Caltech was a new and rising star. Arnold got offers from all three. It says much about his attraction to the West that he chose to go to California, despite its being nearly 3,000 miles from Long Island and Mabel.

Onward to Graduate School

The California Institute of Technology was a very new, very small institution in 1923, but it had already attracted some very prominent scientists. Arnold Beckman had a spirit of adventure, an affinity for the West, and two personal connections to the new school. One was Richard C. Tolman, a former faculty member in physical chemistry at Illinois who had left soon after Beckman arrived. He ended up at Caltech in 1922. Beckman had contacted Tolman for advice about his choices, and though he had known Tolman only briefly, Tolman's presence at Caltech was a "big factor" in his own decision. Tolman took pains to extol the virtues of a small school, and as Beckman later put it, "I followed him."

Arnold and Mabel with Bill Hincke and friend at the beach in the 1920s.
Courtesy Beckman family.

Beckman's other personal connection was his close friend and classmate William Hincke, who had also been made an offer by Caltech and had accepted. Hincke offered Beckman the prospect of a traveling companion, a friend in a new land, and a scientific compatriot, for he, too, intended to get a Ph.D. in physical chemistry. Beyond the academic attractions of Caltech and these personal connections, Beckman recalls how important the draw of the West was: "This fabled country of California, land of milk and honey and oranges and all that. I just wanted to see it."

Beckman and Hincke took in the scenery during a rambling road trip from Illinois to Pasadena in Hincke's Model T Ford. They traveled through the northern Great Plains, then into the Pacific Northwest, then south through California, ending up in Pasadena. By the end of their trip the western scenery and climate were a little more familiar, though no less enchanting. Majestic vistas and more mundane sights rewarded them as they struggled to get the stall-prone Model T over the dirt roads and mountain passes that made up much of their path to Pasadena.

Beckman and Hincke arrived at a heady time. The young Caltech was intellectual home to just 458 undergraduates and a mere 62 graduate students. Owing in no small part to the influence and example of its leading figure, Robert Millikan, the faculty and graduate students formed an easy mix, a community. Millikan called all new graduate students into his office when they arrived, as the first step in their socialization into the community. Beckman recalls: "I looked up to any professor with a good deal of awe. . . . When I went to Caltech I remember that when Millikan called me in to see him, I went in with a great deal of trepidation. Later on, when I got to know Millikan, those feelings disappeared. I found that the faculty and the student body worked closely together. A student had no difficulty seeing a professor. He was always welcome. That was one of the positive features of being in a small school like Caltech."

Millikan set the standard for accessibility and collaboration. He set the example for open social interactions as well. Each domain of easy communication fostered the other. Beckman remembers that Millikan and his wife Greta "used to have Sunday afternoon meetings at their home and invite a bunch of students over for tea and conversation—ten to fifteen at a time—just to sit around and chew the fat. He was very friendly." Similarly, on the campus but outside of offices, lecture halls, and laboratories, the faculty and students mixed over shared lunches in the faculty club. The conversations did not stick to technical matters and academic intrigue: "We talked over everything from politics to auto racing to science—almost anything."

Beckman had a graduate fellowship that covered his tuition. He earned both experience and a small salary as a teaching assistant in freshman chemistry, and he took the spate of courses typical for the chemistry graduate student. He knew fellow students well and developed close ties to two important faculty members—Richard Tolman and Roscoe Dickinson—both of whom bridged the gap between chemistry and physics. With them, he explored how the new physics of quantum theory could be combined with the new chemistry of the physical chemist. Through this shared endeavor with the faculty, Beckman began a course of research that combined these two realms, building specialized instruments of his own creation as the research required them. This endeavor solidified the understanding with which he later launched a new industry based on a new instrument of his own devising.

As Beckman later explained, chemists at Caltech (students and faculty alike) had to work their way through the new physics of quantum mechanics that radically altered familiar ideas about the nature and behavior of atoms and molecules.

> This was when quantum theory was in its very controversial stage. Our text was Arnold Sommerfeld's *Atombau*, which we had to read in German, which was bad enough in itself, especially since Sommerfeld's style was not particularly clear. To try to get this controversial quantum theory—that was a tough job, but it was exciting. We had visitors, of course. Einstein was there, Sommerfeld himself was there, Heisenberg came in, Bohr, the real chief actors in the drama [of quantum mechanics] visited Caltech. This was undoubtedly due to the preeminence of [the Caltech faculty]. . . . If we were going to be in a discipline, we wanted to be second to none.

Despite this intellectual ferment and close interaction with leading scientists, Beckman became restless as the year wore on. Other desires and dreams were at play in his life. California he loved. And Caltech he loved. But he also loved a woman who was a continent away. To ask his fiancée to abandon her home and

**Robert Millikan and
Albert Einstein at Caltech.**
*Courtesy of Institute
Archives, California Institute
of Technology.*

family while his resources were meager and his prospects uncertain was unthink-able. Mabel herself was gainfully employed back East, working in Manhattan as an executive secretary for Equitable Life Assurance Company of New York. He longed to be close to her. Yet unless he earned a better salary, there was little chance that they could start their life together. The answer was simple. He would drop out of Caltech. With the self-confidence gained from his summers tramping about the West, Arnold bade good-bye to graduate studies in 1924 and set out, believing that he could find a well-paying job in New York, near Mabel.

New York and the Beginning of Bell Labs

The oil-refining business was booming in Southern California in the 1920s. Standard Oil of California was a major presence, opening up oil fields, building refineries, and producing new products. From his education in chemical engineer-ing and from his California experience, Arnold Beckman knew that Standard Oil needed chemists and chemical engineers. He also knew that one of the largest Standard Oil refineries was in Bayonne, New Jersey, outside of New York City, and not too far from Mabel. Better still, he also knew that close connections existed between Caltech and the Manhattan-based Engineering Department of Western Electric, which was hiring technical staff at a vigorous rate. Specific job prospects were not the first consideration. "In all honesty, I wasn't thinking seriously about the future. I needed some money to go back to school and had a girlfriend there. Those were the thoughts uppermost in my mind." Fully confident that New York wanted chemists, he left Pasadena on the cheapest passage he could find, an old steamer that sailed down through the Panama Canal and up the East Coast to New York. The room that his hundred-dollar fare paid for was so uncomfortable that he made most of the passage up on deck.

When Arnold reached New York, he and Mabel enjoyed a happy reunion. The reality of finally being together was a welcome change from communication by let-ter, and Arnold set about finding a job that would allow him to stay. He made extraordinarily short work of the task. After a single morning's interview at Standard Oil of New Jersey's Manhattan offices, he had a solid offer of a job as a chemist at the Bayonne refinery. He then made his way over to West Street, to Western Electric's Engineering Department, the research and development center for the whole of America's telephone monopoly, the Bell System. Western Electric Engineering was busy with a host of innovations, not the least of which was its organizational restructuring into what would become the most famous of all industrial research laboratories, Bell Laboratories. Beckman knew a student from Caltech, Todd Nies, who had left California shortly before to take up a position with the famed telephone system engineers. Nies and Beckman had arranged to meet and "chew the fat."

As soon as Beckman reported his job offer, Nies responded, "Oh, you don't want to work out in Bayonne, the mud flats. Why don't you get a job right here in New York with Western Electric?" That very afternoon Nies introduced him to a colleague who was vigorously launching a new line of research. Walter Andrew Shewhart, later known as the father of statistical quality control, was just nine years older than Beckman and an Illinois native as well. Shewhart had earned a Ph.D. in physics from the University of California at Berkeley in 1917 and taught physics for a year at the University of Illinois. His work on quality control is well known today, in part because of the activities of his colleague and disciple W. Edwards Deming, who lectured in Japan in the 1950s. Those lectures are widely credited as sparking the revolution in efficiency and quality in postwar manufacturing in Japan, a revolution that later spread to the United States. But when he hired Beckman, Shewhart was just getting started.

Previous accounts of Arnold Beckman's career have duly noted his two years in New York before he returned to Caltech to complete his Ph.D. in chemistry. Yet this period is largely treated as a sidelight, a diversion from the main course of his life. When viewed from the perspective of Beckman's own future as an industrial entrepreneur, however, those two years hold great significance. One of his special gifts has always been the ability to sense the "sweet spot" where excellence and opportunity come together. His choices of the U.S. Marines, of the University of Illinois, of the West, and of Caltech provide early illustrations. So too does his arrival on Walter Shewhart's doorstep in time to be part of the founding research group at Bell Labs, as it began its fabled career as a distinct entity and Shewhart began to lay the basis for modern quality control.

Bell Labs introduced Beckman to the forefront of thinking about electronic technology and quality control in manufacturing, and to the structure of research and development as practiced in the most renowned of industrial research centers. He learned to seek the cutting edge in science, long before the phrase became commonplace. His years at Bell Laboratories elevated his sights beyond anything he had yet seen, and the combination of Bell Labs with Caltech had a formidable effect on the development of his technological imagination. Many nineteenth- and early twentieth-century scientists, technologists, and even toolmakers counted as a formative experience the time they spent, however short, in the "invention factory" of Thomas Edison. From the 1920s on, Bell Labs provoked a lifetime of similar mental ferment for those who worked there—and Beckman was no exception.

Lessons in Quality Control

Arnold O. Beckman was Walter A. Shewhart's first technical employee in the new Inspection Engineering Department. Their task was immediate, for there was a growing sense that something was very wrong with Western Electric's approach to standardizing products and testing quality. Quite simply, what percentage of a

The Bell System was one of the first American corporate enterprises to have a research branch, encompassing a wide area of responsibility, and for very straightforward reasons. Alexander Graham Bell invented the telephone in Boston in 1875. Five years later his corporation provided service to 54,000 telephones.

By 1892, when most of America was still without phone service, the company was offering, with difficulty, long-distance calls from New York to Chicago. Bell's quest to expand and improve service depended on one central resource: science and technology. In 1881 American Bell started an Electrical Department, followed by a Mechanical Department three years later. Each had experimental labs and a growing population of employees with doctorates.

In 1897 Bell brought in George Campbell, an engineer and mathematician. Campbell and the physicist-inventor Michael Pupin independently figured out that magnetic coils placed at intervals along a telephone line increased the distance a signal would travel. With such coils positioned every eight miles, calls were successfully transmitted from New York to Denver by 1911. Bell then aimed for San Francisco by 1914. To reach that distance, Lee De Forest offered an improved amplifier as a replacement for the coils: the "Audion," or triode tube. Bell System scientists and engineers radically improved De Forest's technology, creating the now-famous powerful vacuum tubes that amplified telephone conversations and later amplified much more. Equipment with vacuum tubes installed in a special booth allowed visitors to the 1915 San Francisco Exposition to listen to the Atlantic surf.

Such amazing feats led to further investment in the research, development, design, and engineering depart-

The Bell Labs building, at 463 West Street, New York. While this photograph was taken in the 1950s, the building's facade remained as it had been during Beckman's time there in the early 1920s. *Courtesy AT&T Archives.*

ments of the Bell System. Those departments were then consolidated into a single organizational entity at a single location: the Engineering Department of the Western Electric Company. Western Electric itself was the manufacturing arm of the Bell System. Western Electric produced in great quantities the equipment that Bell customers used in their homes—the telephones themselves—as well as equipment to build the Bell telephone network, including central switches, fuses, protection devices, wire, repeaters, and amplifiers. Other parts of the Bell System were responsible for putting up the network, maintaining it, and serving customers, but Western Electric designed and built the components that made up the system, and research and development was concentrated in its Engineering Department.

In the 1910s this department already comprised several hundred scientists, engineers, and technicians—all gathered at 463 West Street in Manhattan. The staff had grown still further by the time Arnold Beckman arrived in 1924. He joined just as the announcement was made that a separate Bell Telephone Laboratories would be organized to do research for the Bell System and invent devices for Western Electric to manufacture. Beckman was on the staff the very first day Bell Laboratories became an official entity. The decision to create Bell Labs was due, in no small part, to the Western Electric Engineering Department's success in developing the vacuum tube. The vacuum tube was a technological breakthrough that ushered in not only tremendous advances in the telephone system but also the modern era of electronics. This extraordinarily sensitive and versatile electrical switch put Bell scientists and engineers at the forefront of several new technologies. The creation of Bell Labs was a recognition of this success and of the corresponding need to devote still more time and personnel to basic research.

Frank Baldwin Jewett. *Courtesy AT&T Archives.*

In the mid-1920s Bell Labs was an exciting place. Herbert Ives was using photoelectric cells to send pictures over wires, and in 1927 he used radio waves to send visual images. Harold Black was working on amplification techniques to minimize feedback. J. P. Maxfield and H. G. Harrison developed orthophonic high fidelity, adding an octave on each end of the recordable sound range. The Vitaphone technique allowed synchronized sound between a set of sound discs and the John Barrymore film *Don Juan*. There was a good deal of interest in quantum physics at Bell Labs. Karl Darrow wrote articles for Bell's in-house journals, while Clinton Davisson and a graduate student, Lester Germer, showed that the famous thesis of quantum physics, the "wave-particle duality," could be extended to electrons—to matter as well as to light. Davisson won the Nobel Prize for this work.

The first president of Bell Labs was Frank Baldwin Jewett. Born in Pasadena, Jewett graduated from Throop Polytechnic Institute—the forerunner of Caltech—in 1898. He earned a Ph.D. in experimental physics under Albert Michelson at the University of Chicago, where he met Robert A. Millikan, who became one of his closest lifelong friends. Jewett taught at MIT, and in 1904 he joined the Bell System via American Telephone and Telegraph, of which he became chief engineer in 1916 and vice president in 1922. Jewett and Millikan kept a close relationship between their two laboratories. Millikan sent Jewett some of his best students, and Jewett often consulted with Millikan on breakthrough technologies like the vacuum tube. (By the early 1920s, of course, Millikan was—in all but name—president of Caltech.)

Jewett shaped Bell Laboratories on the model of the academic departments he had known at Chicago, MIT, and, through his connection with Millikan, Caltech. Jewett's plan for Bell Labs gave it a feeling not unlike a university faculty, with senior scientists engaged in research, giving seminars, and publishing in in-house journals. By 1925, when Bell Labs began its official existence, Arnold Beckman was part of an enterprise that itself was the world leader in the scope, scale, and quality of its work in every aspect of electronics. ∾

Walter A. Shewhart, as he looked when he hired Arnold Beckman in the early 1920s. *Courtesy AT&T Archives.*

production run should be tested to ensure quality? And what was to be tested? Tests that determined whether a piece worked or not were simple enough, but with vacuum tubes there was the additional question of variation. How did a production line distinguish between normal, acceptable variations and those that revealed critical manufacturing problems? Moreover, the requisite test sometimes ruined the object, making it impossible to test every piece, and tests took time and cost money. Beckman was now part of a division that sought maximum quality combined with maximum economic results. He and Shewhart turned to math and probability theory.

When Shewhart began his work, engineers already realized that earlier attempts to refine manufacturing processes to eliminate deviations from the standard product often paradoxically resulted in *increasing* the amount of variation. They needed to develop a new technique for assessing the quality—the standardization and variability—of manufactured products that would determine when they should make a change to a process, what that change should be, and when they should simply leave the process alone.

Shewhart, who had taught physics at the University of Illinois, conceptualized his new role as being analogous to eliminating errors in a scientific experiment. Experimenters had long used mathematical techniques to analyze the errors inherent in making measurements, developing tools to differentiate random from systematic errors in measurement. Random errors were caused by a wide variety of transient causes, and analysis showed that they clustered around an average value. Other errors graphed differently. These were regular and systematic and pointed to a persistent cause or cluster of causes acting in predictable ways over time, all of which skewed experimental data. Systematic errors made measurements unreliable, but once the errors were identified, their causes could be ferreted out and eliminated. Mathematics and graphs allowed scientists to manage an experiment. Would the same system work for production at Western Electric?

When Beckman and Shewhart first met, Shewhart had been thinking along these lines for some time. Beckman's background seemed right for a number of reasons. Here was a bright, young experimental scientist, familiar with the problems of error in experimental measurement, who had been immersed in mathematical statistics through quantum mechanics, statistical mechanics, and physical chemistry. In short, Beckman possessed the expertise and sensibility Shewhart needed. Beckman in turn learned from Shewhart. "I've often said that one important thing, whether in science or business, is to have intellectual integrity. Don't allow yourself to have wishful thinking. And that was what Shewhart did: He would not go on until he found some results that agreed with his preconceived ideas. He'd go along, just as completely objective, I think, as a person can be. And I think that probably I got a little bit of the spirit of that type of investigation from him."

Control Charts and Intellectual Integrity Put to the Test

Shewhart's solution to the quality control problem was the control chart, a graph that displayed the boundaries for acceptable and unacceptable variation in the quality of a product such as a vacuum tube. For example, Western Electric wanted to make vacuum tubes with a consistent level of sensitivity. Ideally, one of Shewhart's control charts would allow an inspector to test a small percentage of the production run and determine whether the sample tested displayed acceptable random variation or whether it fell within an "action area," signaling the need to root out some damaging systematic cause. Data in action areas prompted managers to inspect the production line, or the design concepts, for faults.

Such charts were conceptually straightforward and relatively easy to employ, but creating reliable ones was no simple matter. What statistical tools would differentiate trends from random fluctuations? What statistical techniques would yield the most valid results from the minimum number of tests? Minimizing the number of tests was of primary importance, for great savings and efficiency depended on it. It was the problem of creating the control charts themselves—finding statistical tools that would work in the real world of high-technology manufacture—that Beckman and Shewhart collaborated on.

Beckman later recalled the difficulty and the excitement of his efforts, first with Shewhart and later with a handful of other colleagues in the Inspection Department.

> You see, in the Bell telephone system, there is a tremendous inspection problem. Innumerable inspections of soldered joints, relay contacts, and fuses, et cetera; and on some things—take fuses for example—you cannot have a 100-percent inspection because you destroy the fuse in testing it. And so you have to bring in probability theory. How accurately can one rely on test results of a 50-percent sample or a 5-percent sample? Well, we worked, theoretically and experimentally, on experiments to apply probability theory to testing. This was an interesting thing; although I was not a mathematician, I found that it appealed to me.

Beckman and Shewhart were committed to testing their methods outside the laboratory walls, and Beckman was often sent out into the field to see how their theories fared in the messy realities of real installations. One early trip was to a production facility for vacuum tubes that Western Electric had on Hudson Street in Manhattan. As he and Shewhart had suspected, "when we applied the inspection techniques, we found out that Western Electric was throwing away its money doing inspection on tubes because all of them fell within the limits. There were no defects. It was one of the first applications of this technique." According to the control charts for the vacuum tubes that they had developed, all the variation in the tubes was caused by inherent, random differences in the manufacturing process. Sampling and testing could therefore be curtailed to an absolute minimum—just enough to let them know that no new systematic cause of variation had emerged. This change in operation translated into significant savings in material and time.

On another occasion he traveled to Philadelphia, where the telephone company was installing an exchange—an extraordinarily intricate complex of switching hubs for routing hundreds of telephone calls. Beckman investigated the freshly soldered joints and the relay switches to see how different statistical methods and different kinds of sampling techniques compared with one another. While an experimental scientist was relatively unconstrained by cost and time in the battle against error in measurement, this was not the case with industrial quality control.

On this same excursion Beckman had a chance encounter that taught him a lesson about the persuasive powers of print.

> I was down one summer evening with nothing to do and walked down a street . . . where they had the medicine shows. . . . Anyway, here was a fellow going to sell snake oil to the public. He had a banjo player out there bringing a crowd. . . . I like banjo, of course, so I started listening to the fellow—he was good. Pretty soon, the barker came out with his oil. He was going to sell this medicine—a bottle of it will cure everything from falling hair to stomach pains or whatnot, you know. We got a very impassioned pitch—for only a dollar you can get this thing—but not a single buyer. I thought, gee, that fellow must be discouraged after all the good banjo show there, and then not a first buyer. Then he broke out in a great big smile and said, "Folks, you don't know how happy you've made me. You don't know me. I could tell you anything. But I'm glad to see that you're smart enough not to be taken in by that. But folks, you don't have to take my word for it, you can read it on the label yourself." And he passed the stuff out, and the money began to come in like that. Well, from that I learned the value of the printed word over the spoken word.

The Bell Labs Experience

Arnold Beckman's most profound experience during his two years at Bell Laboratories was his exposure to the vacuum tube. That exposure taught him the potential of electronics, the necessity of quality control, and the possibilities encompassed by the interaction of the two. Working with Shewhart, he was steeped in the emerging field of statistical quality control. Many of its pioneers worked in the Bell System and with Shewhart, some of whom—Harold F. Dodge, for example—Beckman got to know personally. Statistical quality control became a hallmark of high-technology product manufacturing in the United States in the 1930s and increasingly in the 1940s. Indeed, some interpreters have seen it as ushering in an entirely new phase in industrial development, a third wave of the Industrial Revolution. Bell Labs and Shewhart were at the center of this new industrial revolution, and Beckman was there for a period of extraordinary intellectual ferment. Not only was he introduced to new techniques of creating and assessing quality in manufacturing, he also found himself at the forefront of a movement that raised the expectations for quality in products to an entirely new level. This experience helps explain his commitment to quality and his unflinching approach to the quality issue once he established his own enterprise for the manufacture of instrumentation.

An early telephone switching station, similar to that which Arnold Beckman worked on in Philadelphia. *Courtesy AT&T Archives.*

Mabel Meinzer visits the shore. *Courtesy Beckman family.*

This experience at Bell Labs had another enduring effect. It immersed him deeply in the cutting-edge electronic technology associated with the vacuum tube. He worked in a building organized around a belief that electronic wonders were only beginning and that research could achieve one advance after another. As he later put it, "That was an important stage in my career. If I'd never gone to Bell Labs, I might not have developed any interest in electronics." Bell Labs had an academic atmosphere, complete with a seminar series and in-house journals. Through those journals and seminars, and by working side by side with scores of electrical engineers, Arnold developed a serious interest in where the vacuum tube might lead. He learned about circuit design and electrical communications and saw first-hand the amazing array of new devices and new possibilities that electronics had opened. He gleaned practical experience, picking up enough knowledge to allow him to build his own radio using vacuum tubes. He even began to build radios for others as well, notably his fiancée Mabel's friends on Long Island.

No interview or document records such a perception, but one cannot but wonder: Did Arnold Beckman leave Bell Labs with the half-formed idea of making electronics do for chemistry what Bell Labs was making it do for communication? His initiation into electronics research at Bell Labs opened his eyes to its broad possibilities. Less than a decade later he would launch his own journey and make the marriage of chemistry and electronics a reality.

Mabel and Marriage

Mabel Meinzer remained the focus of these New York years. Arnold was living near Mabel, out on Long Island. He commuted to Bell Labs on the Long Island Railroad, often riding with two of the secretaries from the Inspection Department. Mabel, too, commuted to her work as an executive secretary and clerical supervisor with the actuarial department of Equitable Life. They saw each other constantly.

After years of waiting for a solid future, they decided within months of Arnold's arrival that their financial situation and his career prospects were well enough in hand to allow them to embark on their life together. They each had carefully saved from their earnings, and the Meinzer family arranged to give them a generous gift of cash and property as a wedding present. The wedding took place in All Saints Church, Bayside, Long Island, on 10 June 1925. Arnold took a vacation from Bell Labs, and he and Mabel left on a ten-day honeymoon in his Model T Ford. The newlyweds visited Niagara Falls and took a boat tour on the Great Lakes. Afterward they started a new household together and returned to their jobs.

New York offered plenty of variety. Mabel's parents were close by. Bell Labs was full of challenge. But somehow, the sweet spot of opportunity and excellence that would bring together chemistry, electronics, and business was not in New York. Arnold Beckman was restless for the West.

Arnold's Model T, 10 June 1925. *Courtesy Institute Archives, California Institute of Technology.*

Arnold and Mabel's wedding party. Walter Meinzer and Bill Hincke, the best man, stand to Arnold's right. To his left stand Frances Partenheimer, one of Mabel's cousins, and Charles Meinzer. Mabel is seated in front of Arnold with a bridesmaid to her right. *Courtesy Beckman family.*

Arnold and Mabel on their honeymoon, 1925. *Courtesy Beckman family.*

Professor Beckman lecturing
at Caltech in the early 1930s.
Courtesy Beckman family.

3 Professor Beckman

I've been given far more credit than I deserve as a scientist. As an instrument maker, a toolmaker, fine. I get credit as a businessman, and I don't consider myself a businessman. . . . I still think I was a damn good teacher.

Home to California

In the spring of 1926 Arnold Beckman had been married for a year. Although settled in his home life and immersed in the world of Bell Labs, he was ready for a change. An unexpected visitor from Pasadena served as catalyst. The visitor was none other than Arthur A. Noyes, not only the chairman of Caltech's chemistry division, but also a member of Caltech's ruling scientific trio. It was no accident that he was known in Pasadena as "the King." Noyes informed Beckman that he would be in New York for a number of meetings, staying at the Plaza Hotel, and wanted "to have a chat." Such a summons from the King was not to be ignored. Noyes's interest documents the impression that Arnold made in his brief time at Caltech. It also reveals the continuing connection between the Bell Labs of Frank Jewett and the Pasadena of Millikan and Noyes. Noyes and Beckman duly met. Noyes was not one for coming straight out and telling you what he thought you should do. He wielded his power differently. As Beckman later remembered, Noyes gave his command in the form of a question: "He said, didn't I think I ought to go back and finish my degree."

Caltech's chemistry faculty in Gates Library. This group photo includes Stuart J. Bates, Roscoe Dickinson, A. A. Noyes, James H. Ellis, Howard Lucas, and James Bell. *Courtesy Institute Archives, California Institute of Technology.*

Mabel and Arnold Beckman are off to California. *Courtesy Beckman family.*

Arnold Beckman patching one of the many flat tires that slowed the trip across the country. *Courtesy Beckman family.*

Arnold weighed the possibilities. He and Mabel had saved carefully from their paychecks from Bell Labs and the insurance office. Uncle Charlie Jewkes back in Cullom would loan him some funds. A teaching assistantship would provide a guaranteed salary. Financially, he could afford to go back to graduate study.

Returning to Caltech was not simply a problem of money. Motivation mattered too: "[By] that time I was getting a little nostalgic for the smell of the chemistry lab, and I did want to get my degree anyway." Undeniably, the wide-open spaces of the West still held their appeal. Mabel understood and endorsed her husband's ambitions, even if leaving home and her mother would be hard for her—and even harder for her mother, as a surviving letter reveals.

Dearest Mother,

What can I say at a time like this to let you know how I feel? If it made it any easier for you to go away without saying goodbye, then I'll try to be a little happier. God knows it didn't for me. Surely you must know and realize that I love you and no one can ever take your place in my heart, no matter what happens or where I am. Don't ever forget that Mother darling.

Since I am Arnie's wife, tho, I must make myself realize that my duty is to be with him. Please, Mother, don't think unkindly of him, for after all, it's really best for him to finish his doctor's degree—and then the road will be much clearer and brighter for everyone. Without the degree, there'd always be a regret in both his life and mine—as I don't want to feel that I'm standing in his way. Won't you wish him luck to get it in two years? This past year has sped—and may the next two go as quickly—for I'll be an awfully lonesome girl in the meantime.

Won't you start in planning to come out by October, at least? Try, try, try, and you'll be able to avoid the snow and cold this winter and we'll be happy together again. Charlie said you had left something for me, but I can't take it. Mother, you've done too much already for us, so won't you take it with the enclosed and start getting a few things ready for your trip out—a little hat, or shoes, or maybe a dress.

Please write, Mother dearest. Walter has the address, but I want to hear from you direct, at least a line or two will help lots!

With my deepest love, to my wonderful little Mother,

Always your little girl

Mabel

X

In any case, the two set out for Pasadena in the fall of 1926. Arnold Beckman was returning to Caltech.

The journey together to California was a typical Beckman adventure. It was also Mabel's introduction to another facet of her husband's life: When it came to travel, the simple or fully predictable lacked charm. They packed their Model T with household goods, to which Arnold added camping gear, and set off on a combination cross-country move and camping trip. This was no small undertaking

Mabel poses on the Model T; Arnold digs it free; the journey continues. *All courtesy Beckman family.*

for Mabel, who was more accustomed to the streets of New York than to dirt roads and canvas tents. Intended or not, the trek took six weeks.

Of necessity, Model T drivers were adept at tire changes and repairs. On this journey they must have seemed the rule, and Arnold set a personal record for one day in the Badlands of South Dakota: They suffered nineteen flats. The first eighteen were bothersome, but reduced to a familiar routine: Take out the seat from the car, get out the jack and equipment underneath, raise the car, take the wheel off, fight the tire off the wheel, locate the leak, patch it, put the tire back on the wheel, inflate the tire with a hand pump, replace the wheel, lower the car, put the jack back under the seat, restore the seat, and start off again. They began the day with plenty of patching material, but flat number nineteen found them patchless and miles from anywhere. One method did suggest itself: Arnold could stop the car, pump up the tire as hard as he could, jump back in the car and drive fast, until the tire went flat. Then repeat the procedure, again and again. It was hot, Mabel was fainting, but persistence got them to Spearfish, Montana, where they found much-needed water at an exorbitant ten cents a glass.

This was the nadir of man-machine interaction. In more benign contexts Beckman's thoughts also turned to the performance of the Model T. He was never content with the state of its art. Seemingly, he rarely accepted the limitations of existing devices in laboratory equipment or automobiles, always asking "How can I do this better?"

In the hills of South Dakota he found one answer to this question, for his car. The Model T had a gas tank below the level of the carburetor, which meant that as the car went up a hill, gravity cut off the gas supply. Many drivers solved this problem by driving backward up steep grades, a solution that did not appeal to Arnold, perhaps in part because of the extreme risks it entailed. He improved his Model T in one elegant step by having a bicycle valve put through the gas cap. Thus he was able to pressurize the gas tank enough with his tire pump to negate the force of gravity when the need arose. Other drivers gaped in amazement as he drove straight up a hill.

Mabel learned a lot about her husband and the American landscape on the trip. She also learned how to drive. Wyoming's lonely roads seemed the ideal place to start. Things went very well, and soon Arnold felt able to sleep while Mabel drove—a refreshing change, since he had driven all the way to Wyoming. When he awoke, the practiced and practical scientist noticed that the sun was not where it should be—it was off the opposite side of the car. A check of the map and a review of the turns showed that a town or two ago Mabel had started heading back toward New York. Both of them laughed about her unconscious homing instinct for many years. Couples certainly learn much about each other when one teaches the other to drive. Mabel learned still more about Arnold when they stopped in one of the places that her husband held dear to his heart: Ashton, Idaho.

There she met Togo and Jerry Manning—his camping and fishing companions from the summers of 1919 and 1920. Arnold made a great show of unpacking the fishing rod that Togo and Jerry had given him years earlier, still a prized possession. Mabel liked both men immediately. After a few hours of conversation Arnold and Mabel set out by themselves to camp along the Snake River. They set up their tent and went to bed in peaceful isolation. Naturally, they were alarmed when roused from sleep in the dead of night by shouts of "Whitey!" Arnold must have remembered that "Whitey" was the nickname the Manning brothers had coined for him because of his blond hair and fair skin—but this was the dead of night, and Mabel at least was terrified. It was indeed the Mannings. They were determined to find

Arnold Beckman snapped this photo of one of the makeshift ferries used to cross the Snake River near Jackson Hole, Wyoming. *Courtesy Institute Archives, California Institute of Technology.*

Pasadena, California, situated in the foothills of the San Gabriel Mountains. *Courtesy Library of Congress.*

Arnold wherever he was and at whatever hour. He had left his fishing rod on the counter in their shop. "They knew I'd be disappointed when I went to fish the next day. So, not knowing exactly where I was, they went out in the middle of the night to find me and bring the rod back."

Leaving Idaho behind, the young couple wound their way across Nevada and through the Sierra Nevada to Southern California. When they finally arrived, Mabel must have been taken by the beauty of her new hometown. Pasadena is nestled at the foot of the San Gabriel Mountains, about thirteen miles northeast of Los Angeles. In 1926 Pasadena was a stylish resort and tourist destination, speckled with fashionable hotels and stately homes. Clear signs of its history as a productive agricultural community still showed in its many citrus groves and grapevines, and Caltech was an ambitious if still small institution.

The Crucible of Caltech

Caltech was an unusual place. Like the Harvard College of three centuries earlier, it was organized around a vision—but the vision now was technological, not theological. Science and rationality would provide good things for all mankind, through selfless labors by individuals of extraordinary talent, chosen on the basis of neither birth nor belief but of scientific ability. That vision had been rearticulated as recently as 1920–1921, when three scientists who worked together on scientific research for the war effort during World War I took over the reins at what was then—briefly—the Throop Institute.

That ruling triumvirate comprised George Ellery Hale, astrophysicist; Arthur Amos Noyes, who joined the faculty part-time in 1915 while still teaching at MIT; and Robert Millikan from the University of Chicago. As trustee, Hale had engineered Throop's refocusing of its efforts to students in its College of Science and Technology and had encouraged Noyes to leave MIT altogether in 1920 and move to Pasadena. That same year he and Hale agreed that the name of their institution needed to be changed, and the college's student body, which by then had grown to over three hundred young men, learned at an assembly that the school was now the California Institute of Technology. Millikan left the University of Chicago to join Noyes and Hale at the new "Caltech" in 1921. He brought with him much more than his reputation. He had a triple appointment: He would be director of the

The Gates Laboratory at Caltech, which housed the chemistry faculty and labs. *Courtesy Institute Archives, California Institute of Technology.*

Pasadena today is a scientific and technological powerhouse, with Caltech at its center—justifiably so, given the central role it has played in the growth of Pasadena's scientific and business endeavors. Yet Pasadena was a far different place at the opening of the twentieth century.

A bird's-eye view of downtown Pasadena, circa 1908. *Courtesy Library of Congress.*

Agriculture and tourism were then its mainstays, and Caltech did not exist as such. Filled with citrus orchards, grazing pastures, and vineyards, Pasadena was a relatively isolated agricultural and ranching community until 1885, when the California Southern Railway connected it to Los Angeles. The town, incorporated in 1886, began civic improvements befitting its growing reputation as a winter resort for the well-to-do from California and the East. Paved streets, electrical street lighting, and sewers all supported the real estate developers who built grand hotels and grander houses. In 1890 the local riding and foxhunting association, the Valley Hunt Club, began the tradition of holding a midwinter picnic with competitive riding tournaments that culminated in a parade of flower-festooned horses and carriages. Soon after, the Tournament of Roses Association took over the festival.

As Pasadena's size increased, so did its reputation. Construction noise was a constant presence as the population tripled to thirty thousand between 1900 and 1910. And noise, construction, and growth continued through the 1920s, as word of Pasadena's mild winter spread.

Amos Gager Throop. *Courtesy Institute Archives, California Institute of Technology.*

Education naturally grew with the town. The year after the Valley Hunt Club's first parade, Amos Throop established Throop University. Throop, originally from Chicago, was a wealthy businessman and former mayor and councilman of Pasadena who was drawn to the community via Los Angeles. Universalism brought him to Pasadena when he found a group of like-minded individuals who wanted to start a Universalist church. Toward the end of the 1880s he and other leaders agreed that Pasadena needed higher education comparable to that springing up in nearby communities. In 1891 he answered the call himself, and Throop University opened the doors of its single building. The start was small, but that building was planned as the nucleus of a full university.

Two years later, a major economic downturn nationwide led the trustees to reorient their plan. Schools in nearby communities, among them Pomona College and the University of Southern California, were already competing for traditional students, and Throop's trustees redefined their mission, and thus their market, to "manual training"—the education of young people not only in traditional subjects but also in badly needed industrial and mechanical skills. Here was a real unmet need with practical appeal in financially troubled

Students, faculty, and staff of Throop Polytechnic Institute, circa 1918. *Courtesy Library of Congress.*

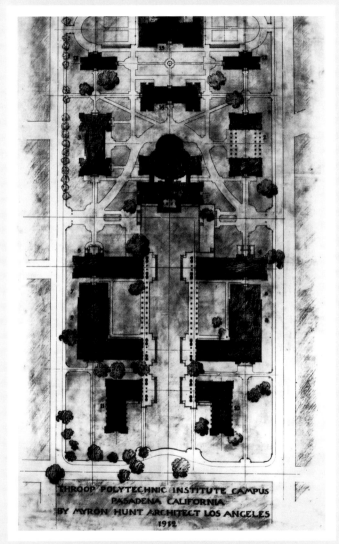

Architectural design for the expansion of the Throop Polytechnic Institute campus. *Courtesy Institute Archives, California Institute of Technology.*

times, one that went well with the great explosion of new methods of manufacturing and factory production—the so-called American system of manufactures. To capitalize on this market, Throop University became Throop Polytechnic Institute, with a curriculum organized around manual education in new, more appropriate accommodations in Pasadena.

As Throop Polytechnic Institute, the school grew, but erratically and in many directions. By 1908 it had six separate units serving all ages of Pasadena's students. There was an elementary school, a grammar school, a high school, a teacher-training school, a business school, and—at the top of the pyramid—the College of Science and Technology offering studies leading to a bachelor's degree. Each of the schools was very small, and the total enrollment of the College of Science and Technology hovered around twenty-five young men. Soon Throop would experience a third transformation, and the catalyst for it was the famous astrophysicist and astronomer from Chicago who had come to Pasadena five years earlier to build an observatory atop Mount Wilson. His name was George Ellery Hale.

George Ellery Hale (1868–1938)

Hale, like Beckman, had enjoyed an Illinois boyhood centered on his very own laboratory and workshop. While Beckman pursued his interest in chemistry, Hale followed his passion—building tools for the study of the heavens. He was born in the generation preceding Beckman's, the son of a very successful Chicago businessman. From his youth Hale was fascinated by astronomy and the nascent field of astrophysics, opened up by spectroscopy, an offspring of the marriage of chemistry and physics. When growing up, Hale built a simple device for viewing stellar spectra and their patterns of dark lines—a spectroscope—as well as a number of ordinary telescopes.

Hale later put the matter thus: "I was born an experimentalist, and I was bound to find the way of combining physics and chemistry with astronomy." By experimentalist, Hale meant that his passion, since his earliest days, had been to build the instruments that would make this combination of disciplines possible. He became one of America's greatest telescope builders. He went to college at MIT, then returned to Chicago, where, enjoying the prerogatives of wealth, he established his own private observatory. Besides telescopes, Hale stocked his observatory with instruments of his own creation to photograph spectra from the Sun. On the strength of that research he was made professor of astrophysics at the University of Chicago when it opened in 1892. A restless instrument builder, he soon founded the University of Chicago's Yerkes Observatory, overseeing the construction and installation of the then-largest refracting telescope in the world. A decade later he embarked on an even-more-ambitious project when he arrived in Pasadena in 1903 with a plan to build an observatory atop nearby Mount Wilson.

Hale settled in Pasadena. With his extraordinary political and persuasive prowess, he secured a commitment from Andrew Carnegie to underwrite the grand observatory on Mount Wilson. Construction itself was a major engineering feat, to say nothing of equipping it with special observational equipment. As the years of planning and construction went on, Hale became an ever-more-active member of the Pasadena community—not least through becoming a trustee of Throop Institute.

Hale came to believe that Throop Institute was spreading itself much too thin and that it should prune back its primary and secondary educational branches, leaving only the College of Science and Technology. He envisioned transforming Throop into a first-class training ground for makers of new technology. Its mission should be to "educate men broadly and, at the same time, make them into good engineers." He wanted a center of scientific and technical learning to match the wonder he was building on Mount Wilson.

In 1911, while Beckman was in Cullom in his laboratory qua clubhouse, Hale brought the rest of the Throop trustees around to his vision. Reduced to its College of Science and Technology, Throop moved to another new (and final) location in town, hired its first engineering faculty member, and concentrated its resources on the very few students in the college. Hale, buoyed by his initial success in changing Throop, saw that realization of his dream for the transformation of the institute depended on his ability to bring in other major scientific figures. He would remake Throop by building it around a very few leading American scientists. To this end he had the prescience to contact his former chemistry professor at MIT, Arthur Amos Noyes, for advice on developing this vision. Noyes was by that time the undisputed doyen of American physical chemistry.

Arthur Amos Noyes (1866–1936)

Noyes was a son of the Bay State, born in Newburyport, Massachusetts, and just two years older than Hale. He earned a bachelor's and a master's degree from MIT, and in 1890 he earned a Ph.D. at Leipzig under Wilhelm Ostwald, the central figure in the genesis of physical chemistry as a discipline. Noyes returned to MIT and a professorship, and he succeeded in establishing the first physical chemistry laboratory on American soil. Noyes enjoyed great prominence from his excellence as a teacher, the bright students he gathered around him, and his contributions to ionic theory. He was president of the American Chemical Society in 1904, and from 1907 through 1909 he was the acting president of MIT. If Hale had any institution in mind as a template on which he would fashion Throop, it was MIT. Who better to involve in his Pasadena plans than the leader of American physical chemistry who was deeply knowledgeable about MIT?

Noyes was not altogether satisfied with his situation in Cambridge. He had experienced frustrating constraints in the establishment and the running of his laboratory there and was further frustrated at times with MIT's resistance to a broad humanistic and scientific curriculum for all its engineering students—an ideal he and Hale shared. In his conversations with Hale, Noyes found that there was much in common in their visions for what a scientific and technological school could be. By 1915, with assurances from Hale that funds for the establishment of a new physical chemistry laboratory in Pasadena were at hand, Noyes agreed to join Throop on a part-time basis.

Before Hale and Noyes could make much of their vision for Pasadena, the European war drew them to Washington, D.C., where they joined with America's most prominent physicist, Robert Andrews Millikan, in mobilizing American scientists and engineers for war.

Robert Andrews Millikan (1868–1953)

Millikan had been director of physics at the University of Chicago since 1900, working with America's first Nobel laureate in the sciences, Albert A. Michelson. Millikan and Michelson quickly established their department's prominence within the world of physics. Their specialty was creating instruments and equipment for highly exacting, ultraprecise measurements. Millikan, starting in 1909, conducted a series of experiments in which he refined to greater and greater precision the fundamental unit of electricity, the charge of the electron. In 1915 he followed this feat by a tortuously exacting experimental check on Einstein's theory of the photoelectric effect. He had been a skeptic but convinced himself and many others of the theory's validity through his experimental results.

Millikan shared with Noyes a deep commitment to basic, or curiosity-driven, research, but both knew that such research could prove vitally important to America's industrial development. Noyes had financed his laboratory at MIT in part through the proceeds of a chemical process company he had started and then sold. Millikan knew firsthand that university researchers could be of great help to large corporate enterprises. He had for many years been a consultant and expert witness for Western Electric, especially in the field of vacuum tube research. Millikan's best friend was Frank B. Jewett, the chief engineer for Western Electric, who was responsible for the transformation of the Western Electric Engineering Department into Bell Labs. As president of Bell Labs, Jewett was Beckman's ultimate boss during the latter's tenure in Manhattan. Millikan and Jewett exchanged researchers, problems, and materials between the laboratories they ran, to their mutual benefit.

Dedication to basic science and the realization that it could be yoked to innovative technology were ideals that Hale, Noyes, and Millikan shared, and it made them natural candidates to lead the new National Research Council. Created by the National Academy of Sciences, the NRC was recognized by President Woodrow Wilson as the body officially responsible for organizing and promoting war-related research in America's scientific and technical communities. Through their feats of coordination and planning, Hale, Noyes, and Millikan fostered breakthroughs for the war effort ranging from submarine detection to artillery ranging and aviation instrumentation. By the end of the war, as Arnold Beckman was meeting Mabel Meinzer for the first time in Brooklyn, the trio of leading scientists had forged an extremely productive working relationship. The trio, or, as they came to be known, the "triumvirate," A decided to build on their wartime experience through a continuing joint venture in Pasadena: Caltech. ⌒

The triumvirate in front of Gates Laboratory. From left: Arthur Amos Noyes, George Ellery Hale, and Robert Andrews Millikan. *Courtesy Institute Archives, California Institute of Technology.*

George Ellery Hale at his desk at Throop Polytechnic. *Courtesy Institute Archives, California Institute of Technology.*

Norman Bridge Laboratory, which had been built for him; he would be professor of physics; and he would be chairman of Caltech's Executive Council. In his role as chairman, he was president of the college in everything but name.

Beckman was one beneficiary of the vision these three had of Caltech, a vision he was to embrace, to respond to, and to develop over the next seventy-five years. And since the triumvirate of Millikan, Hale, and Noyes, no one has more profoundly influenced Caltech than Arnold Beckman.

When Beckman returned to Caltech in 1926, none of this was yet apparent, but it was everywhere evident that Hale, Noyes, and Millikan were well on their way to realizing their dreams for their adopted school. The small Institute had a growing collection of impressive young faculty, and judging from the number of visitors from the national and international scientific community, it was clearly on the map. As Arnold reintegrated himself into the Gates Laboratory of Caltech's chemistry division, he was reentering Noyes's program of research in physical chemistry, one that relied on modern instrumentation and looked to the future. Leaving behind ionic theory and more traditional areas, he planned to situate his department at the crossroads between chemistry and the new physics, where his researchers would focus on questions of atomic and molecular structures and radioactivity. To carry out this program, Caltech's chemists had to master the new theories of relativity and quantum mechanics and demonstrate an equal mastery of instruments and equipment, the physical tools that made experiments at the crossroads exciting and possible. By the time of Beckman's return the department was already the center of X-ray crystallography in the United States and had begun extensive probes of molecular structure.

Beckman quickly found his plate quite full. He was studying physical chemistry under his old mentor Richard Tolman, who had advised him to come to Caltech, and he was spending long hours mastering statistical mechanics and thermodynamics. He had a teaching fellowship and the duties that attended it. He also had the question of what to pursue for his own doctoral research. His self-identity as an experimenter was as strong as it had ever been. In Caltech's Gates Laboratory he saw all around him the buzz of experimental research using X-ray crystallography, but he was more intrigued with the prospect of experiments that related to Tolman's theories about chemical reaction, heat, light, and the new theories from physics.

As he carefully made his way through his studies and formulated a research plan, Beckman often worked long hours at home after his labors in the lab. He and Mabel had rented a modest house in Pasadena on South Grand Oaks, not far from Caltech, where he had a study with a simple desk on the upper level. Also sharing the house was a tiny bird, a cedar waxwing, that the Beckmans kept as a pet. Arnold arranged a goodly portion of his personal library of books on the stairway of the house, to provide little intermediate steps between the permanent ones for the use

Richard Tolman was another MIT chemist; he had earned a bachelor's degree in chemical engineering there in 1903 and a Ph.D. with Noyes in physical chemistry in 1910.

He had studied in Germany and had taught at Michigan, Cincinnati, and Berkeley. He then came to Illinois, shortly before Beckman's time there, though Tolman was present only infrequently, as he was also running the federal government's Fixed Nitrogen Research Laboratory on the East Coast. In 1922 Noyes persuaded Tolman to join him at Caltech.

Tolman enjoyed a high stature among physical chemists as a master of the mathematical theories of physics and their application to chemical questions. Indeed, in 1909 Tolman co-wrote one of the first introductions of Einstein's special theory of relativity for an American audience. Not only was he a well-known and much respected academic, but his efforts to mobilize chemistry for public service during World War I and immediately thereafter had bestowed on him a measure of fame.

When Tolman arrived at Caltech, he wore two hats, as a professor of both physical chemistry and theoretical physics. He also assumed responsibility for Caltech's graduate students in physical chemistry, many of whom, quite naturally, shared his own two research interests. On the physics side he worked to combine the mathematical theory of thermodynamics with Einstein's revolutionary theory of special relativity. Within physical chemistry he tried to make a similar marriage of the new with the old. In the mathematical theory of chemical kinetics or chemical reactions in gases, Tolman used new theories of statistical mechanics and even quantum mechanics to produce theoretical visions of the inner workings of both thermal and photochemical reactions. That is, Tolman was building an abstract, theoretical account of how exposure to heat and light affected the course of chemical reactions within gases, knowledge critical to such processes as the fixation of nitrogen. ∽

Richard Chace Tolman. *Courtesy Institute Archives, California Institute of Technology.*

Just six years Beckman's senior, Roscoe Dickinson—like Tolman—had gone to MIT as an undergraduate and stayed on there for graduate studies under Noyes.

In 1917 Noyes sent Dickinson to Caltech while he was still a relatively new graduate student. There his assignment was to begin structural studies using the new X-ray crystallographic equipment that Noyes had already obtained for Caltech. It is a testimony to Dickinson's experimental skills that Noyes gave him this opportunity. First research endeavors with new and untested equipment are often more about mastering, tinkering with, and coaxing the instrumentation than anything else. In 1920 Dickinson received Caltech's very first Ph.D., with a dissertation based on his crystallographic studies. He stayed on in the department as a research associate and was promoted to assistant professor in 1926, the year Beckman returned.

Dickinson was the gifted experimentalist who could make cranky apparatus work, spot the virtues and flaws in an experiment's design, and teach newcomers the fundamentals of good technique. He was also the trusted adviser for graduate students wishing to pursue X-ray investigations. In fall 1922 he began to teach crystallographic experimentation to an extraordinarily gifted new graduate student—Linus Pauling. Pauling, who would become one of the most visible scientists and public intellectuals of the twentieth century, came to Caltech as a new chemical engineering graduate of Oregon State College in Corvallis. He was already curious about using X rays to determine

Roscoe Gilkey Dickinson. *Courtesy Institute Archives, California Institute of Technology.*

molecular structure, and Noyes set him to work under Dickinson. Pauling was skilled indeed. He collaborated with Dickinson on the first publication of his career—a paper detailing a crystallographic determination of structure—during his first year of graduate school.

Dickinson began to develop an experimental research program in photochemistry. Chemists knew that light, like heat, could produce chemical changes in a substance. Also like heat energy, the energy transmitted by light to a gas could break apart molecules of the gas into its various constituents—exposure to light could "decompose" a chemical substance. Untangling the specific steps in this decomposition was a complex matter, as the initial products of a decomposition would routinely undergo further chemical reactions with one another and with the remaining molecules of the original substance. Nevertheless, Dickinson felt that photochemistry held great promise as an area where quantum theory could be applied to the understanding of chemical reactions. The quantum theory of light was by then well understood. The theory stated that light came in discrete elements, or "quanta," called photons, and that the energy carried by each "quantum" of light was related to its wavelength—the color of the light. Since Dickinson believed he could handle the quantum side of the question, he strongly hoped to decipher the role of light quanta in chemical decomposition. ～

of their pet. When Arnold was studying, the bird would often hop its way up the path that he had set for it and join him at his desk.

For his doctoral dissertation Arnold Beckman opted for experimental work exploring the connections between quantum theory and theories of chemical reaction, and Richard Tolman sent him to Roscoe Dickinson. If Tolman was the leading theorist of physical chemistry at Caltech, Dickinson, a new assistant professor, was the most respected experimenter. Photochemical research was Beckman's particular choice, and Dickinson welcomed him on the research frontier. Tolman even secured a grant for Beckman's research, through the auspices of Noyes and the Carnegie Institution of Washington.

Beckman began by breaking down his research into constituent steps. First, he would have to select a substance to study. Second, he would have to determine a method to measure the photochemical decomposition of the substance—the different chemical products that would be produced when he exposed the substance to light. Third, after unraveling the complex photochemical reaction, Beckman would have to come up with a way to measure how much of the substance was decomposed for each incoming "quantum of light," that is, for each incoming photon. In this way he would be able to determine experimentally the precise relationship between a quantum action and a chemical reaction.

Photochemical apparatus in Arnold Beckman's Caltech lab. *Courtesy Beckman family.*

With Dickinson's help Beckman selected hydrazine as his compound. Hydrazine would later become familiar even to school students as the rocket propellant

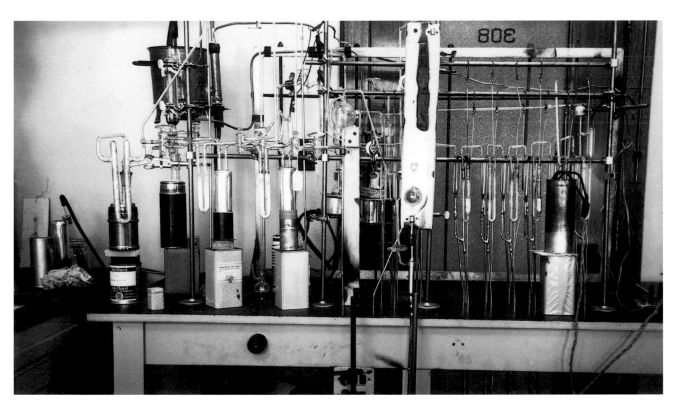

of the Apollo space program, but when he started, it was just a simple explosive whose photochemical decomposition would earn him a Ph.D. in 1928. Soon after he entered Dickinson's lab, he produced his first papers on the equally explosive hydrogen azide. Like any rational experimenter, Beckman prepared hydrogen azide a drop at a time, using ultracold liquid air to condense the volatile gas. The procedure was quite delicate, especially when he would convert his liquid sample back into a gas by taking the storage flask out of its frigid liquid-air bath.

During one preparation the burst of pressure as the compound expanded rapidly from liquid to gas inside the one-liter glass storage bulb blew the whole thing up into his unprotected face. Shards of glass flew everywhere, including into his eyes. In extreme pain, he had to hold his eyelids out to prevent further damage from the embedded glass as a colleague at the Gates Laboratory led him to the doctor. The doctor set to work on the eye that hurt the most, using faint scraping sounds as indicators for the presence of a shard. Ever the scientist, Beckman, even in the 1980s, remembered: "It was difficult because glass has about the same index of refraction as tear fluid, so glass fragments can't be seen." Luckily, the bits of glass went only into the whites of his eyes, not the pupils. As he left with a patch, his thoughts were not so much on his sight, or future safety precautions, or his luck as on the party he and Mabel were giving that evening for graduate student friends. The party was agony, and he was back the next day for the doctor to take fragments out of the other eye. He decided to start using a safety shield.

While Beckman had more than enough to keep him busy at the lab bench, his student life was enriched by other experiences outside of his research. Dickinson enjoyed taking his graduate students with him on camping trips into the great variety of natural environments—from desert to mountainsides—within easy reach of Pasadena.

Another Caltech experience might be labeled social, but at the time it felt more like a public exam. For each week's seminar Professor Noyes assigned a new graduate student the task of making cocoa. This was no simple "bring refreshments" venture. As though it were an exercise in quantitative analysis, explicit instructions were posted on the back of a door in the laboratory. Cocoa beans were to be weighed in a precise way (no preground cocoa allowed) and the mixture boiled for a precise length of time, then strained. Noyes's cocoa procedure ran in part:

12:30 P.M.	Buy three quarts of milk and one quart of whipping cream at Safeway on Lake Avenue, and buy cakes or cookies for 36 people costing not more than 60 cents. Return bottles from previous week.
2:00 P.M.	Put 6 cups of water into 8-quart pot, and heat it to boiling.
2:10 P.M.	Add 1⅓ quarts of cocoa beans, cover the pot, and turn down gas so water boils only *very gently* (for 2 hours).

Beckman and Dickinson chose to study the photochemistry of hydrogen azide because its volatile nature would allow them to work with it at very low pressures—and working at low pressures was key to the experimental system they had devised.

Further, the gas was colorless and thus immune to the effects of normal visible light. Beckman could work on his experiments in regular daylight without the worry that his results would thereby be spoiled. Hydrogen azide underwent photochemical changes only in the presence of highly energetic, ultraviolet light. Having found an appropriate compound for his photochemical research, Beckman began by inventing a new piece of apparatus, a quartz-fiber manometer. He published a description of this instrument in the *Journal of the Optical Society of America* in 1928—his first scientific publication.

A manometer is an instrument for measuring pressures, a form of a pressure gauge. In its simplest form a manometer takes the form of a U-shaped tube—the pressure difference between one end of the tube and the other being measured by the rise or fall of the level of liquid in the tube. The manometer that Beckman devised was far more complex, using changes in the vibration of a fiber of quartz as a precise measure of pressure. Beckman's manometer also used an electromagnet and a small iron bob to pluck the quartz fiber into a standard vibration without the experimenter's having to touch it directly. Thus his manometer was specially suited to low-pressure work—it could be incorporated into a system of glass tubes

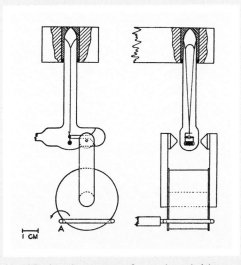

Arnold Beckman's manometer. *Courtesy* Journal of the Optical Society of America.

and containers, the interior of which could be airtight and at low pressures.

On 11 April 1928 the editors of the *Journal of the American Chemical Society* received the first paper coauthored by Beckman and Dickinson, on the photochemistry of hydrogen azide. The quartz-fiber manometer was just one element on the crowded laboratory bench top as they assembled the complex equipment they needed to determine the manner of decomposition by ultraviolet light. The bench was also laden with glass tubes and containers, pressure gauges, supply lines for the frigid liquid air, electrical transformers, and electrodes: "The photochemistry was more or less a happenstance [for me]. That was what Dickinson was interested in at that time. Quantum theory was just beginning to be applied to chemical reactions, and it sounded like an interesting thing. Also, I've always liked to do experimental work—I like to blow glass, and do things like that—and this involved a lot of such apparatus—a vacuum bench we called it in those days. So it was a type of work that I enjoyed. I liked to make different things." The experiment was as much a reflection of Beckman's manual skills as it was of his mental craftsmanship. Using older analytical methods combined with the readings of his new instrument, Beckman—with Dickinson—uncovered which wavelengths of ultraviolet light given off by an electrical spark set photochemical decomposition into play and identified the stages and chemical products of decomposition. ～

| 4:10 P.M. | Pour off cocoa through strainer into coffee urn. Add 2 cups of sugar, and stir thoroughly with a large spoon. |
| 4:12 P.M. | Take 54 cups one by one from racks, fill with cocoa from urn, place in saucers. |

Noyes's palate was the final arbiter of how well the student had performed his task. There is neither written nor oral tradition on how fifty-four cocoa drinkers were satisfied with thirty-six cookies, an average of 0.666 cookies apiece.

In 1927 Beckman had a chance to do far more than make cocoa with Noyes. He was about to complete his Ph.D. with Dickinson when Noyes invited him to help in synthesizing the growing chemical and physics literature on the electronic structure of the elements into a new form of periodic table. Part of the brilliance and utility of the traditional periodic table is its ability to express, in condensed visual form, an enormous amount of information about the properties, similarities, and differences of elements. Noyes thought that the accumulated studies on the electrons and associated energies of the first twenty-odd elements (and their ions) might be graphed into a new, electron-based periodic table that might likewise reveal interesting patterns and relationships.

Beckman and Noyes had created their new periodic table by the early summer of 1927, and they traveled to Reno to present it at a meeting of the Pacific Division of the American Association for the Advancement of Science. No great fanfare followed. The reaction seems to have been one of quiet appreciation for the labors that it took to create their charts rather than shouts of "Eureka!" Nevertheless, Noyes published their results in the *Proceedings of the National Academy of Sciences*, and an expanded treatment appeared the next year, 1928, in *Chemi-*

Beckman and Noyes's periodic table. *Courtesy National Academy of Sciences.*

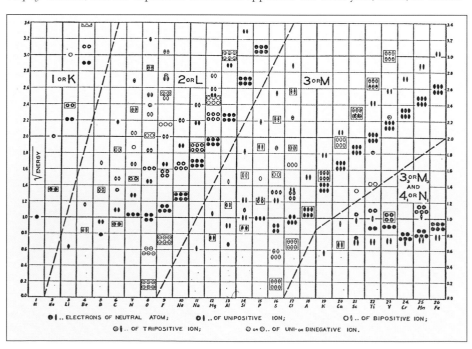

Noyes behind the wheel of his famous Cadillac, 1917. With Noyes are, from left, David F. Smith, Gilbert N. Lewis (on the running board), an unidentified man, Mrs. Lewis, James E. Bell, and Mrs. Bell.
Courtesy Institute Archives, California Institute of Technology.

cal Reviews. More important to Beckman was the time this project allowed him to spend with Noyes, even if a part of it came by accident.

There was a memorable adventure as a dividend. Noyes, Beckman, and another graduate student were driving back from Reno in Noyes's large Cadillac, the "Brown Betty." The route crossed some irrigation ditches, and either the water level was unexpectedly high, or perhaps Noyes took the ditch too fast. Either way, water splashed into the engine, bringing it to an abrupt stop. Forced to wait for a mechanic to set the engine to rights, they had to camp overnight along the lonely road. Noyes impressed his young colleagues by cooking cornbread for them over an open fire, even as Beckman—perhaps being informally reviewed for a faculty position at Caltech—continued to impress Noyes.

First Patents and Other Diversions

Not content with teaching, experimenting, and creating apparatus, Arnold Beckman at this time began his formal career as inventor. With the help of his brother Fred (by now a lawyer), he prepared a patent application for a device of his own invention as early as 1927. U.S. Patent No. 1,684,659, Beckman's first, was for a "signaling device," a buzzer that could be attached to a car's speedometer that would signal when a preset speed had been reached. Beckman was even then becoming notorious as a fast driver, a reputation he has maintained all his life. Perhaps motivated by the number of speeding tickets he had to pay—or perhaps inspired by the realization that other drivers, unlike him, might actually want a contrivance to help them curtail their penchant for speed—he came up with the design for a speed alarm. Fred helped him prepare the patent application and negotiate the byzantine patenting process. Amazingly, he received an offer from the Chrysler Corporation to purchase a license for the patent.

Beckman also kept up the interest in radio he had acquired at Bell Labs, and he and a fellow student, Henry Fracker, built radios of their own design. At that time there were two kinds of standard radio—the crystal set and the battery-powered direct-current version. Beckman and Fracker wondered if a radio could be run on common household alternating current. They wound wire for their own power transformers, "ran the filaments of peanut tubes in series," and built their own speakers. Their private source for the crucial vacuum tubes was one of

Beckman's first patent, 1927. The diagram details Beckman's signaling device.

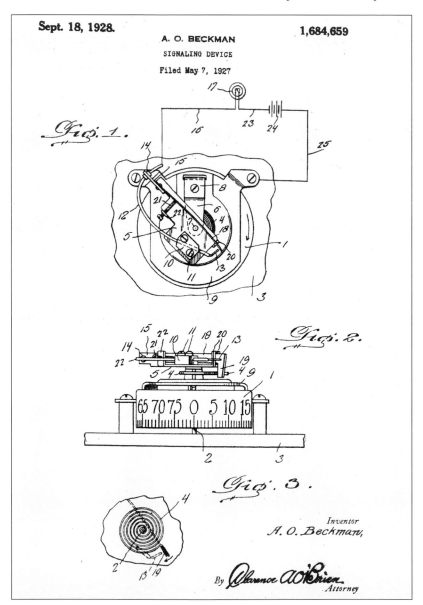

Arnold's old friends at Bell Labs. When they finished, there operating before them was the first radio that to their knowledge ran on household current. Characteristically, by this point in his life, Beckman could not be content with simply building a radio on his own: His had to be of an original design that pushed the boundary between the actual and the possible. This driving desire to improve upon the extant, whether machine or instrument, has stayed with him through his entire career. His tinkering, however, was not of the ordinary garage sort. Rather, his extensive knowledge of current science allowed him to devise designs on the cutting edge.

Radios and speedometers were just a tiny subset of his creative ruminations, and he often envisioned devices he never tried to build. Indeed, ideas came so fast that he began to keep a journal at Caltech, enumerating and capturing his "various ideas, designs of apparatus, etc., which are thought to be patentable if completely worked out." In the journal pages Beckman recorded his thoughts about a stopwatch based on the same mechanism that he had used in his chemical manometer—a vibrating filament and an electromagnet. He recorded ideas for other electrical signaling devices like the one he had patented for a car's speedometer—including an alarm for a typewriter that sounded when the bottom of a sheet of paper was approaching.

There were all manner of electrical and electronic appliances as well: an idea for using beams of electrons to record soundtracks onto rolls of movie films; a switch to turn electrical appliances on and off at preset times; a recording device for capturing sound on a metal wire through the use of magnetic fields; ideas about using electron beams for an image broadcasting system like television; and an electronic organ. Last, there were ideas for inventions of the building-a-better-mousetrap variety, designs that sought to improve existing devices by dispelling their particularly bothersome aspects. These included a plan for an appliance to maintain butter in an optimally spreadable state, a mechanical system of springs to raise or lower car windows at the press of a button, a whitening toothpaste using dyes instead of bleaches, a contrivance to keep mosquito netting taut above a bed, and a "self-sharpening pencil." Save for the mosquito netting device, others would invent every one of these in later decades of the century.

In 1928, with dissertation complete and further investigations with Dickinson well under way, Arnold had one last hurdle to face before he could be called "Dr. Beckman," the name by which he has been known ever since. He prepared for his final oral examination with his usual care, but wise graduate students learn that a doctoral program is over only when the last examination is completed. Even

The desperate search for jobs—a characteristic scene during the Great Depression. *Photo by Arthur Rubenstein. Courtesy Library of Congress.*

friendly professors can create unexpected problems, and he surely must have counted Tolman an old ally when he took his seat at the examination table. Quantum theory was in the air at Caltech, occupying the thoughts and labors of chemists and physicists alike. Tolman sat across the table in a reflective pose. Before saying anything, the professor leisurely filled his pipe, lit it, then placed his box of matches on the table. Suddenly he flipped the matchbox across the table to Arnold along with his first question. "Now, Arnold," he intoned, "tell me about the entropy of that matchbox going across the table." Beckman nearly panicked. What could Tolman possibly mean? After a few additional gentle questions, he realized, finally, that Tolman wanted him to talk about quantum theory, using the skittering of the matchbox across the table as a loose illustration. Beckman passed.

Dr. Beckman Joins the Faculty

Almost immediately after he had earned the title "Dr.," Beckman was invited to stay on in Caltech's chemistry department as an instructor. The salary was competitive, $250 a month, and roughly what he had earned at Bell Labs a few years earlier. More important, both he and Mabel had formed a vision of their future with Caltech and California as its backdrop. Arnold did no comprehensive review of career opportunities, nor did he and Mabel contemplate moving elsewhere. They would stay in Pasadena and advance along the academic ladder at Caltech: "Yes, I liked the idea of staying here. I liked it out here, and Mrs. Beckman did, too. I've forgotten whether I had other offers. I don't think I ever applied for any other job, because I was asked to stay on, and I decided to stay."

In Beckman's early years on the faculty at Caltech, the course of his later career began to lay itself out: He found increasing demand for his mechanical and technical skills, while continuing the research that interested him. In 1928 the transition from life as a graduate student to life as a faculty member must have seemed at once minimal yet great. No longer a student, he was still working in the same building with the same men—now his faculty colleagues. He had acquired the title of "Dr.," but was still teaching much of the same material that he had taught as a graduate student instructor.

Within a year Beckman had been promoted from instructor to assistant professor, a promotion that earned him a fifty-dollar raise, giving him a monthly salary of three hundred dollars—just as the stock market crash heralded the worst economic depression in American history. Caltech suffered with the rest of the country and indeed much of the world: By 1932 all construction on the campus had ground to a halt, and faculty members had agreed to take a 10-percent pay reduction. Millikan, Noyes, and Hale led the school in no small part through their personal example. Indeed, the triumvirate went so far as to finance research from their own pockets, allowing some projects to continue that otherwise would have had to be shut down.

The chemistry faculty group at Caltech, 1937. Professor Beckman is standing, second from left; Roscoe Dickinson and Linus Pauling are seated next to each other, at left. *Courtesy Institute Archives, California Institute of Technology.*

Professor Beckman and His Students

Dr. Beckman must have been thankful that his new job was secure and that his experimental budget was not cut. He was following a fairly straightforward line of research in photochemistry, one that took account of quantum theory and was propelled by improvements he made in experimental design and apparatus. Even so, his research was not the overriding center of his life, or even of his career.

For a start, there was the time and energy he devoted to teaching—of graduate students and undergraduates alike—and teaching was a job that he loved and treated with the utmost enthusiasm. Beckman was colleague and mentor to his graduate student Ralph R. Wenner, as figures like Noyes, Tolman, and Dickinson had been for him. Ralph went on several camping trips into the desert with Professor and Mrs. Beckman, including a particularly memorable outing to Yosemite National Park. When they made camp, it was much colder than Ralph could bear, and as the night wore on, he grew colder and colder. Finally, he spread his blanket where they had built the campfire hours earlier. The spot was still warm, warmer than Ralph realized, and soon his blanket went up in flames. Fortunately, he escaped unscathed. Beckman was fond of the young chemist and was greatly saddened

91

Arnold and Mabel Beckman enjoyed many camping trips throughout California and the West. *Courtesy Beckman family.*

when just a few years later Ralph's life and promising career were tragically cut short by a fatal automobile accident. Another of his graduate students was Albert E. Meyers, who went on to an industrial career; Beckman continued working with Meyers on quantum yields and photochemistry through the mid-1930s.

Beckman was assigned to teach freshman chemistry, in tandem with his colleague James E. Bell. Freshman chemistry at Caltech was nothing if not rigorous; the chemistry being done by the eighteen-year-old freshmen was at the same level of sophistication as the courses taken by twenty-one-year-old seniors at the University of Illinois when Beckman was there. The Caltech students who excelled at the difficult chemistry taught in their first year were promoted to honor sections. Beckman usually taught one of those sections as well, something he actively sought out rather than avoided, because "it was really a stimulating experience to teach them." As a precocious student of chemistry, Beckman had benefited from a series of teacher-mentors who had worked with him and encouraged his interests. Now, as Professor Beckman, he felt for himself the personal rewards that come from encouraging young chemists.

Some academics revel in teaching graduate courses and strenuously avoid undergraduate work, particularly freshman courses. Beckman was far different: Chemistry 1 was his main area of professional joy. "I just liked it," he says. "I liked to try to explain things in a way that can be understood by other than experts. Also, I liked the excitement of young minds coming on, learning new knowledge—I had the feeling I was doing something worthwhile. The essence of teaching is not teaching, it's learning on the part of the students." Standing at the front

By the summer of 1929 Beckman and Dickinson had reached the stage in their investigations of the photochemistry of hydrogen azide at which they could combine, in a direct way, knowledge of the new quantum theory with knowledge of chemical reactions.

From their earlier work they knew the details of the way in which hydrogen azide was broken apart by shining ultraviolet light upon it, and in 1929 they measured how much light energy was absorbed by the hydrogen azide gas as it was decomposed. These observations allowed them to establish a link between quantum theory (governing the energy of the ultraviolet light) and their knowledge of decomposition.

They could calculate from their experimental measurements the ratio of the number of molecules of hydrogen azide broken apart or decomposed by each photon of ultraviolet light that was absorbed into the sample—the "quantum yield."

This was pioneering work, for their quantum yield measured the direct contribution of a phenomenon governed by quantum theory (the energy of a particle of light) to a chemical reaction (the decomposition of hydrogen

Photochemical apparatus in Arnold Beckman's Caltech lab. *Courtesy Beckman family.*

azide). Beckman and Dickinson had figured out the experimental problems of measuring the chemical reaction in their earlier work, but for this research they had to develop means for very delicate measurements of energy that could not be made directly: Beckman needed to be able to measure the energy of the beam of ultraviolet light that he was shining into his sample. To make his measurements, he built an instrument. His new thermocouple translated the energy of the ultraviolet light into a signal by generating an electrical response in proportion to changes in temperature that could be read in precise terms with a common galvanometer.

This use of the thermocouple is more than a technical achievement: It represents a migration, or perhaps a translation, of an interest in electronics into his personal creation of chemical instrumentation. Beckman was familiar with electrical measurements in chemistry from his early days studying physical chemistry at the University of Illinois. He was also deeply familiar with electronic and electrical technology from his time at Bell Labs and from his tinkering with radios as a graduate student. But here, in this work on quantum yields, he first incorporated electrical technology into his very own chemical investigations. Thermocouples were not new to science, but in 1929 they were new to the chemical equipment that Beckman had built for himself. This combination of electrical circuits and chemical instrumentation allowed him to truly connect quantum theory with knowledge of chemical reactions, and his paper was again published in the highly respected *Journal of the American Chemical Society*. Here, as later, he saw how data might be derived from an experiment by transforming them into measurable electrical currents.

Beckman was so pleased with this kind of photochemical investigation that he refined his experimental system over the next few years and carried out studies of other substances with graduate students of his own. In 1932, with Ralph Wenner, he determined the quantum yield of ultraviolet light for the photochemical decomposition of the compound hydrazine. Hydrazine was that same compound he had studied for his dissertation in 1928—the one that sent glass shards shooting into his eyes.

For this project with Wenner he followed much of his earlier procedure and used much of the same apparatus. The major change came in improvements to the instrumentation employed. He and Wenner replaced the thermocouples with *thermopiles*, a more complex and sensitive assemblage of several thermocouples. Better galvanometers were also used to measure the electrical signals given off by the new thermopiles. New equipment made the old formula work better at each end.

Significantly, Beckman connected his galvanometers to another mechanism of his own devising—an automatic recording device that captured the galvanometers' readings. This device was a photographic plate, moved by a motor, that caught the light reflected off small mirrors attached to the galvanometer's measuring mechanism. As these mechanisms moved, the reflected light from them recorded curving lines on the photographic plate. The plate could be developed and the readings of the galvanometers (and the difference between them) directly measured from the photograph. This was a complex, sensitive, ingenious recording device, and it is a testimony to Arnold Beckman's commitment to inventive excellence that he devoted so much effort to creating it. This early effort reveals Beckman's deep understanding that a chemical instrument must not only give good measurements, but must also deliver them to the user in a simple, comprehensible, and usable form. ✑

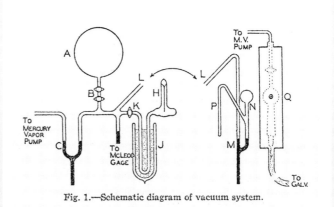

Fig. 1.—Schematic diagram of vacuum system.

Arnold Beckman's photochemistry experiment. The thermocouple is at the far right. *Courtesy American Chemical Society.*

of the classroom, he used simple analogies and metaphors to illustrate complicated chemical theories; for example, in explaining the migration of ions, he went to the blackboard and drew pictures of boats crossing a channel. The banks of the channel, he explained, represented electrodes, and the different-sized boats represented differently charged ions. "The idea of ion mobility is kind of complicated and dull if you just take the mathematics alone," but giving his students a vivid mental tableau, a scene for them to let their intuitions run with, made even the driest theory accessible and comprehensible. Former students would often say to him, "Remember the boats you got across the channel?"

Beckman also taught graduate courses. One was Chemistry 176, a seminar in photochemistry that he team-taught with Dickinson. Within the seminar the attending students made reports to one another and held discussions on the latest research and news in the field.

In all his courses Beckman demonstrated an almost irresistible urge to create devices to aid the learning process. Rather than simply lecture about electrophoresis (the movement of electrically active particles suspended in a liquid under the influence of electrical forces, an important technique for coating metals and for performing chemical analyses), he designed and built a U-shaped glass tube in which electrophoresis could take place. The tube was fashioned specifically to fit into a slide projector. While Professor Beckman described the science of the phenomenon, his students could see the activity itself.

His teaching style was creative in other ways. Robert C. Barton, a longtime Beckman Instruments employee who had also been a student at Caltech, remembered that in the classroom his boss "had a wonderful sense of humor. He was a hit with all the undergraduates because he spoke their language." When instructing students on how to fold a paper funnel, he would quip that the tip could be opened by tearing off a small piece or by biting off the piece—it was all a matter of taste. Apparently some of that practical joking rubbed off on the students. A prank that could have had disastrous results occurred one day while Beckman was working in his office, directly under the freshman laboratory. He heard the sound of breaking glass and looking up saw test tubes flying by his window. He rushed upstairs to find that one of his students had been trying to make a batch of nitroglycerin and was testing his results by throwing the tubes out of the window. Another time, he remembered, two students decided it would be fun to grind together all the chemicals on the lab shelf to see what would happen—and the mortar blew apart! Fortunately, neither student was seriously hurt. Professor Beckman must have been given a moment of pause when such foolish experiments were undertaken by his students. As a youth he too had been nearly as cavalier in his play with the power of chemistry, but his new role demanded that he enforce the boundaries of reasonable behavior.

Professor Beckman Hits His Stride

In the early 1930s Beckman's career at Caltech took on a regular pattern. He was largely responsible for freshman chemistry, while his other courses delved into experimental techniques and instruments for research in chemical engineering or industrial chemistry. There was a natural connection between his teaching about industrial chemistry and about the equipment and instruments of chemical research; the same kinds of problem-solving skills are required for grappling with tangible, material puzzles at the workbench, on the laboratory counter, or on the plant floor. More immediately, he carried instruction in experimental technique and instrumentation on his own shoulders because he was the recognized faculty virtuoso in these areas. His growing reputation as master of experimental apparatus and instrumentation brought a stream of problems and requests for help through his office door, just the sorts of questions and puzzles that held a strange power over him. Questions of invention matched wit and skill of hand and eye against the toughest challenges presented by the material world.

Such questions competed with photochemical research for his attention. As he later put it, "It wasn't just a case where I was sitting there doing research. I was doing lots of miscellaneous things." But this "miscellany" had its own order—Beckman was tackling a hodgepodge of challenges, but they all had to do with the construction of instruments and apparatus. Glassblowing was now a continuing resource. He had studied it at the University of Illinois, and he had used the skill for his experiments with photochemistry. His "vacuum bench" covered a laboratory table with a tangle of glass tubes, bulbs, stopcocks, and traps. Glassblowing was an essential element of his ability to envision and make instruments for his research: Both his vibrating-fiber manometer and his thermocouples for rendering light into electrical signals involved glass chambers within glass chambers.

His highly visible skills in glass led to many interruptions from other inhabitants of the Gates Laboratory, asking for his assistance. They wanted his help, or even better, they came for finished pieces. Caltech had a resident glassblower, Mr. Clancy, a highly respected artisan much in demand. But physicists as well as chemists wanted glass equipment, and at that time Caltech, and hence Clancy, gave physicists priority. Thus more and more chemists asked Beckman for help, and it was partially an act of self-preservation that led him to offer a course in glassblowing.

Beckman met with his students in a lecture hall in the Gates Laboratory. They covered the lecture table with a protective plank and ran tubing for compressed air and burner fuel across it. Professor Beckman and the students sat on high stools, elbow to elbow, while he gave them individual guidance in the craft. It was not enough that he teach them just how to get by. His goal, as with all aspects of his life, was to strive for excellence. If he was going to instruct people in glassblowing, he would make them truly skilled. Thus he insisted that they learn on "soft glass,"

Examples of the glass-blower's art. *Courtesy Institute Archives, California Institute of Technology.*

lime-soda glass. In the 1930s Pyrex glass was becoming widely popular, in part because it was a very forgiving material for the glassblower. Professor Beckman kept his students on the more cantankerous lime-soda glass, knowing that if his students could master the older material, they would have no problem with the new. The instruction made a great impression on the students who undertook it, and many years later he would still encounter Caltech alumni who would ask, "Do you remember when I took that course in glassblowing?"

In similar fashion he became responsible for the chemistry division's "instrument shop," actually a collection of units in a common home. In the "student shop," which had limited equipment and tools, students could develop basic skills in creating experimental equipment. The "regular shop" was the domain of Fred Henson, the resident instrument builder for the chemistry division. Last, there was the instrument cabinet, which safeguarded the precious supply of instruments that could be signed out. As administrator, Professor Beckman had to make sure that supplies were ordered, requests filled properly, and demands for limited tools carefully rationed. He also had to protect Henson from faculty who insisted that their job be given top priority—no small task since Henson had an astounding reputation. "He was an extremely good mechanic. In fact, they used to have a term back then that you could have a good fit, you could have it to a thousandth of an inch or a ten thousandth of an inch. If you really wanted to, you specified a 'Henson fit.' That was the ultimate precision you could get."

The experience with this shop further refined Beckman's sense of the importance of instrumentation to the process of science. The training of chemists and advancement of research depended on instruments. Either instruments acted as a restrictive bottleneck for scientific development, or they opened a wide vista of possibilities for entirely new achievements.

Beckman soon combined his responsibilities in the glassblowing class and in the instrument shop to create Chemistry 169, Research Manipulations. The students in 169 would be taught how to blow glass and use the tools of the instrument shop. He also lectured them on advances in research in physical chemistry, describing how he and others were using electrical measurements and appliances, vacuum systems, and other techniques. He taught a parallel, less-advanced course in instrumentation for students of industrial chemistry or chemical engineering, introducing them to the basic tools of the trade, the standard chemical instruments that could be found in any laboratory, whether industrial or academic. That course had "nothing in the way of theoretical development or anything like that. Just a practical course primarily for industrial chemists. Those who go around and work in the sugar mills, for example, have to know how to use a refractometer."

Through the 1930s Beckman concentrated increasingly on questions of measurement for the experimenting chemist. What was the best way to measure a chemical property? What questions could be answered, what new paths for science could be opened, with new kinds of instruments? Yet he also pondered how instruments could meet pressing concerns in industry. Both academic duties and personal curiosity gave the young professor a broad awareness of chemical theories, experimental frontiers, and instrumental developments in electronics, optics, materials, mechanical engineering, and electrical engineering. Although he barely knew it, he was once again in the "sweet spot," his experience as professor prefiguring the essential genius of the creator of Beckman Instruments.

The Lure of the Practical

Caltech's catalog for 1934 showed how much the Institute had changed in the course of a decade. Under the leadership of Noyes, the chemistry division was becoming ever more devoted to pure science, despite its official title of "Chemistry and Chemical Engineering." The single professorship in chemical engineering was held by William Lacey, who found himself working more and more with his younger colleague Arnold Beckman. Although applied chemistry was being de-emphasized by the department, Beckman continued to teach courses in industrial chemistry and instrument analysis, as well as his ever-popular glassblowing, now incorporated into Chemistry 169. That course also had exercises in machine-shop operation, discussions of high-vacuum technique, vacuum-tube circuits, and measurement of pressure, temperature, and radiant energy. Beckman taught 169 for the remainder of his time at Caltech. As the 1930s went on, he also became responsible for the engineering instruction offered by the department. He took over Lacey's old course Chemistry 61, Industrial Chemistry, which reviewed not only the chemical processes but also the "conditions and equipment necessary to carry on these reactions." The text was Emil Riegel's *Industrial Chemistry*. He also taught the companion Chemistry 62, Engineering Chemistry, which focused on the application of chemical principles to engineering problems and of engineering to chemical industries.

Arnold Beckman was not the only man on the Caltech chemistry faculty in the 1930s whose name would come to be associated with greatness. There was also Linus Pauling.

Linus Pauling. *Courtesy Institute Archives, California Institute of Technology.*

Pauling had finished his Ph.D. at Caltech just before Beckman. The similarity went further, for Pauling also had Roscoe Dickinson as his adviser and had conducted experimental work with him. After he earned his degree, Pauling too was invited to stay on at Caltech, and like Beckman he accepted. Beckman and Pauling traveled similar paths at Caltech, but at this crucial stage in the 1930s, their careers began to diverge. Through his graduate research Pauling saw the previously hidden world of molecular structure opened up by the X-ray diffraction instruments that he and Dickinson worked on. Like Beckman, Pauling began with an experimental, instrumental approach to putting the worlds of chemistry and quantum theory together. But as the 1930s progressed, Pauling increasingly pursued the theoretical meanings that arose out of and could be validated by the use of instruments and experimental results. The results of Pauling's use of experimental information was astounding, and in the early 1930s he developed a mathematical theory of the chemical bond that truly wed quantum theory to chemical theory. This work secured him a place in history. Beckman, on the other hand, became ever more intrigued by and talented in solving the more immediate and practical questions that truly fired his imagination: questions about instrumentation and measurements. His own research in photochemistry had shown how quantum theory could be connected to chemical theory using sophisticated new instrumentation. As Pauling became more interested in ways to use instruments to create new, revolutionary understandings, Beckman dreamed of creating instruments to open up new vistas for future Paulings. ◞

In his teaching and in running the instrument shop, Beckman made the acquaintance of many Caltech students, including undergraduates like William Shockley. Shockley would win the Nobel Prize in physics in 1956, as one of the inventors of the transistor. He was a seminal figure in the early days of the semiconductor industry in California, but as an undergraduate he needed help on complex electrical equipment. Beckman helped Shockley build some thermocouples—the same devices he was using to measure the energy of light in his photochemical research. Twenty years later their paths would cross again in a very different context but toward the same end: the invention of new devices.

Of more immediate importance were the contacts that Beckman was developing with individuals outside of Caltech. Millikan and Noyes were committed to keeping the Institute strong, even in the depths of the economic depression of the 1930s. Millikan was the consummate ambassador and promoter for Caltech in Pasadena, the surrounding region, and beyond. He had a vision of Caltech as a real centerpiece in the community and in the state, a vision that has largely been realized. Part of that vision was a mutual support between Californians and the Institute. Caltech itself might value basic research over industrial application, but it could offer industrialists advice and expertise about their problems, while these Californians could support Caltech through financial gifts and in many other ways. Thus Millikan was open to being approached by leaders of government and business who had scientific and technical questions. He was more than happy to pass them along to the appropriate member of the faculty.

Left: The machine designed by Arnold Beckman to coat 35-millimeter film with metallic silver. Lee De Forest commissioned this apparatus as part of his attempt to construct a television projection system in the early 1930s.

Right: Another view of Beckman's film-coating machine. *Both courtesy Beckman family.*

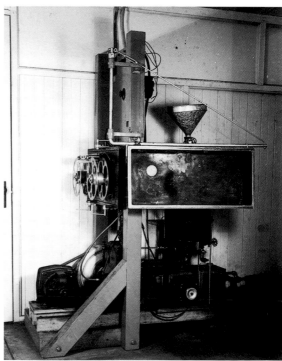

The chemical questions that came across Millikan's desk were increasingly routed to Professor Beckman and his colleague in chemical engineering, Professor Lacey. Noyes, leading the chemistry division, was not interested in such outside questions and consultations. His focus was much more on fundamental research, and the great success of Caltech chemists like Linus Pauling in this direction is a testament to his unwavering stand. This said, Noyes realized that it was important for his professors who were teaching industrial chemistry and chemical engineering to be engaged with the world beyond Caltech. "Because we [Beckman and Lacey] were teaching chemical engineering and applied chemistry, [Noyes] thought we should keep in touch with what was going on in the real world of chemistry. That was applied chemistry. That's why many outside requests for help came to us. We did this work with Dr. Noyes's specific approval, and in fact, with his urging."

Some of these contacts developed into larger relationships. Lee De Forest enjoyed fame among the scientific and technical community as the inventor of the vacuum tubes that Beckman had studied in detail at Bell Labs. Many years later and with a far different project, he sought Beckman's help. De Forest was focused on developing a television-like system that could project a picture onto the screen of a movie theater. A Yale-educated physicist who had written his dissertation on radio waves, he had already seen two of his start-up business ventures end in failure by the time he made it to the West Coast. Over the course of his career he worked for or was affiliated with many institutions (Caltech among them), but he did most of his inventing as a freelance scientist. Despite a checkered history of failed attempts as a businessman, constant embroilments in lawsuits, and crumbling marriages, De Forest did a great deal to promote radio and television as modes of increasing the American public's cultural awareness. For instance, as early as 1910, he broadcast a live performance by the famous tenor Enrico Caruso from the Metropolitan Opera House in New York City.

In the early 1920s De Forest began work on a system for recording and reproducing motion pictures with sound: "talkies." He found a way to record sound on film in 1921 and spent the next six years attempting to sell his Phonofilm recording system to movie studios. His second attempt at a business venture, the De Forest Phonofilm Corporation, folded in 1925. Two years later Warner Brothers Studio released *The Jazz Singer*, the first feature-length "talkie" film. In the 1930s De Forest was living in Hollywood. Others had been more successful at adding sound to movies, but he was determined to engineer important developments in a new field—what is now called television. As part of a new attempt to construct a television projection system, De Forest needed 1,000-foot-long, 35-millimeter-wide strips of film that were uniformly coated with metallic silver. Beckman, in his consulting hours, built an apparatus that coated the film for De Forest's system automatically and precisely. Beckman set up a production lab on Vine Street in Hollywood as part of a company called Market Television. The film strips worked

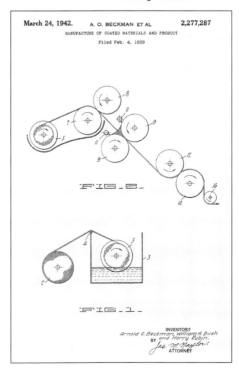

Beckman's patent for a device that applied special coatings to rolls of paper, making heat-sealing packaging for foodstuffs like loaves of bread. Beckman based this invention on his film-coating machine.

Left: Pattty Beckman.

Right: Arnie Beckman.
Both courtesy Beckman family.

parents, among them Pearl S. Buck, Bob Hope, George Burns, and Al Jolson. Applications came from couples across the nation, building an excruciatingly long waiting list, but in 1936 the Beckmans' name finally reached the top of the list.

Mabel traveled by train to Chicago and then to Evanston on Chicago's North Shore. There she stayed in nearby Kenilworth with Lettie Stein and her husband Herman, one of Arnold's old fraternity brothers from the University of Illinois. The Steins and Beckmans have maintained a close friendship over the decades. At the Cradle, Mabel was faced with what must have been an emotional tightrope act: She had to choose which child or children would become her own. She visited and played with two young brothers and, in Beckman's words, "a very pretty little red-haired girl" who was just three years old. Mabel left with Gloria Patricia, the little girl. Lettie Stein helped Mabel work her way through the adoption papers and procedures at the Cook County Courthouse, and then Mabel and her daughter, now Gloria Patricia Beckman or Patty, quickly made their way home to California.

In less than a year the Beckmans received more good news from Evanston, and in August 1937 Arnold, Mabel, and Patricia sped, through the West and Midwest, to bring home the infant who would be the newest member of their family. The Beckmans stopped in Cullom on the trip, visiting relatives, perhaps even making it there for the "Cullom Days" celebration in mid-August. At the Cradle the Beckmans met their new son, Arnold Stone Beckman or Arnie, who had been born on 23 July. On the return to California there were now four happy Beckmans headed for the house in Altadena.

Left: Sister helps brother pose for the camera.

Right: Father and daughter enjoy a conversation. *Both courtesy Beckman family.*

A Brush with Death

Not long after their return the mood changed with the news that Mabel had contracted tuberculosis. She became ill, so much so that she was admitted into the care of the Pottenger Sanatorium in Monrovia, about ten miles southeast of Altadena. *Sanatorium* to the modern ear carries connotations of mental health care and resortlike hospitals for the emotionally troubled well-to-do. This was not the case in the late 1930s. Although most commonly a disease of the lungs, tuberculosis, caused by tubercle bacilli, can affect almost any organ or system in the body. An epidemic scourge during the nineteenth century, especially in the crowded neighborhoods and apartment houses of America's growing cities, tuberculosis evaded successful drug treatment until the mid-twentieth century. Before the 1940s treatment involved a long rest and relaxation period, usually in an isolated area. Tuberculosis patients of means could enter sanatoriums, the first of which in the United States was founded by Dr. Edward Trudeau, in Saranac Lake, New York, in 1884. There the patients underwent carefully supervised regimens, including special diets, ample fresh air, and enforced rest.

Medical science had little to offer a sufferer when it came to pharmaceuticals and medicaments. The first effective antibiotic for tuberculosis, streptomycin, would not be discovered until 1943—almost a decade after Mabel Beckman was stricken with the dreaded disease. During the 1930s the best that caregivers could do for tuberculosis patients was prescribe a rest cure in the dry and warm climate of the American West, where the air was thought to be particularly healthy for the

Patty helps Arnie celebrate his first birthday in 1938. *Courtesy Beckman family.*

lungs. Sanatoriums like Pottenger's sprang up across the West, and sufferers from around the nation flocked to them in search of recovery.

The Pottenger Sanatorium was founded by Dr. Francis Marion Pottenger, who had lost his own wife to tuberculosis. It was built in the foothills of the San Gabriel Mountains behind Monrovia to take advantage of Southern California's clean, dry air, and it accepted its first patient in December 1903. Several years later, the Los Angeles Sanatorium, a treatment center for impoverished patient would open nearby. However, the Pottenger Sanatorium was a more upscale facility, with sculptured flower gardens, private bungalows, and printed menus for each meal. Careful attention was paid to the diet of the patients at Pottenger; the founder's son, Francis, Jr., was a pediatrician and an active researcher in nutritional deficiencies. As a staff member at the sanatorium he advocated eating uncooked foods. Mabel certainly absorbed the nutritional pointers she received: Some time later, following a consultation with Francis, Jr., she put her small son on a diet of raw foods in the hopes of improving his constitution.

Although most patients were confined at sanatoriums for extended periods of time (many doctors did not hesitate to recommend that tubercular patients undergo at least a year of treatment), many did recover, including Mabel. She stayed at Pottenger's, separated from her family, for seven months.

Mabel's absence from the home necessitated a major reorganization of family life. Arnold himself was extraordinarily busy in his role as Professor Beckman and with a separate new venture of his own. (That venture, the beginning of Beckman Instruments, is the subject of the following chapter.) Mabel Beckman gave many

Patty and Mabel Beckman.
Courtesy Beckman family.

aspects of herself to her family, not the least of which was her hard work, care, and thoughtfulness in raising her children and caring for her husband. Mabel was also very much a partner to her husband. She was his confidante and his primary discussant, and through their conversations he made many decisions about his career and his entrepreneurial ideas. She was sorely missed in both roles while away at Pottenger's, as a series of hired household assistants looked after Arnold and the children in her absence. The separation must have been particularly difficult for Arnold Beckman. Not only was he devoid of his closest confidante, his helpmate, and the mother of his two young children, but the gravity of Mabel's illness brought back memories of the loss of his own mother at a young age. These memories, and the possibility that such a tragedy might repeat itself in his family, cast a dark shadow over the Beckman household during those seven months.

Happily, Mabel recovered. However, when she returned home to Altadena, she was still weak, and she stayed close to her room for fear of infecting her children. Consequently, the Beckmans kept on one household assistant, a German woman named Martha, who cooked delicious apple desserts, which little five-year-old Patty greatly enjoyed. This extra presence in the home was a welcome help for Mabel, but not one she could accept without complicated feelings. She was an expert cook, priding herself on preparing three nutritionally balanced meals a day for her family, and she relished early mornings before the other sleepers awoke as time she could devote solely to herself. It was hard for her to see others responsible for the things that she enjoyed doing and took deserved pride in doing so well. She was frustrated at not being able to resume these activities immediately.

The domestic life of the Beckmans at this time began to run counter to convention. As Mabel regained more and more of her health, she insisted on less and less domestic assistance in the home at just the time Arnold's commercial enterprises were growing and bringing in more money than ever. Over the next twenty years, as the financial fortunes of the Beckman family rose, the family paradoxically used less rather than more help at home. Taking back the jobs that gave her real feelings of satisfaction and accomplishment, Mabel Beckman again became the chef and the executor of most household duties for the rest of her life.

Mabel was justifiably shaken by her brush with tuberculosis. She had lost her own mother, to whom she had been very close, only a few years earlier, which could not have been reassuring. Alice Stone Meinzer was gravely ill in 1928, and Mabel took an extended leave from California to be with her. She traveled by boat, through the Panama Canal, stopping briefly in Cuba, on her way to her mother. Unfortunately, she barely made it to Brooklyn before her mother died. Alice's son-in-law had just earned his Ph.D., but she would see neither the fruition of his

Arnie and Patty in front of their Christmas tree, December 1938.

Courtesy Beckman family.

Mabel, her children, and guests enjoy the barbecue Arnold built in the backyard. *Courtesy Beckman family.*

career nor the extraordinary results of her daughter's devotion to him. For Mabel the pain of that loss must have made her own illness all the more frightening. Mabel also became very concerned about the health of her children, concerned to affirm regularly that they were free from tuberculosis. Her fears may have been heightened by her own experience, but they were far from irrational. Tuberculosis is particularly insidious in its ease of communicability. Just as Mabel had to return often to Pottenger's to have X rays taken of her lungs to monitor her full recovery, she was duly cautious in having X-ray films of her children's lungs taken from time to time to make sure they had not unknowingly contracted the disease.

Mabel's concern may also have been elevated by early worries about the constitution of young Arnold S. Beckman. Arnold S. was thin as a child and had a slight heart murmur. However, Mabel refused to let him grow up an invalid. Some fifty years later Pat remembers how her mother put him on a diet rich in raw meats and bean sprouts—a combination then thought to build strength and vitality. Mabel would freeze raw ground round and serve it like shrimp cocktail! Mabel further saw to it that Arnold S. had a swing set and climbing pole in the backyard, for, ahead of her time, she believed in the combination of careful diet and exercise recommended by her pediatrician. Her care and encouragement of her son paid off: He now stands six feet tall, a vigorous and healthy man.

Illness and health concerns by no means dominated the Beckman home, though. The children enjoyed much outdoor recreation, whether on planned excursions or in their own backyard. They played on their own badminton court; their neighbors had a pool (small, but a pool); and they had a grand barbecue, which

Dr. Beckman built himself. Pat well remembers the cats they always had and regular hikes into Eaton Canyon with Arnie and their dogs. Their childhood was filled with trips with their parents, visiting relatives and the places their parents loved best. Most of these vacations incorporated one of Arnold Beckman's favorite leisure-time pursuits—camping. And he naturally took his family to the Ashton, Idaho, region that had meant so much to him as a young man.

In Altadena, Patty had the bedroom upstairs, while Arnie had a room on the first floor. Pat remembers that they could see all the way to the Pacific Ocean in one direction and the top of Mount Wilson in the other. The Beckmans loved to garden, no one more so than Arnold Beckman himself. There were vegetable plants, a grape arbor, flower beds, and always a rose garden, which Arnold cared for personally. Because theirs was one of the first houses in the neighborhood, they shared their living space with many wild animals, and they found that to protect the garden in which they had invested much time and energy they needed a pile of small stones on the balcony as ammunition to drive hungry deer away.

Mabel enjoyed needlecraft and cooking, and Arnold gardened, took care of household repairs, and worked in his woodshop in the basement of the house. He taught his son to use the many different woodworking tools—lessons that the father may have mildly regretted when the young Arnold employed his skills to build exploding toy rockets. Nonetheless, Beckman instilled in his son the manual dexterity and skill with tools that had been keys to his own success. A self-proclaimed tomboy, Patty was athletic and enjoyed riding horses, swimming, diving, and tennis. Like her father, she was a pianist, and her younger brother recalls that she spent a considerable amount of time on the piano bench.

Every Sunday, Mabel drove herself and her children to the local Episcopal church (accompanied by her husband only on Christmas and Easter). Sunday at noon the family would sit down to a big midday dinner in the tradition of Mabel's mother. The remainder of the afternoon was spent in family activity: a visit to a museum or a drive in the mountains. On Sunday evenings the family gathered around the radio. With four years between them, Arnie and Patty generally got along well, though Arnold S. still remembers one incident when, particularly enraged with each other, they donned boxing gloves, and Pat "beat the tar" out of him. Of course this beating elicited much sympathy from his mother, and Mabel bandaged young Arnold's head, after which he proceeded to "strut around with my hero mark up there, with the little tiny Band-Aid on my forehead!"

Dr. Beckman was happy at Caltech and happy at home once Mabel was back. The 1930s were the natural time to build his academic career. The gray pall of the Depression affected Pasadena less than many areas, and by 1940 both the world and Arnold Beckman's agenda had assumed radically different complexions. His was indeed the prepared mind, and chance favored it mightily, not least through a visit from an old friend with a problem.

Arnold and his children. *Courtesy Beckman family.*

A Santa Monica investor grew suspicious when he found that Cox had no patents, either for his process or for his miracle clay catalyst. He demanded that Cox file patent applications or face being reported to the local district attorney for fraud. To start the patent process, Cox sought out Leonard Lyon. Cox described his process in a barrage of idiosyncratic language that left the attorney completely befuddled. Lyon had already learned to call on Arnold Beckman for translations, and he now sought aid in untangling Cox's science, so he could file clear patent applications. Lyon had no suspicions.

Arnold Beckman became deeply involved in the matter in the summer of 1933, a normal seasonal lull in the academic year. He learned to commute between Southern California and Cox's refinery near San Francisco, taking his first airplane rides in the process, probably with Pacific Air Transport, which flew the route in small two-passenger planes. A few years later Pacific Air would merge with other lines as United Air Lines, but at the time Beckman was at a leading edge in both transportation and chemical consulting. On each of many trips he would be promised a demonstration at the Hayward plant, a strange scene surrounded by a moat of sorts, complete with a drawbridge and a guard armed with two six-shooter pistols. Yet each time he arrived, the demonstration was canceled; a truck broke down, or there was a problem with the oil supply. The reasons varied, but the demonstration was always postponed. Suspicions grew about Cox's confusing language and his claim to a secret catalyst. By summer's end Beckman was convinced that Cox and his cohorts were frauds, and he was determined to reveal them.

A characteristic note to Mabel in August 1933 from the Claremont Country Club in Oakland runs

> Dearest, Just a note before I rush out to the [Cox] plant. . . . We had a session here [at the Country Club] last night. . . . Cox came liquored up a little and wouldn't do or say anything. He left early. After he had gone, I told the others that the process didn't amount to much. So everyone is pretty low. The others think Cox hasn't shown me the real thing, so today they are coming out to witness a demonstration by Cox. Well, it won't be long now. I shall probably catch the noon plane tomorrow as I'm all fed up on this job. I'll wire you early, so there will be time for the W. U. [Western Union] to find you at the beach or elsewhere?? Well, it's about 9 o'clock and I have to grab a bite of breakfast and go out to the plant. I hope the weather has been cool down there. It has been cold up here. . . . Good-bye, sweetheart. See you tomorrow, I hope. Your own, Arnie.

He closed the note with a simple "X," a literary kiss. Mabel was one of the very few who ever referred to her husband as "Arnie." For the rest of the world he was always "Dr. Beckman."

Beckman devised a comprehensive testing procedure for the plant operations, with instructions for every detail to be recorded and samples taken at every stage in the process. One evening Cox and company finally agreed that the test could be made. Beckman was taken into town for dinner and for an evening at a nightclub while the test was being performed. On returning to the refinery, he was handed

Mabel and Arnold Beckman don flying gear for a journey aloft. *Courtesy Beckman family.*

Arnold Beckman's subpoena
for the Cox case.

the results along with self-satisfied boasts about the extraordinary gasoline yields that had been attained that night. Quickly analyzing the data, he concluded that the extraordinary yield came from a truck unloading gasoline into the process at a spot near a loading dock! The plant was a complete fraud, a visual structure to explain what really came from a truck.

Beckman confronted Weatherill, the flamboyant financier, with the evidence of fraud. Weatherill pronounced: "Beckman, I'm glad you found it, because Cox didn't think you knew what this was all about. He did this deliberately to see whether you were smart enough to catch him. . . . Now, since you won his respect, we will show you [the real process]." Beckman was unswayed, and after Cox and Weatherill tried several more times to pass off doctored tests, he finally had had enough. He wrote a registered letter to Cox and to Lyon telling them that he wanted nothing more to do with the matter, and that the process was below meritless—he was sure it was out-and-out fraud. But this was only preamble to what was yet to come. Back at Caltech that fall and well into the term, he was confronted by the sight of a sheriff's deputy headed straight toward him, delivering a subpoena with his name on it. Cox and Weatherill had been arrested up in Alameda County, and they were on trial for fraud, prosecuted by Alameda's district attorney, Earl Warren. This was the same Earl Warren who later enjoyed three terms as governor of California before becoming chief justice of the Supreme Court. He was then a serious crime fighter and a tough prosecutor, and he now considered arresting Beckman. Cox and Weatherill had gone on a renewed bonanza of stock selling later that summer, telling investors that they had a certain Dr. Arnold O. Beckman, a Caltech professor, working *with* them to improve their process.

Weatherill had also convinced Warren's office that Beckman was their consultant rather than consultant to the patent lawyer Lyon. Beckman, however, was always the careful scientist who kept detailed and dated notebooks, and these soon persuaded the prosecutors that he should be a key witness for the state rather than a suspect.

Beckman's testimony was damning for Cox and Weatherill, so their lawyers began to besmirch his good name and by extension the credibility of his expert testimony. They accused him of having affairs with a secretary in the Cox operation, and they said that he had fabricated his notebooks and his testimony for money. Even though Warren and his staff had prepared Beckman for the

Arnold Beckman working with his apparatus for making ink. *Courtesy Beckman family.*

Beckman found the problem quite simple. The ink clogged because the particles of pigment settled out of the ink solution. An ink that did not settle would solve the problem, and he soon devised a new formula based on butyric acid. Lyons was happy for the moment, but he was back when he found that no ink company would use the formula because of its smell. Butyric acid gives rancid butter its unique and powerful odor. Here was a challenge. Even major producers of specialty and bulk inks like California Printing and Ink Company refused the business. Beckman saw two options. The obvious one was to come up with another formula. As he mulled the question, there was another choice. With all the entrepreneurship of his piano playing in movie houses, his dance bands, and his home chemistry lab behind him, he saw the manufacturers' refusal as a personal opportunity. He could make the ink himself.

People of confidence and talent often embark on new endeavors with little concern for practicalities or negative outcomes, both of which inhibit others from even contemplating something new. In 1934 Arnold Beckman was a full-time assistant professor at Caltech, engaged with teaching, research, and other departmental responsibilities. He had his consulting work through Caltech channels as well. He had just built a house for himself and his wife, and he planned to start a family. This was certainly a full plate for anyone, but Beckman was a man of unusual energy and dedication to work. He was sure, intuitively, that he could add the title of "specialty ink manufacturer" to his dossier without diluting the energy he would need to advance in his other roles. He was convinced that he could produce the postage meter ink "on the side," a "pin money" project as he would later describe it.

Beckman's apparatus for producing the rancid-smelling, but nonclogging, ink for National Postal Meter. *Courtesy Beckman family.*

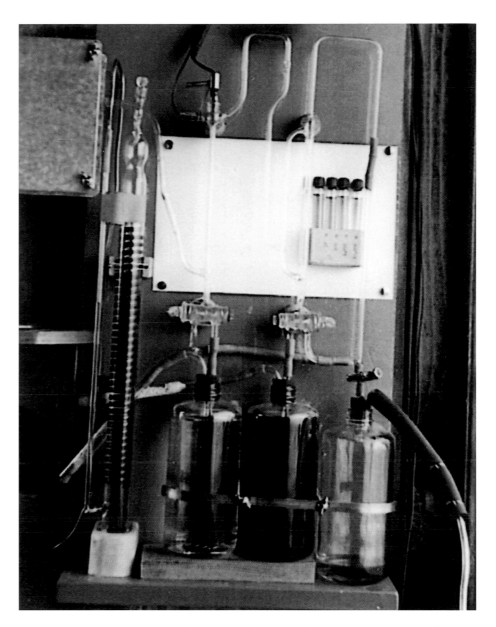

As Beckman's thoughts about manufacturing the meter ink were developing, his relationship with National Postal Meter deepened. The company was taken with the young professor and his simple, if odiferous, solution to its inking problem. He began discussions with National Postal's resident inventor, a "fellow named Jewell," about other needs and opportunities. Hector W. Jewell had an idea for an invention to meet an untapped market; a device to reapply ink to typewriter ribbons, putting ink back on just as quickly as the typist could transfer it to paper with each keystroke. The device would keep a new ribbon performing optimally for a long time or rejuvenate an old, depleted ribbon. Such a reinking device, if also used in National Postal Meter's newest models, could give the company an advantage over the competition.

Beckman became convinced that the idea did have some prospects. In no time he came up with not one, but two ways to apply the idea. The first of his solutions was simplicity itself. The ribbons of typewriters, adding machines, and postage meters came wound on reels, in much the same way as the film of movies are wound onto spools. To reapply ink to old ribbon, and to keep new ribbon well saturated, he proposed installing ink-soaked felt disks on the interior of either side of the reel. It was a simple, direct solution, and one that turned out to be patentable. With the counsel of Leonard Lyon, Arnold Beckman filed for his second patent on 8 May 1934. The application for his "Inking Reel" was granted.

The second of his solutions to the reinking puzzle was much more novel. He devised a solid spongelike pad that could be inserted into a variety of typewriters, meters, and printing devices. The sponge pad would be filled with special ink, formulated not to dry out. As the ink ribbon advanced, it would rub against the delicate "porous, friable material" of the pad, removing layers of it and exposing new ink with each layer. He applied for a patent on this "Inking Device" on 8 June 1934, again with Lyon as his patent attorney. Again the Patent Office approved.

To translate the patents into reality, National Postal Meter started a subsidiary company called the National Inking Appliance Company on 26 November 1934. Its goal was to manufacture the nonclogging meter ink and the ribbon reinking devices that Beckman had developed. Beckman was named vice president and manager of the National Inking Appliance Company. A detail to complete the corporate picture notes that National Postal itself was half owned by the Jergins Oil Company of Long Beach, California. In short, Beckman was now running a subsidiary of a subsidiary.

This arrangement was new for Beckman. National Inking was the smallest of operations, but it was no simple consultancy. Beckman was in charge of a company, however small. No longer just an enterprising professor, he was now professor and entrepreneur, responsible for a business based in part on his own patents. Even though he ran a billion-dollar corporation later, Beckman has said repeatedly of himself that he is no businessman, a comment that goes back to this first arrangement. In retrospect, he sees himself as very naive. He was running National Inking Appliance, a subsidiary with a very definite

Illustrations from Beckman's patent applications for his Inking Reel and Inking Device inventions.

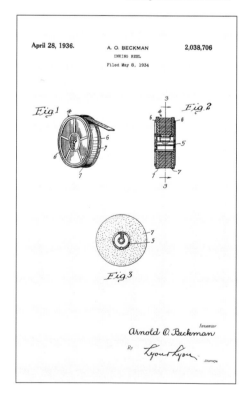

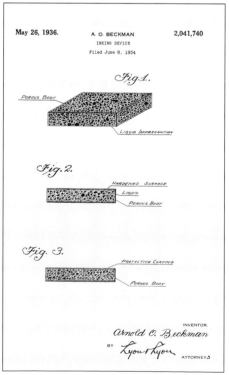

Fred Henson's garage, the first home of the National Inking Appliance Company.
Courtesy Beckman Coulter, Inc.

parent corporation. The president of National Postal Meter and owner of the other half of its stock was John J. Murdock of Beverly Hills, who had once owned a large vaudeville theater circuit. Murdock and his fellow directors would stay involved in Beckman's early business career far longer than he could have imagined when he first came home at night smelling of rancid butter.

Beckman found space for his new company through a Caltech connection. His old friend Fred Henson, the resident instrument maker, had left the Institute earlier in 1934 to start a business of his own. He had a large sheet-metal garage along an alley in Lamanda Park, now a section of East Pasadena. There he kept his Studebaker truck and a stock of lumber. Beckman worked out a deal with Henson to rent the back area of his garage, a space about ten feet by twenty-five feet, for five dollars a month. Next he needed employees. Very much the professor, he hired two Caltech students as his first staff. Robert Barton and Henry Fracker were happy to have part-time work, given the harsh realities of the mid-1930s. Barton, who had recently finished his Ph.D. and who later went on to manage a refinery for Shell Oil in Anacortes, Washington, remembered the garage shop in which he, Fracker, and Beckman worked side by side. "It didn't amount to much . . . it was equipped with a few basic things: laboratory glassware, Bunsen burners, a hood to exhaust fumes, and not much else."

In these simple quarters Beckman, Fracker, and Barton began producing meter ink for National Postal. Product development of the patented reinking pads was also crucial, and market testing "in the field" was a high priority. The field was, of course, nearby offices. There the reaction was devastating: "It became apparent that [the inking device] was not going to be a success. The last thing that secretaries wanted to do was to get their fingers dirty with ink to save the boss a seventy-five-cent ribbon." Beckman learned an early lesson: A feasible technical solution without commercial appeal has little future. He led the recommendation to other investors that the plans for the "inking device" be abandoned. They agreed.

Far from disheartened, he was probably delighted. He now had the capacity to produce something else, and by early 1935 he knew exactly what it was thanks to Glen Joseph, his old undergraduate friend and colleague on the *Illinois Chemist*.

Of Lemon Juice and the Birth of an Industry

Oil and gasoline production took place all over the country, but citrus growing was a distinctly Californian enterprise in the eyes of most Americans. Indeed, Southern California growers were transforming farming into agribusiness, through corporations like the California Fruit Growers Exchange, which marketed more than three-quarters of California citrus production. Its unified corporate structure took the fruit of many local growers to national markets under the Sunkist brand. The Exchange also ran lobbying efforts, notably for increased irrigation through public works.

Chemistry is crucial to the citrus industry. The trees themselves are quite sensitive to the acidity of the soil and water on which they depend. Chemistry and the chemical industry were also key in the Exchange's exploration of fungicides and insecticides for use in citrus groves. The industry even worked under a chemico-legal definition of ripeness: a specific ratio between the amount of solids and the percentage of citric acid in the juice. Chemistry was also critical to creating uses for vast amounts of lower-grade fruit that did not rate the Sunkist label. Great quantities of fruit were processed into two key by-products, pectin and citric acid, and both were produced by industrial chemical means.

Because of the complexity of its operations, the Exchange had started a research operation at its laboratories in Ontario, California, not long after World War I. The lab's director in the mid-1930s was William Baer, a Caltech alum, who was dedicated to serious research and had Caltech itself in his mind. And by then Glen Joseph, former business manager of the *Illinois Chemist*, was one of the lab's chemists. Joseph found himself wrestling with how to get consistent measurements of the acidity of lemon juice as part of his research into by-product processes. Acidity determined which by-products could be made from a given batch of juice and the design of the chemical processes to use. The difficulty of the measurements was matched only by their importance. None of the standard techniques would work consistently. The problems stemmed in part from the sulfur dioxide added as a preservative, which kept the juice usable but played havoc with the attempt to determine acidity.

By the 1930s acidity was no longer judged by mere impressions. Many labs measured acidity by colorimetric methods; to a practiced eye the color of litmus paper could give a measure of acidity. Small slips of paper were, and still are, saturated with litmus—a mixture of organic compounds derived from certain species of lichen—and then are dipped into the solution under examination. Litmus turns red in acidic solutions and blue in alkaline solutions, and the color changes of standard litmus paper can be matched against color charts to gauge the acidity of the solution tested. But the litmus test—the cheapest and most common method for measuring acidity—could not work for the California Fruit Growers Exchange: Sulfur dioxide acts as a bleach and makes reading litmus paper hopeless.

Chemists could also measure acidity by electrochemical methods. These rely on one of the central theories of physical chemistry, the ionic theory, which defines acidity in terms of the concentration of hydrogen ions in solutions. The more hydrogen ions, the more acidic a solution. This measure is codified in the pH (standing for "potential of hydrogen") scale, introduced in 1909 by the Danish biochemist Søren P. L. Sørensen. His numeric scale calibrated pH in values that ranged from 0 (an extreme acid) to 14 (an extreme base). The pH scale was quickly adopted around the world and provided a convenient and economical language for chemical scientists investigating acidity and alkalinity. Both Joseph and Beckman had used hydrogen electrodes to measure pH at Illinois. Being a well-trained chemist, Joseph tried to measure the hydrogen-ion concentration in lemon juice by using a hydrogen electrode in a standard, if complex, electrochemical measure.

A Leeds and Northrup set for measuring acidity similar to that used by Glen Joseph. *Courtesy Thomas Scientific, formerly Arthur H. Thomas.*

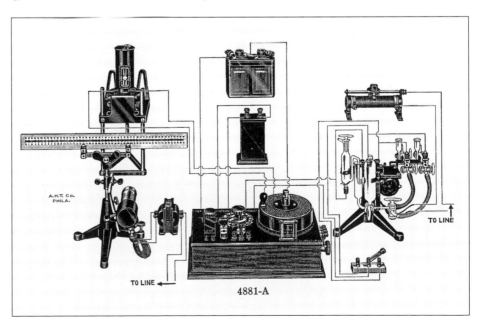

TO LINE

A.H.T. CO.
PHILA.

TO LINE

4881-A

The hydrogen electrode method for measuring acidity had severe drawbacks, and Joseph encountered a fatal limitation of the method in his work on the Exchange's lemon juice. Again the culprit was the sulfur dioxide preservative, which "poisoned" hydrogen electrodes and other closely related electrodes. In despair Joseph turned to a much more delicate, but sulfur dioxide–tolerant, electrode to replace the hydrogen electrode: the glass electrode.

Joseph found that a glass electrode gave reliable results if the equipment did not break. The problem was that the electrical signal produced by a cell with a glass electrode was very weak. That signal could be increased in strength if the electrode were larger, with very thin walls—maximizing the contact area and minimizing the pathway through poorly conducting glass. But such electrodes seemed made to be broken in a production line or a lab, frustrating managers and researchers. Moreover, even if the electrode did not break, the sensitive galvanometer used to measure the current was equally delicate and often failed from vibrations and jolts. Not good equipment in an active plant! The high-sensitivity galvanometer that Joseph used, one of the few commercially available, was manufactured by Leeds and Northrup. Repairs meant sending the whole device to headquarters in Philadelphia, with the loss of two or three weeks.

For Joseph, electrochemical methods worked well in theory, but they were almost useless in practice. Naturally enough his boss, Baer, suggested he look to Caltech for help. It was simple for Glen Joseph to ask his old friend Arnold Beckman whether he could suggest a better way. He could. Once the question was posed, the answer seemed to come by immediate intuition: Joseph was not doing anything wrong with his equipment; he had simply chosen the wrong tools for the job. "Get rid of that galvanometer," Beckman ordered, "and put in a rugged vacuum-tube voltmeter."

Galvanometers were based on very old principles, and making them more sensitive required making them impossibly delicate. Joseph was trying to operate beyond their threshold for sensitivity. Basic, radical rethinking of Joseph's problem led Beckman to resort instead to an entirely new route: *amplification*. If small currents were at the root of Joseph's problems, why not make the current bigger while still representing the same information? A "rugged" amplifier would allow sturdier glass electrodes, even though sturdier glass was invariably more poorly conducting and would give weaker signals. If the amplifier were strong enough, this would present no obstacle. With a rugged amplifier and a rugged glass electrode, Joseph's prayers would be answered.

What kind of amplifier could deal with such minute currents and still be a relatively rough-and-tumble device? Beckman was familiar with just such an amplifier: the vacuum tube. Joseph left Beckman's office with a sketch in hand.

Joseph must have thought his problem was solved. He returned to the plant intending to create a new glass electrode himself and ask a friend who was a ham

Litmus was useful for quick determinations of pH, but in the 1930s the standard for highly accurate work was the electrochemical method. An electrochemical determination of acidity, or pH, could be made by building an electrochemical cell—a battery of sorts.

One half of such a cell was variable, the other half of the cell was a standard. Each of these halves was called an "electrode." Most commonly, the variable part of the cell was the hydrogen electrode, which comprised a container of the solution under investigation and a special type of electrical contact, one sensitive to the concentration of hydrogen ions in the solution and hence to its acidity. Thus the amount of energy that this variable part of the cell could contribute to the overall energy produced by the cell was directly proportional to the acidity, the pH, of the solution within it. The other half of the cell, the standard component, was most often the "calomel electrode"; it comprised a standard solution and a standard electrical contact and conveyed a reliable, constant amount of energy to the overall cell. Within the overall cell the electrodes were connected by a junction, a meeting point, between the solutions inside the cell's two halves. An experimenter could thus connect the two ends of the cell (the two electrodes) *externally* with a wire and measure the amount of electrical energy (the current) that the overall cell produced. By subtracting the contribution of the standard electrode from the measured electrical current, the experimenter could determine the contribution of the variable hydrogen electrode and, through a very simple mathematical formula, compute the acidity—the pH—of the solution under investigation.

The glass electrode differed from the hydrogen electrode in its special electrical contact. Rather than the much more common metal wire or plate, the contact placed into the solution under investigation was a small glass bulb, hence the name "glass electrode." But this glass bulb itself contained a standard electrode—like the calomel electrode—immersed in a solution of *known* pH. The glass bulb, with its interior cargo, was then placed in the solution of *unknown* pH, the solution under investigation. As early as 1909, with a glass bulb blown from glass of the appropriate chemical composition, chemists had found that the energy that this electrode could make available varied directly with the pH of the solution under study, exactly as in a hydrogen electrode. The difference was that it was the chemical interaction between the outer surface of the glass bulb and the solution that accounted for this sensitivity.

The electrode components used in measuring pH, from Beckman's early acidimeter.
Courtesy Beckman family.

This glass-solution interaction had many attractions to chemists, for it was immune to many kinds of poisoning—like that from sulfur dioxide—and it could work with very small samples of solution. By adding a second electrode, a standard calomel electrode, to the solution under investigation, one had a complete electrochemical cell. The amount of electrical energy produced depended on the pH of the solution, and thus measurements and calculations could be made just as with cells with hydrogen electrodes. ∽

Arnold Beckman's ability to seize so swiftly on a solution testifies to his inventive insight and intuition and to the familiar dictum "Chance favors the prepared mind." He knew the galvanometer was wrong because he knew another instrument would work better.

Ten years earlier he had been at Bell Labs, ground zero for vacuum-tube technology. He knew vacuum tubes well from quality-control projects, seminars, and lectures, and he had continued to use them in his own radios, teaching, and projects. Over and over, vacuum tubes had proved themselves as amplifiers of weak electrical signals.

Internal structure gave the tubes their power. There were three components—the cathode, the grid, and the anode—all placed inside the vacuum of a sealed glass bulb. The cathode and anode were straightforward electrical contacts, designed to transmit and receive electrical currents and connected in one circuit with a powerful electrical source, like a good battery. The flow of current from the cathode to the anode was restricted by the space between them in the vacuum tube. In this space stood the "grid," a small mesh of metal connected to a different electrical circuit. The electrical charge on this grid could serve to control the flow of electricity in the other circuit, the one between the cathode and the anode.

Very small changes in the electrical current reaching the grid caused much greater changes in the amount of electrical current flowing in the other circuit, between cathode and anode. In this way very small changes in the current in the circuit connected to the grid were amplified into much larger changes in the circuit connecting the cathode to the anode. Beckman's idea was to put the glass electrode used for pH measurement into the grid circuit of the vacuum tube. The slightest current produced by the glass electrode would be enormously amplified in the cathode-anode circuit. The information, the pH measurement, itself would remain unchanged; it would simply be

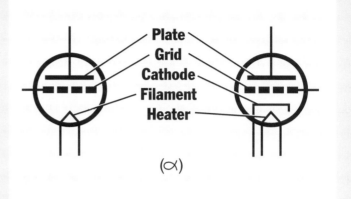

Schematic representation of the kind of vacuum tubes used by Arnold Beckman in his vacuum-tube amplifier.

easier to "hear." The amplified signal could in turn be measured with the sturdiest of ammeters, the simplest of electrical meters for measuring currents.

Beckman armed Joseph with the design for a vacuum-tube amplifier. He sketched a circuit diagram using not one but two vacuum tubes to amplify and then re-amplify the signal. Such a two-stage design could work with the smallest and most fleeting of electrical currents, and it was more or less immune to jolts and vibrations. The diagram showed Joseph where to attach his new sturdy glass electrode, the necessary batteries, and the voltmeter for reading the amplified signal. Beckman may have been familiar with earlier attempts to use vacuum-tube amplifiers for electrochemical experiments. A few had made their way into the chemical literature (e.g., Ellis and Kiehl's article in the *Review of Scientific Instruments 4* [1933]), but even so, these publications were mainly "proofs of concept." No standard designs had emerged that dealt with the difficulties of building vacuum-tube amplifiers appropriate to electrochemical experimentation. Whatever the earlier articles, Beckman was venturing into the unknown with his two-stage circuit design. ∾

radio operator to build the amplifier according to Beckman's schematic. But he was soon back at the office door with a frown and a box of parts for the amplifier. "This thing doesn't work," he announced. Beckman, however, was confident it should. He determined that Joseph's radio-operator friend was not familiar with important aspects of circuit design and had made the amplifier with the wrong voltages. Beckman decided to build the amplifier himself. In a short time it was ready, and it worked.

All was well. Yet Joseph was back again at Beckman's door in just a few months. This time the complaint was different: The amplifier worked so well that he hardly had a chance to use it himself! Too many of his colleagues were borrowing it. He now asked a simple question with great implications: Would Dr. Beckman be willing to make him another unit exactly like the first? Beckman views this as the moment when the innovation that has earned his name a place in history truly began. His reasoning quickly went beyond the amplifier unit he had built for Joseph. He thought, "Gee, if he could use two of these things in that little laboratory he has, maybe there's a market for them." So straight away he built two more units, one for Joseph, the other to "test the market."

In a further vital step Beckman reconceptualized the whole project. He came to see the amplifier not just as a device in itself but as the "essential part" of an integrated instrument for measuring pH. "Maybe you want to call that entrepreneurship or invention," he later reflected on this change of conception, "I don't know. But anyway, I thought, well, heck, let's make it a complete instrument then. Get rid of all the stuff spread on the desktop and make it in a compact unit." By these acts Arnold Beckman was launching a revolution in instrumentation, creating the first chemical instrument with electronic technology at its very heart. Chemists before him had certainly combined chemistry with electrical equipment in highly productive ways. Indeed, such combinations were central to the development of physical chemistry, as particular scientists married "off-the-shelf" electrical equipment to their chemical experiments in their own particular ways. Normally the chemist purchased a given piece of equipment (like, for example, Glen Joseph's galvanometer) that then had to be integrated with other pieces, wires, and electrodes. Once the equipment was assembled, the chemist worked out the intricacies of use and of the mathematical calculation of results. What was lacking were electronic instruments a chemist could buy in the marketplace—complete, assembled, and ready to answer chemical questions by analyzing the electrical properties of matter.

Arnold Beckman's instrument for measuring pH was revolutionary in two senses. First, the amplifier itself was an electronic innovation—compact, robust, and (because of its two-vacuum-tube design) highly sensitive to even the smallest of electrical currents. Nothing like it was to be found in the marketplace. Second, his idea of building an integrated chemical instrument around the amplifier was

The patent diagrams for Beckman's pH meter, including the electrodes, vacuum-tube amplifier, and other components.

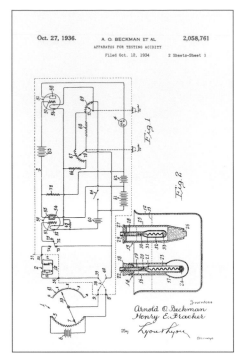

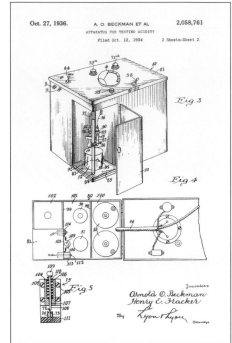

equally new. Now a scientist could purchase a precision instrument and start making quick, simple, and reliable measurements. The frustrations of assembly, then measurement, then mathematical calculation all vanished. With the disarmingly simple-looking box Beckman designed, the chemist had only to prepare and position his sample, then read "pH 3.7" off a dial. Not only had the chores disappeared, but the instrument itself required of its users no special expertise in either electrochemistry or electronics: The expertise was in the box. In this sense Beckman made "the opening commercial move" in the instrumentation revolution of the twentieth century, a revolution that has made the research frontier ever more accessible to ever greater numbers of investigators and that has hence made possible the exponential growth of scientific knowledge.

His new device posed a moral dilemma for Beckman. What should he do with it? He still talks about the question, because in 1934 Caltech, unlike the University of Illinois, was self-consciously a bastion of pure science. It was unthinkable for a Caltech professor to conduct research with an explicit commercial orientation. Beckman shared that ethos. His consulting work was done off campus, and it would have seemed strange to develop postal meter inks or the prototype for a commercial instrument on the grounds of the Institute.

Millikan touted the virtues of pure science as twofold: It was a moral good in itself, increasing our understanding of the world, and it also laid the basis for applied science and industry. Applied science, Millikan held, was the force underlying industrial progress. Even so, applied, commercially useful research was not really appropriate for the Caltech faculty. If they carried it out at all, it should be off

campus and in their private hours. Beckman scrupulously upheld these distinctions, following his own sense of moral integrity. Yet he was more interested than ever in the charm and utility of his acidity-measuring instrument. The answer was to make the instrument a part of his small, outside business, National Inking Appliance. Henry Fracker and Robert Barton could assist in the back of Fred Henson's garage.

By October 1934 they had come up with a design for an "Apparatus for Testing Acidity," as they would describe it in a patent application that same month. More simply, Beckman and his colleagues called it an "acidimeter." The acidimeter had the two-stage vacuum-tube amplifier at its core, but it also incorporated a glass electrode, a standard calomel electrode, electrode holders, a container for holding test solutions, adjustment knobs or rheostats—like the tuning controls for a radio or TV—and the ammeter, all within one housing.

Beckman had come up with an *integrated, portable instrument.* Through the winter of 1934 and into the spring of 1935 he and his colleagues worked to refine the prototype of the acidimeter that they were seeking to patent. Progress was steady, even with Beckman's Caltech duties, which included keeping his own line of photochemical research alive. His extraordinary drive and industriousness were fully employed as he sought to fulfill Caltech duties, continue production of meter ink, and develop the acidimeter.

The Birth of National Technical Laboratories

Work on the acidimeter was one sign of Beckman's broadening and deepening ambition. Another was a change in a name. On 8 April 1935 National Inking

Appliance Company became National Technical Laboratories. The name change signaled the move from reliance on one product to reliance on a program—technical, laboratory-based knowledge that would result in novel, salable products. Equally significant was the new corporate structure. Unlike National Inking Appliance, National Technical Laboratories was not a subsidiary of National Postal Meter. The old group was involved, but in a new fiscal pattern. National Technical Laboratories, NTL, as it became known, accepted nine thousand dollars from its former parent company as working capital in exchange for 90 percent of the stock. This controlling stock was split between the Jergins Oil Company and John Murdock, the owners of National Postal Meter. The great difference from the old arrangement was that Beckman now had a 10-percent stake in the ownership of NTL as well as a modest salary. In later years he bemoaned signing on to a new role for only 10 percent of the stock. He would cite it as further evidence that he was not, and never had been, a "businessman." "You see how stupid I was. . . . We made back that nine thousand dollars the first year. They put peanuts into the thing and [eventually] made several million dollars. . . . I was so naive." Yet that nine thousand dollars was critical start-up capital, the equivalent of over a hundred thousand dollars in the year 2000.

NTL started with great enthusiasm, though it had only one product: the postage meter ink that it delivered to National Postal Meter in batches measured in bucketfuls. In April 1935 the acidimeter still had no confirmed patent, no manufacturing plan, and no orders, but it did have Beckman's clear vision of what it might become. He knew he had a far better product than a device to reink typewriter ribbon. And making scientific instruments fit Beckman's core interests. He was a natural entrepreneur in any field that presented itself, but here was an opportunity to be an entrepreneur in chemical apparatus. He had an intuitive sense of marketing savvy, evident as early as his boyhood creation, "Bloomington Research Laboratories," and the stationery announcing "Beckman's Orchestra: Dance or Concert Musicians" for his high school band. And he had learned a lesson in the power of words from the medicine salesman he saw on the streets of Philadelphia during his field inspections for Bell Labs.

Beckman was doubly happy to have a fresh focus on instruments, because things were shaky at National Postal Meter in 1935 and it had little to do with the Depression. National Postal had its development staff hard at work on an improved postage meter. Management was excited about the product and stopped selling the old model while developing the new. The expenses continued, while sales and revenues plummeted. Beckman could only be pleased he was on a separate course.

Development of the acidimeter continued through September 1935 at NTL in the back of Fred Henson's garage. By then Beckman and his assistants had achieved a refined, well-functioning instrument housed in a simple, good-looking case—complete with carrying handle and latch. Timing was perfect, for by good fortune

Left: The acidimeter closed, wth a ruler to show its dimensions.

Right: The acidimeter with its components opened for use. *Both courtesy Beckman family.*

the American Chemical Society was just then holding its national meeting in San Francisco. Accompanied by Mabel and the acidimeter, Arnold Beckman headed north.

As a young, successful chemistry professor at Caltech, Beckman was a common sight at ACS national meetings and at local section gatherings. Moreover, he had built quite a reputation for himself—perhaps even notoriety—on the basis of his extremely popular and quite irreverent performances at these meetings. They were part lecture, part demonstration, and part entertainment. One performance that he refined over the years was a parody of the serious technical presentations his fellow professors made on new analytical methods.

His topic was the separation of colors. Professor Beckman would begin by demonstrating the ability of a prism to resolve white light into the colors of the rainbow. Next he would announce that through the ancient chemical process of distillation he could separate colors from one another just as a prism did. Pouring a green liquid into the top of a fake still, he would pause dramatically to let the solution cook. With a flourish he would then open two taps at opposite sides of the still, producing blue liquid from one spout, yellow liquid from the other, and laughs from his audience. He would next proclaim that colors could also be separated mechanically, by a grinding machine. He would feed green paper into one side of a box, stare at it intently while it groaned, and marvel at the sheets of blue and yellow paper it spat out from the other side. Last, claiming that his new device could handle any object, even ones with multiple colors, he would invite the audience to prove him wrong. An audience member who was in on the joke would then stand and challenge the machine with a ridiculously vivid tie or scarf. Dr. Beckman would place the garment into the machine, a bell would ring, an explosion would boom, and the box would fly apart. In mock discouragement he would announce the limitations of his device to boisterous applause and laughter from the normally staid ACS audience.

But Beckman's visit to the September 1935 ACS meeting was not for comedy or scientific exchange. It was an outing for the acidimeter. He proposed a price of $195 each for his acidimeters, no insignificant sum, and roughly the monthly salary of a starting chemistry professor. Would there be a market for the instrument at such a price, in direct competition with common litmus paper that cost mere pennies per sheet? He showed the prototype to one of his professors from the University of Illinois, G. Frederick Smith. Hobart Willard of the University of Michigan studied it, too. Others clustered around. None of them said the acidimeter was a certain commercial failure, for all were fascinated with its integrated design, its ease of operation, and its electronic heart. Yet all agreed that they lacked the expertise to give him a definitive answer about commercial prospects. They urged him to show it to the leading instrument houses and apparatus dealers.

A Journey of Faith

The Beckmans took this semiencouraging advice to be positive and left San Francisco immediately on an ambitious national tour. Before they returned to Altadena, they visited the Denver Fire Clay Company in Colorado; Central Scientific, E. H. Sargent, and Chicago Apparatus, all in Chicago; Fisher Scientific in Pittsburgh; Eimer & Amend in New York; and Arthur H. Thomas in Philadelphia. It was a who's who tour of America's scientific equipment dealers.

The trip was Beckman's initial market survey, his first extended foray as an adult into the world of sales. The dealers were in the business of selling scientific equipment in the midst of the Depression. Their judgments would be critical to success, for in the 1930s few scientists or engineers purchased equipment directly from a manufacturer. It was dealers who stocked America's labs, and they provided service and advice together with their weighty catalogs. Weighty is no figure of speech—the Eimer & Amend catalog of 1936 had 895 pages and weighed eight pounds. Would the acidimeter find a welcome place in such tomes?

The dealers were almost uniformly discouraging; $195 was a lot for an instrument that did only one thing, however well. But prospects brightened considerably in Philadelphia at the Arthur H. Thomas Company, one of the most visible national supply houses. There Ed Patterson, Jr., son of the sales manager, was optimistic, at least compared with the other dealers. He thought the pH meter did indeed have commercial potential. It might find as many as six hundred customers over a decade before the market would be completely saturated. Patterson knew his markets. He was already selling the desktop sets of equipment that had befuddled Glen Joseph.

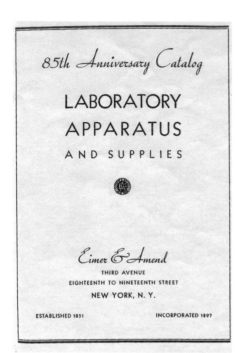

The title page of the Eimer & Amend catalog for 1936. A major instrument dealer, Eimer & Amend carried Dr. Beckman's pH meter in this catalog. *Courtesy Fisher Scientific.*

In the Arthur H. Thomas catalogs of the early 1930s one can find listings for all the components necessary to create a complete "hydrogen ion outfit for precise measurements," including a high-sensitivity Leeds and Northrup galvanometer, transformers, batteries, shakers, electrodes, potentiometers, and similar equipment. This complete outfit, if purchased all at once, cost five hundred dollars. Patterson understood that Beckman's invention could offer the same or higher levels of precision, plus integration, miniaturization, durability, and versatility—for less than half the price.

The Beckmans returned to California encouraged, for Ed Patterson and Arnold Beckman had reached an understanding. Patterson's estimate of a market for six hundred instruments was enough to justify his carrying the acidimeter in the eight-hundred-plus pages of the Arthur H. Thomas catalog. Having Arthur H. Thomas, a very well-regarded distributor, carry his invention would give Beckman a foot in the door of the instrument business. If an instrument was popular with one distributor, chances were that others would want it too.

The prospect of selling six hundred pH meters over a decade had a more personal meaning for the Beckmans. If the invention proved successful it would bring in welcome money as they planned for a family. And, too, this was the fall of 1935. The economic gales of the Great Depression continued to sweep the globe. Nearly half of America's banks had failed, manufacturing levels had fallen to just 50 percent of the late 1920s, and approximately 30 percent of the American workforce was unemployed. Always using understatement to great effect, Arnold later recounted that Patterson's optimistic estimation of "a chance to make a little extra income" came "during the Depression, so that even a few dollars looked pretty good."

Into Production

Arnold Beckman returned from his sales trip to the normal academic duties of Caltech. The year also promised major developments at National Technical Laboratories. Taking an optimistic view of what he had learned, Beckman decided that NTL had outgrown its rented garage space. Once again Caltech connections provided the solution. A Professor Ernest Swift owned 3330 Colorado Street and rented it out to a dry cleaner, and the tenant went out of business just as NTL sought new quarters. Beckman, however, worried at a tenfold increase in rent, from five dollars a month to fifty dollars. Colorado Street was, in Beckman's words, nothing less than Pasadena's "Main Street."

The new quarters did offer ample space for NTL's growing staff, but it had one initial drawback. "We couldn't use the phone if a truck was going by." Mabel Beckman had long kept the books for Arnold's consulting work and business ventures, and she now stepped in to solve the noise problem. The large plate-glass windows running along the front of the Colorado Street building allowed in generous amounts of the warm California sunshine but also served as amplifying resonators

The second home of National Technical Laboratories. *Courtesy Beckman Coulter, Inc.*

for traffic on the busy street. Mabel's new monk's-cloth curtains gave Arnold the option of streaming sunlight or peaceful quiet.

Manufacture of the acidimeter began in earnest in the fall of 1935. Confirming Beckman's confidence, orders started to come in quickly and steadily. By the end of the year—that is, in something on the order of three months—NTL had sold eighty-seven of his pH meters. This brought in $11,200 in gross sales in just one fiscal quarter, and a profit of $2,000. It was a remarkable debut, especially when viewed in the context of general misery throughout the American economy.

Patterson had been right in one thing. Scientists wanted Beckman's instrument, even if it cost the equivalent of a professor's monthly salary. As Beckman later explained, this early flurry of orders allowed production to get off the ground: "We didn't have any venture capital. We took earnings from the first instruments to buy parts for the next ones. We finally got up to large production where we could make [pH meters] in batches of twelve!"

What Arthur H. Thomas started, other dealers were quick to follow, just as Beckman had hoped. The Eimer & Amend catalog of 1936 gave the "pH Meter," as it was now called, a two-page spread. Soon it was carried in the catalogs of all twenty-eight major American instrument dealers. Beckman must have remembered that his brother Roland brought him his first bona fide chemical equipment from E. H. Sargent in Chicago. The path came full circle when Sargent began to sell the instrument created by Professor Arnold Beckman. One footnote on the instrument: Though it was produced by National Technical Laboratories, catalog readers sent in orders for "Beckman Glass Electrode pH Meters." Beckman's name was on his invention from the very first, even though a house like Eimer & Amend might add theirs as well.

As distribution networks expanded through 1936, Beckman could see that the initial success of his instrument was not a fluke reflecting a temporary spike of interest in a new offering. NTL produced and sold 444 pH meters in 1936. Gross sales rocketed to nearly $53,000, yielding a profit of $2,700 despite the ballooning requirements of expanded production. On the last day of December 1936, after only fifteen months of production, Arnold Beckman had sold 531 of his pH meters. The "optimistic" Ed Patterson had underestimated the market; in little over a year NTL sold what Patterson thought it could sell in a decade. There were no signs that demand for the pH meter was abating. The sky seemed truly to be the limit.

Beckman faced and overcame major challenges to orchestrate the creation of so many of his pH meters in such a short span of time. Each meter was built by hand, each electrode and vacuum tube was carefully checked by Barton or Fracker, and each completed instrument was individually calibrated and inspected. To meet the demand and Beckman's insistence on quality, additional staff members were hired. To the handful now working on production, he added a "one-man sales

Early advertisements for the pH meter. Although the company was called National Technical Laboratories, Beckman gave his own name to its pH meter, beginning the association between the name "Beckman" and quality precision instruments. *Courtesy Beckman Coulter, Inc.*

force" to coordinate the orders flowing in from the instrument dealers. At the same time he was still very much Caltech's Professor Beckman. His days were filled with research, teaching, and faculty responsibilities, leaving nights, weekends, and the occasional weekday hour free for devotion to his new business.

Beckman achieved economies in production by buying component parts for the pH meter rather than making them. Using ready-made vacuum tubes for the instrument's electronic heart, the amplifier, allowed production to keep up with the flurry of demand, and it kept costs down. Relying on an outside supply also brought tense moments. Vacuum tubes had a wide range of behaviors dependent on their individual design; some were suitable for an application like the pH meter amplifier and others were hopelessly unsuited. Beckman had early on found a source for tubes that worked well, but when the manufacturer changed the design for the tube, it no longer worked for the pH meter. He faced the prospect of shutting down production and leaving orders unfilled if replacement vacuum tubes could not be found. His staff scoured manufacturers for a tube that would fit the bill, and luckily they quickly found an available model that did. Less crucial than the vacuum tubes were other off-the-shelf components like the adjustment knobs (in more technical language, potentiometers) for controlling the amplifier circuits and making a pH measurement.

Always thrifty, Beckman had an eye for economy and adaptations. One part he borrowed was really made for a common household appliance. The pH meter was housed in a wooden case whose lid opened to reveal the operating panel with dials, knobs, and switches. On the face of the case was a small door behind which lay a white enamel cubbyhole with the pH meter's electrodes. It was into this enamel box that the chemist inserted the sample to be tested. Beckman saw no need to produce these enamel boxes himself when he could order them in quantity from the Gaffers and Sattler stove company, which produced them as salt-and-pepper containers for their gas cooking ranges. "We didn't have money to buy our own dies in those days, but we found the little cans to be about the right size, so we bought them from the stove company. When they remodeled the range, we bought

Left: A view of the top of the pH meter, showing the milliammeter and precision tuning dials.

Right: A close-up of the pH meter's electrodes, housed in the "salt-and-pepper" recess lined with white enamel, on the front of the instrument. *Both courtesy Beckman family.*

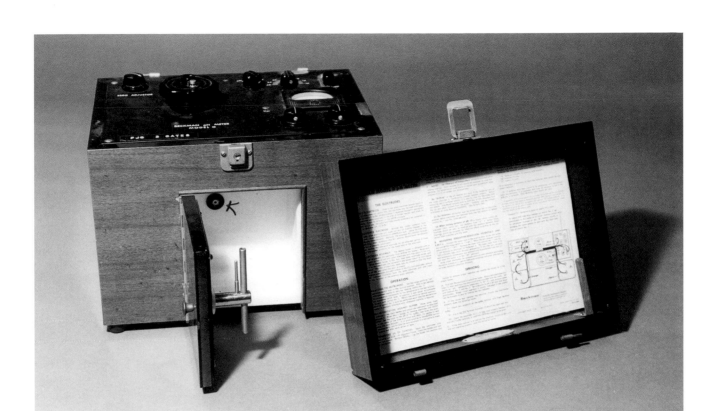

The Model G, perhaps the most successful incarnation of the pH meter. *Courtesy Institute Archives, California Institute of Technology.*

the die at its scrap metal price. We had to make every dollar count." In later years Beckman would assert that the Great Depression provided an advantageous atmosphere for starting a business, for it taught the importance of imaginative economy.

Some design aspects had nothing to do with economy. In 1937 NTL began to produce the Model G pH meter, of which thousands and thousands were eventually made. Beckman decided that the Model G should, as its predecessors were, be enclosed in a walnut case. Walnut was as much a question of aesthetics as it was of function. A walnut case was indeed light and durable, suited for housing an instrument designed to be used in the rough conditions of the outdoors or the plant floor or used many times every day by many hands in the laboratory. But walnut was also beautiful, and Beckman loved the wood and woodworking. His personal sense of craftsmanship in wood was passed on to the business. As the staff grew, Joe Wolf began a long, distinguished career as head of the cabinet shop. Even today, Dr. Beckman can explain that the first twenty-five or so pH meters had walnut cases with interlocking joints by which they still can be identified. He should know, for he made several of them himself.

If the heart of the pH meter was its electronic amplifier, the eyes of the instrument were its electrodes. In 1937, as Model G meters left Colorado Street in ever-increasing numbers, Beckman realized that these electrode eyes were just as crucial to the continued success of the instrument as its electronic heart. While the glass electrode of the pH meter solved many technical problems (for example,

Early staff members of National Technical Laboratories posed in front of their headquarters on Colorado Street. Arnold Beckman is at the far right; standing next to him is Howard Cary. *Courtesy Beckman family.*

allowing a far wider variety of substances to be tested than did the hydrogen electrode), it was a truly complex component with its own subtle problems, which grew directly from the glass from which it was made. Beckman soon realized that overcoming these vexing puzzles of electrode glass could ensure the success of his pH meter and lead to an additional business—the manufacture of electrodes themselves.

By the end of 1937 he had assembled a small development group at NTL to tackle these problems and others. Howard H. Cary, a Caltech alum of 1930, joined the staff that year as chief design engineer, just when other new issues had to be addressed that cast unexpected doubts on the whole future of the pH meter. A professor at Stanford had suggested that glass electrodes like Professor Beckman's did not truly measure pH levels but instead were influenced by the depth at which they were immersed into the liquid sample. This was a troubling report indeed, for it called into question the accuracy of the instrument. As Beckman remembers, the report was "devastating to us; we finally looked into it and found out that, sure enough, it was true."

Beckman and the NTL development group realized that the Model G minimized this immersion error because the holder for the electrodes always maintained them at a constant depth in the sample for any individual measurement. The error was thus at least regular and fairly small. Eventually Beckman and the group at NTL ferreted out the underlying cause. The glass electrode design contained an opening, and an electrical current could leak into the interior of the electrode by traveling up the exterior surface of the bulb, through the opening, and down the interior surface of the bulb. This leakage would affect the electrical current produced by the electrode and thus cause error in the final reading of pH. The deeper the glass electrode was placed in the sample, the shorter the path for the electrical leakage.

While the consequences of this leakage could have been devastating indeed, Beckman took the issue in stride. Here was a scientific, technological problem of the sort that he so delighted in solving. His response was not to throw up his hands in panic but to set his development team to work in crafting a solution. At first they tried coating the glass electrodes with different kinds of waxes, resins, and shellacs in an attempt to increase the electrical resistance of the surface of the glass—to create a barrier to electricity following the leakage path. Soon, however, Beckman became unhappy with this family of possible solutions. They were temporary, stop-gap. Instead, he proposed that the team redesign the entire glass electrode, eliminating the leakage path itself. By the early fall of 1937 such a solution was in hand. NTL filed a patent for factory-sealed electrodes, without any openings that would allow the immersion error to rear its ugly head. This solution became a financial boon: Because NTL was now producing the most error-free line of electrochemical electrodes available, the firm gained a distinct edge in a new marketplace. Beckman later surmised that the sealed electrode solution "really gave us a stranglehold on the glass-electrode business."

Beckman and his team noticed other properties of their electrodes as well. "We found that when you start measuring a high pH, the electrode begins to function as a sodium electrode [an electrode for measuring sodium ion concentrations] as well as a hydrogen electrode. So we started our glass electrode research. We studied thousands and thousands of compositions to come up with glasses that are specially suited for this or that." Again, a new technological business evolved out of a creative response to an unexpected challenge. Sales also got an extra, unexpected boost from the very industry that caused the invention of the pH meter. Mutual Citrus Products had a regular stream of commercial customers who complained that its pectin did not produce jelly. In self-interested defense Mutual countered that its pectin always worked if the pH in the mixture was right—"get yourself a pH meter and test it" was easy advice. Mutual thus asked Beckman for the right to sell his equipment along with its pectin. "There was a market that never entered our mind."

At the end of 1937 Beckman reviewed the figures for the performance of his "side business." They were again extraordinary. NTL had sold over five hundred more instruments and had brought in almost twenty thousand dollars in additional sales of accessories and supplies, like electrodes. NTL's operating expenses nearly doubled to fifty-four thousand dollars, reflecting the expanded activity of the development team. Despite the Great Depression, the investment in research and development paid off. NTL again made a profit in 1937.

Even with the abundance of work at NTL on production and technological problem solving, and although running NTL was only Professor Beckman's spare-time second job, he managed to direct several other research-and-development projects that year. There was work on a chemical thermometer, a new kind of steam iron, and a variety of specialized inks like those he was still producing for National Postal. By now it was impossible for him to conduct all this work himself or even to closely scrutinize those he hired to work on the various projects. Instead, these lines of research and development went forward because of his style of organization and management.

Beckman hired a leader for each project in much the same way that he and his faculty colleagues assigned dissertation topics to graduate students. "I try to select the right man and then let him run the show." Dr. Beckman would set the problem, identify the goal to be pursued, and find the right fit between the challenge and the individual. He would suggest possible plans of attack, ideas about potential solutions and methods, and then stand back. If the solution that the project leader came up with differed from his original suggestions but worked, Beckman was more than contented. He and his organization were solution oriented above all else.

Going It Alone

Sales of pH meters and electrodes through 1938 drove an explosive growth in revenue and profits for National Technical Laboratories. Sales increased 41.4 percent, and after-tax profit by an astounding tenfold to $20,356. To give an idea of the magnitude of this profit, it was approximately ten times what a young professor or an entry-level engineer might have expected in annual salary, and Oldsmobile V-8 convertible sedans started at $880. In the following year, 1939, sales and profit recorded further respectable increases, with sales up by 16 percent, and after-tax profit by 9 percent.

Beckman had been running NTL with the formal title of vice president, but on 11 May 1939 the board of directors approved a document creating a new, full-time position at the four-year-old firm: that of "president," someone to run the company that was now bringing in $140,000 in sales per year. The president would have a salary of $10,000, stock, and a profit-sharing bonus, and the name of the new president of National Technical Laboratories was Dr. Arnold O. Beckman, newly hired from Caltech.

Chance favors the prepared mind, and Arnold Beckman was confident that his scientific knowledge, his craft abilities, his experience with electronics, and his eye for opportunity were resources enough for this next step in his life. His pH meter could generate a sideline in electrodes, but that was only a first step. A full decade before, in 1929, as he filled his journal of ideas for inventions, he had seen several

**Arnold Beckman in a
formal portrait, late 1930s.**
Courtesy Beckman family.

The staff of NTL gathered for the Christmas photo, 1938. *Courtesy Beckman Coulter, Inc.*

connections between electronics, pH, and health. "I have . . . nearly worked out a cell for lowering into the stomach to determine pH values. This will be recorded soon, when time permits." If many stomach ailments, like ulcers, are from imbalances of acidic juices, then perhaps measurements of pH levels within the stomach would help the clinician—damage could be prevented and treatments could be evaluated. Other potential inventions sprang to mind, connecting the realm of health to chemical instrumentation: a "thermocouple to determine temperatures in the stomach," an "automatic temperature recording device which will travel through the alimentary tract," and a "pellet to be swallowed which will travel through the alimentary tract and which will discharge medicine at any given point." If ideas are raw material, his warehouse was full long before 1939.

In that year he finally made a momentous, life-altering decision. NTL was enough of a challenge to occupy the full time of even so industrious an individual as Arnold Beckman. Running the company and being a professor of chemistry were mutually exclusive careers, not only in terms of time. Today we are familiar with and laud the professor who begins his start-up company in a rented garage. Not so at Caltech, in the 1930s. If Beckman presciently saw how the future lay with novel combinations of academic knowledge, hands-on experience with electronics, and entrepreneurial tenacity, he also paid a price for being so clearly ahead of his time. Leaving pure science for the workbenches of business posed an acute moral dilemma for a Caltech professor. "Here I was going out applying science, making instruments. I worried about it a great deal. Was I prostituting my scientific professional training by getting over into business, making things for profit?"

5 | Battles on Many Fronts

When you're faced with the necessity to do something, that's a stimulus to invention.

New Beginnings

Five years after his "pin-money" enterprise had started in half a garage, Arnold Beckman gave up his professorship. Confident that he had the "mental makeup involved in invention," he would cast himself as instrument maker and entrepreneur. With characteristic humor he once explained that "inventors are, by and large, a little bit goofy. They have a different cast of mind from non-inventors. They'll improvise all sorts of ways to overcome problems. When you're faced with the necessity to do something, that's a stimulus to invention. If Dr. Joseph hadn't come in with his lemon-juice problem, chances are I never in the world would have thought about making a pH meter."

World War II would press that necessity of invention far more than he could have imagined. Barely twenty years after the "war to end all wars," Hitler's army invaded Poland, an omen of suffering and slaughter. Scientists watched with an eye as wary as that of any general.

The year 1939 had been a buoyant one for National Technical Laboratories. The odd diversions and smaller incomes of inks and steam irons were now dwarfed by the more reliable market and more certain yield of chemical instrumentation. Not only was Beckman in charge of a new organization, but the enterprise had grown so much that it was time for another move. Confident of his ability, Dr. Beckman planned boldly. This time he would not seek a rental. He would build a spacious factory.

Although the company was called *National* Technical Laboratories, Beckman's pragmatic conclusion that a location closer to Los Angeles could be useful led him to focus on South Pasadena. He went to his bank to borrow half the cost of the plant. Though the bank knew his prosperous business record, it refused to make any real estate loan in South Pasadena—it was a "dead city." Undaunted, he approached the South Pasadena branch of Security First National Bank of Los Angeles. When the manager, Clyde Church, heard that other banks pronounced his city "dead," he asked Beckman only how much he wanted. That eighteen-thousand-dollar loan began a long, fruitful relationship between Beckman as a businessman and Security

Helipots: one of Arnold Beckman's wartime inventions. *Courtesy Beckman Coulter, Inc.*

147

The burgeoning staff of National Technical Laboratories, in front of the first building built for the company at 820 Mission Street in South Pasadena. *Courtesy Beckman Coulter, Inc.*

First National. With the bank's help, NTL moved into a new 12,000-square-foot plant in 1940.

Beckman had planned every detail, but he was still "aghast at the amount of space" as they moved into the new plant. Memories of empty space soon dimmed as the building more than filled with staff and equipment to meet the demands of a nation at war. Like its original parent company, National Postal Meter, which turned to making parts for the M-1 rifle during World War II, NTL stepped up to the challenge of the war effort with a number of critically important innovations, most of them organized around light.

Since the end of the nineteenth century wars have been fought by industrial enterprises as much as by battalions. Indeed the fate of armies has increasingly depended as much on their technological capabilities as on their valor. Beckman's business experienced a vast expansion, thanks to its critical role in the war. His efforts helped planes land and kept soldiers and submariners healthy, and he provided vital parts for radar and the Manhattan Project, which created the atomic bomb. At war's end commendations came his way, yet no one read headlines about him. In secret scientific work he had made advances that continued contributing long after war surplus was scrap. And no advance was more important than the work that culminated in the DU spectrophotometer.

The A, B, C of Innovation and the DU

The DU spectrophotometer was the first ready-to-use tool for determining the makeup of a given substance by analyzing the appearance of its absorption spectrum—the characteristic pattern of light wavelengths it absorbed. The DU focused on the ultraviolet range owing to the new importance of that region to biochemistry. Vitamin A, for instance, was found to have "fingerprints" in that range.

Just as "hydrogen-ion outfits" had filled whole tabletops before Arnold Beckman's creation of the integrated pH meter, so by 1940 an astounding three thousand dollars might begin to cover a lab bench with equipment that, if hooked up correctly, offered a chance at the ultraviolet range. Even then this equipment only produced sets of awkward-to-handle photographic plates, from which a graph of absorption could be cumbrously plotted. In 1940 an instrument set did find its way into dealers' catalogs when Coleman offered off-the-shelf ultraviolet absorption spectrophotometry using phototubes and electrical signals. This spectrophotometer captured Beckman's attention immediately.

The Coleman Model DM used an optical and phototube assembly to translate the ultraviolet absorption fingerprints of chemical substances into weak electrical signals that were then read with a separate Coleman product, its pH meter. Coleman pH meters were very similar to Beckman Model G pH meters, with variations in amplifier and electrode design that avoided direct patent infringement. The immediate lesson was that in producing the pH meter Beckman had created more than the pH meter. The Coleman spectrophotometer set showed once again that pH meters like Coleman's or Beckman's Model G could be used as very sensitive instruments for measuring any kind of weak electrical signal.

Realizing in a flash that a Beckman pH meter could amplify the weak electrical signals of ultraviolet spectrometers just as the Coleman pH meter did, Arnold Beckman turned his attention to this new class of analytical instruments. Beckman was never one to let a technological challenge and opportunity pass him by, especially one that had emerged in principle from his own innovations. With chemical researchers of all stripes eager to work on ultraviolet-absorption spectrophotometry, he lost no time in establishing a research-and-development program.

Leading this effort was NTL's vice president in charge of development, Howard Cary. Cary had distinguished himself in early work on new pH meters and associated electrodes, and had been quickly promoted to vice president for development. Both he and Beckman now focused on the quest for a spectrophotometer.

Early in 1940 they agreed that the most promising strategy for quick entry into the spectrophotometer business would come with a partner firm: NTL could adapt its pH meters for use as amplifiers for the phototubes, while another firm could produce the optics. Beckman approached Bausch and Lomb, then the premier American firm in optics. The company had long built spectrographic instruments for the visible regions of the spectrum, and its instruments were uniformly respected for quality of design and manufacture. America was teetering on the edge of war, and Bausch and Lomb, already the major American producer of optical glass, foresaw the pressures of war work. The firm anticipated overwhelming demand for glass for bomb sights, binoculars, cameras, range finders, and thousands

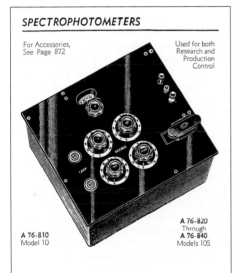

The Coleman spectrophotometer, designed to be used with the Coleman pH meter. *Courtesy Burrell Scientific.*

Chemistry is a science built on the ability to identify the unknown building blocks—the "stuff," the elements—of all material things. Early in the twentieth century "wet-bench" chemistry was the main way of identifying unknowns.

The college student and the senior chemist both practiced a disciplined series of reactions, precipitations, filterings, and dissolutions to identify an unknown by test after test. To find what a given substance consisted of, the analysis was qualitative. Further refined to identify the exact percentages of each component making up a compound, it became quantitative.

Gradually chemists developed a whole sequence of investigations beyond the wet-bench work, as unknowns, even molecules and atoms, revealed their identities through spectra, their signatures written in light. The most familiar spectrum is the rainbow spectrum produced when white light falls on a prism. In this phenomenon the many wavelengths (or colors) that make white light are spread apart by the prism, resulting in the blended stripes of the colored band. To one end of this spectrum lie the longest wave-

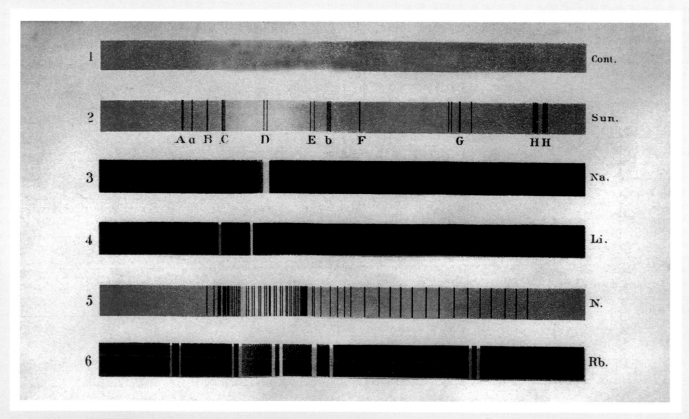

The frontispiece to Steele's *Fourteen Weeks in Chemistry* showing a variety of spectral lines.

lengths of light, the invisible infrared. From this invisible region one moves across ever-shortening wavelengths, passing through the shades of red, to oranges, yellows, greens, blues, indigos, and then violets. Above the violets lies another invisible realm of the spectrum: the ultraviolet.

Chemists found two kinds of spectra useful in analysis: emission spectra and absorption spectra. Emission spectra are created when an element—sodium, for example—is burned; the light so produced is then passed through a prism to reveal a spectrum marked with distinctive patterns. These distinctive patterns are the result of any given element's particular structure—a sort of visual fingerprint. In the case of sodium there are two bright yellow lines within a band of darkness, always at the same position. Such bright lines came to be known as emission spectra. Just as elements can only emit specific colors, so too they absorb light of specific wavelengths. For example, instead of burning sodium, one can shine white light through sodium vapor and then through a prism to create an absorption spectrum, the familiar band of the colors of the rainbow, but punctuated throughout by distinctive black lines. These black lines or holes in the spectrum are caused by the sodium absorbing light of particular colors. Other elements have equally distinct absorption patterns, making different chemical fingerprints.

Chemists became extraordinarily interested in these spectra, as they began to provide the keys to identifying unknown substances with remarkable accuracy. Spectra revealed chemical compositions that would have eluded traditional methods of wet chemistry. Spectral fingerprints allowed scientists like George Ellery Hale to ascertain the chemistry of the sun, the planets, and the stars. But despite the known usefulness of the method, the spectrometers, spectroscopes, and spectrographs that scientists had developed by 1940 left much to be desired.

Such delicate pieces of optical equipment were very temperamental—complex to operate and difficult to master. Even worse, results varied from chemist to chemist, based as they often were on subjective color perception and individual visual acuity. And these instruments were confined to the visible spectrum, nestled between the infrared and the ultraviolet. This was a growing limitation as chemists grasped the analytical significance of those invisible spectra on either side.

In the 1920s and 1930s a new type of spectrophotometer escaped some of these limitations. The new instrument relied not on photographic plates or observer's eyes to chart the dark lines of absorption spectra but on phototubes instead. Looking and acting like a sort of vacuum tube, phototubes worked rather differently, for their flows of current depended on the fact that for many substances electrical resistivity is changed by light. Some substances are very sensitive to particular colors of light, and they can be made to transmit current at a rate that varies with the intensity and color of the light that falls on them. Such photosensitive material was the chief component of this new electronic technology.

The new spectrophotometers used a prism to spread light out into absorption spectra, a phototube to "read" the spectrum by translating it into changing electrical signals, and some means to "listen" to these faint electrical changes. Thus a spectrophotometer allowed a scientist to "see" the characteristic fingerprints of matter electrically, regardless of whether the lines of the fingerprints fell within the visible or invisible—infrared or ultraviolet—ranges of the spectrum.

Probing the ultraviolet range became particularly vital in the 1930s as researchers learned that vitamin A has chemical fingerprints in that range. Yet there were no phototube instruments commercially available to explore the absorption spectra that now seemed so vital. The classic method still obtained. The individual researcher built or commissioned laboratory equipment if he had an adequate budget supplemented by skilled hands and deep knowledge of both optics and electronics. Only a very few "handmade" ultraviolet spectrophotometers existed by 1940, and all were based on emission spectra. These emission spectrophotometers were easier to build, but they were of no use in finding the critical ultraviolet absorption spectra of biochemical materials like vitamin A. ∽

of other applications: This was no context in which to explore spectrophotometers, and Bausch and Lomb was not interested in Beckman's proposal, little suspecting how critical his new instrument would be for war work.

Beckman was undeterred. Now he would direct Cary, NTL, and indeed himself to produce the entire spectrophotometer. Such scientific and technical challenges appealed to his mental makeup as an inventor and entrepreneur. "We dusted off our physics textbooks to learn about optical ray-tracing and such and ended up with what has proved to be an enduring optical design for the spectrophotometer." The technological push led to several false starts before NTL found the way to a successful creation. But only the fourth version would fully satisfy its inventor.

At the heart of any spectrophotometer is its optical design, the system that can select out light of a specific wavelength, transmit this light through the sample under investigation, and direct the resulting, partially absorbed light to the detecting phototube. And prisms are the center of this optical design, the means by which light is separated and specific wavelengths selected. Spectrometers of the 1930s commonly had glass prisms. They were the easiest to come by, and Beckman and Cary started with glass in their first design, their Model A. Within months they discovered that the glass prism, while suitable for investigations using visible light, was useless in the ultraviolet region of the spectrum. After considerable frustrations they

Quartz for making prisms for the DU spectrophotometer. *Courtesy Beckman Coulter, Inc.*

found that a quartz prism worked well, allowing ultraviolet light to be manipulated without any chemical reaction.

By the opening weeks of 1941 Beckman's NTL team had succeeded in creating the Model B spectrophotometer, with a quartz prism for handling ultraviolet light. It was designed to be attached to a Beckman Model G pH meter to read the output of weak electrical signals from the phototube. Only two of these Model Bs were ever made, and only one made its way to the outside world. NTL sold its first ultraviolet spectrophotometer in February 1941 when a Model B went to the Department of Chemistry at the University of California, Los Angeles.

Beckman soon grew dissatisfied with the optical design of the Model B. The quartz prism worked well for ultraviolet work, but the mechanism by which the prism could be turned to adjust the wavelength was difficult to set. Beckman demanded consistent, highly precise readings plus simplicity of use, and the Model B relied too much on its user's skilled hand and focused attention. An instrument so dependent on user skills was not part of the plan.

Through the winter and spring of 1941, as Londoners suffered through the Blitz and German U-boats threatened U.S. convoys, Beckman and his colleagues were hard at work on the Model C in the NTL building in Pasadena. The Model C was like the Model B in most respects including the mechanism that controlled the position of the quartz prism and the dependence on the pH meter for electronics and readout. The Model C included a new drive system for the prism that allowed easy, precise, and accurate selection of wavelengths without special skill or caution from users. It also had a linear, rather than circular, cell compartment to accommodate long-path sample cells, along with large, easy-to-operate controls for setting wavelength and slit width. NTL produced only three Model C spectrophotometers before Beckman gave the order to halt their production. All three had been sold: one to Caltech; another to a large citrus industry research facility in Riverside, California; and the last to the Vita Foods Company. The Model C had proved itself capable of attracting the attention of academic and industrial researchers alike, but Beckman was still not satisfied.

As he later explained, "It quickly became apparent that having the amplifier and readout in separate housing was economically and technically undesirable." The genius of his pH meter lay in part in the way he had replaced an entire set of apparatus with a single instrument. Now he applied the same thinking to spectrophotometry, leading his NTL team to create a single instrument for ultraviolet spectrometry that contained both optics and electronics and that no longer required a pH meter to serve as an amplifier and readout. Theirs would be a simple and complete instrument for searching out the ultraviolet fingerprints of vital substances. The user would only have to insert a sample, dial up a desired wavelength, and read on a simple meter the amount of absorption. In one or two minutes a number of wavelengths could be investigated, and the presence or

The electrical design of the Model D as presented in the paper Arnold Beckman and Howard Cary wrote for the MIT conference. *©1941* Journal of the Optical Society of America.

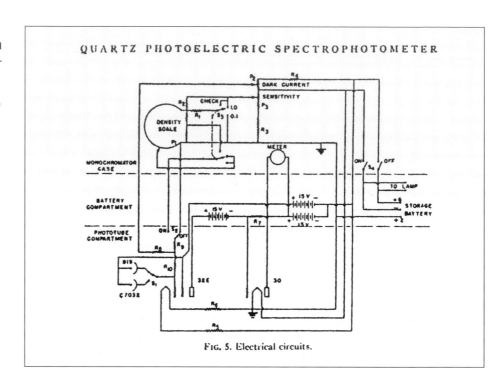

FIG. 5. Electrical circuits.

absence and quantity of a particular compound in a sample substance could be certified. The Model D would be a powerful tool for chemical analysis, available truly off the shelf and requiring a minimum of specialized skill. Beckman had every certainty it would usher in a whole new era of chemical research.

By July 1941 Beckman, Cary, and the development team had produced the new integrated design. Beckman sent off the first Model D to Ed Patterson at Arthur H. Thomas in Philadelphia on 12 July. Patterson—the salesman who had encouraged him to press forward with the pH meter—would now preside at the public unveiling of Beckman's new creation, at MIT. MIT had held regular conferences on spectroscopy since the 1930s, and Beckman and Cary had prepared a paper about their revolutionary new spectrophotometer for the conference on 21 July. But travel by air was severely restricted since President Roosevelt's declaration of an "unlimited national emergency" in May, and they could not find a way to get to Cambridge in time to present their paper. Patterson could simply take the train from Philadelphia, so he both presented the paper and displayed the wonders of the Model D.

Even as Patterson presented the new instrument, Beckman and Cary were wrestling with components back in South Pasadena. A reliable source for ultraviolet light still remained a technical challenge. From his own work in photochemistry Beckman knew that a particular variety of hydrogen lamp was the best source for ultraviolet light, but no such lamps were available commercially in 1941. As was becoming customary, he decided to manufacture the lamps himself, and in December 1941, the month of Pearl Harbor, NTL began production based on its own design. By the end of this fateful month NTL had delivered eighteen Model D spectrophotometers at a price of seven hundred dollars each, and orders were pouring in from the nation's instrument dealers. Arnold Beckman had another winner.

Early in 1942, as the new product took off, the war brought two challenges that threatened to shut down production. NTL needed high-grade Brazilian quartz for the prisms, and Beckman found himself competing for this quartz, which was much in demand for radio components needed for the war effort. Yet the new ultraviolet spectrophotometer was assuming its own critical role in American mobilization as a fast and powerful tool for discovery and production in fields ranging from pharmaceuticals to foods to chemical manufacture. Orders for the instrument were rising rapidly, and Beckman met his first challenge by having the government classify production of the spectrophotometer as high priority, though he had to pay the prices for quartz that scarcity demanded.

Phototubes provided the second challenge to production. NTL's design used an experimental tube produced by RCA that was particularly sensitive to ultraviolet light. RCA produced these experimental tubes only in small batches, and their performance varied greatly. NTL had been working around the problem but had nearly exhausted its supply of acceptable tubes early in 1942. Seeing that RCA could not keep pace with his production needs, Beckman set Howard Cary and Warren Baxter, another NTL researcher, on a new project of the highest priority: to design and bring to production a high-quality, sensitive ultraviolet phototube. Within a few months NTL began to manufacture its "Beckman type 2342 phototube." To emphasize the now-enhanced ultraviolet capability, the instrument's designation was changed to Model DU.

The Beckman DU spectrophotometer was a revolutionary instrument that had profound consequences for Beckman's enterprise and for the chemical sciences. After 1942 the DU was produced in ever-greater numbers for the next twenty-two years, for a total of 21,000 units, before it was discontinued. A key ingredient in what historians have called the "second chemical revolution" (the first was that of Antoine Lavoisier in the late eighteenth century), through its speed, precision, accuracy, and affordability the DU greatly increased the pace of chemical research. It brought powerful analytical techniques to growing numbers of scientists, and complex, delicate procedures that had once taken hours or days to perform could now be performed simply, with a single instrument, in a matter of minutes.

As the DU opened whole realms of investigation in biochemistry, it also taught organic chemists the great difference that new, electronic analytical instruments could make. Analysis allowed synthesis, and the DU foretold a golden age in which no substance would be beyond the ability of the organic chemist to analyze and then to create synthetically. That dream may exaggerate, but only slightly. Many years after the DU was introduced, Bruce Merrifield, a Nobel laureate in chemistry, called it probably the most important instrument ever developed toward the advancement of bioscience.

Its impact, however, was visible immediately. As early as September 1942 chemists browsing through *Industrial and Engineering Chemistry* saw an article that must have grabbed their attention. A high-profile feature on vitamin A showed what the DU could do for vitamin research, all the more striking because the published article appeared only three months after NTL had delivered the instrument to the author's lab. No wonder orders poured into South Pasadena.

The DU had an immediate role, for vitamins were a critical need in wartime. By the early 1940s researchers had determined that vitamin A was an essential dietary component, but the first laboratory synthesis would not be achieved until 1947. The primary source of vitamin A was cod liver oil, imported from the Scandinavian countries. As the war in the Atlantic curtailed shipments, scientists began a feverish quest for domestic sources of vitamin A. Biological assay by primitive means was then the standard test for the vitamin A content of a food. Juvenile rats were run through a period of deprivation, then fed a test substance (initially shark liver oil) for a period of four weeks. Sections of their tails were clipped, and the bone was tested. If the bone was healthy, the test substance probably was high in vitamin A. If not, the scientists ran tests on something else for four weeks. It was tedious, critical, hit-and-miss work. Vitamins, however, have characteristic absorption peaks in the ultraviolet range, and with the DU, biochemists could skip the rats and in minutes analyze any food for vitamin A content. Children who were grateful for alternatives to cod liver oil—and no doubt the rats—surely celebrated quietly.

At this point the National Bureau of Standards ran tests that certified the reputation that the DU was already building on its own. Would different laboratories produce identical results with the same instrument? The Beckman DU performed quickly, with reproducible precision, in test after test. As the government agency responsible for certifying units and methods of measures, the National Bureau now stipulated that the DU was the proper instrument for ultraviolet spectroscopy in large and important projects that required measurements to be absolutely interchangeable between research centers and individual investigators. The report was more than a guarantee of sales of the DU: It was official government certification of NTL's excellence in the manufacture of high-technology instrumentation, a guarantee that if other new instruments were needed, Beckman's firm could be relied on to produce both quality and accuracy. Walter Shewhart, Beckman's old patron at Bell Labs, would have been pleased.

Penicillin, TNT, and Rubber

No wartime project of medical science was more closely guarded than the Anglo-American effort to produce a "miracle drug"—the antibiotic penicillin. The development of penicillin and the technology of its mass production were critical.

A World War II propaganda poster publicizing the need for vitamin A. *Courtesy National Archives.*

Top: The American war effort would not have succeeded without the many women inducted into the workforce. Here a worker checks penicillin fermenting tanks.

Bottom: A technician running an infrared analysis of penicillin. *Both courtesy National Archives.*

Penicillin prevented a casualty from becoming a fatality, lessened long-term consequences of war wounds, and sped recovery.

The great potential of penicillin was known, but large-scale production was proving to be a technological challenge. The Beckman DU was an unexpected and critical tool for one group of workers involved in the project—those seeking to reveal the chemical structure of penicillin and thus to make the "miracle" a reality through synthesis. After the war, data from the DU led scientists to see that "penicillin" comprised a whole family of antibiotics, each containing the structure of the "beta-lactam ring" that confers their great medicinal power.

Penicillin work might have been secret, but the DU spectrophotometer was an immediate and undoubted success in many areas, as published papers and the stream of orders confirmed. Orders themselves revealed potential uses, and thus Dr. Beckman was alerted to the DU's power for a wholly distinct realm: petroleum refining and the production of petrochemicals, another industry at the very heart of America's ability to wage war on a global scale.

Crude oil is a veritable soup of different substances, the vast majority of its constituents made up of just two elements, hydrogen and carbon. From these hydrocarbons of crude oil come gasoline, motor oil, and a wide variety of other petroleum products. As the exigencies of war aggravated pressures from the normal economy, refiners sought any tool that could provide more knowledge of hydrocarbons.

Gasoline, kerosene, and oil were visible products of refining, but crude oil was developing a secret profile as the logical source for a significant wartime need: synthetic rubber. Jeeps ran on rubber tires, planes landed on rubber wheels, and rubber was used throughout every tank. Japanese successes in the Far East cut off America and its Allies from their traditional sources of natural rubber, and the race was on to find a reliable synthetic substitute. Butadiene, one of the hydrocarbons in crude oil, offered great promise, but scientists and engineers needed a tool to identify it. The Beckman DU was just such a tool, providing a means to assess the presence and quantity of butadiene through its ultraviolet signature. Throughout the war, scientists and engineers used the DU to tackle the chemical challenges inherent in producing ton after ton of butadiene for synthetic rubber.

Eclipsing the demand for synthetic rubber and even for gasoline was the call for nearly unimaginable stocks of explosives. Key to the high explosives of World War II was toluene, another hydrocarbon in crude oil; and the second *T* in TNT—trinitrotoluene. Just as petroleum refiners found Beckman's DU a powerful tool for producing butadiene, they also found the instrument could pull double duty in identifying toluene.

Ultraviolet spectroscopy enhanced research on butadiene and toluene, but Beckman and most American chemists already suspected that research on these two hydrocarbons and many others would be even more fruitful if focused on a different part of the spectrum, in another invisible realm, the infrared. There toluene, butadiene, and many other crucial chemicals had their most distinctive wavelengths of absorption. The government was soon persuaded to make development of infrared spectroscopy one of its own wartime campaigns.

Infrared Spectroscopy and a Call to Arms

The uses of infrared were no secret. *Industrial and Engineering Chemistry* carried the latest news and research on instruments and techniques for industrial chemists and chemical engineers. The journal was also the leading American Chemical Society publication in its attractiveness to advertisers, since it was the forum for discussion of industrial applications of chemical instrumentation. In January 1941 the journal ran a pathbreaking article by a chemist at Dow Chemical, Norman Wright. His "Application of Infrared Spectroscopy to Industrial Research" was surely a mandate to a wartime government and a stimulus to every instrument manufacturer in America, especially to alert readers in South Pasadena.

Wright emphasized that infrared spectrophotometry was exceptionally important for at least twelve reasons. It was the ideal tool for the identification of compounds; the detection of impurities in organic compounds; the quantitative analysis

One of the great successes of science and technology during World War II was the mass production of the antibiotic penicillin. *Courtesy National Archives.*

of such impurities; the study of reaction mechanisms and speeds; the detection of intermediates; the study of isomerism and tautomerism; the study of association and compound formation; the study of polymerization and copolymerization in plastics; the determination of chemical structures, bond lengths, and moments of inertia; the determination of force and dissociation constants; the calculation of specific heats and other thermodynamic constants; and the study of crystal structure through use of polarized radiation. Almost any one of the pursuits that Wright listed could have alone supplied a market for a small industry in infrared spectrophotometers. To be safe, however, Wright added, "There are no doubt other applications."

Invisible infrared radiation is also a source of heat. Scientists conducted experiments in the infrared throughout the nineteenth century, using measurements of heat rather than traditional optics. By 1881 techniques existed for converting that heat into photographic images, ushering in the use of infrared spectroscopy in the opening decades of the twentieth century. What infrared spectroscopy could teach the chemical researcher in this period was largely qualitative, as chemists learned to read infrared absorption spectra for the characteristic lines that revealed the presence of specific chemical elements, of certain bonds within molecules, and of other chemical structures. Only in the late 1930s did chemical scientists make infrared spectroscopy a quantitative as well as qualitative method.

Wright made headway by transforming infrared's invisible light into electrical signals. At Dow Chemical, with assistance from researchers at the University of Michigan, he developed an infrared spectrophotometer much like the instruments used to measure ultraviolet absorption spectra before Beckman developed the DU: a tabletop full of equipment that worked together in the targeted area. Wright's instrument used a rock salt prism to select out particular wavelengths of infrared light for study, just as Arnold Beckman's DU used a quartz prism for the ultraviolet. Absorption information about infrared wavelengths was converted into weak electrical currents with a thermopile, then read by a testy high-sensitivity galvanometer of the sort that had bedeviled Glen Joseph. Complicated and extremely delicate, the Dow instrument did produce quantitative data from infrared absorption spectra. Wright's article showed that the instrument was producing real results in all the categories of industrial usefulness he mentioned. When Beckman read the article, he saw it as an invitation to a whole new product line ripe for the picking.

Wright's chosen technology, the thermopile, was old news for Arnold Beckman. He had used thermopiles—devices that measured quantities of light by the heat they produced, translating heat into an electrical signal—in his dissertation research at Caltech in the 1920s. As the DU project moved toward success, Beckman began to think about a shift to the other end of the spectrum.

The government helped that shift. Wright's article appeared during a war in which rubber was an essential material. Japanese invasions of the Dutch East Indies

The war effort jump-started the American economy after the slump of the 1930s, but it did not eliminate competition. This poster makes clear that NTL was not the only manufacturer of the instruments necessary to such programs as the Synthetic Rubber Program. *Courtesy National Archives.*

SYNTHETIC RUBBER PLANTS
THEY NEED BRISTOL INSTRUMENTS·LIKE THE PYROMASTER pH CONTROLLER-- TO SPEED PRODUCTION, GUARD AGAINST MISTAKES.

THE "RUBBER" THAT ARMIES ROLL ON.
FAULTY INSTRUMENTS MEAN BREAK-DOWNS AT THE FRONT. ACCURATE INSTRUMENTS KEEP 'EM ROLLING. BRISTOL PRECISION CHARTS GIVE VITAL OPERATING DATA TO WAR PLANTS.

NTL employees responded to the call of this poster, feverishly building infrared spectrophotometers to be used in the manufacture of synthetic rubber.
Courtesy National Archives.

PHOTO BY U.S. ARMY SIGNAL CORPS

THESE BOYS NEED GOOD TIRES.   YOU CAN HELP THEM GET THE BEST BY LOSING NO TIME IN TURNING OUT THE INSTRU-MENTS NEEDED TO MAKE MORE SYNTHETIC RUBBER

and Malaya had severed connections between America and the natural rubber plantations of the South Pacific in 1941. A limited stockpile of rubber had been conserved, and rubber could be rationed and recycled, but the government's primary objective was to develop a synthetic rubber. President Roosevelt had already declared rubber a strategic and crucial material when he formed the Office of Rubber Reserve in 1940. One of the organization's first acts was to seek alliances with petroleum companies to guarantee supplies of butadiene, the key ingredient for synthetic rubber.

Well aware of the evolving success of the DU spectrophotometer in this area, the Office of Rubber Reserve contacted Arnold Beckman after Pearl Harbor to see whether his company could make an infrared counterpart. For his part Beckman knew that any national synthetic rubber program desperately needed precise, accurate, and reliable infrared spectros. The effort would require producing instruments at the cutting edge of technology, with negligible variation from instrument to instrument. It was another grand technical challenge, as well as an opportunity for a natural extension of his expertise. In early 1942 Beckman agreed to build infrared spectrophotometers for the American synthetic rubber program.

A secret meeting that the Office of Rubber Reserve convened in Detroit sealed his commitment. Key leaders in the development of spectrophotometry were

Even though the United States built up a synthetic rubber industry between December 1941 and August 1945, scrap rubber was still needed for the war effort. *Courtesy National Archives.*

A Gas Mask requires 1.11 pounds of rubber

A Life Raft requires 17 to 100 pounds of rubber

A Scout Car requires 306 pounds of rubber

A Heavy Bomber requires 1,825 pounds of rubber

America needs your SCRAP RUBBER

invited, among them Robert Brattain from Shell Development Company in California, who had concentrated on instrumentation after earning his Ph.D. in physics at Princeton. (His older brother, Walter Brattain, later shared the Nobel Prize in physics in 1956 with William Shockley and John Bardeen for the invention of the transistor.) Another industrial scientist present was R. Bowling Barnes of American Cyanamid. Both Brattain and Barnes had been hard at work developing infrared spectrophotometers specifically for analysis of hydrocarbons and petroleum products.

The steadfast consensus of the meeting was that the infrared was key to realizing synthetic rubber production on a vast scale. The debate was not *whether* infrared spectrophotometers should be produced but *which* variant should be perfected and manufactured. Industry needed a standard instrument with standard readings so that results could be both trusted and easily shared between laboratories and production facilities. The government wanted a hundred such instruments distributed among researchers and plants. These were to be secret scientific tools, closely guarded and powerful. Users were forbidden to publish or to divulge any details about them or the research results to anyone outside the Synthetic Rubber Program.

The Detroit group met to act rather than merely to plan, and it selected both design and manufacturer. Robert Brattain was a strong advocate of the design he had created for Shell. He had already described that instrument and the results it could produce at a meeting of the American Physical Society held in Pasadena in 1941. Brattain's design was a simple, single-beam spectrophotometer, the most basic type of this class of instruments. "Single beam" meant that the instrument made use of just one beam of infrared light. Looking for absorption of a particular wavelength involved two measurements. The first was a reference measurement of the intensity of light at the infrared wavelength produced by the instrument without any sample. A thermocouple with a high-sensitivity galvanometer provided the readout. The second measurement was a measurement with the sample in place. By comparing the two measures, the absorption for that particular infrared wavelength could be calculated. In theory a double-beam instrument could produce two paths of light and allow users to make the reference measure and the sample measure simultaneously. Nevertheless, Brattain's infrared spectrophotometer had the great virtue of existing, and it had proved that it could produce reliable measurements. The Office of Rubber Reserve adopted Brattain's design.

From IR-1 to IR-4

The Rubber Reserve asked Arnold Beckman to manufacture a hundred instruments of the chosen design. The early reputation of the DU, seconded by the National Bureau of Standards' independent investigation, left NTL few competitors for the contract. Beckman's would be a secret manufactory, and few people would know that he was one of the very first producers of infrared spectrophotometers. When Brattain's design plans arrived at NTL, the company quickly set to work. Though Brattain had produced an instrument that worked, Beckman engineers reviewed every detail of his plans themselves, producing a set of manufacturing blueprints some three inches thick. Clayton Rasmussen, one of Beckman's machinists (and later a systems engineer for the firm), then turned these prints into parts for the first instrument. Rasmussen knew at the time that he was working on an infrared spectrophotometer, but the secrecy was such that only later would he learn that it was a special project for synthetic rubber.

By September 1942, less than half a year after the Detroit meeting, Arnold Beckman's enterprise shipped off the first infrared spectrophotometers, known as the Model IR-1. Yet Beckman and his colleagues could not help seeing many ways to improve it. Both the pH meter and the DU spectrophotometer substituted rugged vacuum–tube amplifiers for testy galvanometers. The original Model IR–1 of Brattain's design still required a galvanometer. That using electronics circuitry would improve the design was obvious. Once production began on the contracted one hundred IR–1s, Arnold Beckman initiated designs for an infrared spectrophotometer that took advantage of his experience with the DU.

Beckman began work on Model IR–2, his own improved infrared spectrophotometer, just after Howard Cary had invented a reliable phototube for the DU spectrophotometer. That achievement made it only natural that Dr. Beckman would call upon him now. Cary took as much technology from the DU spectrophotometer as he could for the infrared device, and over the next two years, under Beckman's direction, Cary and others at NTL developed the IR–2 into an instrument that visibly, conceptually, and technologically drew on the DU spectrophotometer, which the firm was already producing as fast as it could.

Like the pH meter and the DU, the IR–2 did away with galvanometers and attached apparatus, such as photographic plates, by using an electronic amplifier. Beckman's firm also developed a highly responsive thermocouple tube for detecting infrared light, just as it had developed its own phototube for ultraviolet light in the DU. Moreover, Cary and his team built the IR–2 in a rugged metal housing with simple controls that looked virtually identical to the housing and controls of the DU. The IR–2 went into production in 1945. Despite the design, it was not as easy to use as the DU, for its delicate prisms and the difficulties of infrared spectroscopy required skilled researchers at its controls. The IR–2 sold for upwards of four thousand dollars, and Arnold Beckman's firm sold over four hundred

Steve Murphy, the supervisor of NTL's infrared assembly department, makes a precision adjustment on an IR-2A in the late 1940s. *Courtesy Beckman Coulter, Inc.*

instruments in the next eleven years. While this would have been highly impressive by the standards of NTL in 1935, in the postwar context it was a modest success at best.

Wartime achievements like the making of an infrared spectrophotometer came as Beckman's enterprise grew rapidly and as he and his colleagues gained valuable experience and new skills in the process. The work had its paradoxical costs. NTL's efforts in the field of infrared spectrophotometry were unsung, for the production and use of the IR-1 instruments were government secrets. Meanwhile other infrared instruments appeared, and neither instruments nor research results were covered by secrecy restrictions. Bowling Barnes, the scientist from American Cyanamid who had been at Detroit, decided to go into business and produce a sophisticated double-beam spectrophotometer. He and others who used his instrument were free to publish their results, even during the war. Barnes worked with Perkin-Elmer to bring out a commercial version of his instrument immediately after the war, around the same time that Arnold Beckman launched his IR-2. Researchers "didn't know that we had actually made more spectrophotometers than Bowling Barnes had: We had nothing in the literature! We had one heck of a sales problem when the war was over. People wanting to use new instruments referred back to the literature to see what so-and-so used, and it was a Barnes instrument. We had an uphill battle for years."

Reviewing NTL's unsatisfactory struggle to regain lost ground, Beckman posed himself a direct question in 1953: "Are we going to be in the infrared business or not?" Less than fifteen years earlier he had been a professor of chemistry at Caltech, instilled with the Caltech spirit of being second to none. This same ethos he brought to bear on his own firm. Beckman positioned his company to explore new avenues in technology, for he was convinced that one never knew where the "next big thing" would emerge. Yet he did not pursue technology for the mere sake of having a presence in the "big things." He wanted to be in business only if he and the firm could create superior products or push the envelope of scientific and technological development. He wanted both firm and instruments to be second to none.

"I made the decision that, yes, we were going to be a leader in the infrared business, and we spent a tremendous amount of money on development and subsequent models of the infrared spectros," Dr. Beckman later explained. By 1956 his development team had come up with the IR-4, a radically redesigned scanning instrument. The user could select with a switch whether the instrument would operate in single- or double-beam mode. It was a sophisticated, high-performance instrument, and it fulfilled Beckman's intention of regaining leadership in the realm of infrared spectrophotometers: The IR-4 was the archetype of an evolutionary family of spectrophotometers that ultimately spanned some seventeen years of production from 1956 to 1973. Through these infrared instruments and his growing

The optical design of Beckman's IR-4 infrared spectrophotometer.
Courtesy Beckman Coulter, Inc.

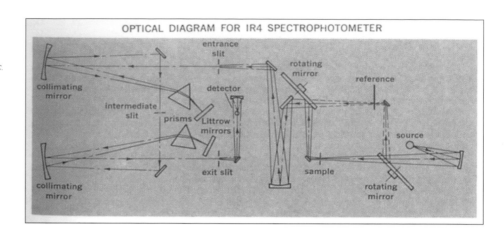

OPTICAL DIAGRAM FOR IR4 SPECTROPHOTOMETER

The IR-4 spectrophotometer depicted in a Beckman Instruments catalog.
Courtesy Beckman Coulter, Inc.

array of ultraviolet spectros, Beckman further stoked the fires of revolution in the conduct of chemical and life sciences research. He provided devices that married electronics with analytical probes and extended human understanding and control of the molecular world. In the immediate context of their introduction, Beckman's spectrophotometers were also valued aids to America's victory in World War II.

The Helipot

While Arnold Beckman was in Detroit at the secret meeting with the Office of Rubber Reserve, he received a mysterious phone call from Paul Rosenberg, a professor of physics at MIT's Radiation Laboratory. Rosenberg had joined the "Rad Lab" immediately after earning his Ph.D. from Columbia University. He told Beckman that for some time he had been trying to get information from the staff at NTL about one of the components in Beckman pH meters. Rosenberg was

The exterior of the Radiation Laboratory at MIT. The roof of the building holds receiving equipment. *Courtesy MIT Museum.*

The steering committee of MIT's Rad Lab in 1945. Notable figures include I. I. Rabi, Nobel laureate in physics, seated at far left; Lee DuBridge, future president of Caltech, seated eighth from left, at the head of the table; and Britton Chance, seated front right. *Courtesy MIT Museum.*

secretive and unwilling to discuss any details over the phone. Stressing the seriousness of his inquiry and the crucial need for information, he made the astounding suggestion that Beckman go directly from Detroit to meet with him in Cambridge; there would be no problem in getting a flight to Massachusetts and then back to California. With commercial air travel under the government's control, that assurance meant connections—and it plainly implied a summons to another secret wartime project.

With this call hovering between a puzzle and a command, Beckman set out for Massachusetts, confident—though somewhat wary—of what traveling from one secret meeting to another would ultimately entail.

In the hastily constructed wooden buildings that collectively housed MIT's Radiation Laboratory, Beckman first heard the word *radar*, a watchword that initiated him into the closed ranks of American and British scientists, technologists,

The British began work on radar in the 1930s. They knew from World War I that airborne bombing rendered geographical barriers and national borders obsolete.

A technician studying a radar screen during World War II. *Courtesy MIT Museum.*

Britain watched the German rearmament program in 1935 with growing trepidation, anxious to develop a system to detect approaching enemy aircraft. The science behind radar was a half century old when the British launched their efforts. In the late 1880s the German physicist Heinrich Hertz conducted experiments on electromagnetic radiation, trying to test earlier theories of James Clerk Maxwell, a Scottish physicist who worked during the mid-nineteenth century. By formulating his famous "Maxwell's equations," Maxwell established that light waves and radio waves are alike varieties of electromagnetic waves and therefore governed by the same fundamental laws. In 1888 Hertz went on to demonstrate that radio waves, like light, can be reflected and refracted. That is, Hertz showed that electromagnetic radiation in the form of radio waves and even microwaves could be broadcast and reflected and most important that these broadcasts and reflections could be detected.

The early 1930s brought reports of interference in radio broadcasts from passing planes, cars, and steel ships. In 1935 Robert Alexander Watson Watt, a Scottish engineer working as the superintendent of the Meteorological Office of Britain's Royal Aircraft Establishment, drafted a memo on using radio to detect aircraft. (Watson Watt took up radar only after giving up on his plans for a "death ray" to kill enemy soldiers from long distances.)

His memo spurred Britain to develop a serious radar system, and by the fall of 1938 the country had its first twenty-four-hour radar operation system, named the Chain Home. This system operated on a relatively low frequency, about 30 megahertz, making it less accurate than later systems, but it nevertheless functioned and protected Britain for the duration of the war.

Only a year after the Chain Home system was installed, physicists at the University of Birmingham invented the cavity magnetron oscillator. This small, unimpressive-looking device generated electromagnetic waves of higher frequencies than early transmitters—microwaves, in fact. England declared war on Germany in September 1939, and although the Chain Home was up and running, British physicists pressed ahead with the new research, knowing that German radar technology could not be far behind.

British military intelligence sent the blueprints and a working cavity magnetron across the Atlantic to the United States, hoping to speed radar development by recruiting American scientists. Vannevar Bush, an electrical engineer trained at MIT, was responsible for coordinating the National Defense and Research Committee (NDRC), and in August 1940 he met the British diplomat who literally carried with him this vital military secret to Britain's most important ally. Both sides were aware how necessary cooperation was to creating a viable microwave radar system. Meanwhile, in September 1940, the resounding defeat by the British of the Luftwaffe in the Battle of Britain proved the value of radar.

Tracing a course on a radar screen, World War II. *Courtesy MIT Museum.*

The next month the NDRC allocated $455,000 to construct and fund a "Radiation Laboratory" at MIT. The nation's radar lab needed a cover name because a host of new wooden buildings suddenly springing up would not be ignored. The misleading name was deliberately picked to evoke an East Coast equivalent of Ernest Lawrence's renowned Radiation Laboratory—centered on the cyclotron atom smasher—in California. Scientists of all stripes were recruited to join the Rad Lab in pursuit of microwave radar: physicists, biochemists, electrical engineers, and any others who had expertise in invention and electronics. The physicist Lee Du Bridge (who later became president of Caltech) was appointed to head the MIT team. By January 1941 the Rad Lab's wizards had installed their first radar system across the rooftop of the lab and had it up and running. ～

and soldiers who were privy to the true, secret raison d'être of the complex. *Radar* stood for "radio detecting and ranging." While now a commonplace technology that suffuses many aspects of daily life, including all commercial aircraft and shipping, radar was born during World War II, the fruit of a massive project that crossed the Atlantic from Britain, charged with the energy of wartime necessity.

A jumble of receiving equipment at the Rad Lab, where Beckman's Helipot would bring needed order.
Courtesy MIT Museum.

As Rosenberg explained the Rad Lab project, Beckman puzzled over what such an effort required from him. What NTL achievement could be so important, given all the Rad Lab's sophisticated electronics gear? The answer lay in the hundreds of mundane-looking tuning knobs that the staff used to control their creations. Radar requires precise adjustments for transmitting and receiving signals, just as one needs to tune a radio set to particular frequencies. While they may, on the surface, have looked inconsequential, the tuning knobs—"potentiometers," in technical language—were vital to the operation of the radar systems. They had to be extremely accurate, able to hold their settings, and extraordinarily rugged for use on airplanes and ships. It must have delighted Arnold Beckman when he learned that the Rad Lab had found the potentiometers of his pH meters to be superior to any others.

Beckman's early pH meters had used two off-the-shelf control knobs designed by their manufacturer for controlling the tuning and volume of radio sets. The

Beckman pH meter needed two potentiometers to control the vacuum-tube amplifier, one for gross adjustment, the other for fine-tuning. Beckman and his NTL colleagues quickly grew dissatisfied with these radio parts, for they were too crude for such an accurate instrument. He and his staff set out to make the best potentiometer possible, a single unit that would combine a broad range along with fine control. They had an ingenious solution ready for mass production by 1940 and trademarked their innovation as the "Helipot," a contraction of "helical potentiometer."

The name expressed the very essence of the new cylindrical component, which contained a piece of wire wound into the spiraling shape of a helix. A shaft ran down the center of this wire helix, and the knob was attached at the top. As the knob turned, the central shaft turned, and a small electrical contact was made to wind its way up and down the spiral of the helix. Moving this contact varied the length of the coiled wire that an electrical current would flow through: the greater the length, the greater the resistance. By varying this resistance, one could adjust, tune, and control electrical circuits connected to the Helipot. The design provided just what Beckman had intended: an excellent, precise, electrical controller that covered a wide range of settings while affording the finest possible tuning. Without realizing that this improved component for the pH meter was one of the finest potentiometers available in the world, Beckman directed NTL to install the Helipot in all new pH meters and to build up a stock of them for sale as spare parts.

This little creation, the Helipot, brought Beckman to the center of one of the most technologically important projects of the twentieth century. Rosenberg needed to know if NTL could create a new class of Helipot that would live up to military specifications. At this juncture Beckman's seems the traditionally prepared

The Model A Helipot, later adapted by Beckman for the radar project. *Courtesy Beckman Coulter, Inc.*

This sketch of the Helipot shows the resistance coils that made the device finely tunable and the groove that secured the contact.
Courtesy Beckman Coulter, Inc.

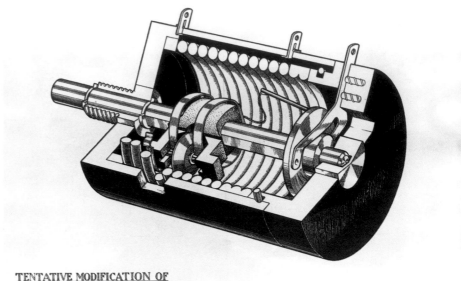

TENTATIVE MODIFICATION OF
BECKMAN HELIPOT
TYPE 680

NON-RESTRICTED

RADIATION LABORATORY, M.I.T.
11-22-43-23-I-6334-B-PRINT Nº

life. He makes solid moves, he is reflective, he has had confidence in the developments that have preceded the present moment, and when sudden questions arise, he is ready with quick but solidly grounded answers. Could he build a new potentiometer for the radar program? "Of course," he said immediately, only adding to the story forty-three years later, "not realizing what I was getting into."

Beckman explained further. "We made this [Helipot] just as a component for our instruments. We never thought of going into the electronics business; we were in the chemical analysis instrument field. Then [Rosenberg] said that they had found our Helipot much more precise than anything else on the market, by a factor of ten or so. We didn't know that." What Rosenberg needed for the new radar was a design that could withstand shocks and jostlings. Rad Lab staff had tested existing Helipots stripped from pH meters and found that when given a blow to the side, the electrical contact carried by the shaft would momentarily break free of the wire helix. Not only did such a blow disrupt the setting of the Helipot, it rendered it inoperable for a split second. The rumbling vibrations of a propeller-driven airplane would be like a continuous stream of such blows: "A redesign was necessary."

Back at NTL not everyone was enthusiastic about the new commission. The research department was gearing up for work on infrared spectrophotometers, under a pressing government contract. Asking the group to work on what looked to be a minor electrical component was distracting and, the staff seemed to think, moderately insulting. Beckman could not announce that this redesign was needed immediately for national defense. He could describe the part to be made, but he

The first page of Arnold Beckman's patent diagrams for the Helipot.

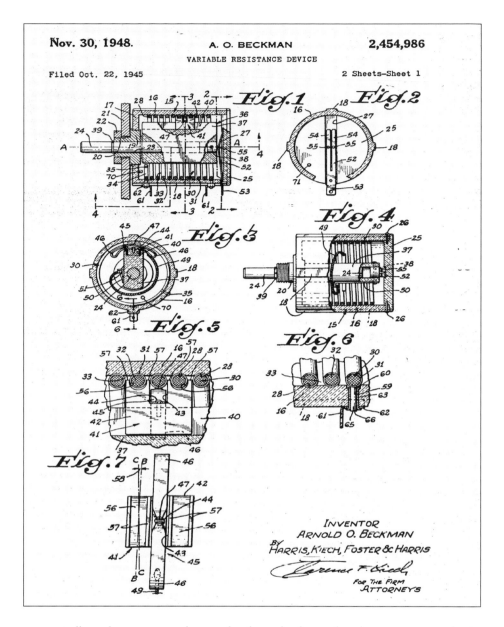

Nov. 30, 1948.   A. O. BECKMAN   2,454,986
VARIABLE RESISTANCE DEVICE
Filed Oct. 22, 1945   2 Sheets—Sheet 1

INVENTOR
ARNOLD O. BECKMAN
BY
HARRIS, KIECH, FOSTER & HARRIS

FOR THE FIRM
ATTORNEYS

was not allowed to even use the word *radar*, as both word and concept were classified. He simply had to appear determined to do something that seemed, to his employees, more like a needless whim. As he remembers, he was faced with "almost an in-house mutiny" in his own research department, with his engineers saying to him that they did not want to work on the "stinking little radio things." After a few weeks he began getting irate calls from the military's top brass demanding to know where the "blankety-blank Helipot" was. They had warships held up in ports because they had no potentiometer for their radar systems.

Never one to stay baffled, Dr. Beckman began to envision the redesign possibilities himself. The more he turned the problem over in his mind, the more it seemed like a mechanical puzzle. The problem was that a small spring pressed the sliding electrical contact to the resistance helix. A sharp jolt could easily overpower the spring. What different mechanical arrangement of parts could let the contact slide but make it impossible for the embrace of the contact and helix to be broken? As he tells the story, his solution came in a moment of inspiration after hours and hours of mental perspiration. "One sleepless night a design evolved in my mind. [This redesign involved replacing the spring with a groove in which the contact would ride—the contact could not leave the groove, and it could not be knocked away from the wire helix.] The next morning I went directly to a shop mechanic, bypassing the engineers, and asked him to make a part from my rough pencil sketch. . . . In two days we built what was called the Model A Helipot."

Since the Model A Helipot satisfied every requirement that the military wanted, Beckman was immediately faced with overwhelming orders. Within the first year of its production the Model A was responsible for 40 percent of NTL's total profit, more than even the spectrophotometers had brought in. As president of NTL, Beckman was gratified that his personal innovation was responsible for so much of the financial health of the firm and that he was making such a contribution to the American war effort. Yet the enormous demand for a single product and from a single customer—the military—was a growing cause of concern. He feared that his innovative success might mean a loss of control of the firm, if demand for the Model A Helipot led government and military officials to declare production of the "pots" a military priority, compelling him to devote all of NTL's human and material resources to the production of the Helipots alone. He feared further that he might be compelled to shut down the production of other instruments and his research-and-development programs for the duration of the war.

To ensure that the military could receive the Helipots they desperately required and that NTL could continue to supply and develop its powerful analytical tools—the pH meters, the DU spectrophotometer, and the infrared spectros—Beckman made a characteristically bold proposal to the other directors of NTL. He would set up, own, and run the Helipot business in a separate, subsidiary company: the Helipot Corporation. Helipot in its turn would pay NTL royalties on a license for the Helipot itself. The other directors, increasingly nervous over Dr. Beckman's apparently insatiable appetite for new ideas, cutting-edge technology, and remorseless hard work, readily agreed. Beckman's ability to ride two horses was facilitated by an agreement that the Helipot Corporation would sublease space in NTL's Mission Street complex. Under these new corporate auspices, production of the Helipot grew at a feverish pace. With the Helipot Corporation, Arnold Beckman simultaneously gained a company of his own and became a major electronics component manufacturer during World War II. Eventually, in the mid-1950s, the corporation would be reintegrated into its parent firm, by then named Beckman Instruments, as the Helipot Division. Through the war and after, Helipot's scientists and engineers produced a dazzling array of advanced potentiometers and other kinds of electronic components, maintaining for decades Dr. Beckman's position as an important electronics manufacturer.

The Model A Helipot has enjoyed a spectacular technological career. From the time of its invention through the mid-1970s over six million were produced. Even today the company that eventually evolved out of the Helipot Corporation, BI Technologies, continues to manufacture the Model A Helipot to Arnold Beckman's original design.

The Manhattan Project and the Micro-microammeter

Monumental efforts can fail for want of small parts, and NTL made its own critical, if small, contribution to one of the war's biggest: the Manhattan Project. Like the Rad Lab, the Manhattan Project was based on hundreds of scientists gathering in secrecy, in this case at varied sites. Men and women at elite universities and secret spots in Los Alamos in New Mexico, Oak Ridge in Tennessee, and Hanford in Washington were expending vast amounts of brain power and economic resources to create the first nuclear weapons. Producing the explosive material itself, the highly radioactive elements uranium and plutonium, was essential.

The Manhattan Project—as it came to be known, after its cover name "Manhattan Engineering District"—was funded by the War Department through the Office of Scientific Research and Development (OSRD). Two leading architects of American wartime and postwar science and technology headed the OSRD: the engineer Vannevar Bush, president of the Carnegie Institution, and the chemist James Conant, president of Harvard University. On the military side General Leslie Groves was in command. Bush, Conant, and Groves oversaw a vast project that had two major components.

The scientific elite who would lead the Manhattan Project, at a lighter moment at a meeting on the giant cyclotron, an atomic particle accelerator, at Berkeley, California, in April 1940. Seated, from left to right: Ernest O. Lawrence, Arthur H. Compton, Vannevar Bush, James B. Conant, Karl T. Conant, and Alfred Loom.s. *Courtesy National Archives.*

The small groups working on bomb design and techniques for producing the radioactive materials were balanced by the vast operations thrown together to make the bomb. The "big science" of the Manhattan Project was in large measure "big industrial chemistry." The DuPont company oversaw the construction and operation of the uranium and plutonium production facilities in Hanford and in Oak Ridge. The Hanford complex was the single largest construction project that America undertook during World War II, employing sixty thousand workers to build the plutonium production complex.

Hanford's reactors were critical for producing a plutonium bomb, and running them at anything less than full strength meant delay in accumulating sufficient plutonium. To measure radiation, and thus operations, scientists developed instruments they called "ionization chambers," gas filled and electrically charged so that radiation passing through a chamber would produce an electrical signal. Some MIT scientists had been commissioned to develop an instrument to measure and record the output of electrical signals from the ionization chambers. However, they were having trouble making a device that could measure these weak signals accurately—a reliable micro-microammeter. Ultimately the group turned to Arnold Beckman and NTL.

Below: Hanford Works, the first chemical facility for the extraction of plutonium.

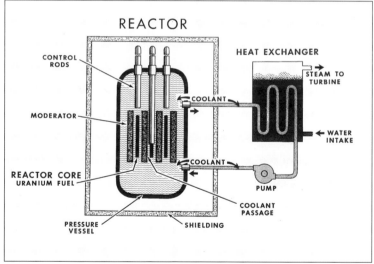

Right: A simple diagram of a nuclear reactor issued by the Atomic Energy Commission. The statement released with the diagram reads: "Basically, a reactor is an atomic furnace in which the fissioning, or splitting, of atoms of nuclear fuel can be controlled and put to useful work." *Both courtesy National Archives.*

Beckman describes how the micro-microammeter was "an outgrowth, again, of the pH meter amplifier. I recall we had a visit from a couple of professors from MIT one day. They were visiting Professor Royal Sorensen, and he suggested they come over and see me." (Royal Sorensen had taught electrical engineering at Caltech since 1910 and was well acquainted with the former Professor Beckman and NTL's technical achievements.) "Well, they [the MIT group] had a project of trying to build a recording micro-microammeter, something that would record from 10^{-15} amps up to 10^{-12} amps. . . . They had several Ph.D.s working on it, and they'd

Beckman's micro-microammeter. *Courtesy Beckman Coulter, Inc.*

spent umpteen thousand dollars back there and still didn't have it. They came over and talked to me, and I said, 'Well, we'll sell you one off the shelf for $750.' This was our recording pH meter. By merely substituting an input-load resistor for the glass electrode, you have a recording micro-microammeter. That opened up a whole new field. It never occurred to me to exploit the pH meter as a micro-microammeter."

Once again the electronic amplifier at the center of the pH meter proved capable of technological evolution. The MIT group was appalled that a capable instrument had been available all along, that the group had failed to recognize it, and that Arnold Beckman had failed to proclaim its versatility. Astonishment became annoyance, and the MIT group, in Beckman's words, "chewed him out" for not having come forward earlier with news of the pH meter doubling as a micro-microammeter. Said Beckman in the 1980s, "They accused us of hiding our light under a bushel. I guess at the time we weren't thinking very deeply about wide-spread applications of our equipment. We were measuring pH."

Nonetheless, adaptation was a well-established Beckman trait, and once the pH meter was also called a micro-microammeter, he had a new business. Thereafter his firm produced a whole line of micro-microammeters that were used to assess the nation's plutonium in wartime—and for much else beyond.

Radiant Bodies: Beckman's Quartz Fibers and the Dosimeter

While the micro-microammeters supplied by NTL allowed scientists to monitor the radiation within the nation's wartime nuclear reactors, the Manhattan Project needed yet another instrument—one to warn personnel when their bodies encountered radiation that had escaped. This project did require imaginative design.

The challenge of recording human exposure to doses of radiation again fired Beckman's inventor's mindset: The result was the Beckman dosimeter. Not unlike a heavy pocket flashlight in shape, complete with clip, the new dosimeter was a miniature ionization chamber charged with 170 volts. It had a calibrated scale that could be observed through the top of the dosimeter itself, as though through a small telescope. Inside the dosimeter's chamber was a platinum-covered quartz fiber that was the needle to the scale. As radiation changed the ionization in the hermetically sealed tube, the position of the needle allowed individuals to keep track of levels of exposure. Over the years Arnold Beckman made thousands of dosimeters.

Of all his instruments the dosimeter was a personal favorite: "It's such a complete neat little instrument, just a vibrating quartz fiber." The dosimeter worked well, though it was very fragile, especially in shipping. Beckman jokes that the first profits came from insurance claims. While the neat design of the dosimeter—and its value to the workers it protected—satisfied Beckman, nostalgia must have increased his partiality for the instrument. His first publication, as a graduate student at Caltech, was on a pressure gauge based on the vibration of a small quartz fiber. Now, as Dr. Beckman, he saw his student experience at the laboratory bench paying off with a tangible application in the world of action.

Beckman manufactured these dosimeters at yet another company he established during the war, Arnold O. Beckman, Inc. That company's original purpose was to handle a secret project that could not fit within NTL, the oxygen meter, discussed later. Besides their secrecy, the oxygen meter and the dosimeter shared a common technology, as they both contained near-invisible quartz fibers as basic components.

Witness to a New Age

Beckman's role in the Manhattan Project eventually earned him a front-row seat at one of the era's eerier spectacles. He was invited by military officials to travel to the deserts of the American Southwest, where he observed one of the first postwar tests of atomic weapons and bore witness to the tremendous powers released by the scientists and engineers he had assisted. Decades later he still has the special protective goggles that shielded his eyes for the awesome sight. I. I. Rabi, a physicist who worked on both radar and the Manhattan Project, witnessed a similar detonation, another of these harbingers of a new age. Rabi later described the scene from the observation trenches—and some of the emotions that accompanied the detonation of the first atomic device outside of Alamogordo, New Mexico, on 16 July 1945:

> We were lying there, very tense, in the early dawn, and there were just a few streaks of gold in the east; you could see your neighbor very dimly. Suddenly, there was an enormous flash of light, the brightest light I have ever seen or that I think anyone has ever seen. It blasted; it pounced; it bored its way right through you. It was a vision that was seen with more than the eye. It was seen to last forever. You would wish it would stop;

Above: "Trinity," the first atomic bomb detonation, at Alamogordo, New Mexico, in July 1945.

Right: The raising of "Jumbo." Los Alamos scientists originally planned to detonate the first atomic bomb within this massive steel jug. If the bomb fizzled, Jumbo would contain the plutonium. In the end, Jumbo was not used. *Both courtesy National Archives.*

altogether it lasted about two seconds. Finally, it was over, diminishing, and we looked toward the place where the bomb had been; there was an enormous ball of fire which grew and grew and it rolled as it grew; it went up into the air, in yellow flashes and into scarlet and green. It looked menacing. It seemed to come toward one.

For Arnold Beckman, witnessing the atomic genie let loose from its bottle was indeed a grave experience, but one that led him to ruminate on the horrors of war in general, rather than the particular horrors unleashed by atomic weapons.

I didn't have any feelings against the A-bomb. That was just the next step. We had gunpowder and then nitroglycerine and TNT, and this was the next stage in the development of more powerful weaponry. I think the people who witnessed it were pleased because most of them had something to do with it, and they felt this was successful. That's the feeling I had. A-bombs are powerful weapons, but I don't have any feeling they are morally improper. I don't know that I'd have any preference on whether I was going to be torn to pieces by shrapnel, by a bomb, or by a nuclear bomb. It's all a horrible business; war is a horrible thing.

Arnold O. Beckman, Inc.

In South Pasadena, Arnold Beckman was never far from Caltech, and if the government turned to him for technical solutions, so too did his old colleagues in Pasadena.

Caltech was also deep in war work. On 3 October 1940 the National Defense Research Committee—the main organization directing American scientific and technical talent to the needs of a nation at war—called an urgent meeting in Washington, D.C. The NDRC saw pressing need for an instrument that could measure the oxygen content in a mixture of gases. The committee wanted first to use the device on gas samples in the laboratory and eventually to adapt it to monitor oxygen levels within the military's deep-diving submarines and high-flying aircraft. Linus Pauling was present at the October meeting, and just a few days later he submitted an initial design to the NDRC. Pauling and Caltech then secured NDRC contracts for the development and the production of what quickly became known as the "Pauling oxygen meter." It was a secret project.

Arnold Beckman learned of the Caltech effort through a request for help. "Holmes Sturdivant, who was an assistant to Linus Pauling, came over one day and wanted to know if I would provide him with a hundred wooden boxes for an oxygen analyzer." Beckman soon became well acquainted with Pauling's design: "It was a very simple instrument; you just had a magnetic field with a field gradient. They put a little glass ball in there, two of them, like a dumbbell . . . suspended on a quartz fiber." Oxygen gas has the peculiar characteristic of being strongly attracted into magnetic fields. The small glass dumbbell delicately suspended within a magnet's field would thus be shifted to and fro by oxygen gas rushing into the field, pushing the glass balls out. Measuring this twisting with a mirror, a small light, and a scale was thus a measure of the proportion of oxygen in gas samples

The Pauling oxygen analyzer, manufactured by Arnold O. Beckman, Inc.
Courtesy Beckman Coulter, Inc.

Arnold O. Beckman, Inc., located four blocks from NTL in South Pasadena in the early 1950s. *Courtesy Beckman Coulter, Inc.*

admitted into the instrument. Pauling's Caltech team planned to make a hundred of these instruments, and Beckman immediately agreed to supply them with housing boxes.

Sturdivant was back a few days later, this time asking Beckman whether his company would be willing to manufacture the instruments in their entirety. The Caltech scientists had discovered that mass-producing a consistently accurate and reliable instrument was very different from designing one demonstration model.

Beckman had learned well the lesson that the new age of analytical instrumentation required complementary dedication to excellence in design and excellence in manufacturing. Beyond new kinds of inventions combining chemistry, electronics, and physics, the growing instrumentation revolution required that these inventions be reproducible, that they be manufactured with the utmost standardization and reliability. By the time of the plea from Pauling's Caltech project, Beckman was justly confident in his firm's skills in instrument manufacture. The oxygen meter would prove invaluable to the war effort and would open up a new realm for his enterprise. In early March 1942 he told Caltech that he was ready to take up production of the Pauling oxygen analyzer in the most serious way.

There were two complications. The first was organizational: Because the project was classified, the production must be secret. Hence all that Beckman could tell his corporate board, as he attempted to convince them of the virtues of the "Caltech project," was that the matter was a war priority and one he thought could be

A magnified image of the delicate glass dumbbells suspended from an almost invisible quartz fiber. The dumbbells composed the heart of the oxygen analyzer. *Courtesy Beckman Coulter, Inc.*

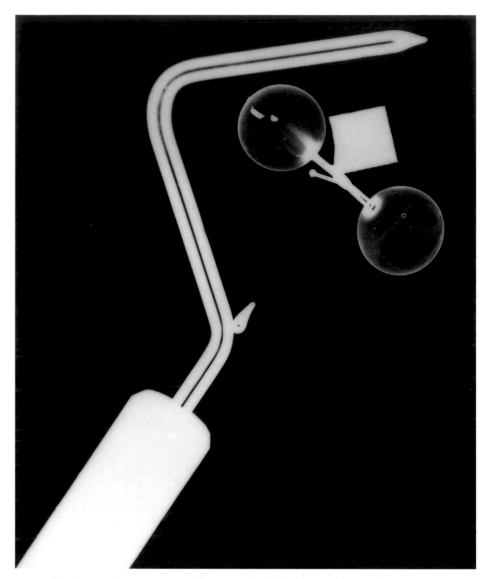

as productive as the pH meter. The second difficulty was that at this very moment he was also coming to NTL's directors with a second classified project, the "Shell Company instrument" (i.e., the IR-1 infrared spectrophotometer). The board, still more attuned to the old "low-technology" world of National Postal Meter, was increasingly bewildered by high-technology projects, wartime secrecy, and Arnold Beckman's breakneck pace. On 18 June 1942 the NTL board decided to proceed with the Shell Company project "but not to go ahead with the Caltech instrument."

Arnold Beckman has always believed that "where there's a will, there's a way." If the directors of NTL would not allow their firm to take on production of the oxygen meter, he would take responsibility for the secret project. At the 2 September board meeting he reported that he had personally provided funds to go ahead with the Caltech instrument and urged NTL to take over the project. The board refused. "I feel some obligation in this thing," Beckman told his board. "If you want to turn it down, may I manufacture them?" The board members could find no further objections and passed a resolution stating: "The Company has no objection to Dr. Beckman's investing his money in any enterprise, so long as he does not use corporation time or facilities."

Thus Arnold O. Beckman formed a new corporate entity to take up the oxygen meter work. Arnold O. Beckman, Inc., was wholly owned by Arnold Beckman, with Mabel Beckman included in the enterprise as one of its legal officers.

Beckman's oxygen analyzer, a modification of the earlier Pauling analyzer, emblazoned with the company logo. The compact size and durable construction of this instrument made it highly portable. *Courtesy Beckman Coulter, Inc.*

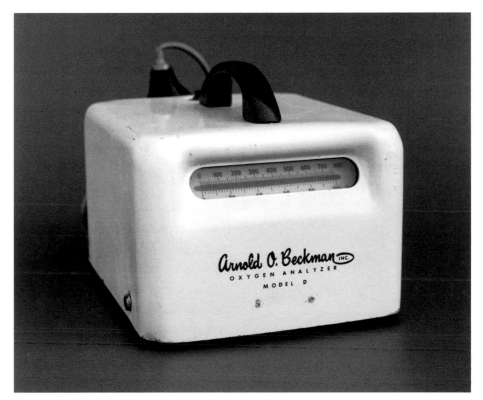

Throughout the war Arnold O. Beckman, Inc., handled projects that Beckman could not fit within NTL, often secret projects like the oxygen meter and the dosimeter. After the war Beckman's handpicked manager, Joseph Lewis, brought Arnold O. Beckman, Inc., into profitability, and the firm produced a whole line of oxygen meters and other devices. Eventually Beckman folded Arnold O. Beckman, Inc., into Beckman Instruments during the 1950s, receiving in payment $1 million.

The oxygen meter carried technical as well as institutional challenges. The miniature glass dumbbells, though beautiful when seen in a display today, proved hideously difficult to make. They had to be precise, and they had to be tiny. The balls of the dumbbells needed to be an eighth of an inch in diameter and joined together in such a way that they were perfectly balanced. To make the dumbbells, a tiny glass tube was heated to close the end, and then a bulb could be formed by a puff of air. The problem arose in regulating this puff of air, which had to be precisely controlled lest the small bulb burst with too much air. Beckman recruited the best glassblower he could find, a Caltech graduate student named Herb Sargents. Sargents could make the pieces, but out of every hundred attempts, he would get only one or two intact bulbs.

The NDRC wanted a hundred instruments, and it needed them quickly. That Sargents was about to finish his Ph.D. and go elsewhere did not add stability to the production planning. In what was becoming his usual modus operandi, Beckman sat down and tackled the problem personally. "I realized what was wrong. We had a mismatch in the capacity of this small bulb and that of [human] lungs. What [was needed] was a blowing machine that had a small bulb or small source of compressed air in which the pressure would drop down automatically. I went down to the shop one weekend and made probably what was the world's smallest glass-blowing machine. It was nothing more than a sliding valve with which you could transfer a small volume over from a tank of oxygen." With this new invention Beckman soon had almost a 100-percent yield of glass bulbs, much more efficient than Sargents's one-percent yield.

There was still one other practical, hands-on complication, not so much a problem as a tricky detail. The dumbbell was suspended from a quartz thread, in thickness about a tenth of a human hair. The thread itself was easy to make. The glassblower heated a quartz rod half a millimeter in diameter and pulled it in half until a piece broke. An ultrafine quartz fiber would be hanging from the broken piece; however, it was thin to the point of being invisible to the naked eye, thus making it very difficult to find. Surrounded by new technology, Beckman solved the invisible fiber problem with a primitive technique, one he had learned at Illinois and taught at Caltech: "You take an ordinary gum label, wet it, and put it where you think the fiber is. If the label stays there, you've found the strand. If it falls to the floor, you try again. Once you've put labels on the two ends, you can work with the quartz fiber under a microscope."

When the oxygen analyzer appeared, it bore the label "Pauling Oxygen Analyzer." Most of the oxygen analyzers that Arnold O. Beckman, Inc., produced during the war were the laboratory instruments designed by Pauling. Beckman and his associates did succeed in designing and producing several other varieties of oxygen analyzers, including recording models and outfits for submarines and aircraft, and after the war Arnold O. Beckman, Inc., developed and produced an expanded range of improved oxygen analyzers for military, industrial, and laboratory markets. By 1955 Beckman Instruments integrated this technology with its infrared analysis and other technologies in the Mark II Atmosphere Analyzer, and these units found extensive service in the nuclear submarine fleet of the U.S. Navy.

Beckman's oxygen analyzer also took an interesting turn away from military uses after the war—an early foray of a Beckman instrument into the world of clinical medicine, which would ultimately become the major market for the firm. The analyzer made this debut when an anesthesiologist at Huntington Memorial Hospital in Pasadena borrowed a protoype from its inventor. The anesthesiologist's granddaughter had been born prematurely, and although from the early 1940s on well-equipped and modern hospitals routinely put premature babies in oxygenated incubators to combat the "blue baby" condition, the baby was still not faring well. Concerned, the anesthesiologist measured the oxygen levels in the incubator and found them very low. Knowing this, he built a makeshift incubator out of a cardboard box and a pillow and fed oxygen into it, carefully monitoring levels with the oxygen analyzer. The infant survived, and the anesthesiologist earnestly tried to convince his hospital to invest in one of Beckman's oxygen analyzers. At two hundred dollars, though, the hospital refused to buy one, as it was considered too expensive.

Hospitals changed their tune in the mid-1950s, however. Inexplicably, a significant number of oxygen-tented premature babies went blind; doctors were baffled.

The Beckman oxygen analyzer, being used to monitor oxygen levels in an incubator for premature infants. *Courtesy Beckman Coulter, Inc.*

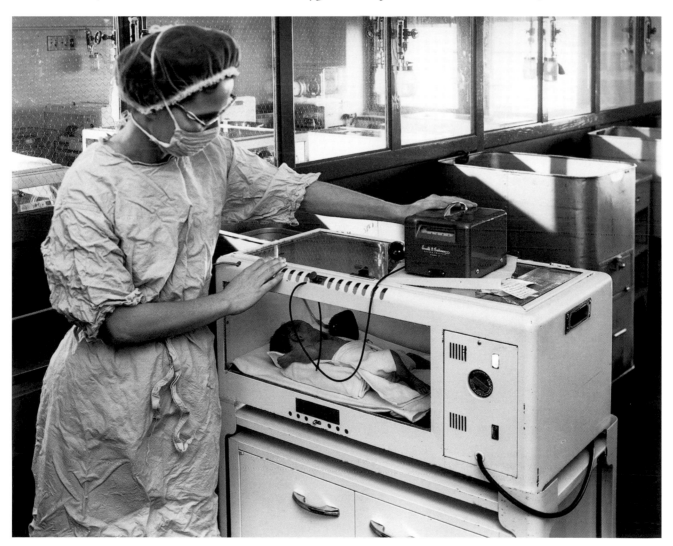

Retrolental fibroplasia, the name given to the condition, indicated a fibrous growth at the back of the lens that caused blindness. In the early 1950s the connection between oxygen levels and retrolental fibroplasia was finally elucidated. Ironically, the pure oxygen needed to keep babies alive also caused retinal tissue to wither when too much was administered.

The explanation of retrolental fibroplasia—and especially an article on its cause and the means of prevention published in the *Saturday Evening Post* in June 1955—brought an almost instant flood of requests for Beckman's oxygen analyzer from hospitals around the country. "Estimating the concentration [of oxygen] on the basis of the flow per minute from the oxygen tank has been found to be grossly unreliable. Recommended instead are oxygen meters which give an accurate and instantaneous reading of the actual concentration in the incubator," the *Saturday Evening Post* article noted. Designed to measure oxygen levels in the hermetically sealed environment of a submarine, the analyzer worked equally well in the smaller, but likewise sealed-off, incubators. Doctors at Johns Hopkins used the precise calibrations of the Beckman instrument to recommend healthy oxygen levels in incubators, thus guaranteeing a safe environment. "Not surprisingly, sales of our oxygen analyzer spurted. Our greatest reward, however, was not the modest profit from sales, but the realization that this instrument helped preserve eyesight for thousands who might otherwise be blind." Although Beckman's company did not seriously enter the world of clinical and biomedical instruments for another decade, this early application of an instrument to improving human health foreshadows that entry.

A Harvest Born of Sorrows and Sweat

Certainly neither Arnold Beckman nor anyone associated with him would ever have wished upon the world the horrors and sorrows of World War II. Nevertheless, while the war years brought many personal tragedies to the lives of the men and women who worked alongside him, these were years of remarkable growth for his enterprise. It was a time of feverish invention, of a technological harvest of powerful new instruments and tools quickly brought to secret and open markets, and of the transformation of Beckman's role from supplier of first-rate pH meters to director of a large and diverse technological enterprise, comprising three separate corporations by war's end.

The pH meter and the DU grew from rational development of market opportunities. But infrared spectrophotometers, Helipots, oxygen meters, and dosimeters emerged at forced speed, rushed ahead to meet the needs of war. The cumulative effect of all these developments was to consolidate the instrumentation revolution that Arnold Beckman had initiated with the pH meter. Assumptions changed during the war. Scientists in academia and even in industry might still build one-of-a-kind instruments to run an experiment, but thanks principally to

A group of civilian air raid wardens. *Courtesy National Archives.*

electronics, they began looking to the instrumentation industry to provide ready-made products in which they could insert the sample and read out the results. Science, skillful technique, and precise analysis were all built into the box, leaving the scientist to focus on discoveries rather than tinker with wires and meters. Wartime projects showed the power and potential of this instrumentation revolution, and the whole nation began to see science in a new light. Precision research was the basis of better lives and new industries.

The Beckmans had spent the war in their house on Crescent Drive, with its clear view of the Pacific Ocean. The glory of California in peacetime, the coast was a strategic weakness in war, a likely point of attack from the Far East. Like many other Californians, Arnold Beckman joined a local civil defense organization. As an air raid warden in Altadena, he was issued a helmet and billy club. During the occasional blackout his duty was to go outside and stand guard. He later made light of the task, saying his job was to "sound the alarm, I guess, if we saw any aliens."

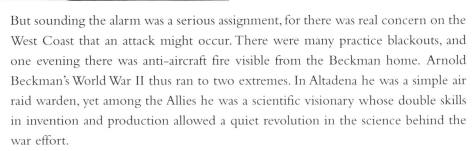

Clockwise: Arnold and Mabel Beckman in the 1940s; the Beckmans' home in Altadena; Arnie Beckman enjoying a company gathering in the early 1940s; Patty Beckman practicing her roller-skating in the early 1940s.
All courtesy Beckman family.

But sounding the alarm was a serious assignment, for there was real concern on the West Coast that an attack might occur. There were many practice blackouts, and one evening there was anti-aircraft fire visible from the Beckman home. Arnold Beckman's World War II thus ran to two extremes. In Altadena he was a simple air raid warden, yet among the Allies he was a scientific visionary whose double skills in invention and production allowed a quiet revolution in the science behind the war effort.

Coming home to peacetime is always a challenge, as soldiers adapt their military skills to civilian use. In 1945 Arnold Beckman was ready and eager to find new uses for the skills he had refined in the crucible of war and forced innovation.

A call to arms for Arnold Beckman and his companies. *Courtesy National Archives.*

it was remarkable that Beckman was able to surround himself with so many long-term and loyal colleagues. But he also experienced firsthand a drawback of being at the helm of a dynamic firm at the forefront of so many emerging technologies: Many of your best people left. Like it or not, some of your most highly capable associates wanted to begin their own enterprises, often in direct competition. Your firm would inevitably produce "spin-off" companies, perhaps to the detriment of the parent but to the great expansion of the industry as a whole.

In the postwar years Beckman lost two of his most important employees and colleagues in succession. The first to leave was Howard Cary, his director of research and development. Cary had been tremendously important for the design and the production of Beckman's spectrophotometers, both ultraviolet and infrared, and he left to start his own firm in the spectrophotometer business in 1946. The end of this close personal and professional collaboration was fraught with tension, heightened by the fact that the two would soon be tough competitors in an important field. Both men, perhaps unavoidably, emerged from their collaboration with feelings of having been wronged. Cary's spin-off firm, Applied Physics Corporation (later named Cary Instruments when it became a part of Varian), did expand the instrumentation industry, producing a number of notably successful spectrophotometers. A reconciliation took place in 1958, when the American Chemical Society selected Cary to win the award in chemical instrumentation that Beckman had established and that was named after him.

Roland Hawes, Cary's successor as leader in research and development, also left Beckman Instruments to form his own company. Beckman reacted to Hawes's departure much as he had to Cary's. He felt that the bounds of loyalty had been crossed. By 1951 Hawes had abandoned his own venture and joined Cary's Applied Physics Corporation, where he would stay for the next twenty years. While these were early and dramatic departures, they were certainly not the last that Beckman had to face. Through the mid-1950s a healthy portion of his senior staff left to create new companies. One reason, no doubt, was Beckman's own frugal approach to compensation: The main reward, he felt, was in the intellectual challenge of the job.

While these spin-offs caused Dr. Beckman consternation, they were signs of health in the industry he had done so much to develop and to promote. In a way they were the unavoidable consequences of success. Such "employment migration," to use a much later turn of phrase, was an outlier in the general culture of American industry, but it became a signature feature of the new business culture emerging around electronic technologies. Owing in no small part to Arnold Beckman, the American instrumentation industry was an integral part of those electronic technologies, an economic sector that was already on its way to defining the second half of the twentieth century. Beckman's firm was ahead of the curve in experiencing the phenomena of spin-off, job-hopping, and entrepreneurialism that are central to the most important new industries of today.

A Beckman Instruments trade show display from the 1950s. *Courtesy Beckman Coulter, Inc.*

Dr. Beckman, breaking ground for Beckman Instruments' Mountain Side facility in New Jersey, 1952. The company had become truly national. *Courtesy Beckman Coulter, Inc.*

Devotions, Public and Private

Beckman Instruments continued to grow apace through the 1950s because of the devotion of many people who came to work at the firm's offices, laboratory spaces, and shop floors in South Pasadena day in and day out. Arnold Beckman himself exemplified the kind of devotion that he expected his colleagues to aim for. He worked long hours in his office and his home, helping to give to his enterprise the intelligence, creativity, energy, and enthusiasm that he was sure were the keys to its advance. His days were filled with asking questions, struggling for answers, and envisioning new directions—days of interactions with colleagues in research, development, and finance; with operators and assemblers on his plant floor;

and—stretching well beyond the plant itself—with hosts of scientists and engineers in universities, industries, and government and even in rival instrumentation firms.

Each year Beckman became a more visible public figure, but when he left his office to return home, he returned to a private space that was relatively untouched by the waves of change sweeping over his career. Arnold, Mabel, Pat, and Arnold S. continued to live in the Altadena house the couple had built in the early 1930s. As the corporation grew, the Beckman residence came to be more and more a domain—a focus point for an active family—that depended for its very existence on the work and will of Mabel Beckman. Perhaps because of her husband's devotion to his work, his schedule filled with long hours and frequent trips, and the increasing number of her husband's business colleagues, Mabel deliberately made her house into a refuge, a place apart from Beckman Instruments, a center devoted almost exclusively to the family.

Pat Beckman has vivid memories from these years of just how busy her father was—of how often his commitment to building Beckman Instruments required

Left: The Beckman family in the late 1940s. *Courtesy Beckman family.*

Right: Dr. Beckman works the phone in a 1956 telethon. By the mid-1950s he was an active and visible member of the Southern California community.
Courtesy Beckman Coulter, Inc.

him to travel. She recalls that she, her brother, and her mother "did a lot of back and forth to the Burbank Airport when I was a child—a lot of picking Dad up from the airport and taking him back."

Both Pat and Arnold S. remember the grueling daily schedule that their father set for himself between these frequent travels. Arnold Beckman left the house in Altadena early in the morning, returning home in the evening. After a few quick greetings to his family he retired to his study for an hour or so, continuing to work on the projects that he had started at his office. He would emerge from his study promptly for dinner, however. This was a time when the entire family was together at the table, catching up with one another on the day's events and upcoming plans, as well as enjoying the fruits of Mabel Beckman's culinary labors. It was a daily time for Arnold to fill Mabel in on the events and activities of his day: speeches he had given to employees, visitors he had seen and the purposes of their meetings, and looming challenges and opportunities.

Mabel had abiding interests in the science of nutrition and in the art of cooking, interests that she combined in the meals she prepared for her family and in a daily question that became almost a family joke. At every family dinner Mabel asked her husband what he had had for lunch that day—the only meal whose nutritional value she could not be certain of. Arnold would also ask questions at the table, often lightly teasing his children with impossible queries like, "What did you do for the world today?" He also enjoyed posing mathematical word problems. After this time together he would frequently turn his chair sideways to the table and read the newspaper before returning to his study for several more hours of work.

Even as Mabel made her home a center for her family, Beckman Instruments became a constant presence in the lives of everyone in the Beckman household. Mabel played a special role. It is a constant refrain among the Beckmans' friends and associates that she was Arnold's most trusted confidante, the person with whom he could—and did—discuss everything. Thus Beckman's devotion to his firm brought him and Mabel closer together, even as it separated them in time and in place. They developed an intimacy that neither shared with anyone else, in part because Arnold trusted Mabel with his innermost thoughts about the work that so consumed him. As Arnold S. Beckman remembers of his mother, "She really supported Dad." Pat Beckman shares this memory: "She was very supportive of Dad on anything and everything he did. She was his champion, and she believed in Arnold Beckman."

Despite her wholehearted support of her husband and her commitment to his work, Mabel Beckman had quite a mind of her own. She was content to have her husband's devotion to his work structure most parts of their shared life together. She did not object when she and the children often had to wait for him outside the plant, while he completed a project and the children ran around talking with the employees, whom they had come to know well. She understood when the family had to stop by the plant before leaving on a family trip or a Saturday's excursion together. But she did insist that she take the children to Sunday school and that the family spend Sundays together. Although Arnold Beckman's mother had been a devout Methodist, her son did not follow her in this path but looked to the intellectual challenge of scientific thought to enrich his life. Throughout his adult life his personal attitude toward organized religion has been ambivalent: He realizes the great benefits it has given to society but also sees all-too-frequent excesses. Mabel Beckman, however, was a devout Episcopalian, and despite her husband's reservations, she and her children attended church each Sunday. Further she insisted that the family carry on the practice her own mother had overseen, of eating

Mabel and Arnold Beckman, 1955. *Courtesy Beckman family.*

a large Sunday meal at midday, relaxing together in a common room, listening to radio shows, reading, talking, and going out for family excursions.

While others might be awed by his accomplishments, to his children Arnold Beckman was an ordinary, even-tempered, scrupulously honest, albeit extraordinarily busy father. He helped them with their homework, even if the children had to schedule the help in advance. Indeed, Beckman was sometimes a little overzealous. He did not just help; he did their homework for them, as their teachers occasionally suspected.

When the children were small, Beckman told them bedtime stories that he made up on the spot. With Horatio Alger and *Peck's Bad Boy* never far from his mind, he wove morality plays starring two fishlike creatures, Peewee and Goggle-eye. Childlike Peewee drew himself and the more parental Goggle-eye into misadventure and trouble. But the pair would always escape from trouble in the end, and the resolution of their difficulties would close with a lesson near to Beckman's heart, a moral about integrity or honesty.

Beckman seemed constantly busy with the company, yet he still found days for family outings. Camping trips were a perennial favorite, the family Ford loaded with tents, supplies, children, and pets. Pat Beckman remembers long hikes with her father on these trips and his indulging in his passion for photography, taking snapshot after snapshot. Arnold S. Beckman fondly recalls times at home with his father, in his father's wood- and metalworking shop, learning to master lathes and other machines. In this, Arnold O. Beckman was doing for his son what his own father had done for him—giving him the space, tools, lessons, and encouragement to build creative manual skills. He also facilitated the younger Arnold's interest in the power of chemistry, on occasion bringing home chemicals his son had requested. Arnold S. remembers his father's remarkably nonjudgmental temperament, even when he used the supplies for making rockets or explosives.

In the 1950s sailing was a growing interest for the Beckmans. The Newport Harbor Yacht Club became a common destination for the family—the point of embarkation for daylong sailing trips aboard a thirty-seven-foot sloop, the *Lady Pat*, co-owned with Gray Phelps, a lawyer and former fraternity brother from the University of Illinois. In the late 1950s Beckman commissioned the family's very own forty-one-foot fiberglass sloop, *Aries*, named for his birth sign. Phelps then helped Arnold and his children sail the *Aries* from the Sausalito boatyard down to Newport Beach, its new home. As the passion for the water grew, camping trips gave way to sailing and a vacation house on Lido Isle, but these were still family outings focused on the outdoors. The family cars evolved to Mercurys, then to Lincolns—always with the Ford Motor Company, like Beckman's very first car. Despite his expanding resources and diminishing free time, Beckman still found time to drive all the way from Detroit each time he bought a new car, avoiding the dealership by buying directly off of the factory production line.

Arnold, Mabel, and Pat aboard the *Lady Pat*, an R-class racer.

Courtesy Beckman family.

While Dr. Beckman enjoyed the personal financial success that attended the blossoming of his firm, more income was never his ultimate goal nor his immediate care. As ever, his true passion was the excitement of the invention, design, and manufacture of the instruments he was producing. Financial success brought no dramatic changes to new heights of luxury. Rather a simplicity and practicality of manner continued to mark him, announcing him as a Midwesterner and a survivor of the Great Depression.

Paths of Technologies

In the decade from 1945 to 1955 Arnold Beckman and his firms developed a profusion of new instruments and accessories. Beckman himself saw them all as pursuing logical paths from the initial pH meter. While that expresses one truth, another is that as Beckman Instruments—and Helipot and Arnold O. Beckman, both of which he still owned personally—originated new product lines, they grew in four directions.

First, there was the continuous drive for the high-end instrument of new sensitivity that opened research frontiers. These were the instruments associated with the term *cutting edge*, a phrase actually coined in 1951 to describe just such products as Beckman produced—and the research done with them. The cutting

edge—a new frontier of scientific discovery moving ever forward to new levels of understanding—was the place Beckman sought to be throughout his lifetime. Being there was the focus of his business. Later it would become the focus of his philanthropy. Through both, he has sought instruments, techniques, and research that offer significant advances on the known.

The second theme in the business was the simplification of earlier, more delicate instruments into versions that were more portable, more durable, or cheaper. This second theme surely grew from wartime observation of how his products were employed, as one use led to demand for another. That was a pattern to be nurtured, not just observed, and both the corporation and science labs at many levels profited. Simpler versions sold well.

One postwar example of simplification is the ultraviolet spectrophotometer. Throughout the 1940s and 1950s Beckman's Model DU built a reputation and sales that would be difficult to overstate. Quite simply, the DU was an indispensable tool for chemistry. The options it opened became a symbol of the new promise of chemistry at mid-century. Now, after the war, Beckman resolved to bring the kind of knowledge afforded by the DU to a much wider audience by producing a lower-cost ultraviolet spectrophotometer, less sophisticated and less sensitive than the DU. This second instrument would still offer fast and simple analyses. In 1949 Beckman's engineers succeeded in bringing the Model B ultraviolet spectrophotometer to market. The Model B was a spectacular success in industry and medicine, and it enjoyed brisk sales across the next quarter century.

For the ultraviolet, the Model B represented the move from remarkable sophistication to remarkable accessibility. The course of the firm's infrared work was more difficult. Beckman had virtually invented the ultraviolet field, but there were competitors in infrared from the first, among them the commercial infrared spectrometer designed by Bowling Barnes that Perkin-Elmer introduced shortly after the war. Only in the 1950s did Beckman develop a series of successful IR models for the experienced, skilled researcher; these established the Beckman name and sold well into the next decade. Once the firm captured a hold on the cutting-edge market, Beckman could apply the simplification strategy to infrared as well. He decided to have infrared spectros aimed at industry rather than the research laboratory in 1955, but rather than develop the infrared equivalent of the ultraviolet

Beckman's sales engineers at the Liston-Becker company, which Beckman Instruments acquired in 1955. *Courtesy Beckman Coulter, Inc.*

Model B, he followed yet another strategy. As a well-regarded public company (in 1955 its sales would reach $21.4 million and its profits, $1.4 million), Beckman Instruments could buy the technology housed in other, smaller, innovative companies instead of inventing it. The Model B had been an in-house project; the new infrared technology would be a corporate acquisition for the Beckman name, thereby introducing the third theme in Beckman's growth: acquisitions.

The most obvious choice when buying technology was to purchase licenses for patents held by other firms. Dr. Beckman preferred the bolder course of finding new technology by acquiring outside firms in their entirety. This means of propelling the growth of Beckman Instruments went well with his conviction that skilled, creative, intelligent people are a corporation's greatest asset, holding the key to still further technological breakthroughs.

Beckman Instruments turned to the Liston-Becker Instrument Company and acquired it in June 1955. Max Liston had founded Liston-Becker in 1950 to manufacture a line of infrared gas analyzers that proved highly popular for industrial applications. Liston, who had a hand in creating Perkin-Elmer's first industrial infrared spectrophotometer, was now an established designer of scientific instruments. His analyzers worked on the same basic scientific principles as Beckman's infrared spectros but were simpler, designed to measure concentrations of specific gases of commercial significance, like carbon dioxide.

With the purchase of Liston-Becker, Arnold Beckman was not only acquiring a leading line of analytical infrared instruments for the industrial, military, laboratory, and medical markets, he was also bringing the skills and talents of Max Liston into his company. Liston worked as a director of research at Beckman Instruments until his retirement in 1965. More than a simple expansion of products, purchases were a means for expanding Beckman Instruments' roster of creative, able researchers—the talent behind the products.

The military market was important for the fourth area of the firm's growth: electronic components. Beckman surveyed his firm's involvement in electronics in a 1976 talk before the Newcomen Society. He noted that at first blush electronics manufacturing seems "a far cry from a pH meter, yet along the way each step was a logical extension of something we were already doing. As someone said about sin, 'One thing leads to another!'" The pH meter led to the Helipot, and as demand increased, his designers at the Helipot Corporation produced an ever-widening variety of Helipots. With this diversification Beckman entered the business of electronics components proper. Just as he had invented the helical potentiometer itself, so he would encourage his colleagues to invent new means for the manufacture of these important devices, such as high-speed continuous winders for spinning the coils of wire at the heart of the Helipot.

By the mid-1950s Beckman potentiometers enjoyed a wide range of application as controls and sensors. Used in one way, as a volume control, for example, the

Breaking ground at the Newport Beach facilities of the Helipot Corporation, 6 March 1956. Donald Duncan, the head of Helipot, stands with his foot on the shovel, Beckman is on the tractor, and the mayor of Newport Beach, Dora Hill, stands to the right. *Courtesy Beckman Coulter, Inc.*

Arnold Beckman's acquisition of new technologies through purchase of outside firms in their entirety is nicely illustrated by his purchase of the Berkeley Scientific Corporation.

In September 1945 W. K. Rosenberry started Berkeley Scientific in a modest basement in Berkeley, California. Rosenberry's shop developed and manufactured highly advanced, precision "counters." These were high-technology instruments for recording with exactitude numbers of "events" as they occurred over time—events like each turn of a high-speed winding machine, the passage of an object past a detector, or the incidence of a radioactive particle upon a sensor. Some Berkeley Scientific counters were designed to record as few as six thousand "events" per minute. Others could keep track of thirty thousand, even a hundred thousand, events per second.

Moreover, some of the firm's most advanced counters could perform these extraordinarily rapid counts while they tracked the passage of time, giving the researcher exact counts per second or minute. These devices were known as EPUTs, instruments for measuring "events per unit time." Berkeley Scientific enjoyed a brisk demand for its counting machines, and by 1950 had built its own factory in Richmond, California.

Another product line spurred the growth of Berkeley

A radiation counter manufactured by the Berkeley Division of Beckman Instruments. *Courtesy Beckman Coulter, Inc.*

Scientific: Geiger counters that incorporated the firm's sophisticated equipment. Geiger counters measure radiation levels, and Berkeley Scientific's provided very accurate and sensitive readings for applications ranging from nuclear science to medicine. One instrument was even designed to check for radiation contamination on the human body, with a cavity in which one could insert hands and feet. In the atomic age such instruments were in great demand.

Arnold Beckman decided to acquire Berkeley Scientific in the middle of 1952. He struck a favorable deal with Rosenberry (who stayed on for a time as manager of the Richmond operation), with a purchase price around the $1 million mark. This was not an unreasonable figure, given that Berkeley Scientific recorded $825,000 in sales during 1951. With this acquisition Beckman put Beckman Instruments at the forefront of the Geiger counter business and brought EPUT technology into the firm to be integrated in new development projects. With the dosimeter and the micro-microammeter, the Geiger counters helped position Beckman Instruments to meet technological needs in the atomic age. ❧

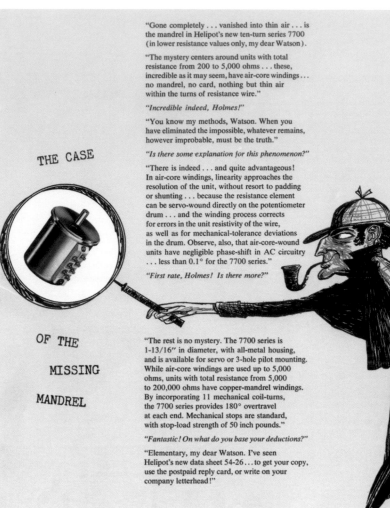

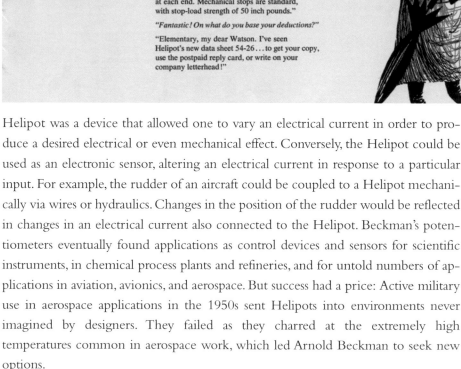

Two advertisements put out by the Helipot Division of Beckman Instruments in the late 1950s. *Chemical Heritage Foundation.*

Helipot was a device that allowed one to vary an electrical current in order to produce a desired electrical or even mechanical effect. Conversely, the Helipot could be used as an electronic sensor, altering an electrical current in response to a particular input. For example, the rudder of an aircraft could be coupled to a Helipot mechanically via wires or hydraulics. Changes in the position of the rudder would be reflected in changes in an electrical current also connected to the Helipot. Beckman's potentiometers eventually found applications as control devices and sensors for scientific instruments, in chemical process plants and refineries, and for untold numbers of applications in aviation, avionics, and aerospace. But success had a price: Active military use in aerospace applications in the 1950s sent Helipots into environments never imagined by designers. They failed as they charred at the extremely high temperatures common in aerospace work, which led Arnold Beckman to seek new options.

Failures were not so much faults as indicators for Beckman. First, occasional failures showed that engineers were pushing research to the very limits of human and technological capabilities, at the frontier of the "cutting edge" the period was learning to discuss. A certain amount of well-intentioned failure was a sign of health in his research-and-development staffs. They were trying new things—not all would work. Second, he welcomed failures of his technology as signal flares—blazing markers hard to ignore. Long ago the technological failure of Glen Joseph's pH apparatus was the signal of opportunity for the acidimeter and pH meter in turn. Failure of the Helipot now pointed to a new option, a version designed for very high temperatures.

Beckman directed the staff of the Helipot Corporation to explore high-temperature options, using newer noncombustible materials. The Heliport researchers soon began to focus on ceramics, long known for their tremendous ability to withstand heat in glass and pottery manufacture. New ceramic-metal compounds, known by the contraction *cermets*, had just the properties that the Helipot researchers were looking for—the electrically conductive properties of a metal combined with the heat resistance and versatility of a ceramic. By 1956 Beckman's teams had developed a specially formulated cermet to replace the coil of metal wire within the Helipot. Potentiometers made with these new winding pieces of cermet answered the demands of high-temperature applications and opened up a whole new field—and a whole new range of technical products—in electronic components.

In 1958 the Helipot Corporation was reincorporated into Beckman Instruments proper and renamed the Helipot (or the Components) Division. The division started to use new, versatile cermet processes to create an expanding array of electronic parts: cermet-trimming potentiometers (small devices used as "presets" to control the properties of electrical circuits now ubiquitous in all manner of

Management at the Helipot Division of Beckman Instruments. Arnold Beckman is at the center. *Courtesy Beckman Coulter, Inc.*

electronic devices), capacitors, and resistors. The wonder of the new material went beyond its heat tolerance, for cermet components could be manufactured in ways more akin to silk screening than to welding. This made them easy to produce in volume, in mass batches. Cermet components gave Beckman Instruments an edge in the marketplace, speeding the company's expansion beyond the borders of the United States. That same year, 1958, Beckman traveled to Scotland to attend the opening ceremonies for a new Beckman Instruments plant dedicated to electronic components. Over the next decades cermets would become more and more common, hidden within the interior of the countless electronic devices on which society has come to depend.

Beckman was in many respects a restless, demanding director. He was not simply content that Helipot develop cermet processes and products. It was not enough to provide a few classes of highly desired electronic components. Beckman next wanted to explore and exploit the possibilities for parts, attachments, and accessories—as he had done first with the pH meter, then with the DU. Eventu-

Some Beckman electronic components available in the 1950s. *Courtesy Beckman Coulter, Inc.*

ally the Helipot, or Components, Division of Beckman Instruments would produce turns-counting dials, servomotors, precision gears, magnetic clutches, and voltmeters, among other things. The lesson that the pH meter was valued for its parts as well as its whole was never forgotten.

This profusion of electronic and related products explains why Arnold Beckman was frequently referred to as an "electronics executive" or an "electronic manufacturer" in newspaper accounts of his company's growth in the middle to late 1950s. While the manufacture of electronic components (including, eventually, microcircuits) remained a part of Beckman's corporation through the early 1980s, it receded in the firm's overall profile as medical research and clinical instrumentation became its most visible products in the late 1970s. But in the heady days of the first explosive development of electronics in the 1950s and 1960s, it looked to observers—both within Beckman Instruments and without—that electronic components and devices held great promise as the defining business for his firm's future.

Strategies for a Technology Company

The war years had taught Beckman the importance of planning for the unpredictable. In the late 1940s and early 1950s he found how to take complete command and expand both the electronic and the instrument motifs of his enterprises. His overall aim was to position his companies on the technological ground floor of the unpredictable "next big thing." His technique was to move his firms into a broad array of cognate scientific fields and technological businesses. While Arnold Beckman relied on the production of bread-and-butter instruments like pH meters, spectrophotometers, and electronic devices from counters to Helipots, he also initiated a broad range of research-and-development activity. In so doing he transformed Beckman Instruments and its outliers into a true technology company, a firm with the competence to solve technical problems in general, but one that still emphasized electronics, chemistry, and instrumentation in particular.

Government work fit in this strategic mix, for it was one activity that kept a corporation at the cutting edge. Despite limited production runs, high unit costs, and very particular specifications, government contracts kept a firm well ahead of the curve in technological development. Military contracts called for the newest of technologies in the face of national security concerns, and Beckman knew that by continuing such specialized work, his firms would gain expertise in a broad range of the latest technologies, allowing them to craft the finest of instruments and then in turn to develop simpler products to serve the civilian market of scientists and engineers when the time was right.

In keeping with this broad strategy, and at a time when plans for a public stock offering by Beckman Instruments offered a future of growth through both internal R&D and external acquisitions, Beckman set up "Special Projects," a permanent organization within the firm to handle high-technology government contracts.

Special Projects as a group reported to the corporation's new vice president, Jack Bishop. Bishop joined the firm in 1951, coming with a background in engineering and an M.B.A. from the Harvard Business School. His arrival reflected Dr. Beckman's determination to build a true technology company and to push for still more rapid growth in the firm he now controlled. In short order Bishop was responsible for managing half of Beckman Instruments, including Special Projects and the firm's flagship analytical instrumentation. In keeping with the dynamism of Beckman's main company and its activities, Bishop was only twenty-nine years old in 1951.

The first of Bishop's special projects was the design and production of mass spectrometers for the Atomic Energy Commission (AEC). Mass spectrometers are dazzling analytical tools for understanding the chemical realm. Where spectrophotometers dispersed light across a spectrum in order to identify clues to chemical compositions and structures, mass spectrometers dispersed matter itself across a spectrum in order to identify these very same clues. In mass spectrometers a sample of material is ionized (broken apart into electrically charged fragments, or ions), and the ionized matter is "flown" through a complex arrangement of electrical and magnetic fields. The result is a dispersion of material, a very precise separation of the ionized components according to their weight and charge—in other words a spectrum based on mass rather than color. Read by an electronic detector, mass spectra reveal characteristic "peaks" indicating the presence and abundance of elements and compounds. Mass spectrometers were new and promising instruments for a variety of fields, including the nuclear chemistry at the heart of both peaceful and military uses of atomic power.

Mass spectrometers played an important part in the Manhattan Project, both in the production of radioactive material for atomic weapons and in a wide array of investigations that lay behind that effort. Other manufacturers were already producing commercial machines for the small market that existed in the early 1950s, but as the government planned a wide expansion of its atomic program in the early days of the Cold War, it wanted mass spectrometers of its very own, built to its own specifications and performance requirements.

Government specifications for mass spectrometers after the war were similar in one way to those for infrared spectrometers during the war: standard instruments of the highest quality, manufactured to a rigorous standard of excellence. Since Beckman had done well during the war, he knew he had a good chance to persuade the AEC to turn to him for the new order of mass spectrometers. Beckman and Bishop guided Special Projects to success on the mass spectrometers, and by 1953 Beckman Instruments was installing instruments of its own design and manufacture in the nation's most important nuclear sites, most notably the massive complex in Oak Ridge, Tennessee, dedicated to the production of weapons-grade uranium and plutonium.

Arnold Beckman and Beckman Instruments executives Taylor Fletcher, kneeling, and Jack Bishop inspect a Beckman mass spectrometer manufactured for the Oak Ridge nuclear facility in 1953.
Courtesy Beckman Coulter, Inc.

Through the AEC mass spectrometers, Beckman Instruments developed considerable in-house expertise applicable to other projects. The firm did not launch its own commercial line of mass spectrometers, since Beckman and Bishop believed that other manufacturers were better positioned to maintain their leadership in the business. Yet in the mid-1950s Beckman Instruments had translated mass spectrometer technology into two related applications for industrial use. The leak detector used a sensitive mass spectrometer to detect even the most minute of leakage points in everything from steel drums, television picture tubes, or vacuum tubes to large-scale vacuum or high-pressure systems like those in chemical plants. Amazingly sensitive, it was able to detect "a leak so small it would require 300,000 years for a quart of helium to escape through it" in the words of one company bulletin. The gas analyzer similarly used a mass spectrometer to detect small concentrations of up to six gases in a sample of material. It was designed for routine but highly precise analysis and was used for applications like "monitoring refinery gas streams, on-the-spot analysis of drilling mud gas, control of air reduction products, and analysis of stack and exhaust gases in air pollution studies." Here once more was the strategy of transforming cutting-edge work into extremely precise industrial tools.

Fast Cars and Clear Skies

As Beckman entered his fifties, his activities often seemed to reflect the character of a man who left little room for anything but serious thinking, difficult decision making, responsibility, and industriousness. But there was more. He was a man with a sense of humor about the world and himself. He had had a playful streak since his youth, even a touch of the thrill seeker. As a child he had earned a spanking for venturing on a train bridge as a locomotive passed by only feet from his small frame. As a youth he had taken off on formative trampings out West. As an adult in California he had even conducted a surreptitious climb to the top of the San Francisco–Oakland Bay Bridge to take photographs of a view as breathtaking as the ascent was dangerous. As a mature adult, sailing held many opportunities for thrills and braving the unexpected. But beyond all of these adventures, he indulged his playful streak most in a single, daily activity. Dr. Beckman drove his car at the speed of a bat out of hell.

In the 1940s and 1950s Beckman's propensity for remarkably fast driving was happily congruent with the demands and pressures of his work life. He could excuse his driving "style" through the demands of his enterprise. He needed to be many places at many times, and his schedule simply would not work with lengthy transit times. He relished pushing himself and his machines to the limit, just shy of danger or recklessness. Indeed, he would often quip that safety considerations necessitated fast driving. Once, when kidded about the number of his accumulated speeding tickets, he rejoined: "Well, you see, I had to do that in self-protection. I wanted to cut down my chance of being involved with an accident. If you go faster than the rest, you'll probably never get hit from the rear. So you cut it down, probably by a factor of two."

On occasion he would make such high-speed trips a group activity for his family. His children remember times when they and their mother would wait restlessly in the car while he would get ready, with only a few minutes left before they were due elsewhere. Then their father would suddenly emerge from the house to join them. The children would be assigned to look out vigilantly for the "cops" while he shot through traffic, smoothly, calmly, and—as he explained to his son—always thinking many cars and great distances ahead. Arriving at their destination with moments to spare, he would tease Mabel and the children about their apparent lack of faith.

In a broader frame, Beckman's driving style adapted to the changing driving conditions in his region. Between 1940 and 1950 California's population rose from

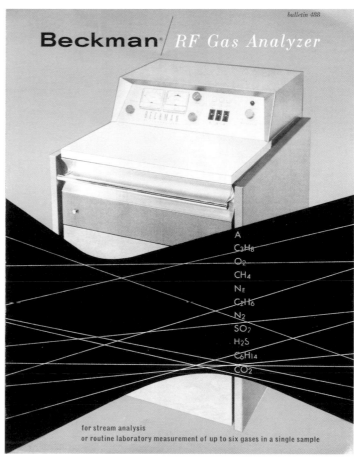

Left: An avid amateur photographer his whole life, Arnold Beckman is captured on film as he takes a photograph. *Courtesy Beckman family.*

Right: The Beckman RF gas analyzer, which used a mass spectrometer.

Courtesy Beckman Coulter, Inc.

7 million to 11 million, while the number of registered motor vehicles skyrocketed from 2.8 million to 4.5 million. These numbers quantify what everyone in Southern California experienced ahead of the rest of the nation—urban sprawl made possible by the automobile.

The human flood that descended on the area was driven by booming local industries, like aviation, refining, chemical production, shipbuilding, and heavy manufacturing, all tied inextricably to the war effort. The influx that the pressures of war had driven earlier was now propelled by the lure of Southern California itself. As the longtime editor of *The Nation* Carey McWilliams put it: "The climate of Southern California is palpable; a commodity that can be labeled, priced and marketed. The climate is the region. It has attracted unlimited resources of manpower and wealth. . . . It has given the region its rare beauty, for the charm of Southern California is largely to be found in the air and the light."

McWilliams's identification of Southern California with its climate, its "air and light," was one expression of the grip that California holds on the public imagination. But numbers, industry, and war brought a severe jolt to the California vision: smog. Smog became a postwar issue, one where Arnold Beckman would make a considerable difference.

In the summer of 1943 residents of Los Angeles County found an unexpected hostile environment as a noxious haze hung over the region, cutting clear western vistas to a murky range of visibility of just three city blocks.

This stinging haze brought tears to the eyes of all and for some nausea and even vomiting. Los Angelenos did not have a ready language to describe the phenomena, and they drew on wartime fears in calling the change in climate a "gas attack."

From 1944 through 1947 the citizens of the Los Angeles region adopted a new name for the air pollution that refused to leave them, *smog*, a term first coined in London, England, in 1905, to describe the noxious combination of "smoke and fog." Looking around, Californians sought remedies by pointing fingers at possible culprits. There were the stacks and the effluent of refineries, industrial plants of all stripes, and power plants. Moreover, the region was peppered with hundreds of thousands of backyard incinerators. Residents burned their rubbish, freely releasing smoke.

One of the first mobile air-quality sampling vans built for the Air Pollution Control District of Orange County. Joe Lewis is second from left, and Arnold Beckman is fourth from left. *Courtesy Beckman Coulter, Inc.*

Even more numerous were the more than four million "smudge pots" in the vast citrus groves and orchards that surrounded the urban center. Smudge pots were portable stoves designed to generate thick clouds of heavy black smoke by burning old tires and motor oil. Growers used them because during California's rare frosts the smoke cover and the heat the pots generated protected their citrus trees. Also numbered in the millions were the cars, trucks, and buses (many of them diesels) that crowded the region's growing roadway system.

Southern California's initial reaction to the "gas attacks" of 1943 was to cast suspicion on conspicuous newcomers to the region rather than more accustomed presences like smudge pots, backyard incinerators, and automobiles. Residents and leaders alike focused on the new industrial plants of the war years built to produce butadiene, the key petroleum product in synthetic rubber.

Removal of the cause did not end the effect. The region could no longer point to butadiene plants as villains when these operations were cleaned up (some were even closed) and the smog continued. New theories were necessary. Los Angelenos turned to sulfur-laden smoke produced by coal burning and other industrial processes as a likely culprit. Here analysis followed the logic of the term *smog* itself—smoke mixed with fog must produce smog. Smoke was also at the heart of the precedents available in the United States for air pollution; sulfurous smoke produced by coal fires or metals smelting was certainly familiar to towns like Pittsburgh, Pennsylvania, and Gary, Indiana.

Los Angeles created a Bureau of Smoke Control. Industrial concerns in the region invested greatly in plants and processes to remove sulfur and prevent visible smokes from leaving their stacks. Still, in 1947, California smog continued.

That summer California Governor Earl Warren signed a new Air Pollution Control Act. The act gave counties the ability to create Air Pollution Control Districts (APCDs), organizations with the legal muscle to enforce air pollution measures and licenses on a regional scale. In October 1947 Los Angeles County's Air Pollution Control District became America's first air pollution control program and a much-emulated model across the nation.

The Los Angeles APCD was a political production in the truest sense, a compromise between different segments of society, each with its attendant interests and each with its vision of the common good. Smog touched sensitive nerves throughout the region; at stake were climate, health, continued prosperity, industrial development, population expansion, and the place of science and technology in society.

A regional board with power to control the inexplicable was sure to activate the political forces of the wary. Quick to be heard was the Los Angeles Chamber of Commerce, in league with the region's oil companies, both suspicious of granting broad regulatory powers over industry to a new governmental body. Any chamber of commerce promotes business and industry. Here was a paradox. Regulation might curtail industry, yet smog threatened the national lure of sunny California. At this juncture the Chamber found a new resource in an active member of rising reputation, Arnold O. Beckman, the instrument maker in South Pasadena. ∽

A brochure detailing the smog elimination plan put forth by the Los Angeles Chamber of Commerce. *Courtesy Beckman Coulter, Inc.*

LOS ANGELES CHAMBER OF COMMERCE SMOG ELIMINATION Action Program

PREMISES

We are informed by the scientific authorities who have studied the problem that:

1. The pure air supply of *metropolitan areas throughout the world* is becoming increasingly polluted as a result of man's activities. The problem in our community is accentuated during periods of inversion. The very factors, *meterologic and physiographic*, which make this climate unusually pleasant, also insure that air movement is sometimes slow, thus restricting the rapid ventilation of the area.

2. The natural forces affecting this pure air supply are so great that there is no apparent way to modify them.

3. A continuation of our present rate of air pollution poses serious threats to living values, business values and property values in the Los Angeles Basin.

4. Therefore, we must limit pollution of the air supply now available to this Basin.

5. The most important contributors to smog, in the order of the size of their contribution, are:

AUTOMOBILES AND OTHER MOTOR VEHICLES
INDUSTRY
INCINERATORS

6. In the light of this knowledge, we should proceed as rapidly as possibly in the reduction of air pollution from the three major sources.

7. We believe the citizens of the Los Angeles Basin will support intelligent action to reduce substantially the air pollution from these major sources.

The Los Angeles Chamber of Commerce will work toward the early reduction of smog in this Basin by the following methods:

1. Declare to the automobile industry that this Metropolitan area (and eventually every large city) must have automobiles and other motor vehicles with vastly improved fuel combustion to prevent the continued exhaust into the atmosphere of increasingly large quantities of hydro-carbons and strongly urge greatly accelerated research and development by the automobile industry to that end.

2. Recommend the establishment by business and industry of ride-sharing plans to operate during the early fall months of greatest temperature inversion.

3. Support studies and early action looking toward the establishment of at least some non-smog producing rapid transit services on major routes which will assist in the mass movement of our people to the principal centers of business and industry concentration.

4. Urge the early completion of air pollution control installations on all equipment now operating under variance.

5. Support a policy that new industries to which adequate smog control devices cannot be applied, shall not be permitted to locate in the area.

6. Urge and support the early inauguration of area-wide collection and disposal of combustible rubbish.

7. Continue to support the most competent research, seeking a more conclusive understanding of the conditions which form smog and of the practicable means of reduction in smog forming emissions to the atmosphere from all sources in the Los Angeles Basin.

8. Review these recommendations periodically in the light of experience and knowledge as developed by competent public and private research.

Important Progress to Date

It is recognized that the automobile industry is expending very great sums of money for research and development of improved fuel combustion.

It is also recognized that a great many industrial establishments throughout the area have already expended large sums to reduce air pollutants from equipment now operated under variance; also that many industries which are now operating in compliance with existing law and air pollution rules and regulations are never-the-less actively and voluntarily still expending large sums to further reduce air pollution wherever it exists.

Progress has also been made by householders and some communities in the collection and disposal of combustible rubbish.

But in all of these things, there is urgency for greatly accelerated action.

The purpose of this program is to stimulate that action. We know it can succeed if the people of the community will give it wholehearted support.

Request for Cooperation

We urge that civic, commercial, industrial, service and other organizations in the Los Angeles Basin give maximum attention to the smog problem and join in a united attack along the lines herein recommended.

We further urge that all such organizations in the Los Angeles Basin join in a united effort to promote the best possible understanding by the citizens of the Basin of the causes of smog and the problems involved in its control, including an understanding of the time required to perfect correction.

We have worked in cooperation with others in the earlier phases of this smog problem—to promote research, legislation and the initial control activities. This policy statement is designed to further implement the joint efforts of the community and to stimulate increasingly vigorous action.

We are ready to work wholeheartedly with any responsible organization in an organized program of action to rid this area of smog.

The Civic Apprenticeship of a Scientist

In 1946 Arnold Beckman was fully occupied at National Technical Laboratories. However, he somehow found the time to become involved with the Los Angeles Chamber of Commerce when its scientific advisory group began looking into the problems of smog, problems that had first surfaced in 1943 and that refused to go away. The Chamber had natural confidence in Beckman, for he was both chemist and entrepreneur. As public sentiment moved toward creation of an Air Pollution Control District to somehow define and remove this trouble in paradise once and for all, the Chamber asked him to serve as its representative in the scientific, political, and pragmatic negotiations with the Los Angeles County board of supervisors over what the Air Pollution Control District, or APCD, would be, how it would operate, and what powers it would have.

Beckman arrived at these talks with an unblemished reputation of integrity as business leader, as scientist, and as scientific consultant. His calm, authoritative, measured approach to problem solving quickly helped the board of supervisors and community leaders reach an agreeable compromise, creating a control district with limited but very real powers, supplemented with a thorough scientific analysis of smog. The proposals giving Los Angeles County the ability to create its control district thus found no opposition in either house of the state legislature. The board of supervisors and the leadership of the new APCD were so impressed with Dr. Beckman that he was signed on as scientific consultant to the new Air Pollution Control Officer. He served in this capacity from 1948 through 1952, crucial years for the air pollution battle and for the scientific understanding of Los Angeles smog.

The Air Pollution Control Officer in these years was Louis C. McCabe, a geologist with a Ph.D. from the University of Illinois and a background in chemical engineering. While Beckman's skills in chemistry and in analytical techniques and methods outstripped McCabe's, the two shared a common background and spoke the common language of science. Their relationship was tremendously productive. McCabe directed his early attention to sulfur dioxide released from the stacks of the district's chemical industry, power plants, factories, and refineries. From studies on coal and its combustion earlier in his career, McCabe was sensitive to sulfur dioxide pollution, an instinct reinforced by popular conceptions at the time. In short order he announced a radical and expensive proposal. The district could turn sulfur dioxide pollution into crops by buying up closed synthetic ammonia plants nearby, using polluting sulfur dioxide to create vast amounts of sulfuric acid and then using that acid to transform ammonia into usable fertilizers. Pollution would be turned into a product.

Beckman was taken aback. Yes, McCabe's plan did offer to mitigate somewhat the enormous costs of further reducing sulfur dioxide emissions into the district's atmosphere. But to have the county government buying and operating ammonia

A Beckman mobile air quality laboratory of the early 1960s. *Courtesy Beckman Coulter, Inc.*

plants was an enormously expensive proposition. Beyond cost, Beckman could not get past one key question. Was sulfur really the culprit responsible for smog? Was there truly an exorbitant level of sulfur dioxide in the region's atmosphere? He thought not. In forming his opinion, Beckman relied on a common, though powerful, instrument of analytical chemistry: the human nose. Sulfur dioxide has a distinctive odor, recognizable even in very small amounts.

The Los Angeles APCD adopted regulations to reduce the sulfur dioxide released by industrial stacks to no more than two-tenths of a percent (by volume). Beckman knew that work was already under way in Gary, Indiana, to deal with sulfur dioxide. Perhaps he might learn something useful by going to Gary. He did. U.S. Steel Corporation's Gary Works was the world's largest steel-making complex, replete with seemingly innumerable smokestacks. Sulfur dioxide emissions from those stacks had been of concern to the workers and managers of the Gary complex for many years, and the factory was well advanced in control techniques. As he walked around Gary, Beckman learned an important lesson. Concentrations of sulfur dioxide in the atmosphere around Gary were well below the limit proposed by the Los Angeles APCD, yet the old chemistry professor could smell the distinctive scent of the pollutant. Back home his nose detected no sulfur dioxide in the smog.

Beckman now knew that sulfur dioxide was not the major culprit and that McCabe's expensive plan for transforming sulfur dioxide into fertilizer, while potentially beneficial, would not do anything to solve the smog problem. He marched in to see McCabe. "Lou, for the love of Pete, you don't have sulfur dioxide in the air. Your nose is one of the best sensors for that; you can smell a few parts per thousand long before it gets up to two-tenths of a percent. Before you spend millions of dollars putting in recovery or replacement plants, you'd better find out what's in the air." In short order McCabe came to accept Beckman's position that scientific investigation was required to further the battle against smog in the quickest and most efficacious manner. He relied on Beckman for a research design, and Beckman in turn invoked his Caltech connection. Soon they were talking with Arie J. Haagen-Smit, a professor of chemistry who had been conducting his own research into smog and believed that he was on the trail of the offending agent: ozone. Accumulated research over the several decades following Haagen-Smit's work has proved his suspicions to be correct.

From Haagen-Smit, Beckman and McCabe wanted a careful analysis of pollutants in the regional atmosphere, specifically seeking whatever matter may have been present in addition to the gaseous ozone that Haagen-Smit suspected. After Haagen-Smit agreed, Beckman, McCabe, and two other scientists spent several months obtaining a sample of air pollutants from the Los Angeles atmosphere. They passed prime L.A. air through a system of tubing, interspersed with a series of vessels partially filled with extremely cold liquid nitrogen. The liquid nitrogen caused the heavier molecules in the air to condense out, to fall into the trap. These heavy molecules were those of pollutants. Even using an enormous volume of air, Beckman and his team succeeded in collecting only one or two drops of pollutant condensation, a minute amount of "smelly brown stuff," as he described it. It was enough to run analyses.

Haagen-Smit's analysis of the brown stuff found peroxy organic materials, a class of compounds listed as toxic, not just irritant. These new results also agreed with his findings about ozone: They were just the sort of materials that one would expect to find if hydrocarbon emissions were somehow oxidized in the air above the Los Angeles basin.

Once Arie J. Haagen-Smit had run the analysis on the Beckman team's "smelly brown stuff" that pointed to ozone as the likely culprit, he began drifting back toward the excitement of his other research.

Although still intrigued by the riddles of smog, he was, after all, a regular Caltech professor. Dr. Beckman, however, was not prepared to let him go so quickly. More had to be done on smog, and Haagen-Smit was the best man for the job. Beckman was now as focused on smog as he ever was on any instrument. Smog imperiled, in the most tangible ways, the health—even the lives—of the area's population as well as the health of the region's developmental momentum. Beckman believed he could get Haagen-Smit back on smog by involving his ego as well as his scientific curiosity. He knew just how.

The region's oil and gas producers had commissioned their own examination of air pollution and smog questions. They invited Abe Zarem, a director of the Los Angeles division of the Stanford Research Institute, to visit and look at the brown stuff from the Los Angeles air. Beckman knew that Zarem agreed that the air carried peroxy organic compounds but that he found them to be largely innocuous, certainly not the villains responsible for the odors, irritations, and degradative effects of smog. Knowing too that Zarem was a strong advocate of his position, Beckman, with calculated mischief, arranged for him to give a lecture at Caltech.

Beckman also arranged to sit next to Haagen-Smit at the talk. All went according to plan. Zarem did not hold back. He announced that the peroxy compounds were not the real culprits and that it was "unfortunate that a chemist of Haagen-Smit's caliber could be misled like this." As Beckman tells it, "Haggie was a Dutchman and a damn good chemist. He just said, 'Well who's telling me I don't

Two Beckman scientists run a test using the Beckman automobile exhaust gas analyzer. *Courtesy Beckman Coulter, Inc.*

know what to do?'" Newly motivated to continue his work on smog, Haagen-Smit yielded easily to entreaties that he take a year's leave from Caltech and devote his time to research in a laboratory provided by Beckman and the APCD.

The outcome of Beckman's ploy was momentous, for in this year of research Haagen-Smit discovered the chemistry of smog, presenting his results in 1952. Ozone, responsible for the bulk of smog, was formed by a complex photochemical reaction in the air above the region, a mix of the "air and light" that in the minds of many Californians defined their special climate and hence their home. Hydrocarbons released from smokestacks, oil refineries, automobile tailpipes, and the like would hang in the still air above the region, stuck between the sea and the mountains. There the hydrocarbons would be propelled by the intense western sunlight to combine photochemically with nitrogen oxides also in the air, resulting in the formation of copious amounts of ozone. In turn, ozone played a role in the photochemical formation of the peroxy organic compounds that Haagen-Smit had also investigated. The reaction to Haagen-Smit's conclusions caused a great public stir: Hydrocarbons associated with petroleum and automobiles, cultural icons at the center of Southern California's identity, were responsible in large measure for the region's smog. The larger question remained: What could be done?

The Business of Smog

Through all the discussions of smog Beckman was never one to miss an opportunity for technological advances. As he followed smog research from 1948 through 1952, he saw the need for instrumentation to monitor air pollutants. During this period he personally developed and patented an instrument for the continuous detection, measurement, and recording of levels of different compounds present in the atmosphere. This patent was granted on 7 October 1952; it covered instruments that measured and recorded substances in the atmosphere using colorimetric methods. Devices based on colorimetry would mix the atmosphere with a chemical compound in such a way that the color of the compound would change in proportion to the concentration of specific substances in the atmosphere.

Based on this patent, Beckman Instruments introduced

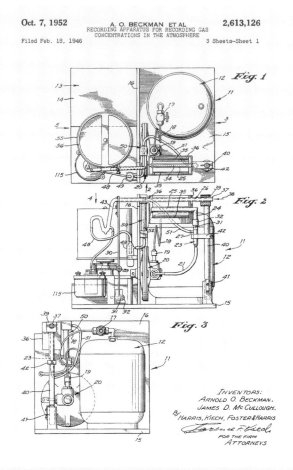

Patent diagram for the apparatus for recording gas concentrations in the atmosphere.

an instrument for the measurement of smog. This "oxidant recorder" tested air with phenolphthalein, a compound that turned pink when oxidants—the constituents of smog like ozone, nitrogen oxide, and peroxy organic compounds—were present. The degree of color change was measured electronically and recorded on a paper chart, giving continuous measures of the levels of air pollution. These Beckman Instruments oxidant recorders were used extensively by the APCD and the Air Pollution Foundation's researchers to monitor the smog problem and to untangle its mysteries.

The oxidant recorder opened the way for a whole host of instrumentation that Beckman's firm produced for the investigation of air pollution. There were new specialized instruments for measuring automobile exhaust, both large-scale devices suited for the production lines of automobile manufacturers and smaller instruments suited for testing at local garages and inspection stations. Beckman Instruments also offered highly specialized research instrumentation for use by automotive scientists in their efforts to develop cleaner technologies. The firm eventually even produced "air quality monitoring vans," customized trucks packed with an array of air pollution–monitoring devices for use by local governments and large industrial enterprises. For many years these Beckman Instruments products were in demand as automobile manufacturers and environmental agencies used them to reduce the contribution of automobile exhausts to air pollution. ❧

His central position in the war on smog brought Arnold Beckman increasing prominence in the Los Angeles Chamber of Commerce. Smog, of course, was topmost on the Chamber's mind, and Beckman had an extraordinary ability to unify the communities of industry, science, and government. In December 1952 a London tragedy made very clear to Californians the need for immediate action to reduce levels of smog, now that the basics of scientific understanding were coming into focus thanks to Haagen-Smit and Beckman. A thick smog enveloped London, cutting visibility down to three feet and cutting short the lives of some four thousand people. California Governor Goodwin J. Knight, justifiably alarmed by reports from London, decided to set up a Special Committee on Air Pollution charged with thinking up immediate plans to control smog. For leadership of this emergency committee he looked south to Los Angeles and appointed Arnold Beckman chairman—asking him to shoulder a weighty and highly charged public burden.

At the end of 1953 Beckman's committee made its findings public. Soon called the "Beckman Bible," the report contained a series of recommendations that set the air pollution control agenda for the Los Angeles APCD and the entire state for many years to come. Beckman and his committee listed the most important steps to be undertaken immediately: cutting vapor leaks from refineries and filling stations to reduce hydrocarbon emissions; establishing standards for permissible automobile exhaust; converting diesel trucks and buses into propane-fueled vehicles; suggesting to the industries contributing the most to air pollution that they consider checking their growth or locate new operations in more remote areas; banning immediately and outright the open burning of trash; and beginning to develop a regional mass transportation system.

Beckman was also active in creating the Air Pollution Foundation, incorporated as a not-for-profit organization in November 1953. Beckman was vice chairman of the new foundation's board of trustees and Caltech President Lee DuBridge was head of the trustees' scientific committee. Beckman, DuBridge, and their fellows set up the Air Pollution Foundation to support research about the most efficacious solutions to the smog problem in the Los Angeles area in a context that removed it from the political fray and suspicions about the trustworthiness of research supported by various interest groups. Further, the foundation was to educate the public about the results of the scientific investigation of smog and the complexity of the issues involved.

With such a prominent role in the war on smog, it came as little surprise that Arnold Beckman was asked by the Los Angeles Chamber of Commerce to take on larger roles and responsibilities in the organization. In 1954 he became a member of the board of directors of the Chamber. That October, Los Angelenos learned the hard way that the dangers of smog had not been abolished, despite strict bans on trash burning and on the use of certain materials in smudge pots. Los Angeles County was stricken throughout the month by a series of terrible "smog attacks,"

A Beckman Instruments trade show exhibit used Dr. Beckman's growing prominence as the springboard for a playful advertising-cum-quasi-political campaign on the theme "Put Beckman in Control," alluding to the firm's process instrumentation and control systems. Here the "candidate" poses with "supporters." *Courtesy Beckman Coulter, Inc.*

to use Beckman's phrase. Schools and industrial facilities were repeatedly closed; residents felt powerless and angry as smog shut down many significant activities for an entire month. The public outcry was deafening, fueled by political activities reaching fever pitch in anticipation of the national election in November. In response the Chamber of Commerce made Arnold Beckman chairman of its own Air Pollution Committee and charged him with crafting the powerful institution's response.

The position taken by Beckman and his fellow directors was to back and even to strengthen the county government's Air Pollution Control District. Beckman suggested that the Chamber throw all its weight behind a program to encourage industry, business, and citizen groups to support the APCD's work. The district was facing severe negative publicity in the wake of the October smog attacks. Politicians, newspapers, and citizen groups were calling for the recall of its leaders and of the county government. Some were even advocating a grand jury inquiry. At Beckman's urging the Chamber of Commerce fought not for crippling the APCD but for strengthening it with new inspectors and enforcement officers. The Chamber amplified the earlier call for stricter controls on hydrocarbon vapor leaks associated with petroleum refining, for retrofitting diesel trucks and buses with cleaner-burning engines, for completing the system of unified rubbish removal, for motivating area industry to step up the pace of voluntary compliance, and for mobilizing civic groups to urge the automotive industry to develop devices to clean up automobile exhausts.

After leading these initiatives, Dr. Beckman was a natural for vice president of the Chamber in 1955. Throughout the year he helped the APCD pass new regulations that set up plans to monitor smog continuously at stations throughout the region, instituted a system of smog alerts based on monitored levels, and established emergency actions that could be deployed if smog alerts reached ominous levels. He helped devise a unified smog campaign for the Chamber, making it the number-one priority of the entire organization. Each standing committee of the Chamber was given a special job for the smog campaign specifically related to its individual area of expertise.

Civic Spokesman

Arnold Beckman became president of the Los Angeles Chamber of Commerce on 25 January 1956. Speaking at the banquet that evening, he emphasized two key issues as the focus for his tenure in this highly public office. They were the battle against air pollution and the fostering of the scientific–technical–industrial–educational nexus then emerging in the region. First, he emphasized the strength and the prominence of the organization he would now lead. "The Los Angeles Chamber of Commerce, with its 5,000 members and permanent staff of 120," he began, "has become the most effective organization of its kind in the entire world. It has become a recognized powerful force for good in this community." He then turned to the challenges that he and the Chamber would face in the coming year.

> Air pollution is generally conceded to be the major menace to our community. It is noteworthy that the Chamber of Commerce has already set forth a realistic plan of action to combat air pollution. As many of you know, the announcement of this plan had a tremendous impact on the public, not only in Southern California but throughout the country.
>
> As a scientist I have been personally associated with various aspects of the efforts to eliminate smog since the earliest days of the Air Pollution Control Act, and I have a deep personal interest, for many reasons, in doing everything possible to accelerate the elimination of air pollution. I trust that no one today deludes himself into thinking that air pollution is a problem to be solved by one man or by one agency. It is an objective of the Chamber to encourage cooperation between the pertinent governmental and private agencies, to review reports on progress, and to consider and recommend new forms of attack on the smog problem.

Beckman knew the need for reasoned patience: "Let us not deceive ourselves. Certainly we shall not lick smog during the coming year—progress will be slow, even if all of the technical problems were to be solved overnight. The tempo of the fight must be speeded up. We must cut out nonsense and time-consuming bickering and get on with the job. In its fight on smog the Chamber is battling for the community as a whole, and it will carry on its fight without bias, prejudice, or fear."

Leaving no doubt about the priority of the smog fight, Beckman then turned to his other special concern for his presidency of the Chamber, one equally near to his personal experience and involvement. Again he showed his uncanny ability to sense, define, and seize opportunity.

He began by dramatizing the dynamic growth of the region with a simple statistic: "Our population is increasing at the rate of some four thousand persons per week. This phenomenal growth creates a multitude of problems—housing, sewers, schools, transportation, etc.—problems which have become almost routine and which must be taken in our stride." He then directed his audience's attention to what he saw as the critical opportunity for the future of the region:

> Within the overall growth there has come a special growth, however, which is of particular interest to the Chamber. A group has been growing in our midst which can exert a most profound influence upon the future of our community and, in fact, upon our nation. This group, not yet defined by a simple designation, is composed of research scientists and technicians in varied fields, as electronics, instrumentation, computers, automation, nucleonics, guided missiles, and the like. We have here one of the most potent and active groups in the nation for developing the new devices and systems which will shape and control our industrial and economic future. The Chamber has an obligation to encourage and aid this group, not only for our own selfish interest but for our nation as a whole.

At the start of the third millennium these words command assent. In 1956 they were equally true, but seemed visionary in the extreme to many.

Beckman's public involvement with the fight against air pollution and with support of the scientific enterprise extended far beyond his year as president of the Los Angeles Chamber of Commerce. He continued both efforts during his leadership of the California Chamber of Commerce a decade later in 1967, and he was appointed to the Federal Air Quality Board in 1970 by President Richard M. Nixon and served four years. Beckman also continued his public efforts to support the scientific community of Southern California and the nation in many ways and in many forms over the following decades. With the perspective of hindsight, and mindful of both the dramatic successes in the abatement of air pollution in Southern California and the nation's realization of the economic impact of innovation, we can appreciate the significance of his early willingness to take on the role of civic leader.

Arnold Beckman's work on air pollution brought national visibility, and a year of Chamber leadership gave him a national platform for a growing interest—education, a subject about which he thought hard and spoke vigorously. In the year before *Sputnik*, on 22 June 1956, he vigorously critiqued American technical education.

U.S. News devoted an amazing five pages to the critique. Dr. Beckman emphasized faults and the things that might be improved, though his overall view was that "public education is a magnificent institution—I wish to make it still better." He pointed out that the Cold War was on, and that the United States and the

U.S.S.R. had about the same number of engineers. Yet the American count was decreasing, while Soviet numbers increased annually. Any business that knew there was a national demand for its product would increase output! Government studies showed that the United States needed more technical personnel, and educators should take this cue. Fewer Americans were studying science and engineering because high school preparation had slipped. Students once had to take physics in high school; now electives made the curriculum less demanding. In Dr. Beckman's view, both colleges of education and state regulations were deficient. Colleges stressed education programs rather than science and math for prospective teachers, although they did so only because states did not demand that teachers really know the science and math they were hired to teach.

A few years earlier the American Chemical Society had offered competitive examinations for scholarships. When the examinations were over, many teachers asked for a list of correct answers in order to discuss them with students. The clear message, said Beckman, was that the teachers could not figure out the correct answers on their own. It seems, he feared, that modern education "tends to destroy competition, eliminate free enterprise, and destroy individual initiative." Giving good grades to all diminishes real achievement. He had even greater worries about a cadre of teachers protected by tenure and getting annual raises regardless of quality, preparation, or results. Merit systems would attract and keep the best teachers.

The concerns Arnold Beckman voiced in 1956 drew considerable attention then and still resonate today. He was learning how to play the role of citizen and leader. Other aspects of that role came home to him as the importance to the Los Angeles economy of foreign markets and investments took the Chamber president to stages as far apart as Tokyo and Moscow.

Los Angeles to Tokyo and Moscow

As president of the Chamber of Commerce, Arnold Beckman was a leading spokesman for the entire Los Angeles region and the industrial engines fueling its growth. Many of the economic trends recently grouped under the name *globalization* were already under way; Beckman was launching his own foreign subsidiaries; and a global perspective was required of him as president of the Chamber.

In 1956 he attended a conference in Tokyo that combined discussion with pomp, circumstance, and, in his retrospective view, inadvertent technology transfer. C. Norris Poulson, the mayor of Los Angeles, had been invited to attend the World Mayors' Conference held in honor of Tokyo's five-hundredth anniversary, but he fell ill and asked Beckman, as Chamber president, to go as his deputy. Beckman made the trip to Japan carrying a most unusual gift, a gift that he has pondered for decades. "The protocol [for such a conference] is that you have to take a gift over there, so what to take? Believe it or not the Chamber of Commerce decided that the thing to take was a transistor radio. At that time they were brand new. We got one of these modest-sized radios, and we put it in a beautiful leather case, embossed the seal of the city of Los Angeles on it, and I took it over."

True, the gift was a fitting one for Beckman to bestow. It was then a high-technology product, with transistors of precisely the kind that he wanted his own company to produce. And semiconductors would soon make California the center of entire new industries ushering in the information age. However, the coin also had another side:

> I missed the grand opening ceremony because the plane was late. They had a protocol officer come on and find out what the gifts were that the guests were going to give. Then they determine the pecking order. I was hoping that I was going to be pretty well down the list because I didn't know what the procedure was, particularly since I missed the opening . . . and I missed the instructions that they had given to the other people. Then I saw some of the gifts that others were giving, for example, the mayor of Tehran had a beautiful bowl made of woven strands of silver and gold. Here was this radio, and believe it or not, this was selected as the number one [gift to be presented], and I had to go to the head of the procession. It was because of the novelty, they had never seen a transistor radio, never heard of it before. I often wonder whether that was what kicked off the semiconductor business! It was only a short time after this that Toshiba became the world's largest manufacturer, at that time, of germanium transistors.

Continuing Chamber connections put Arnold Beckman on the roster of invitees for another trip three years later to Moscow at the height of the Cold War. There he was witness to one of the defining moments of that era—the famous "Kitchen Debate" of 24 July 1959 between Richard Nixon, then vice president of the United States, and the Soviet premier, Nikita Khrushchev.

In the midst of bubbling tensions between the world's two superpowers, centered on hotspots like Berlin and Havana, the United States and the Soviet Union agreed on an exchange of trade and cultural exhibitions in the hope that giving the populations of each country a better view of the other's daily life would ease suspicion and fear. The agreement also stipulated that neither side would impose any form of censorship upon the other and that neither side would propagandize. Beckman was invited by a Chamber colleague to accompany Vice President Nixon on his trip to open the U.S. exposition.

Before joining Nixon's delegation for Moscow, Arnold Beckman traveled to New York to take in the Soviet exposition. The exhibit was installed in the Coliseum, and as he toured the show, he became increasingly convinced that the Soviets had not lived up to their promise to refrain from propagandizing. He thought that the large statue that greeted visitors when they first entered, depicting a Russian beating a sword into a plowshare, implied that the Soviet Union stood for peace and that America did not. He also found the large graphs hung around the exposition, which compared Soviet with American industrial and agricultural output, to be "such blatant propaganda it was laughable." The graphs showed Soviet production dramatically exceeding, or about to exceed, American production at every turn. Similarly, when Nixon, Beckman, and the rest of the delegation arrived in Moscow to open up the American exposition in Sokolniki Park, they were disturbed—but also somewhat amused—by the Soviets' failure to restrain the impulse to censor. The Soviets confiscated a number of publications that the American delegation had brought with them: the Sears-Roebuck catalog, the *World Almanac*, and the latest book by Adlai Stevenson.

For the official opening of the American exposition Richard Nixon and Nikita Khrushchev strolled around the pavilion, surrounded by their respective delegations, television cameras, and the international press. Within this crowded penumbra stood Arnold Beckman. As Nixon and Khrushchev walked through the exhibit, their conversation quickly turned from blithe formalities to an impromptu, sometimes pointed, exchange about global politics.

In the course of their debate, with Arnold Beckman crowded near them, Nixon paused in front of a model American kitchen replete with all the modern appliances that 1959 had to offer.

"You had a very nice house in your exhibition in New York," Nixon remarked. "My wife and I enjoyed it very much. I want to show you this kitchen. It is like those of our houses in California."

Khrushchev pointed toward a washing machine and replied, "We have such things."

Nixon and Khrushchev then used the comparison of houses and washing machines as a metaphor in brash exchanges about the relative merits of the superpowers' ideologies and nuclear arsenals.

The Kitchen Debate, caught on film. Richard Nixon explains the merits of democracy to Nikita Khrushchev. *Courtesy AP/Wide World Photos*

"Don't you have a machine that puts food into the mouth and pushes it down?" Khrushchev asked. "Many things you've shown are interesting, but they are not needed in life. I have heard of your engineers. I am well aware of what they can do. You know for launching our missiles we need lots of calculating machines."

Nixon's reply doubtless had Beckman's full assent: "We do not claim to astonish the Russian people. We hope to show our diversity and our right to choose. We do not wish to have decisions made at the top by government officials who say that all homes should be built in the same way. Would it not be better to compete in the relative merits of washing machines than in the strength of rockets?"

As a witness of the Kitchen Debate, Arnold Beckman returned from Moscow with a new friendship with and a great respect for Richard Nixon.

Growing and Going Global

By the mid-1950s Arnold Beckman had truly hit his stride. He was savoring the responsibilities, pleasures, and burdens of public and political leadership in his adopted state of California. At the same time his days were filled with the challenges and opportunities of leading a growing and esteemed public company that he himself had built. Available capital allowed him to acquire whole technological businesses with research and development completed and products established. They in turn could provide the base from which new heights could be scaled.

Strategies with acquisitions varied with Beckman's goals and the details of corporations to be acquired. Visionary as to the waves he would surf and artful as to the details, he sought out the most exciting new opportunities for instrumentation and technological innovation and then selected the fields and businesses he wanted to move into and could quickly assume leadership of. The strategy of bringing outside firms into Beckman Instruments and retaining top management and innovative talent paid off handsomely. Part of the reward lay in the growth and enhanced stature it brought Beckman Instruments, but what truly fired his imagination was the thrill of producing new tools for science.

Global connections were not something that Beckman heard about in public-affairs lectures after the war: He knew it from his order departments, as Beckman Instruments sent many shipments to Europe. Foreign sales were rising steadily, but fulfilling them was a constant source of difficulty for the firm. Beckman had a penchant for direct, pragmatic action, and the endless difficulties surrounding export permissions, import licensing, and currency exchange were a constant irritant that often delayed and sometimes prevented deliveries abroad. To cure the irritation, he opted for international expansion.

Beckman chose Germany for his first international subsidiary and created Beckman Instruments, GmbH, in Munich in 1953. He selected Germany because he anticipated the quick renewal of the world-class German chemical industries and because Germany was also free of what he called the "worst" of European

Left: Pat, Arnold, and Mabel Beckman disembark in Munich, on a visit to the Beckman Instruments' subsidiary in that city. *Courtesy Beckman family.*

Right: The Beckman Instruments subsidiary in Cape Town, South Africa. *Courtesy Beckman Coulter, Inc.*

labor relations, notably the labor unionism prevalent in the United Kingdom. Although the majority of Beckman's overseas orders originated in Britain, its unionism made him reluctant to establish his first subsidiary there.

Beckman was in fact suspicious of organized labor throughout his active business career. The only facility that had ever been "union" within his enterprises was one factory of the Helipot Corporation, and that voted to go non-union when Helipot reintegrated with Beckman Instruments. Beckman believed that if the management of an industrial concern acted with integrity and in its own best long-term interest, employees would have a better deal than they could compel through union organization. His employees agreed in the case of their particular firm, and given the particular man who led it, this was indeed true. Despite many votes on the matter, Beckman Instruments declined to unionize.

The German subsidiary was a glowing success by every measure, opening the way for Beckman subsidiaries in Scotland, France, Austria, the Netherlands, Sweden, South Africa, Mexico, and Puerto Rico. Beckman also established sales and service offices in many more countries, excepting only the Soviet Union and its closest allies. His worldwide vision and concern in the early 1950s, and his dedication to acting upon them, led to his company's becoming truly a global leader in instrumentation in the following decade.

The Move to Fullerton

Milestones in the development of institutions are often most enduringly marked by structures built to house them, and in 1955 it was time to move again. In the early

An aerial view of the Beckman Instruments headquarters in Fullerton, California. *Courtesy Beckman Coulter, Inc.*

1950s Beckman Instruments made its home in its two South Pasadena plants, but they soon could not contain the enterprise as a whole. As time went on, dozens of other buildings scattered throughout the Pasadena area housed various parts of the firm plus the Helipot Corporation and Arnold O. Beckman, Inc. Space became a true issue, for Beckman could see only greater demand for shop floors and laboratories to keep pace with the growth of his company. The Pasadena real estate market had little to offer, even had he wanted to pay local prices. He sought not only more space but also consolidation of his company's operations at a single site. His matured enterprise needed a new home base.

In 1953 Beckman oversaw, with great pride, the start of construction of an expansive factory, laboratory, and office complex in Fullerton, California. The previous headquarters in South Pasadena had an apple orchard in its backyard, an orchard that Dr. Beckman had cared for with his own hands. In Fullerton he transformed a forty-acre orange grove into a striking facility for incubating innovations. In 1954 the company moved into 220,000 square feet of buildings unified by crisp, right-angle geometries—low, rectangular structures that covered acres. The design was highly modern, centered on the concept of flexibility for further expansion: Additional space could be easily constructed and integrated, and any interior spaces could be reconfigured quickly and efficiently. Such a flexible design befitted a firm dedicated to new instrumentation in a growing array of technologies. The wisdom of providing for future contingencies has been validated for the complex has grown fourfold to contain today's Beckman Coulter, the company that Beckman's enterprise became in 1997. The design of the Fullerton complex is one more expression of Arnold Beckman himself.

The Beckman facilities in Fullerton, under construction. *Courtesy Beckman Coulter, Inc.*

Arnold O. Beckman in front of panels embedded with parts of his instruments. *Courtesy Beckman Coulter, Inc.*

7 | *Visions of Technology*

If you're not taking risks, you're probably not doing very much.

William Shockley and a Shared Vision

One Sunday evening in early August 1955 William B. Shockley, the key individual responsible for the development of the transistor, picked up his telephone and dialed Arnold Beckman's number. There were many reasons for his call. Foremost was his desire to involve Beckman in a new company. Shockley knew Dr. Beckman as a pioneer of scientific instrumentation, for in the mid-1950s Beckman's fame as innovator and manufacturer of electronic devices was nearing its apogee. Furthermore, Shockley and Beckman were connected by Caltech, where Shockley had been an undergraduate physics student in the class of 1932. Young Professor Beckman's reputation as a master experimenter had then brought Shockley to his office for help building thermocouples, and Beckman showed him just what to do.

After going to Harvard for his Ph.D. in physics, Shockley joined Beckman's other technological alma mater, Bell Labs. As the research arm of the Bell System, Bell Labs had an abiding interest in enhancing the transmission of electrical signals. In the late 1930s Shockley began to experiment with *semiconductors*—materials midway between the more familiar electrical categories of *conductor* (a material that allows electricity to pass freely though it) and *insulator* (a material that does not conduct electricity). A semiconductor is a solid, crystalline material that can exhibit a wide range of electrical properties, depending on the addition of slight traces of other substances to it. Researchers believed that by careful control of these trace additions they could produce semiconductors to exacting specifications, possessing just the electrical properties they wanted.

William Shockley in 1938.
Courtesy AT&T Archives.

237

After World War II, Shockley led Bell Labs' research program on semiconductors, exploring what became known as "solid-state physics." The versatility of semiconductors and the precision with which they could be controlled made the solid state an area of great interest to the telephone system's best scientists and engineers. Many at Bell Labs, Shockley among them, saw semiconductors as first steps toward devices that would open an entirely new age in electronics. Working with his colleagues John Bardeen and Walter H. Brattain, Shockley began a research program to develop new electronic devices out of semiconductors to replace vacuum tubes in amplifying and controlling electrical currents and signals. In 1947 Shockley, Bardeen, and Brattain succeeded in building such a semiconductor device—the transistor. Like the vacuum tubes they would soon replace, transistors acted as "electrical valves." But transistors could be miniaturized far beyond the most diminutive of vacuum tubes, and they were more robust and heat resistant.

The commercial use of the transistor in contexts beyond the Bell System began to intrigue Shockley. While exploring possibilities, he spent time at Caltech as a visiting professor in 1954. In that same year Texas Instruments launched the first commercial transistor radio. Shockley's fame attracted the attention of Arnold Beckman and the Los Angeles Chamber of Commerce, where Beckman became vice president at a gala banquet in February 1955. Electronics was an industry of growing importance in the Los Angeles area, thanks to the presence of many defense contractors. The Chamber's banquet honored William Shockley and Beckman's friend Lee De Forest for their groundbreaking labors on behalf of the dawning electronic age.

Not surprisingly, Beckman and Shockley—both Bell Labs and Caltech alumni and both visionaries in the electronic realm—became fast friends. Shockley continued to dream of an industrial enterprise of his own, one that would develop and manufacture new kinds of transistors and semiconductor devices. In August 1955 he picked up the phone to call his former professor with a question that seemed clear enough: Would Dr. Beckman serve on the board of Shockley's dreamed-of company? Beckman needed more information before deciding. He was unquestionably interested in semiconductor technology, and the transistor had been creating quite a stir in the world of electronics for several years. But he had very specific questions for Shockley about the business side of the proposition. "I asked him a little bit more about who else was going to be on the board, and it turned out that he was going to have a board composed of almost everybody who was in the instrument business, all of whom would be his competitors."

To Beckman, this was evidence that while undoubtedly a virtuoso of science and technology, Shockley was "unbelievably naive" when it came to business and finance. Beckman himself was particularly sensitive to this disjunction of talent—it was one of his main criticisms of himself. He rued many of his early business decisions, decrying them as evidence of his own commercial naïveté, of proof that he was "really no businessman."

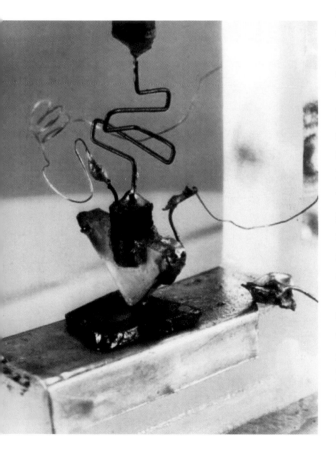

An early transistor built by Shockley, Bardeen, and Brattain. *Courtesy AT&T Archives.*

Arnold Beckman felt comfortable enough to offer Bill Shockley some strong advice. "You just can't do that," Beckman told him over the phone. "You'll have such a thing as conflict of interest, Shockley. If you want to do this, come out and talk it over." Shockley accepted both Beckman's reaction and the invitation that accompanied it. Before the end of August, he was in Southern California. He stayed for a week in Newport Beach, near the yacht club where Beckman went to sail the *Lady Pat*, discussing with his colleague whether to launch a new industrial concern to manufacture a new product by new methods.

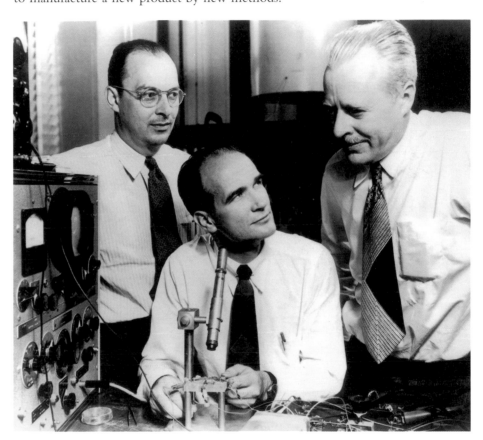

Future Nobel laureates (left to right) John Bardeen, William Shockley, and Walter Brattain at Bell Labs in 1948 with the apparatus used in the scientific investigations that led to the development of the transistor. *Courtesy AT&T Archives.*

Making semiconductor devices involves carefully introducing minute amounts of other elements into the semiconductor material. Shockley proposed setting up a company for large-scale, automated manufacture of silicon semiconductor components—transistors, electronic switches, and the like—using the radical new production method of *diffusion*. This process of diffusion is akin to a drop of cream spreading through coffee. Even when not stirred, the cream will diffuse throughout a cup of hot coffee fairly rapidly, lightening it uniformly. Cream will also diffuse throughout a glass of *iced* coffee, but it will take much longer. The rate of diffusion of cream in coffee can be controlled by regulating the temperature of the coffee.

Shockley proposed to manufacture silicon semiconductors by introducing his trace, or "doping," elements through a process of gas diffusion. The doping matter would seep into the silicon crystal; the amount and extent of this diffusion would be controlled by governing exposure time, temperature, and pressure. Shockley's process might allow mass manufacture of new silicon semiconductor devices, but the technique was still months of research and development away from readiness.

Shockley's goal interested Arnold Beckman. Silicon semiconductor devices had many of the same advantages as the cermet electronic components that he had developed. Like cermets, silicon semiconductor transistors, switches, and other devices could be very small, heat resistant, durable, and amenable to mass production. Beckman had pushed the development of cermet potentiometers to meet the stringent demands and boundless appetite of his military and aerospace customers for advanced electronic parts. These same customers were virtually breaking down the doors of Bell Labs to get semiconductor transistors, and Texas Instruments showed that these transistors could revolutionize the design of electronic products like radios. Beckman wondered what they might do for scientific instruments like spectrophotometers.

If Shockley could develop the mass-production method of "diffusion" with Beckman's help, it would be the dawn of a new technological era for Beckman Instruments. Beckman convinced Shockley to abandon his sketch of an independent company with a board of competitors and instead set up shop within the Beckman Instruments organization. The phenomenal growth of Beckman Instruments in terms of technology, funding for research and development, and creative scientific

The Beckman family, with Lee and Marie De Forest, at the Moulin Rouge, a club in Hollywood. *Courtesy Institute Archives, California Institute of Technology.*

and engineering talent would give Shockley's operation a wealth of resources to draw upon. Perhaps most important, Arnold Beckman and William Shockley held similar convictions about conditions needed to nurture the young, creative scientists and engineers (who were far more familiar with the halls of universities than with the floors of production plants) who would carry out the work of research and development.

Beckman and Shockley agreed that finding the very best people for the job was the most important thing. They wanted people like themselves: individuals who combined a passion for and grasp of science and engineering with a kind of restlessness, a drive to solve practical problems and bring to reality the most far-reaching promises of new technologies. Beckman certainly thought that in Shockley he had found the ablest man for the job and that the best thing he could do was to get him started and get out of the way. In this, he later explained, he was doing nothing new: "I set up an operation, put somebody in charge, and let him run." Backing the best horse and letting it run was his modus operandi in business, and it had produced remarkable results as well as attracting and rewarding some of the best American scientific talent. Beckman's attitude was in turn just what Shockley was looking for, and he claimed to hold the same ideals—finding the ablest talent and then giving that talent the space and freedom to push back the frontiers of science and technology. Unfortunately, as Beckman would soon find out, Shockley was true to only half of his expressed conviction.

By the end of the week Shockley and Beckman had a legal letter of intent to form a subsidiary of Beckman Instruments: the Shockley Semiconductor Laboratories. Drafted by Arnold Beckman with the assistance of a company attorney, the letter stated the plan succinctly: "We propose to engage promptly and vigorously in activities related to semiconductors. The initial project contemplated is the development of automatic means for production of diffused-base transistors." Beckman and Shockley were united in the belief that there is no satisfactory substitute for excellence. With the agreement in hand, Shockley left Southern California for the East Coast to begin a whirlwind tour of technological centers and academic departments, determined to recruit the best and the brightest.

The Shockley Semiconductor Laboratories and the Birth of Silicon Valley

Initially, William Shockley was in the strange position of not being able to tell his recruits exactly where, geographically, he was asking them to move and work. Beckman favored locating Shockley's shop in or near Fullerton, close to the bulk of Beckman's own operations and staff. Shockley, on the other hand, preferred Northern California, specifically Palo Alto, near Stanford University. Shockley's mother had attended Stanford, and Palo Alto was his boyhood home. Beckman acquiesced in short order, in part because of Shockley's success in attracting outstanding young investigators. Help in recruiting came from Frederick Terman, the provost and dean of electrical engineering at Stanford and a powerful, visionary force for science and industry in the Bay Area. Terman also provided something more: a spot for the operation in Stanford's new industrial park.

Beckman, true to form, decided not to block Shockley's wishes or to slight Terman's initiatives. He agreed to sign a lease for space for Shockley Semiconductor Laboratories in Terman's Stanford Industrial Park—a decision that made good business sense as well. The park contained the facilities of another Bay Area firm that Beckman had recently acquired—Spinco. Spinco—the Specialized Instruments Corporation—manufactured ultracentrifuges; it was originally located ten miles away from Stanford in Belmont, California. Housing both subsidiaries in Terman's park would minimize disruption for Beckman's new Spinco workers while satisfying Shockley's needs.

In 1955 the profits of Beckman Instruments passed $1 million for the first time, surging to $1.4 million—an increase of 52 percent from the previous year. The time seemed ripe for bold ventures. Arnold Beckman moved quickly to secure the business tools and resources he and Shockley would need to pursue their grail, the automated mass production of silicon semiconductors using diffusion techniques. Beckman bought patent licenses from Western Electric (the manufacturing branch of the Bell System) that covered production processes for semiconductors, began construction of the new facility, and provided Shockley with a generous budget.

In the broader sweep of history Beckman's decision proved momentous. By placing Shockley Semiconductor Laboratories alongside Hewlett-Packard in the Stanford Industrial Park, he helped set in motion the chain of events that led to the birth of Silicon Valley and the U.S. semiconductor, computer, and Internet industries. Without Beckman's decision the Stanford Industrial Park might never have given rise to Silicon Valley, nor would Terman be known as the father of both.

In February 1956 Beckman threw a luncheon at a hotel in San Francisco to celebrate the launch of Shockley Semiconductor Laboratories, located for the short run in Mountain View, California. Shockley proudly announced: "With the guidance of Dr. Beckman, I plan to build the most creative team in the world for developing and producing transistors and other semiconductor devices." And this he did, recruiting a stunning roster of individuals of unique talent who, in their turn, have become famous for pioneering semiconductor technology and integrated circuits: Julius Blank, Victor Grinich, Jean Hoerni, Gene Kleiner, Jay Last, Gordon Moore, Robert Noyce, and Sheldon Roberts. The group would spearhead the technology underlying the information age.

All indications pointed to a propitious future for Shockley Semiconductor, a feeling reinforced with the announcement in late 1956 that Shockley, the head of Beckman's newest enterprise, had just been awarded the Nobel Prize in physics, along with his earlier collaborators, Bardeen and Brattain. Shockley basked in the

Frederick Terman was Arnold Beckman's exact contemporary, born in 1900. Terman, like Beckman, had earned an undergraduate degree in chemical engineering.

While Beckman went on to pursue physical chemistry, Terman chose a career in electrical engineering. For his Ph.D., Terman selected MIT over Caltech, but he then returned to the West for a professorship at Stanford. Terman's area of expertise was radio engineering and technology. Terman, like Beckman, combined a passion for science and engineering with a drive to engage with these fields of knowledge in the "real world," the arenas of technology and industry.

By the mid-1930s Terman was increasingly dissatisfied with the way his best students left the Bay Area for research centers and industrial concerns on the East Coast. To Terman this was a great loss to Stanford and California; if graduates could stay in the area, building and working in new high-tech businesses, a critical mass of talent and opportunity would propel Stanford and its region to new heights. One of Terman's earliest efforts to combat the drain to the East Coast firms began with his encouragement of two of his students to come back to Palo Alto to start a business manufacturing audio oscillators. The two, William Hewlett and David Packard, agreed. Terman arranged a grant from Sperry Gyroscope for them, and in 1938 Hewlett and Packard started to produce these sensitive electronic devices in a rented garage in Palo Alto. It was a beginning much like that of Arnold Beckman's a few years

earlier in a garage in South Pasadena. Hewlett-Packard, of course, went on to become one of the leading producers of computers, electronic devices, and scientific equipment.

By the 1950s Terman's plans were much more expansive. Stanford University possessed hundreds of acres of unused land, part of Leland Stanford's bequest of his farm. The bequest forbade Stanford from selling the land, but Terman saw that there would be no restriction against leasing it. He established the Stanford Industrial Park to lease large plots of land to high-technology firms right next to a prestigious and eagerly helpful university, where he became provost in 1955. By 1953 Varian Associates had moved into the park, and General Electric, Eastman Kodak, Hewlett-Packard, and Lockheed, among others, soon followed. ∾

Frederick Terman, circa 1952. *Courtesy Stanford University.*

David Packard shakes hands with Frederick Terman, with William Hewlett in the background. *Courtesy Stanford University.*

glory of his achievement. By the start of 1957, however, Beckman was concerned that all was not right with his new venture. Shockley had assured him in 1955 that he could be turning out mass batches of silicon transistors within two years. Eighteen months had passed, with no product in sight. The expenses that the Shockley Semiconductor Laboratories had run up were significant, fast approaching the $1 million mark. While sales of instruments and products flowing out of other Beckman Instruments divisions were brisk, Shockley's expenses were not offset at all by sales revenue. The company's overall research-and-development budget had therefore ballooned to nearly 14 percent of sales revenue, far higher than either Beckman or Wall Street wanted. Beckman Instruments' stock lost 5 percent of its value in March 1957 after the public announcement of these R&D figures.

Beckman sent Jack Bishop to the Bay Area to investigate what was happening; he also made several trips himself to meet with Shockley and his leading staff. While generally loath to tell his research directors precisely how to do their jobs, Beckman had little compunction about reminding them of what the job really was,

Beckman poses with Shockley, who had received a congratulatory proclamation from San Francisco Mayor George Christopher, for his Nobel Prize. *Courtesy Beckman Coulter, Inc.*

of the need to keep the organization's goals clear in their minds. In one meeting he gathered Shockley's group together to broach plans for bringing the team back into focus on innovations in semiconductor manufacture rather than on research on ever-more-sophisticated breeds of transistor. Shockley reacted violently to the suggestion that the laboratory return to its original goal. The newly minted Nobel laureate stood in front of Beckman and the staff and declaimed, "If you don't like what we're doing here, I can take this group and get support any place." The rest sat stunned as Shockley exploded out of the conference room.

In reality Shockley was increasingly besieged not only by Beckman's discontent from above but with growing unease from the staff under him. Many of his best scientists and engineers came to doubt the direction, and the director, of the laboratory. They had come to pioneer new production methods for silicon semiconductors with Shockley, but he scarcely let them work toward this goal at all, and never together in a unified program. Instead, he set them individualized projects, explicitly keeping some of these tasks secret from other members of the staff.

Shockley was directing his researchers toward solving parts of a puzzle that fascinated him personally: the creation of a four-layered diode, a wondrously complex transistor that was proving hellishly difficult to achieve. Shockley's researchers rankled at more than this change in direction away from the goal they had signed on for. They also resented his personal eccentricities and their corrosive effect on the direction of the laboratory. Bill Shockley was prone to loud, embarrassing, public outbursts like the one he had directed toward Arnold Beckman. He acted as though his truly impressive achievements and his genuinely remarkable abilities as a scientist exempted him from the rules of social intercourse, from responsibility for the effects of his words and deeds. More dramatically, however, he began to display behavior that verged on the paranoid.

Shockley suffered from insomnia, worsened by a series of strange phone calls arriving at his home around midnight. If he answered the ringing phone, he was met instantly with a dial tone. Shockley thought a member of his staff was out to get him. When a secretary in the laboratory cut her hand on a small bit of metal sticking out from her door, he let it be known that he felt that this was the result of a deliberate act of sabotage intended to do violence to her, perhaps even to him. His suspicions settled on Sheldon Roberts, who had come to the lab from Dow Chemical. He confronted Roberts, blaming him for both the calls and the metal shard. Roberts reacted to this unsettling situation in a manner befitting a scientist: He examined the piece of metal under a microscope. It was the remnant of a common office pushpin that had lost its cap! There was no sabotage, merely the natural decay of office postings. The absurdity of the situation stood in stark contrast to the ill effects that Shockley's manner and accusations were having on the organization.

The "pushpin incident" became a rallying point for the senior researchers. Despite his scientific gifts, William Shockley was no director, no manager. They could work with him, and they valued his advice, but they could no longer work directly for him. Among themselves, the senior staff members decided that Gordon Moore should act as their spokesperson and that he would contact Arnold Beckman—their ultimate boss—directly. Moore phoned Beckman, who immediately grasped the reason for the call. Instead of skirting around the matter, he tackled reality head on. "Things aren't going all that well up there, are they?" he asked Moore. This simple question reflected not only Beckman's straightforward dedication to solving problems but also his innate grace, as he saved Moore the embarrassment of being first to bring up the reason for his call. "No, not really" was Moore's reply.

Beckman agreed to meet with Moore and his colleagues, in confidence, over several dinners near San Francisco. Sometimes as many as seven others joined them as they struggled to find a solution that would keep the laboratory together and move it back to focus. Moore and his co-workers said the situation was dire: Unless some kind of solution could be found, they all would resign together. They lobbied Beckman to replace Shockley, to make someone else the director of the laboratory, and to move him into some kind of consulting position.

Such a drastic solution went against Arnold Beckman's managerial instincts. If he agreed to the staff's proposal, he and Shockley both would see it as an act of betrayal, for rightly or wrongly he had placed his confidence in William Shockley. Beckman kept to his instincts and to his sense of integrity by choosing to break the news of the resignation threat to Shockley—in person, over dinner. Beckman told him that if something did not change in the leadership of the laboratory, the critical core of the staff would leave. Shockley was stunned by the news. By telling him, Beckman hoped Shockley might handle the situation himself.

It was not to be. In June, Beckman had to appear in person again as a mediator between the director and his staff. No improvements in the working atmosphere had materialized. In desperation Beckman hammered out a deal between Shockley and the dissidents wherein a new position would be created, that of "manager," firmly in between Shockley and the rest of the staff. Beckman considered who would be best to fill this new role. One likely candidate was Joseph Lewis, who had cut his teeth as head of Arnold O. Beckman, Inc. But this solution turned out to be no solution at all, as Shockley and several staff members simply left the dissidents behind, moving into space in the new Spinco building now ready at the Stanford Industrial Park. Shockley and his group continued to pursue the four-layered diode, while the dissidents stayed in the old location in Mountain View, working directly on silicon semiconductor production. The gentler solution had served only to split the organization apart.

Arnold Beckman changed his tack. He expected loyalty from his managers, but he expected no less loyalty from himself for his appointed managers, however

Dr. Beckman details building expansion plans for the new Spinco plant at Stanford Industrial Park in Palo Alto, 1960. From left: F. Clifford, Jr., the Spinco Division manager; Arnold Beckman; Frederick Terman, provost and vice president of Stanford University; and Rear Admiral John Ball, mayor of Palo Alto. *Courtesy Beckman Coulter, Inc.*

bizarre their conduct or poor their profits. He backed Bill Shockley. Looking back, he regrets that he did not learn more about Shockley's capacity as a research director or appreciate more fully the difficulties of his personality. Yet Beckman had to bear in mind the opinions of other leaders in the field of semiconductors, who advised him that removing Shockley from unfettered leadership on the heels of his Nobel Prize would sound the death knell of his career. "With one of my misdirected feelings of loyalty, I felt I owed Shockley and should give him enough of a chance to prove himself. And I said [to the dissenters], 'I'm not going to fire Shockley at this stage of the game.'"

Instead Arnold Beckman installed Maurice Hanafin (whom we shall shortly encounter as one of the founders of Spinco) as manager for the Shockley laboratory, but left Shockley himself with final say over Hanafin. Leadership did not change. The dissenting senior staff felt that they simply could not stay, since the events of the preceding months had produced an unbridgeable rift. On 18 September 1957 the group of eight dissenters—reportedly referred to by Shockley as the "traitorous eight"—resigned. While certainly a grievous blow for Shockley and Beckman, this

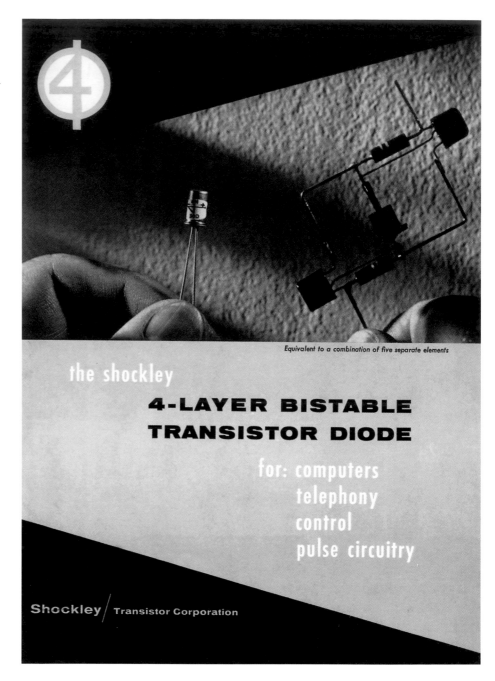

resignation in the end had far broader historical significance. It marked the opening act in the growth of the semiconductor, integrated circuit, and microprocessor industries of Silicon Valley, which rapidly attained global leadership. Moreover, the resignation and subsequent move by the eight was the first distinctly Silicon Valley episode of "exodus and start-up."

The group of eight left Shockley to form Fairchild Semiconductor. Fairchild was significant for a number of reasons. There the Shockley eight achieved their goal of developing a process for mass-producing silicon semiconductor devices: the planar process. Moreover, at Fairchild the eight were able to manufacture integrated circuits on silicon semiconductors. Integrated circuits are systems of extremely small electrical "on-off" switches on a single piece of silicon, and they constitute the very heart of the microprocessors that drive the information age.

The move by Gordon Moore, Robert Noyce, and their colleagues from Shockley to Fairchild set the pattern for Silicon Valley—technology transfer through the rampant migration of individuals, as employees of one semiconductor firm took their ideas, experience, and knowledge and left to establish their own start-up operation based on these resources. This dynamic has been repeated in the semiconductor industry in the decades since 1957, in part because it is impossible to stop. As soon as Fairchild was established, Arnold Beckman's legal counsel, Leslie Duryea, looked into taking legal action against the former Shockley employees. Clearly, the eight had gained valuable knowledge and experience while in Beckman's employ, but there was no clear-cut way to show that they were directly infringing the intellectual property and patents held by Beckman Instruments. Such was the nature of a new industry, based on technological revolutions.

Fairchild, created from the core of Beckman's semiconductor business, in turn gave rise to a phenomenal number of semiconductor firms. By the early 1970s some forty-five companies had been formed by employees who had left the company—an astounding average rate of three start-ups per year. Indeed, ten years after the founding of Fairchild, the two most important members of the Shockley Semiconductor eight—Noyce and Moore—left to found Intel, their own new company. Intel built the first microprocessor, the computer on a chip, and thereby confirmed the reality of Silicon Valley as the cradle of the information age.

William Shockley, for his part, was finally successful in building a four-layered diode and began to produce it, but Arnold Beckman came to realize that this device had no large market and that the future lay with integrated circuits and Fairchild. Shockley Semiconductor Laboratories, renamed Shockley Transistor Corporation in 1958, was a personal research laboratory, not at home within Beckman Instruments. "It was a critical thing. I didn't know enough about Shockley at the time when this group came up to me and said either it's Shockley or us. If I had known what I know now, I'd have said good-bye to Shockley, and I probably would have been very much involved in the semiconductor business. But I didn't. We carried on for a while, and finally it got to the point where we could see that [Shockley] was just incapable of running an operation." Beckman sold the Shockley subsidiary to the Clevite Transistor Company in 1960, ending his formal association with the semiconductor industry.

Arnold Beckman had once again seen, and sought to surf, the wave of opportunity. Their common commitment to inventions of excellence blinded him to the problems of William Shockley's personality. The outcome was not at all what Beckman intended, but his unerring instinct for the sweet spot of opportunity surely started a breeder reactor for the semiconductor industry. As he later recalled, the entire Silicon Valley phenomenon "starts with Shockley and then Fairchild, all composed of people who were employed with some other company who got an idea or were dissatisfied or something, and they go and start their own companies . . . anyway, it started with Shockley"—and with Beckman, he might have added.

The Promise and Pitfalls of Computer Automation

The episode in which Arnold Beckman joined William Shockley in a venture of high promise, which he was then unable to bring to fruition, indicates how, as Beckman Instruments continued to develop and diversify, it became steadily more difficult for Dr. Beckman himself simultaneously to stimulate new technologies, manage the firm, and take on growing roles as citizen and civic leader. His greatest gift lay in his instinct for the possibilities of new technologies, growing out of and feeding the advance of science. Semiconductors, transistors, and integrated circuits offered one such field. Another lay in computers and automation. There too he would pioneer—and there too he would experience the frustration of not being able to institutionalize fully and on a long-term basis the opportunities that beckoned his corporation.

Today the annals of computer development say little of Beckman Instruments, but in the mid-1950s the firm was active as a key player in this new field. By purchasing Berkeley Scientific in 1952, Beckman positioned his corporation in the vanguard of computer development—a position buttressed by Department of Defense contracts for projects that grew out of Beckman work in nuclear instrumentation. By the end of the decade there were a considerable number of civilian installations as well, and Beckman Instruments had established a Systems Division, under Jack Bishop. Bishop was given his head—but precisely because his ideas were shaped by and agreed with Dr. Beckman's restless agenda of opportunity.

Computers and automation were new items in public discourse in the mid-1950s, and both came to public notice in the same period that produced the phrase "cutting edge." The *New York Times* first noticed "automation" as an index item in 1954, the same year the city held its First International Automation Exposition. Seventy manufacturers exhibited at that exposition, and an "electronic computer clinic" offered instruction on both analog and digital computers. Anyone who looked up "computer" in the *New York Times* index was as a result told to "See Calculators." That changed in 1956, when index researchers were told to "See Data Processing," itself a new heading that year. Finally, in 1957, there appeared a short entry on "Computers and Automation," with the concepts joined in indexes as in the public mind.

In that era "automation" evoked a whole cluster of connotations related to a technological future characterized by speed, efficiency, labor-saving machines, and computerized control. Arnold Beckman led his company in the attempt to translate this technological dream into present realities in the area of scientific and industrial instrumentation. Instruments are in a sense machines for producing facts. To transform the facts that they produce into knowledge or understanding involves a number of steps and activities beyond the operation of any instrument itself. The facts, the data, must be collected, interpreted, and compared to readings of other instruments and to theoretical understandings. By transforming facts into knowledge, one gains the capacity to act—to refine scientific research, to control a chemical production process, to operate a complex technological device, or to make a clinical decision in a health care setting. For Beckman and others the ideal

One of the ads prepared for the twenty-fifth anniversary of Beckman Instruments, 1960. *Courtesy Beckman Coulter, Inc.*

Not since the year One ● There's been no change in the scientific method. Only the tools are different. Our job—providing them ● Today a Beckman meter counts events from one a second to twelve billion per second. A Beckman ultramicro analytical system routinely measures cholesterol or chlorides in a split-drop of blood. Beckman high-speed computers can monitor and control everything from a process stream to a satellite launching ● These are the kinds of electronic components, instruments and systems that Beckman builds now…the standard, practical tools of the times. Research scientists, manufacturers, processors, the military—all, in turn, build progress around them ● One day the present science of electronics will be supplemented or replaced. Still newer technologies will need even more advanced instruments to implement them ● Our catalog for the future? We're working on it now.

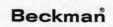

BECKMAN INSTRUMENTS, INC. FULLERTON, CALIFORNIA | ELECTRONIC COMPONENTS, INSTRUMENTS, SYSTEMS…FOR ANALYSIS, MEASUREMENT, COUNTING AND CONTROL | DIVISIONS: BERKELEY· HELIPOT· INTERNATIONAL· SCIENTIFIC & PROCESS INSTRUMENTS · SPECIAL PROJECTS · SPINCO · SYSTEMS | SUBSIDIARIES: SHOCKLEY TRANSISTOR CORP · BECKMAN INSTRUMENTS, G.m.b.H., GERMANY · BECKMAN INSTRUMENTS, LTD., SCOTLAND

© 1960 B.I.I. BC 60143

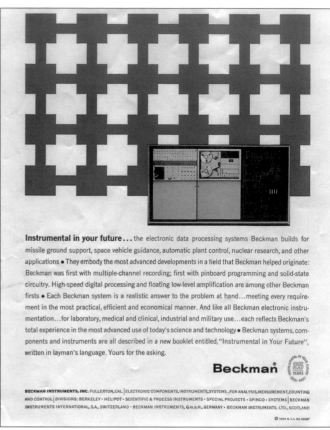

Left: Beckman poses in front of the EASE computer made by the Berkeley Division in the 1950s.

Right: A twenty-fifth anniversary ad for Beckman Instruments' data-processing systems.
Both courtesy Beckman Coulter, Inc.

of automation evoked a vision of building computer-controlled systems that would not only produce and record facts but also turn these facts into knowledge and then act on that knowledge. The computer would be responsible for directing instruments to perform new analyses based on incoming information or to alter the settings and mixtures of an industrial process to optimize yields automatically.

Arnold Beckman took Beckman Instruments into computing, well before the term hit the popular indexes, with the acquisition of Berkeley in 1952. Beckman Instruments created a Berkeley Division, but in advertisements Berkeley was the big word, Beckman in relatively small type. An advertisement in *Scientific American* for November 1953 touted Berkeley's EASE analog computer, an electronic analog simulating system, which could fully mimic the functions of an entire "dynamic system" through accurate readings of the effects of many variables. EASE, the copy claimed, was simple, accurate, compact in taking up a mere eight square feet, easy to install, and "the world's first high-quality computer to be mass-produced in practical commercial form." In 1955 similar ads announced that Berkeley's data reduction system would reduce staff costs, minimize error, and speed data handling. For industrial process control the Berkeley system could monitor at accuracies to 0.001 percent, with recording "on a digital printer, analog recorder, electric typewriter, IBM cards, magnetic tape, teletypewriter, computer, or X-Y plotter."

In September 1956 the Instrument Society of America (which Beckman had helped found some eleven years earlier) held its annual meeting in New York City and dubbed it the "International Instrument-Automation Conference and Exhibit." There were hundreds of exhibitors, and Beckman Instruments was one of the largest. Dr. Beckman's fascination with automation, and his conviction that it was a burgeoning technological realm central to his company's future, are captured in a full-page ad in the *Wall Street Journal* in advance of the ISA show:

> Beckman automation is instruments and systems that integrate the vital functions of production, of business and research, to provide management with essential operating data and controls. Beckman Automation at the 1956 I.S.A. show reveals the tools for sensing, gathering, transmitting, reducing and computing information for production control, tools for computation of data for marketing and finance and for analysis and measurement in research.

More dramatically, the ad spoke of "automatic control . . . the reality of today and the promise of the future."

The instruments that Arnold Beckman led his company to develop in its early decades relied on a marriage between chemistry and electronics. Now he was convinced that his earlier technological successes with electronic instrumentation were but a prelude to far greater success in the new technological fields of electronic processing and handling of vast streams of information. Beckman was personally involved in directing the push through Berkeley into data handling, then into computing and computerized automation. On 9 July 1957 the *Wall Street Journal* reported that Beckman Instruments had formed a Systems Division to "develop and build industrial data systems for automation." Headquarters of the Systems Division was in Anaheim, with a second (Berkeley) plant in Richmond. Systems growth was supplemented, as were other instrument projects, by continuing corporate acquisitions. Statham Laboratories was one such acquisition, made in

Data-handling and computer systems made by Beckman Instruments in the early 1960s. *Courtesy Beckman Coulter, Inc.*

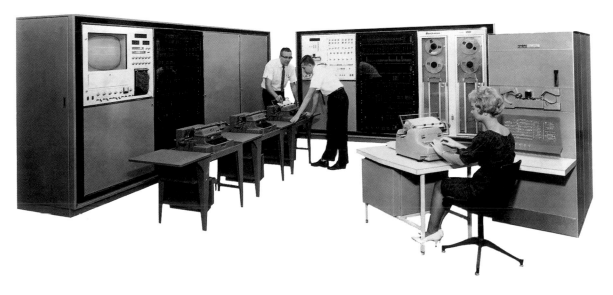

Some examples of Beckman process control systems of the late 1950s.

Courtesy Beckman Coulter, Inc.

DATA PROCESSING

Model 150 Tachometer System
**E. I. du Pont de Nemours & Co.
Martinsville, W. Va.**

A data logger for monitoring motor speeds in a nylon plant, this system operated 24 hours a day, seven days a week for seventeen months without a single system failure. Designed for maximum reliability and ease of servicing, the system pioneered all-solid-state and "plug--in" modular construction. Up to 112 separate speed inputs are scanned by the equipment at the rate of one per second. In addition to periodically logging all speeds, the system indicates an alarm condition should any speed rise or fall below preset limits. A complete log is available at any time upon demand. The system incorporates an automatic self-testing feature to guard against inaccurate readings. Installed in December, 1957.

Model 112 Data Processing Computer
**Phillips Chemical Co.
Sweeny, Tex.**

This, the first 112 system, was installed in December, 1957, at the Phillips Company's ethylene plant. The system accepts inputs from up to 400 standard transducers measuring temperatures, pressures, flow rates and other variables. After scaling, linearizing and zero offsetting the analog input signals — scanned at the rate of five per second — the system makes the mathematical computations pre-programmed for each channel, then prints out the resultant quantities in digital form. Upper and lower limits for each input channel may be introduced via the system pinboard. Both visual and audible alarms indicate when an input is off-limit. Widely publicized, this pioneer system has been described in four different magazine articles.

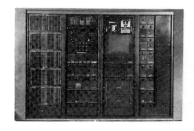

Model 112 Data System
**Socony Mobil Oil Co.
Casper, Wyo.**

Installed in January, 1958, this 200-channel system monitors and logs the operating variables at Socony's new catalytic reformer in the Casper Refinery. Socony's Model 112, used from the day of plant start-up, serves as a valuable operator's tool to assist in rapidly ascertaining plant operating efficiency.

10

February 1956—a very desirable addition because of its precision devices for measurement control, used in aircraft and guided missiles.

By December 1960 Beckman's commitments to and enthusiasm for "systems" had translated into plans for a major new building at the Fullerton site. At a price of $1.25 million, the plant added 100,000 square feet for production of high-speed electronic data-processing systems. With the addition of this facility Beckman Instruments had 450,000 square feet of plant space in Fullerton alone.

Chemical reactions and chemical processes are complex entities, and developing a view of the whole involves collecting information about many parts at various times and locations. Ever the chemist, Dr. Beckman shared and encouraged the vision of Jack Bishop's engineers that data-handling systems would have great potential for industrial and academic chemistry. One of the first devices that the company produced in this new arena was a two-hundred-channel automatic recorder. This machine could take electronic signals coming from a vast array of gauges, convert the signals into digital form, and record all the data on a Flexiwriter. Showing the evolution of one Beckman technology into another, the control panel of the recorder was festooned with two hundred calibrating knobs, each attached to a Helipot.

In the late 1950s and early 1960s Beckman Instruments did produce several data-handling systems, custom-built for monitoring and controlling large petroleum refinery complexes. Those processes are among the most extensive and intricate in chemical industry, and the Systems Division developed computer systems that could measure variables like temperature, pressure, flow rate—hundreds and hundreds of measurements—and control elements of the refinery process in light of these measures. Several petroleum refiners bought such systems, but they proved expensive and temperamental; by the mid-1960s the market was stagnating. It would be at least another decade before the chemical process industries began to clamor for computerized monitoring and control.

The problem on this and other occasions was that Arnold Beckman's vision was ahead of its time. He saw a broad market for computer systems, automating and controlling laboratory equipment and industrial process plants, cutting across the entire spectrum of chemical science. However, the reality he and his colleagues faced was that they were ahead of the technological curve for most of the chemical process industries. As Richard Nesbit, who directed the company's systems work in the 1960s, put it: "We were spending most of our time trying to tell people about things they could hardly imagine."

Beckman found consolation with the discovery that if demand for the two-hundred-channel recorder did not come from chemical engineers and industrial chemists as he anticipated, all was not lost. In practice real customers were in space and defense, among them Watertown Arsenal in Massachusetts (home of the Army Material Technology Laboratory) and the Douglas Aircraft Company near Los Angeles.

Engineers at Douglas used the recorder to collect complex measurements of the performance under strain of the wings of both commercial and military aircraft. Researchers at Watertown sought it out for their work in producing weapons, armaments, and metallurgical technologies for the United States Army. The exigencies of national security and seemingly limitless funds allowed these sectors to embrace and experiment with this novel and expensive technology. Chemical process industries, on the other hand, were much more cautious; they still had to balance the promises of new technology against the bottom line.

Since Dr. Beckman was committed to a major expansion—in terms of facilities, talent, and equipment—for the systems business, Beckman Instruments turned its main attention to the aerospace demand. Each aerospace "system" was a special project, not unlike an organ constructed for a church. Each organ may be similar, in that it consists of thousands of pipes large and small, but the whole instrument is designed for a specific place. Projects for the space program or for defense purposes were the same. The Systems Division was often at work on four to five at once. The division made Beckman Instruments a significant defense contractor.

For instance, in September 1959 Beckman announced delivery of an analog computer system to Boeing Aerospace for use with the Air Force Bomarc IM-99 ground-to-air weapons system. This was perhaps one of the last of the old-style computers, with its five thousand vacuum tubes and sixty-foot length. It weighed ten tons. The Systems Division also contracted with the space program, and Beckman himself told *Aviation Week* in August 1961 that the company expected sizable contracts. And indeed, contracts came in a relatively steady stream. In 1961 Beckman helped develop a Lunar Surface Analyzer for the Jet Propulsion Laboratory's Project Surveyor. Also that year Lockheed Aircraft awarded Beckman two contracts for data-processing equipment for the Air Force satellite programs. Another contract came from North American Aviation for electronic units in an "automatic checkout system for Minuteman long-range ballistic missiles." Beckman received numerous million-dollar government-related contracts in the early 1960s. Three major contracts came in 1963 alone: Grumman Aircraft Engineering wanted a data-acquisition system; Lear Siegler ordered data-acquisition systems and digital computers for the Saturn space vehicle; and NASA awarded a contract jointly to Beckman and Scientific Data Systems for an analog-digital computer system.

Simulators, like the Berkeley EASE, had been a key component in the early systems for refineries. As we have seen, these computer systems mimic the electronic information that will eventually be supplied by the real world. They allow systems engineers to make sure that a computer is handling the incoming data properly, for the simulator provides inputs that are known exactly. Just as the Helipot began its life as a civilian item in the pH meter before becoming an important defense and aerospace device in its own right, so too with Beckman Instruments' simulators, initially developed for petroleum refineries: They found their real role with firms deeply engaged in defense and aerospace work, such as Boeing, Douglas, and General Electric.

By the end of the 1960s America's manned space program was relying on Beckman simulators. The Gemini project had the mission of increasing the duration of space flight (up to two weeks) and improving space walks, docking maneuvers, and reentry procedures for returning the spacecraft to Earth. To meet these goals, Gemini spacecraft needed improved navigational systems and computers. Beckman simulators were used as inputs for Gemini's on-board systems, mim-

Richard Nesbit. *Courtesy Beckman Coulter, Inc.*

icking the data that would later be fed into navigational computers during flight. They allowed the astronauts to get a feel for flying their spacecraft before they left the ground.

The Beckman Systems Division also produced computer systems to handle the vast amounts of data radioed, or "telemetered," back to Earth from satellites and unmanned spacecraft. In principle, these computer systems were much like the two-hundred-channel data recorders that Dr. Beckman had directed his engineers to build in the mid-1950s for applications in chemical plants. Beckman Instruments

The Model 210 transistorized data processor made for Aerojet Corporation in the early 1960s. *Courtesy Beckman Coulter, Inc.*

systems could process these data into usable information whether they came from industrial pH meters installed in a pipe or whether they had been beamed from orbiting satellites or spacecraft to listening stations across the globe.

Telemetric data, that is, data radioed back to Earth from a satellite or spacecraft, were ubiquitous in and crucial to the inseparable worlds of national defense and space exploration in the late 1960s. Satellites, rockets, missiles, and spacecraft all used telemetry to send information back to engineers and scientists, whether they worked for the military or for NASA. This transmitted information was as diverse

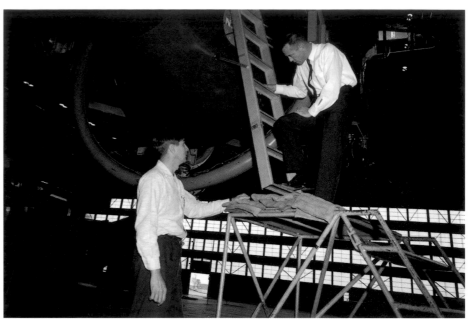

Top left: The Gemini rendezvous docking simulator suspended from the roof of the aircraft hanger at the Langley Research Center in Virginia.
Courtesy NASA.

Bottom: The control room at the Jet Propulsion Laboratory at Caltech where telemetered data were monitored and assessed.
Courtesy Institute Archives, California Institute of Technology.

Top right: Astronaut Alan Shepard, at right, inspects the Gemini simulator at Langley Research Center.
Courtesy NASA.

as it was massive: The vehicle would radio back data from many different kinds of instruments. Besides instruments for conducting scientific investigations in space, a given craft would carry positioning beacons, navigational devices, cameras aimed both inside and outside, sensors to monitor environmental conditions inside the vehicle and the condition of its various components and controls, and a myriad of other devices. Computers were essential for processing telemetered data, since all this information was combined in a single radio transmission to the receiving stations on Earth. Only a computer could unravel these pieces of information and put them in a form that scientists and engineers could use. Systems Division built telemetric-data-processing computers for military missile ranges, NASA satellite control centers, and NASA's unmanned space programs. The division built systems to process the photographs of the Moon taken by the Ranger spacecraft, for example. These unmanned Ranger missions were important first steps in the exploration of the Moon and the development of spaceflight in general.

The only flaw in this story, but a major flaw, was the lack of profits. Arnold Beckman himself might delight in the visions of a William Shockley and in the technological challenge and adventure of computers and automation. But by the late 1950s he was not only a brilliant scientist and entrepreneur but also head of a large (four thousand employee) public company. Both institutional and individual investors had high expectations for Beckman Instruments. Sales that went from $21 million in 1955 to $85 million in 1964 certainly fulfilled those expectations. Profits that lurched from $1.4 million in 1955 to a loss of $950,000 three years later, then up to a $4.8 million profit in 1962 and down to $2.3 million in 1964, were another matter.

What the Systems Division—and Dr. Beckman—needed but did not have was a corporate board of directors that would challenge its CEO and a management forum in which the case for marketing and budget analyses could be made by senior managers. The results of those analyses might then be subject to robust debate *before* decisions were made. Instead Beckman preferred to trust his instincts, keep his counsel, consult with Mabel, and then back his trusted deputies in separate and varied ventures, which agreed with his intuitions. But before treating these realities, we need to lay out more of the riches of Dr. Beckman's inventive vision for Beckman Instruments.

New Instruments for the New Biology and for Industry

Transistors, computers, and automation were new, exciting areas—the very cutting edge of high technology in the 1950s and 1960s. Arnold Beckman wanted his company to be on that edge, and he was willing to bet heavily on William Shockley, on the opportunities to pioneer and to learn afforded by government contracts in defense and aerospace, and on the investments in plant and staff required to develop a viable Systems Division. At the same time he saw new opportunities too good to pass up in Beckman Instruments' core technology of instruments for chemists and life scientists to go alongside pH meters and spectrophotometers.

As mentioned earlier, Beckman Instruments' facilities in the Stanford Industrial Park were designed to house two operations—Shockley Semiconductor Laboratories and Spinco, now Beckman's Spinco Division. Spinco originally joined the company by much the same route as Shockley Semiconductor later on: because a scientific entrepreneur sought Arnold Beckman's advice.

Maurice Hanafin and Edward Pickels had started Spinco in 1947 to produce commercially the first electrically driven ultracentrifuge. Pickels, formerly a scientific staff member of the Rockefeller Institute (later Rockefeller University), was the instrument's inventor; like Arnold Beckman, he had left university life for industry to make available the extraordinary tool for chemical and biochemical analysis he had devised. Hanafin and Pickels anticipated a very small market for their powerful machines, perhaps only ten or twelve leading academic laboratories worldwide. Their plan was to make a few instruments and then go out of business. Like Beckman, Hanafin and Pickels severely underestimated their market. As demand continued, they decided to stay in business and to become leaders in ultracentrifuge production. By 1955 Hanafin wanted to learn how to market their device more effectively. "Who better to ask than Arnold Beckman?" he decided. He admired Beckman's ability at spreading word of his own instruments throughout the industrial and the academic worlds.

Beckman and Hanafin met in Beckman's new Fullerton offices. Initially, their conversation focused on problems of marketing and publicity in the high-end scientific instrumentation business. "We have this centrifuge, and it's a good instrument," Hanafin said. "How do we market something like that?" To answer, Beckman needed to know more about Spinco's ultracentrifuge and what distinguished it from others. In the scientific instrumentation industry, specifications speak volumes. As the discussion progressed, his interest grew. Here was a small firm with solid sales of an extraordinary instrument for biochemical analysis and preparations. Its design was novel, and annual sales topped $1 million. Furthermore, Beckman saw that the ultracentrifuge's success in biochemical applications would fit in well with both his firm's core technology and the success enjoyed by the DU spectrophotometer. Jonas Salk, who introduced his vaccine for polio in 1954, had—famously—used an ultracentrifuge to isolate the poliovirus.

Beckman and Hanafin "talked and talked and finally we said 'Why don't we get together?' So we merged. It was just sheer chance that he happened to come down to see me, and I recognized, of course, that his product line fit in well with

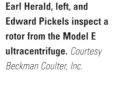

Earl Herald, left, and Edward Pickels inspect a rotor from the Model E ultracentrifuge. *Courtesy Beckman Coulter, Inc.*

A centrifuge is a device that uses rapid rotation to produce a centrifugal force. In turn, the centrifugal force is used to accomplish an act of separation.

For example, the spinning drum of a washing machine is a centrifuge. The spinning of the drum produces a centrifugal force that separates water from washed laundry during the "spin cycle." One of the most common of all centrifuges is the milk separator, which uses spinning to divide milk from cream. As a youth Arnold Beckman had used a hand-cranked centrifuge in the Cullom general store.

Centrifuges had changed a great deal since Cullom. In the early 1920s Theodor Svedberg, a Swedish chemist, developed the ultracentrifuge and won a Nobel Prize in chemistry for the invention in 1926. The ultracentrifuge is like any other centrifuge in principle, but it rotates at far, far greater speeds and generates much greater forces. Svedberg's own rotated at forty thousand turns per minute, producing forces five thousand times the force of gravity. The great virtue of ultracentrifugation is its ability to separate materials with very small differences in density and yet not harm the living processes of the materials. In this sense the technique employed tremendous force but was very gentle.

From the 1920s through the 1950s more powerful ultracentrifuges were developed as scientists made important discoveries using them. The ultracentrifuge proved especially adept at separating and purifying messy, gummy biochemical compounds, the substances most important to biology, biological processes, and, therefore, medicine. Ultracentrifuges allowed researchers to isolate pure samples of proteins and to determine with precision their sizes and molecular weights. Further, the ultracentrifuge allowed researchers to separate parts of cells from one another, to differentiate the components of blood, and to isolate viruses.

By the early 1950s the ultracentrifuge was recognized as a critical tool in laboratories of biochemistry, biology, medicine, and pharmacology. ～

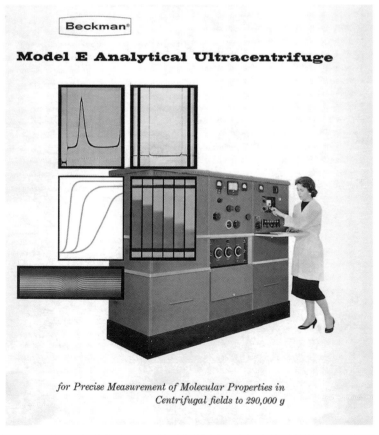

Beckman

Model E Analytical Ultracentrifuge

for Precise Measurement of Molecular Properties in Centrifugal fields to 290,000 g

A 1960s ad for the Model E analytical ultracentrifuge. *Courtesy Beckman Coulter, Inc.*

ours. Their ultracentrifuges were being used in biological research, biochemical research." Spinco became a division of Beckman's company on 1 January 1955.

Beckman recalls Spinco as his greatest acquisition, in part for the ease of its integration into Beckman Instruments, in part for its financial success as Beckman's Spinco Division, and in part for the scientific significance of its work. Acquiring Spinco was another example of Beckman's finding the sweet spot of opportunity for the technological future. Spinco became the technological wellspring for Beckman Instruments in the life sciences. Until the rise of the firm's clinical business in the 1960s and 1970s, Spinco was the most profitable division in the history of the company. Moreover Spinco's innovations for the life sciences laid much of the groundwork for the clinical business—the central mission of the company today.

Spinco's innovations included far more than ultracentrifuges: the Moore-Stein amino acid analyzer and ion-exchange chromatography, for example. The division counted several "firsts," among them commercial peptide sequencing and synthesizing, Tiselius electrophoresis (used on proteins in biological systems), and paper and capillary electrophoresis.

With the financial resources and sales expertise of Beckman behind it, Spinco's sales went to $2.5 million in 1955. By the 1980s Beckman Instruments was selling over $100 million worth of ultracentrifuges per year. Such commercial results are gratifying, but Spinco's true excellence lay in the transformation its ultracentrifuges effected in the biological sciences. The Beckman Model E analytical ultracentrifuge that the Spinco Division produced became an essential tool for the new fields of molecular genetics and molecular biology.

One example illustrates the importance of the Model E. In 1944 Oswald Avery had proved that genes were made of DNA, that it was literally the stuff of inheritance. In 1953 James Watson and Francis Crick published the landmark paper in *Nature* that laid out the structure of the DNA molecule—the iconic, interlaced rib-

Left: The Spinco Division site at Stanford Industrial Park.

Right: The Spinco research team that developed the Model L-2 centrifuge, in 1962. *Both courtesy Beckman Coulter, Inc.*

Left: **Bill Grey of Beckman Instruments makes adjustments on a Model E ultracentrifuge at Spinco.**

Right: **Ultracentifuges and electrophoresis instruments—two of Spinco's great successes.** *Both courtesy Beckman Coulter, Inc.*

bons of the double helix now instantly recognizable. The power of Watson and Crick's discovery of the double helix (for which they received the Nobel Prize in medicine in 1962) lay in its revelation of how DNA might reproduce itself, how genetic information could pass from generation to generation. Roughly put, it seemed that DNA might replicate by first unwinding, with each half strand then acting as a template upon which a companion strand would form, so that from one full strand comes two. In the closing days of 1957, just four years after Watson and Crick's discovery, an experiment was performed at Caltech that proved that theory of DNA replication. The experiment marked a profound leap forward in the understanding of genetics, and the Beckman Model E analytical ultracentrifuge was the tool that made it possible.

With his lively interest in chemical analysis and his eye for the next wave of opportunity, Arnold Beckman was quick to see the possibilities of another tool familiar from the 1930s. In the mid-1950s chromatography took on new life and offered revolutionary possibilities in both the chemical industry and the life sciences. Its appeal was irresistible to Beckman, armed with the acquisition power of his successful, growing public corporation.

He decided to leap over the time, expense, and uncertainty of developing this new technology in-house by acquiring expertise from outside. The gas chromatograph fit in well with his past model of a successful instrument—as indispensable to

Through the early 1950s the chemical world was abuzz with talk of chromatography. If ultracentrifugation worked through speeding things around, chromatography worked by slowing things down.

Chromatography covered a whole family of techniques that separated the components of a sample according to the same principle. In outline, the sample liquid enters a carefully designed tube— the "chromatographic column." Within the column the sample encounters two elements. One is "mobile," a flow of an inert liquid that carries the sample from one end of the column to the other. The second element is "stationary" and forms the column itself; it consists of a powdered solid or a liquid attached to a solid, and it is specifically designed for the sample to interact with, then escape from. This stationary element is the one that slows things down.

Different components of the sample interact with the column material in different ways: They are slowed down significantly if they bond well to or are absorbed by the stationary element, or they pass it by relatively unchecked if their chemistry does not favor such bonding. As a result the sample is separated into its component substances by these different rates of slowing. At the end of the chromatographic column the different chemical components emerge one after the other, from the substance that is least slowed by the stationary element to the substance that is most impeded by its propensity to bond.

Different methods for chromatographic separations had developed in the 1930s and 1940s, and these tools had proved wonderfully capable of isolating and detecting even the smallest portions of important biochemicals. Chromatography proved crucial in chemical studies of vitamins, pharmaceuticals, and amino acids. The 1952 Nobel Prize in chemistry marked the true coming of age for chromatography, as Archer J. P. Martin and Richard L. M. Synge were honored for a chromatographic technique they had developed to study amino acids, the building blocks of the proteins so central to the biological processes of life. The technique was based on a liquid sample carried by an inert liquid through a stationary element that consisted of a liquid-solid mixture. Martin, with the attention of the world's scientific community focused on him after his 1952 prize, announced in that same year that he, in collaboration with A. T. James, had developed a new form of chromatography: gas chromatography.

In this new analytical technique a sample was transformed into a gas before it was introduced into the chromatographic column. The column then separated the sample gas into distinct components. The ease with which gas chromatography separated volatile organic compounds was revolutionary. The technique was best suited to the analysis of volatile hydrocarbons, the chemical components that make up oil and all of the petroleum products made from it.

But without a suitable detection instrument attached to the exit end of the column, one has little more than a peculiar, miniature smokestack. It is the detecting instrument that analyzes the separated components that come out of the column and lets one see and record what the column has produced. Thus the gas chromatograph offered ideal applications for Beckman Instruments' existing technology and expertise in a variety of detectors. It also had applications in the biomedical world.

By the mid-1950s the race was on. If one could transform the technique of gas chromatography into a commercial instrument, a gas chromatograph, then one would have a revolutionary analytical tool, as desirable for the academic biochemist as for the industrial petroleum chemist. ❧

A technician tests a line of Beckman gas chromatographs. *Courtesy Beckman Coulter, Inc.*

the industrial plant as to the academic laboratory. Beckman thought the gas chromatograph might give rise to a whole family of instruments and parts as his pH meter had done; moreover, it offered new possibilities for pushing into biomedicine, in symbiosis with other Beckman instruments.

The Watts Manufacturing Company of Ronceverte, West Virginia, was one of the first firms to produce gas chromatographs, especially those designed for industrial customers. In 1956 Beckman entered the chromatography business by acquiring Watts. Later that same year Beckman Instruments put its first gas chromatograph on the market, the GC-1.

Selling for around nine hundred dollars, the GC-1 was marketed as a tool for large and small laboratories, for those already involved in gas chromatography, and for those looking to enter the field. The GC-1 was compact and had high performance, yet it was significantly cheaper than other chromatographs on the market. It was also designed to work with highly volatile substances, those that boil below 80 degrees centigrade. Arnold Beckman therefore aimed at the industrial market, for such volatile substances were primarily the concern of industrial laboratories. Beckman's marketing firm spelled out in no uncertain terms the fields for which this tool was intended: petroleum refining; natural gas; liquefied petroleum gas, whether for "suppliers of bottled gas" or for "users of LPG for fuel"; petrochemicals; cylinder gases, including anesthetics; plastics; refrigerants; chlorinated hydrocarbons; agricultural chemicals; and "other uses including air pollutants, stack gases, nitroparaffins, combustion products, and low-molecular-weight amines." The GC-1 thus forged immediate links with research on some of the most important classes of products of the postwar American chemical industry.

As with Spinco, the Watts acquisition brought success, and Beckman Instruments produced an expanding range of gas chromatographs through the 1960s. Following the release of the GC-1 for the laboratory market, the company developed a series of gas chromatographs for monitoring industrial processes as they occur at the plant. While the principle behind the operation of these industrial chromatographs was the same, the series offered two notable differences from the laboratory line. First, the instruments offered the attraction of automation. They monitored the amounts of key components in chemical processes and recorded them without requiring a trained technician's attention. Second, Beckman Instruments custom-built their industrial chromatographs, designing each one to best separate and detect the substances of most concern to the particular customer. Gas chromatography, however, did not remain a permanent product for the firm. Commercial competition in this field of instrumentation was extreme, and eventually Dr. Beckman found himself in the position he had faced earlier for infrared spectroscopy. He had to discern whether the company could achieve leadership, and if it could not, it should leave the area. With the growing potentials of and commitments to the biomedical field, Beckman decided to withdraw, since true leadership in gas chromatography had eluded Beckman Instruments.

The Promise of Biomedicine

Both ultracentrifuge and chromatograph brought new customers, customers from academic laboratories to chemical companies and petroleum refineries. These new tools revolutionized whole areas of study, as Beckman's pH meters and spectrophotometers had done before them. Ultracentrifuges and chromatography (ion and liquid) also pointed the way to growing involvement with the newly emerging fields of molecular biology and biomedicine, an involvement that would become a major preoccupation in the later 1960s and 1970s. Dr. Beckman's own personal enthusiasm for those sweet spots where academic knowledge, technological possi-

Stanford Moore (left) and William H. Stein, at their amino acid analyzer in the early 1960s. *Photo by Sam Vandivert. Courtesy Rockefeller University Archives.*

bility, and commercial opportunity meet would in due course produce spectacular results for his company in the biomedical field. Meanwhile, Beckman's acquisition of new instruments of separation kept up the remarkable growth rate for the company, even as business remained strong for the firm's electronic components, pH meters, spectrophotometers, and analytical and life sciences instruments. In 1965 the sales of Beckman Instruments passed $100 million for the first time.

Spinco began at New York City's Rockefeller University, with Edward Pickels. Beckman Instruments' acquisition of Spinco thus gave entry simultaneously to Rockefeller University and to biomedicine. Beckman knew that Rockefeller's standing in biomedicine was similar to Caltech's in the physical sciences. His awareness of the revolution under way in molecular biology and his reflex for excellence quite naturally led him to Rockefeller's Stanford Moore, William Stein, and Darrel Spackman, who were building instrumentation to analyze amino acids. The building blocks of proteins, amino acids are the medium by which the genetic code is expressed in the cell. By 1958 Moore, Stein, and Spackman were building an amino acid analyzer in their studies of ribonuclease, the digestive enzyme responsible for breaking down ribonucleic acid (RNA). While this work would bring Moore and Stein the Nobel Prize in chemistry in 1972, Spinco Division scientists focused on translating that work into an instrument that would advance amino acid research even further. Realizing that the amino acid analyzer would be a useful partner to the ultracentrifuge, Beckman had his Spinco Division license the design of Moore, Stein, and Spackman, and in 1958 Spinco launched its first commercial machine, the Model 120 amino acid analyzer.

Determined to stay at the cutting edge, Beckman began following a promising line of research in Australia in the early 1960s. The director of St. Vincent's Research Center in Melbourne, Pehr Edman had developed chemical

Twenty-five years after its invention, Beckman poses with his original pH meter for a humorous company ad.
Courtesy Beckman Coulter, Inc.

Vass iss vrong mitt $30,000,000.00??? Twenty-pHive years ago even mein best pHriends vouldn't tell me. Dass iss because I hadt only von pHriend...un oldt classmate who didn't know lemon chuice vuss acid. DumkopHt! So I inwented him a machinewerken to pHrove derr iss acid in da lemon-pHruit. Dass iss how I got started in diss pHooey business. Und pHrom da start people vould point derr pHinger at me und say: "Derr goes dot krazy Doktor Beckman." Mitt oudt respect yet. ⋈ Now mein pHamous acidimeter iss a big success und mein pHirst nutty idea hass developed into diss gros pHamily of pH hardvare. Ja? Do dey vaggle derr pHinger at me today? Nein! ⋈ Vass iss vrong mitt $30,000,000.00? Da gotterdam tax man his pHull hand iss pHorever holdt outd! ⋈ Krazy, Man? Like a pHox! Who iss krazy? Our competitors! So iss better epHerybody does business mitt un pHox un notd mitt pHools. Ja? JaWohl! Write pHor Beckman Data pHile 0-00-01. **Beckman**

ScientipHic und Process / *Instruments Division*
Beckman Instruments, Inc.
2500 pHullerton Road, pHullerton, California

techniques for taking apart chains of amino acids within protein molecules. This breakdown of amino acid chains allowed scientists to analyze the building blocks of proteins in more detail. In a characteristic move Beckman flew to Australia to discuss with Edman the possibility of licensing his discoveries for use in an instrument to be designed by Beckman Instruments. Edman, a biochemist and physician, was friendly but wholly uninterested. Like many of Beckman's former colleagues at Caltech, he pursued science for science's sake. Edman wanted to continue his research unimpeded by commercial obligations or commitments. But he gave his consent for Beckman to use his work to develop instruments based on his research.

Arnold Beckman returned full of ideas for his research teams. By 1969 Beckman Instruments' Spinco Division was able to introduce its "protein sequencer," built on principles developed by Edman. For biochemists the protein sequencer was like having an extra senior researcher in the lab. The process of separating, recording, and identifying amino acids went on quickly and automatically, freeing scientists from the tedious precision work the analysis formerly required. Two years later Beckman Instruments followed up with its protein-peptide synthesizer, the fourth in a group of instruments that gave Beckman dominance in genetic engineering instrumentation in the 1970s. The ultracentrifuge, spinning at tremendous speeds, separated biological materials into their molecular components; the amino acid analyzer separated, identified, and measured amino acids, peptides, and other compounds; the protein sequencer determined the arrangement of amino acids; and the protein-peptide synthesizer automated the assembly of amino acids into peptides and proteins. Beckman added another lasting technology to his life sciences business in 1963, when he decided to acquire Sharp Laboratories, which manufactured liquid scintillation counters, important analytical tools for nuclear medicine and pharmaceutical and environmental research.

By a deft series of moves that began in 1955, Arnold Beckman had thus directed his company toward another sweet spot of opportunity, namely, the technologies that would underpin the emergence of biotechnology in the 1970s. In visualizing and stimulating these moves, he brought together a unique blend of elements. First was his own scientific knowledge and talent. Second was his insistence on excellence, and third came his instinct for problems ripe for solution. And what made this combination so formidable was its union with his willingness to act, to bet on his hunches.

Sensitized by these experiences, Beckman and his leaders of research and development noted an expansive trend in a field adjacent to biochemistry and biomedical research: the field of hospital tests and clinical care. Hospitals, clinical laboratories, and medical schools were developing new biochemical tests at an astonishing rate, and these tests called for an ever-greater number of instruments of ever-greater variety to perform the tests reliably and repetitively. Here was the "industrial" analog in the biomedical realm. Just as the chemical industry offered a huge field in which to sell versions of instruments first developed for the chemistry laboratory, so here in the hospital there was a burgeoning realm of technological needs to be fulfilled, a new arena for scientific creativity.

Dr. Beckman knew that the firm's analytical tools combining chemistry with electronics had proved themselves in biomedical research, with direct consequences for human life. In the 1963 annual report of Beckman Instruments he wrote: "With its increasing reliance on instrumentation, the medical field represents one of the most promising avenues of growth for Beckman products and technologies. The company anticipates significant growth in this field." His plans called for long-range research and development projects to develop new technologies and for increased interaction with biomedical scientists of all kinds. For Beckman this was neither a reconception of the nature of his technological enterprise nor an abandonment of any of the other arenas in which his company was at work. Rather, he saw the biomedical strategy as the initiation of the hard work necessary to have his firm be a leader in yet one more expanding field. He was committed to Beckman Instruments as a technology company, establishing and enjoying leadership in multiple areas based on advanced science and precision manufacturing.

Trouble in Paradise

Beckman was in his element, monitoring the wave of technological change and guiding his company into fresh opportunities in myriad new fields. He was also experiencing the pull, and the lure, of public service—not only at the Chamber of Commerce but also at Caltech. And though gifted, energetic, and committed, he

From left: Executives Ed Cherniss, Max Sprechel, Joseph Lewis, and Richard Dozier at a Beckman Instruments, Inc., international sales meeting in the early 1960s. *Courtesy Beckman Coulter, Inc.*

was human. In 1951 his company had little internal organization and $8 million in sales and was entirely based in Southern California. By 1957 it had grown to $38 million in sales and had multiple sites, including two in the Bay Area and one in Connecticut, plus an overseas subsidiary operating in Germany and one about to open in Scotland. Something had to give. And it did. In 1957 profits slumped to $25,000, and 1958 was worse.

The most pressing problem lay with yet another subsidiary. In Beckman's own words:

> In the mid-1950s we decided to go into the high-precision rotating equipment business. We had a policy then—and still have—that if we're going to go into something, we want to make the best instrument. We learned that the best engineers in the country in this field were two fellows named Arnold Rains and Herb Gallman. They had a little company which they called Arga. We ended up buying their company so they could come with us. Well, the orders just poured in—more than we could handle, which was our undoing. We didn't realize that we had accepted more orders than Arnold Rains and Herb Gallman could handle personally. We had to turn orders over to a lower level of engineers, and the tasks were almost impossible for these people. . . . Also we found that some contracts had horrendous penalties for failure to deliver on time. So we were facing deadlines, and we didn't have an acceptable product. We paid through the nose. We lost over $1.7 million, as I recall. Earnings dropped to sixteen cents a share from a forecast dollar sixty, and the following year we lost money—the only year in our history when we lost money.

In the first paragraph of his report to the shareholders for the 1958 fiscal year, Arnold Beckman wrote, "Operations for the year resulted in a net loss of $946,923." It was the only time in his career that he had to lead off an annual report with news of red ink. He attributed the deficit to substantial losses on government contracts, a nationwide recession, and "certain inadequacies in internal organization and controls."

Those inadequacies grew directly out of Arnold Beckman's personal style, as he quite frankly admits. "I've never thought about management enough, probably, to categorize different elements of it specifically. Instead, there are some recognizable aspects in the way I have tried to run the company. One is that I tend to put my faith in the people I employ to do a certain job. I try to select the right man and then let him run the show." This approach—a key to the early growth of Beckman Instruments and to its technological success—was vulnerable once employees numbered in the thousands and sales in the tens of millions. The troubles with Arga coincided with and were compounded by the growing difficulties with Shockley Laboratories, where Shockley was proving not to be "the right man," and by the Systems Division's lack of focus and markets.

Several stark realities stood out in Arnold Beckman's world at this time. Although still deeply in love with scientific advance and technological entrepreneurship, he was approaching sixty—no longer in the flush of youthful enthusiasm. Then again, management issues were now as important to the future success of his company as science and technology. His personal style—sensing opportunities

The winning slogan. Approaching its twenty-five-year anniversary, Beckman Instruments ran a contest among employees to solicit the best slogan to celebrate the quarter century. Arnold Beckman poses with Jayce Vidler, who won the contest with her slogan "Instrumental in Your Future." *Courtesy Beckman Coulter, Inc.*

and backing individuals while avoiding committee meetings and managerial confrontations—was no longer adequate for the corporate reality. Gifted individuals like Jack Bishop, who would quit in 1959, knew what was wrong but could not change it. And though Dr. Beckman owned a little over 50 percent of the stock, Beckman Instruments was a public company, with thousands of shareholders—large and small—who looked for a steady growth in share price and in dividends. At least two other interested parties were also displeased. The board had authorized some $29 million in bank loans between April and November 1956 to finance the growth and opportunity that Beckman saw everywhere around him. Bank and board were equally exercised by the sight of red ink and looked for action.

In the short term Arnold Beckman responded vigorously. The still semi-autonomous Helipot Corporation was fully integrated into Beckman Instruments, and the Helipot plant in Newport Beach was sold. The Liston-Becker operations were brought from Stamford, Connecticut, to Fullerton. Manufacturing operations were consolidated, financial controls tightened, and new executive positions created, under the watchful eye of the bank. At the same time Beckman placed renewed faith in Shockley, in computer systems for aerospace, and in the emerging promise of biomedicine. Only the last of these areas was to fulfill his hopes.

Nonetheless, by 1960 sales had risen to a remarkable $56 million, and profits bounced back to $3.3 million. The rise disguised Arnold Beckman's continuing difficulties in managing the company he had created and grown—and in which he possessed a controlling interest. His green thumb was apparent in the way that sales almost doubled in the next five years, from $56 million in 1960 to $104 million in 1965. Profits, however, were another story. They rose to a peak of $4.8 million (in 1962) and fell to a trough of $2.3 million (in 1964). Shareholders remained uneasy.

Other painful issues arose in these years. For decades American scientists had turned to dealers like Central Scientific when buying all needed equipment from test tubes to spectrophotometers. Indeed, old catalogs from houses like Arthur H. Thomas and Central are wonderful treasures, displaying in great detail which instruments appeared when. In 1963, however, Beckman Instruments disappeared from every catalog, overnight.

Dealers necessarily handled products from many manufacturers. As Beckman and his colleagues analyzed their sales network through the dealers who had supported them since the 1930s, there were three concerns. First, Arthur H. Thomas of Philadelphia and E. H. Curtin of Houston were among the best dealers for Beckman's instruments, but even they promoted everything in their catalogs, selling not only competitors' products but even their own. That hurt Beckman sales. Why should a Central sales representative promote Beckman or even Perkin-Elmer over a Central version of the same instrument?

Second, there was a question of dealer competence in repairs. At the height of the old system there were twenty-eight dealers supplying customers with

Beckman's instruments. As instruments grew more technical in design, they became more complex to repair, and salesmen were having an increasingly difficult time doubling as repairmen. "They could handle a pH meter because they had a little portable tool, and, if you had a service call, at worst you could pick this instrument up and take it back to the shop. You couldn't do that with a spectrophotometer. That's when you had to have a trained service force." Some dealers, like Arthur H. Thomas, began to develop such a force, but other dealers and customers began the simple chant of blaming the manufacturer for anything that went wrong. Beckman realized this was a situation to be corrected.

Third, and more characteristic of the Beckman organization, there was the worry of isolation. Normally Beckman engineers and scientists heard from customers only through distributor representatives, a process that kept them out of touch with what customers were doing. For years it had been part of Beckman strategy to listen to customer comments. What worked, what did not, what could be done better. Listening had still another logic: Sales representatives were agents of discovery. Who was working on what? Who had discovered what? Who had a technology that Beckman might adapt into a whole new line of instrumentation? Arnold Beckman was above all a scientist. He knew that scientists invent new instruments, even as he had in his own doctoral work. The manufacture of those creations was the essence of his business, and lacking a network of his own sales representatives, he was missing opportunities.

For all three reasons Arnold Beckman, following a plan crafted by Joseph Lewis, agreed to drop his distributors, a move not to be taken lightly. Beckman himself felt a great debt to Arthur H. Thomas and E. H. Curtin, yet legal counsel advised that if those loyal firms of so many decades were told of the new arrangement even a day before others, then Beckman Instruments might be acting illegally. Beckman thought it inhuman, yet conceded that all must be informed simultaneously.

The new sales plan was announced on 2 July 1963. The *Wall Street Journal* carried a picture of and a personal message from Arnold Beckman himself over his facsimile signature. Up until 1 July, Beckman Instruments had depended on distributors to sell most of its products, but not all. Infrared spectrophotometers and process instruments had been sold and serviced directly by the corporation, and in those cases good relations between customers and Beckman Instruments had developed, giving one clue to the way forward. Beckman management stated that "the needs of our customers will be served better by direct user-manufacturer relationships than by continued interposition of dealers." The advertisement then announced that Beckman Instruments had established eleven regional warehouses to provide twenty-four-hour delivery in the United States or Canada. In addition there were thirty-three new field offices with 214 specially trained sales and service engineers.

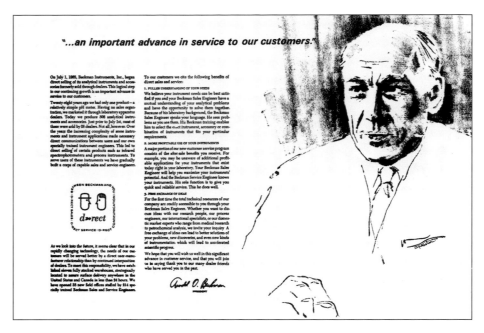

A follow-up article by the *Wall Street Journal* revealed a different angle: "Beckman Expects Gains in Profit by Change to Direct Sales System." The new marketing system would cost $3 million a year, but even so the corporation would still net about $2.5 million by ending its old dealer discounts, which in the past had amounted to about $6 million a year.

Sadly, Ed Patterson, Arnold Beckman's loyal ally at Arthur H. Thomas who had first suggested national marketing of the pH meter, was crushed. He never spoke to Beckman again. The dealers were not the only readers of the *Wall Street Journal* who were disappointed. Investors wondered why Beckman Instruments would drop its distribution network, and the stock fell. As Beckman mused in the 1980s, "They thought we were out of our minds, and we thought perhaps we might have been, too." However, the corporation's assessments paid off handsomely. Though the actual reorganization and creation of the regional distribution centers cost an additional $2 million, within a mere nine months direct sales exceeded anything the old dealer network had produced.

Changing Places

The challenge of steering Beckman Instruments through troubled times and tough decisions shows how Arnold Beckman's world was changing as he entered his sixties. Another change was far more abrupt, when it came.

The place that Beckman called home had remained as one fixed point in his driven, shifting world, ever since 1933. Despite his growing wealth he and Mabel continued to live in the house that they had built in Altadena when they were a young couple. Admittedly, the house had been refined and added to over the years, but in modest ways. Much of the effort came from Beckman's own hands. He built

The back of the Beck-mans' house in Corona del Mar. *Courtesy Beckman family.*

View of the Pacific Ocean from the house. *Courtesy Beckman family.*

a robust backyard barbecue and patio area out of brick, and for many years this spot served as a focal point for gatherings of family, friends, and neighbors. Together, he and Mabel tended to plantings and their beloved rose gardens that surrounded their home, embedding themselves deeper in domesticity.

The house in Altadena was their domestic sphere, their shared space for three decades. It served as a refuge for both Arnold and Mabel during the dramatic changes in other aspects of their lives. That house would always be the site of their children's early memories, but by 1960 the children were gone: Pat to pursue the science and art of occupational therapy and nursing and Arnold Stone to become a successful electrician and eventually an entrepreneur, involved in real estate development and other businesses. With her children thus grown, independent, and gone from her house of thirty years in Altadena, 1960 found Mabel Beckman open to a change.

In a newspaper Mabel saw a real estate notice that caught her attention. A ranch-style house in Corona del Mar would soon be coming up for auction, after sitting unsold on the market for a number of years. The fit between structure and site made her fall in love with the house when she visited it. The house seems like part of a perfectly ordinary suburban street, from the front. In fact it sits well atop a bluff, with wide and unobstructed views, across its tumbling "backyard" of cliffside to the swell and roar of the Pacific Ocean below. It was in many ways Mabel Beckman's dream for a home in California. The house itself was pleasing and well built, and it took full advantage of its location. But its environment was as important as the house itself as a structure. It gave a sense of living with the sea.

Just as important for Mabel, though, was the price. The Beckmans had lived through the Great Depression, and the experience marked them and their generation. They had seen how fickle and unforgiving the economy could be. They were grateful that they had come through the Depression without the serious burdens and depredations that had afflicted so many, and the thought of overly lavish and ostentatious spending repelled them. The house in Corona del Mar was beautiful without a doubt, and its aesthetic joys went beyond the merely functional; but it made no exuberant display of conspicuous consumption. Moreover, Mabel was excited by the prospect that the house would be auctioned. The property had sat unsold for years at the asking price of $250,000. An auction held out the promise that the Beckmans might make it theirs for much less.

Arnold visited the house with Mabel, but he was initially less enthusiastic than she was about moving from their home of so many years. He was certainly not afraid of the new, but he cherished the house in Altadena. Nevertheless, Mabel persuaded him to submit a written bid for the property before leaving on one of his frequent business trips. Beckman bid half the asking price and headed for meetings on the East Coast. When he returned, he learned that his bid had won the auction and that Mabel was already far along with her plans for the couple's move.

Arnold and Mabel Beckman lived together in their new house on the sea until Mabel's death in 1989. Dr. Beckman continues to live there now, together with his daughter, Pat. As with the house in Altadena, Beckman transformed this one with his own hands, installing decks, walkways, and patios from which to contemplate the ocean view and making many other improvements.

The Beckmans' son, Arnold S. Beckman, recalls a telling episode of life in Corona del Mar. He stopped by his parents' house for a visit, only to find them singularly occupied. His father was in the basement, fitting copper tubing for water supply to a new bathroom on the floor above. His mother was in the bathroom, holding the top of the line in place while Beckman secured it below. For one who knew the Beckmans only through their public lives, the sight would have seemed out of place, out of character. For their son the sight was far from abnormal. He was accustomed to his father's pursuit of excellence and dedication to craftsmanship, and to his mother's integral role as his father's partner.

A glimpse of the Corona del Mar house's gardens. Arnold Beckman built the curving handrail to complement his new home. *Courtesy Beckman family.*

The young Arne Beckman with his parents, Arnold S. and Ellyn, enjoys a visit from his grandparents and aunt. *Courtesy Beckman family.*

The years of 1964 and 1965 brought other changes for Arnold Beckman that were even more profound than moving from his home of almost thirty years. These changes were marked symbolically and practically by his acceptance of two very different "chairs." In 1964 he became chairman of the Caltech Board of Trustees. The decision of the Caltech leadership to invest Dr. Beckman with responsibility for the Institute's future and for securing the moral, financial, and material means to develop its tradition of excellence was a vote of confidence in his stature, his ability, and his willingness to commit generous measures of his own time and money. This new role as the steward of Caltech—of its science and technology and of the students it educated—marked him as a leading public figure in the West, responsible for an important part of American science and technology.

As a former professor, Beckman was familiar with and attuned to the idea of tenure to the age of sixty-five, then retirement from one's leading role into new occupations. He knew that with sales approaching $100 million and profits fluctuating uncertainly, there were further hard issues of management to address at Beckman Instruments. The invitation to chair the Caltech trustees was pressing and flattering. And he knew that Caltech sorely needed his vision and calm judgment. He also knew that many other possible roles as a public servant were opening to him, as word got out of his talent and his willingness to work. Indeed it was in the context of an initiative of California's governor, Pat Brown, that Arnold Beckman found a successor to take on the leadership of his company.

Governor Brown had set up a committee of industrial leaders to suggest ways to stimulate economic growth in the state. Committee meetings were naturally held in Sacramento, the state capital. One committee member was William Ballhaus, executive vice president of the Northrop Corporation, a major defense contractor. Another was Arnold Beckman. Ballhaus had the advantage of working for an airplane company. As he recalls, "Dr. Beckman and I were on the same committee. He needed a ride home, and I said, 'Why don't you fly with me on the Northrop airplane?' . . . and as we were flying home, he said, 'You know, I need a young fellow to come in and take over my company, run my company for me.' "

So in 1965 Beckman accepted a second "chair" of an altogether different sort. In this year, his sixty-fifth, Arnold Beckman resigned his presidency of Beckman Instruments—passing this title over to William Ballhaus—and became the chairman of its board of directors. This was a move to a position of stewardship at the broadest level, ensuring that Beckman Instruments would continue to develop powerful tools for science and industry and to make the technology of the future. By occupying these two new chairs, Arnold Beckman moved to a new career stage in his long, productive life. In the next quarter century he would develop inventions of excellence in the fields of science, public service, and philanthropy.

Courtesy Beckman family.

The Beckman Auditorium at Caltech, circa 1965. *Courtesy Institute Archives, California Institute of Technology.*

8 | Citizen and Leader

I'm deeply concerned over the future of humanity. . . . We allow emotions to override rational thinking.

Arnold Beckman was eager to embrace fresh opportunities, at age sixty-five. He had now formally relinquished the presidency of Beckman Instruments and with it the day-to-day operations of the company he had created. Instead, he became chairman of the Caltech board. He was also head of the Lincoln Club. The roster was filled out with other activities he had fashioned for himself over the preceding years. It is not easy to find the right phrase to describe the next three active decades of his life. Citizen and leader is one description. Statesman for science and philanthropist for science both seem accurate, but investor in the future perhaps captures those decades best. The transition from businessman to public figure and then to philanthropist was gradual, and Beckman carefully fashioned these different, though connected, roles. He was not content, even at the age he jokingly called that of "presumed senility," to let his creative energy die down. Isaac Newton once described the nature of the universe by saying that it was "never at rest," and the same could be said of Arnold Beckman.

Caltech, or an Excellent Life's Work

Caltech was one of the earliest institutions to call upon its alumnus for his ability to realize a vision. In fact, Arnold Beckman was the first Caltech alumnus to be elected to serve on the Institute's board of trustees. He received and accepted this invitation in 1953. He had never left the Caltech community, even though he formally resigned from the faculty in 1939 and stopped teaching there after working one more year part-time.

Before World War II, Caltech had been a very small school, devoted to basic scientific research in such a determined way that it was somewhat of a puzzle how engineering and the applied fit within the very notion of Caltech. So central was the figure of Robert A. Millikan that this period of Caltech's history is commonly known as the "Millikan era." The Institute's prewar endowment was small, its operating budget about $1.25 million a year, and much of the funding for the research projects of its faculty came from private philanthropies like the Carnegie

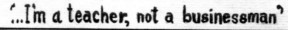

Institution and the Rockefeller Foundation. Millikan saw Caltech through the first, tumultuous years of the war, years of breakneck development in applied, defense-oriented activity.

World War II transformed the school. In many ways it was a new institution. As the historian Judith Goodstein notes, Caltech became nothing less than a "wartime factory" for the government during the conflict. The war swept away private philanthropy as the major support for science and swept in support from the military. One Caltech physicist saw government research and production as so dominant "that a large part of Caltech literally became a branch of the Bureau of Ordnance." Caltech physicists were producing vast numbers of new tactical rockets for use on and against airplanes. The budget for this massive project ran $2 million a month, well over the prewar annual budget for the Institute as a whole. Another war-related program sought to produce proximity fuses. And at the Jet Propulsion Laboratory, administered by Caltech and staffed by faculty members, the military devoted huge sums to developing high-altitude missiles and rocket boosters for aircraft carrier–based planes. Caltech's activities and payroll grew enormously during the war, thanks to the infusion of federal funds.

A new era in Caltech's history opened formally in 1944 when Lee DuBridge was installed as president. DuBridge, an academic physicist, came to Caltech riding the crest of his renown for his accomplishments as director of MIT's Rad Lab and

To Arnold Beckman
Best wishes
Bill Ruckelshaus

Arnold Beckman taking an oath for his service with the Air Quality Advisory Board of the Environmental Protection Agency, 1970. William D. Ruckelshaus (far left), the first administrator of the EPA, delivers the oath to Dr. Beckman (third from left). President Nixon appointed Beckman to this post. *Courtesy Institute Archives, California Institute of Technology.*

its radar program. His immediate mission was to chart what kind of institution Caltech would be in the postwar era. Caltech now needed additional skills from its board of trustees beyond the more or less straightforward services of financial savvy, generosity, and fund-raising acumen. It needed trustees who could help chart the way for the school in a new and uncertain era, trustees who had intimate experience of the novel ways in which science, technology, business, and the government had come together during the war—trustees like Arnold Beckman.

The first decade of the "DuBridge era" was not an easy one. Negotiating the lines between national security and academic freedom and between independence and military contracts was difficult and often involved controversy. The strain took its toll on both the president and the board of trustees. Although Caltech successfully made the transition to the new era of direct support for science by the federal government during the "peacetime" of the Cold War in the early 1950s, the school's administration was also buffeted by the raging winds of McCarthyism.

The Institute's board was still populated by much the same kind of people as had served in the days of Throop Polytechnic: largely prominent businessmen from Southern California, often businessmen who had little contact with science and technology except through Caltech. Early in the Cold War, when Senator Joseph McCarthy was most active, a number of these board members were—in the words of Arnold Beckman—"so opposed to Communism that they were almost rabid on it." This fervor opened up rifts in the Caltech board that spread to its relations with DuBridge, the faculty, and the students.

Three Caltech scientists were at the center of this controversy over domestic Communism in the early Cold War: Lee DuBridge, Linus Pauling, and Robert J. Oppenheimer. As president, DuBridge was vocal and uncompromising in his support of both Pauling and Oppenheimer in the period just before Beckman joined the board. It is a measure of just how important scientists had become to Americans' sense of their national security that both Pauling and Oppenheimer came under suspicion for purported Communist sympathies. Loyalty to any cause that anti-Communists opposed was a basis for doubt, and heated debate surrounded Pauling's public support of such causes as civil libertarianism and nuclear disarmament. That debate engaged trustees as well as faculty. Trustees resigned, private donors to Caltech withheld gifts, and DuBridge still firmly supported Pauling's right to speak out for the causes that moved him. Passions would flare up again in 1954, when DuBridge spoke out against revoking Robert Oppenheimer's security clearance because of his past associations with Communists.

Throughout the 1940s and 1950s Dr. Beckman still lived in the same well-built house in Altadena, just a few miles from the Caltech campus. Even though these years saw the former professor consumed with his entrepreneurial ventures, Caltech never left his life: "We lived right there. . . . We went to parties together, went to seminars. I never lost contact. [What] I lost [was] an official relationship with them." Living within the extended Caltech community and keeping up socially and intellectually with his former colleagues, in 1953 Beckman well knew why he was being asked to renew his official bond with Caltech at this sensitive time. Two reasons stood out. First, he had a long-standing reputation as a man of integrity. He was honest, spoke straightforwardly, and confronted difficulties head-on and without rancor. In short, he could be an effective spokesman and problem solver. Moreover, his history with Caltech positioned him perfectly to bridge the growing rifts between the various communities on campus. As he later explained: "I wore three hats. The students looked on me as being their representative on the board of trustees, as I'd been a student there. The faculty did also; they thought I'd look after their interests because I'd been a faculty member. And, of course, my ordinary trustee hat. I knew and got along well with all the different groups."

In the opinion of Harold Brown, who succeeded DuBridge as president of

Arnold and Mabel Beckman with Lee and Doris DuBridge. *Courtesy Institute Archives, California Institute of Technology.*

Caltech in 1969, Arnold Beckman proved to be just this kind of mediator. Brown saw Beckman build a tradition on the Caltech board of approaching the problems facing the Institute calmly, focusing on overarching goals, and leaving aside the partisan and ideological leanings of the individual trustees. That legacy of sober problem solving and consensus building has served Caltech well.

A second reason to invite Beckman to join the board was that he understood well the complexities of the relationship forged during the war among business, universities, and the government, and he had intimate knowledge of how this interplay worked at Caltech itself. Because Pauling had designed the wartime oxygen analyzer Beckman produced, Caltech held the patents, and Beckman was paying Caltech regular royalties on the analyzer's continuing production. In fact for many years Beckman royalties provided the Institute its largest single source of patent income. Beckman thus sat directly at the intersection of Caltech, Caltech scientists, the government, and private enterprise.

And beyond that unrivaled local knowledge of the burgeoning "academic-industrial-military complex," Beckman understood the interplay between scientific and technological research, academe, and the military throughout the nation, owing to his work on the Helipot, the infrared spectrophotometer, mass spectrometers, and the like.

Although the extraordinary pressures of his growing company also demanded his attention, Beckman's special talents and his appetite for work led him to take on increasing responsibilities on the board of trustees between 1954 and 1964. Many of the tasks concerned Caltech's continuing growth and its dependence on government funding. During these years the trustees watched as the percentage of Caltech's budget that came from the federal government climbed up and up. Beckman posed a difficult but important question to his fellow trustees: "Are we going to lose our independence?" Naturally enough, his reward for posing the question was to be put in charge of a committee to investigate the answer:

> We never did come up with any instance where we could say that the government was responsible for knowingly changing the course of research at Caltech. I think without our realizing it, government funding does exert a pressure, because professors naturally, if they're thinking of two alternative research problems, one for which they can get federal funds and one for which they have to go out and scrounge somewhere else, they're likely to take the one for which funding is easy. So in that sense there's been a subtle and maybe undetectable influence. I don't think it has caused damage to Caltech, because I think the research that the government is funding is worthwhile research [and] quite suitable for Caltech.

As a member of the board Beckman also played the traditional role of a trustee of a not-for-profit institution: He was no stranger to Caltech's fund-raising efforts, and by the time he joined the ranks of its trustees, he had already made significant contributions to those efforts. In the late 1940s the Caltech Alumni Association decided to mount its first ever fund-raising campaign and establish an Alumni Fund that could bring in fifteen thousand dollars a year for the Institute. The timing of this effort owed something to Caltech's newness as an institution. Only by 1947–48 had Caltech accumulated so many as two thousand alumni, enough to make establishing an Alumni Fund a meaningful possibility. The president of the Alumni Association then was Joseph Lewis, an undergraduate alumnus who worked at U.S. Steel. On reviewing information about alumni, he was struck that such a large proportion had earned graduate degrees, not undergraduate degrees, from the school. Clearly, for the Alumni Association to meet its ambitious goal, Lewis would have to find a way to truly engage these alumni.

In his review Lewis was struck by one name: Arnold Beckman. Beckman was unique in having served on the faculty and in leading a thriving company in the Pasadena area. The two met, and Lewis convinced Beckman to lend his name to the effort. Dr. Beckman went beyond sending out a series of letters to his fellow graduate alumni and making a contribution to ensure the initial success of the Alumni Fund: He became the first alumnus to take out a prepaid life membership in the fund at the "Associates" level. Significantly, the life membership was paid in the names of both Arnold and Mabel Beckman. The gift of several thousand dollars constituted half of all moneys raised for the Alumni Fund during its first year.

Lewis and Beckman continued to meet at intervals of three to four months to discuss the fund's goals. By 1951 the relationship between the two had become so close that when U.S. Steel required Lewis to relocate outside California, he asked Beckman whether his enterprises might have a suitable position. Clearly impressed with Lewis's abilities and tenacity, Beckman offered him the position of manager of Arnold O. Beckman, Incorporated. Lewis happily accepted the offer and the challenge. Thus began a business association that lasted until 1967. In later years Dr. Beckman would quip that he decided to hire Lewis because it turned out to be cheaper to pay his salary than to work with him on fund-raising for Caltech.

As a trustee Beckman took on the chairmanship of Caltech's first formal fund-raising drive in 1958. His willingness to pitch in for the Alumni Fund made him a natural choice for the serious work of drumming up major donations from others. Curiously enough this successful endeavor also educated him for the first time, at fifty-eight, in the art and adventure of hitchhiking. Perhaps his cherished memories of hopping freight trains as a youth made him open to this alternative form of transport. His adventure also reflects how seriously he took his commitment to Caltech and his responsibilities as a trustee:

> I had a boat built up at Sausalito [the *Aries*], one of the first large fiberglass boats, forty feet long, and I was sailing it down [to Newport Beach] over the Thanksgiving holiday of 1958. This was right around our fund-raising drive. I was chairman of the

Beckman maneuvers the first shovelful of dirt as part of breaking ground ceremonies for a new building made possible by Caltech's first fund-raising campaign. *Courtesy Institute Archives, California Institute of Technology.*

285

drive, and we had a meeting scheduled at Caltech, and I had to kick this thing off. As I recall, [the meeting was scheduled for] a Monday evening. We realized we were not going to get there by 1:00 P.M., so finally we pulled over at Goleta, which has an old, partly abandoned pier sticking out there. I hopped off and went over to the highway to hitch a ride so I could get [to the meeting in time]. This was my first experience in hitchhiking: It's not that easy! All these cars go whizzing by and whizzing by. Finally, a fellow wearing an old T-shirt stopped. He was a plumber and had been up at Camp Roberts, hoping to get a job. He was coming by, and he stopped to pick me up. I told him I had to get back to Santa Barbara to get to a telephone. It turned out he and I had [something] in common. We were both former marines. We got along well enough, and he [gave me a ride]. When I got to Santa Barbara, I called the vice chairman and told him I was not going to get back in time for this thing, and [asked if he] would go over and hold the meeting. The next day, or day after, the *Los Angeles Times* had a column about Arnold Beckman hitchhiking down from San Francisco. I never lived down that hitchhiking experience.

By 1964 Beckman was the natural choice of his fellow trustees when it came time to select a new chairman for the board. He understood the scientific basis of the Institute's work and its success. He knew firsthand the tangled territory that involved government funding, technology-based companies, and faculty obligations. He moved easily in political circles, and he was well versed in philanthropy as both fund-raiser and donor. He served as board chairman for a decade, before being elected a life trustee in 1974. One of many important contributions that he made to guarantee the growing reputation of Caltech was his shrewd and personal choice of Harold Brown to succeed Lee DuBridge as the Institute's new president, in 1969.

Arnold Beckman's tenure as chairman of Caltech's board of trustees was bracketed by the first two major acts of his and Mabel's philanthropy. In 1964 the Beckmans were present at the inaugural concert of the Beckman Auditorium at Caltech. This grand hall, suited for large gatherings and stagings of the performing arts, filled the Institute's need for a center for art and culture to match existing facilities for science and technology. It was constructed through a gift from the Beckmans to Caltech of $1 million. The gift that made the Beckman Auditorium a reality also gave the Beckmans experience with operating a philanthropic foundation of their own.

In the early 1960s Arnold and Mabel Beckman created their first "Beckman Foundation" to take advantage of a provision in the then-current tax law. That law allowed the couple to set up a foundation as a type of trust in such a manner that the trust could distribute income made from its investments tax-free to the recipients of its philanthropy. By arming their foundation with some of their stock in Beckman Instruments, the Beckmans could increase the funds available for causes that inspired them. The beauty of the Beckman Auditorium itself must have reinforced for them the importance of creativity and the use of foundations for their future philanthropy.

Again, when Arnold Beckman resigned as chairman of the board and became a life trustee in 1974, he and Mabel gave another remarkable gift to the Institute: $6 million for the construction of the Mabel and Arnold Beckman Laboratories of Behavioral Biology. The building completed the "Court of Man" on the Caltech campus, a public space initiated by their creation of the Beckman Auditorium a decade earlier. This major investment by the Beckmans in forward-thinking, interdisciplinary scientific research held out the promise of dramatic benefits for society in the future.

Arnold Beckman and Harold Brown. *Courtesy Institute Archives, California Institute of Technology.*

As we shall discuss, Dr. Beckman's philanthropic and scientific interest in Caltech would reach fresh peaks in the 1980s and 1990s. When in 1999 the annual college issue of *U.S. News and World Report* declared Caltech the nation's number-one university, surpassing Berkeley, Stanford, and Harvard, Arnold Beckman could take quiet satisfaction in his own enduring contribution. It was not simply that by then he was the Institute's single largest benefactor, but that—for over seventy-five years—he had contributed more to Caltech than any other living person, in his

Beckman sailing with the Caltech Graduate Council, July 1969. *Courtesy Institute Archives, California Institute of Technology.*

various roles as student, faculty member, trustee, and chairman. In the words of David Baltimore, Caltech president at the start of the new millennium: "As one becomes more familiar with Caltech, his vast influence behind the scenes reveals itself in myriad ways—in the named professorship and undergraduate scholarships, in the countless hours of wise counsel he has offered Caltech administration, in his continuing involvement in the educational, social, political, and business issues that affect our institution. Just as Dr. Beckman's technological innovations have changed laboratory science, so his personal influence has shaped the destiny of Caltech."

The Lincoln Club and Richard Nixon

Caltech profited from Beckman's growing stature and greater availability in the 1960s and 1970s. So too did political leaders in California and the nation.

In 1960 John F. Kennedy defeated Richard M. Nixon in one of the closest presidential elections in American history. Nixon returned to California and, in 1962, ran for governor against the Democratic incumbent Edmund G. "Pat" Brown. A strong supporter of Nixon as a result of his experience in Moscow in 1959, Arnold Beckman was prompted to make his first, and last, political campaign speech. Much about Richard Nixon appealed to him. Both were self-made

Arnold Beckman's own first major philanthropic gesture came in 1964. That it should be a gift to Caltech ought to be no surprise. That it should be a concert hall may well lift eyebrows.

A sketch of the Beckman Auditorium and the Court of Man at Caltech. *Courtesy Institute Archives, California Institute of Technology.*

The very name Caltech connotes science, engineering, and technology, and over the decades the Institute had made natural provisions for lecture halls and labs second to none. Less visible to the public eye are the arts and humanities at Caltech, for many an accomplished scientist is also a musician. Quite simply, Caltech had world-class labs but lacked a comparable concert hall. The former theater pianist was intrigued.

The Beckmans knew the difference that trustees can make to private institutions. After leading Caltech's major fund-raising campaign, Arnold Beckman knew firsthand how important the beneficence of individuals was to the health of a school. As a trustee and an industrialist with a political sense, he also saw the limitations of government

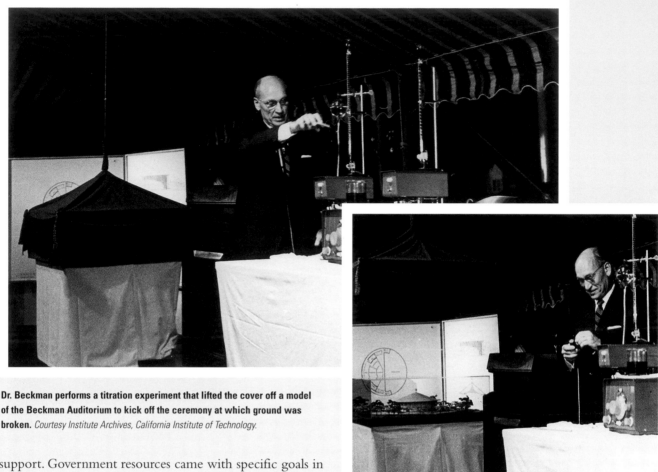

Dr. Beckman performs a titration experiment that lifted the cover off a model of the Beckman Auditorium to kick off the ceremony at which ground was broken. *Courtesy Institute Archives, California Institute of Technology.*

Experiment successful! *Courtesy Institute Archives, California Institute of Technology.*

support. Government resources came with specific goals in mind, with strings attached. Individuals, on the other hand, made longer-term investments in the institution and in science when they built buildings or endowed research funds.

The Beckmans decided that they would give Caltech the concert hall it lacked, and just as he would with many subsequent donations, Dr. Beckman took a close interest in major issues. He certainly knew just who should design the building.

Edward Durell Stone was a well-known architect of the International Style; among his most famous structures are the Kennedy Center for the Performing Arts in Washington, D.C., and the General Motors Building in New York City. Stone, trained in architecture at Harvard and MIT, was inspired during a two-year sojourn in Europe at the end of the 1920s by the modernist movement in architecture. He returned to the United States in 1930 to join the New York firm that had designed Radio City Music

Hall, but left six years later to found his own practice. Stone participated in the design of New York City's Museum of Modern Art (1937), Manhattan's first building in the International Style.

Stone's portfolio of modernist buildings, with their clean design, straightforward geometry, and outward display of underlying engineering and construction, appealed to the scientist and the craftsman in Dr. Beckman. Stone's design for the American Pavilion for the Brussels World's Fair in 1958 brought him much attention within the architectural community and beyond. Anticipating the long-span, domed roofs that cover many stadiums and arenas today, Stone's design relied on complex engineering: Supporting the pavilion's impressive domed roof were two layers of radial steel cables that connected to a steel tension ring placed around the building's perimeter and met at a small steel tension ring at the center of the roof. This combination of modern engineering and design caught Beckman's attention, and he made time to fly to New York to discuss with the architect his own vision for a central auditorium at Caltech. Ever persuasive in enrolling the individual that he believed was the best for the job, Beckman brought Stone aboard.

The circular, brilliantly white hall that Stone designed boasts exquisite acoustics, the result of both aesthetics and science. This acoustic distinction was no accident, for Arnold Beckman helped assemble the experts to address the particular problems presented by a round space. The Beckman Auditorium opened with a gala concert on 25 February 1964. One notable Hollywood resident attending that first concert was the Russian composer Igor Stravinsky, already in his eighties by this time. Stravinsky was so moved by the quality of the auditorium that he sent a telegram to Beckman, thanking him "*de tout coeur* for the best and most sympathetically organized concert I can remember."

Pasadena's reaction to the Beckman Auditorium was just as enthusiastic. President Lee DuBridge called the structure his "little jewel box." A local paper declared it "an architectural gem and a beacon of culture." The city government even went so far as to select Beckman for an award in honor of the building. Speaking for himself and for Mabel, Arnold Beckman declared his own gratitude at the dedication ceremony: "Thank you, Caltech," he declared, "for developing the need which has given us so much pleasure in fulfilling."

The Beckman Auditorium proved to be the first component of a triad of buildings at Caltech now known as the "Court of Man." A Renaissance concept at a school very much dedicated to the physical sciences and engineering, the Court of Man represents the union of the sciences, humanities, and arts. Dr. Beckman was very involved with its planning near the end of his tenure as chairman of the Caltech board. The Court of Man called for construction of a humanities building and a behavioral biology building at either side of a grassy mall, with the Beckman Auditorium anchoring the design at the north end.

In 1971 the Baxter family provided funds for the humanities building, the Donald E. Baxter, M.D., Hall of Humanities and Social Sciences. The behavioral biology building waited—needed, planned, but unfunded. In his last year as chairman, Arnold and Mabel Beckman decided to complete the complex they had helped plan: "Mrs. Beckman and I talked it over and said, 'Well, why not?'" Contrary to the off-the-cuff tone of this account of the decision, Beckman had long been a firm advocate for intensive, scientific study of human behavior, motivated by a long-term vision of the effect science might have on social development. This vision informed many of his actions in the public and the political realms. In 1972, two years before the dedication of the Mabel and Arnold Beckman Laboratories of Behavioral Biology, Beckman expressed his views: "Unfortunately, human behavior is not always praiseworthy. Too often it makes some people criminals, some racists, some warmongers, some beggars, some drug addicts or alcoholics. Why? We don't really know, and this is indeed a sad admission in this age of scientific enlightenment."

The Beckman Laboratory of Behavioral Biology was built with a $6 million grant. It mirrors the humanities building that sits opposite, across the Court of Man. The center complex, with the Beckman Auditorium at the north end, represents the interconnection between disciplines and emphasizes the importance of forging intellectual relationships between the hard sciences, the humanities, and the arts.

The Beckmans' decision to fund another Caltech building meant more than a plan completed. Arnold and Mabel were fast evolving as philanthropists for science, investing for the long term in the knowledge that scientific study might garner for the good of society. They were also expressing Beckman's growing conviction about the importance of interdisciplinary endeavors: "Many new discoveries are made in between the well-known, established fields. . . . The multidisciplinary approach to attacking problems is the most effective." That belief was to find a still richer, fuller expression on the Caltech campus—and elsewhere—a decade or more later. ❧

successes from rather modest backgrounds, and both shared a politically conservative impulse and a strong identification (which Beckman said he inherited from his father) with the Republican Party. But Beckman's political philosophy is not well captured in the simple phrase "conservative Republican." Perhaps his perspective is better captured by the phrase "conservative rationalist" or "techno-scientific conservative."

Arnold Beckman is undoubtedly a conservative in many respects. For example, he supports a shift away from welfare programs to volunteerism and private philanthropy for supporting Americans in need. "I'd get government out of the act," he once said. "In that little town of Cullom, we had poor. We took care of the poor. We didn't have hungry people there. We knew who needed help and saw to it they got it in a way that was not humiliating. That's the way it should be done." But as with nearly all aspects of his life, Beckman's personal politics are suffused with his valuation of science, its understandings, and its methods. "I'm deeply concerned over the future of humanity," he once remarked, "[with the] fact that we refuse to face up to problems that are coming on, and [with the] fact that we allow emotions to override rational thinking."

Unlike many conservatives, Beckman believes that there needs to be frank and open consideration given to voluntary euthanasia and abortion within society, so that their costs and their benefits can be properly assessed. Moreover, he supports many forms of governmental regulation to protect and ensure the common good. He even advocates extending to governmental decision making in general the method the Food and Drug Administration uses in evaluating pharmaceuticals. Much as the FDA weighs the efficacy of a medicament against its potential side effects, Beckman urges the virtue of applying "that same two-sided test to everything that [government does]. We should have a risk-benefit study of every major thing, whether it is a proposal to build a nuclear power plant or another new highway through Orange County or hundreds of new low-cost housing units." Finally, in contrast to many with conservative politics, Arnold Beckman advocates the vigorous and generous support of scientific research by the federal government. This includes support for the basic, curiosity-driven scientific research of the university professor as well as for more applied, directed research, as in government medical laboratories.

Finding in Richard Nixon a strong leader with similar viewpoints and impressed by his personal affability and his ability to stand up to the leaders of the Soviet Union, Beckman backed him wholeheartedly in the California gubernatorial race of 1962. He even prepared and delivered a campaign speech at a rally organized by the Nixon campaign at which the candidate was present. In an act of self-lampooning, intended as a pointed, but lighthearted criticism of the incumbent, Edmund Brown, Beckman took the stage wearing a mortarboard cap. He then delivered a punning disquisition that compared the scientific phenomenon of

"Professor Beckman" presents his Brownian motion lecture in support of Richard Nixon's campaign for the California governorship in 1962. *Courtesy Institute Archives, California Institute of Technology.*

"Brownian motion" to its political analog. According to Beckman, Brownian motion, as practiced by the incumbent, was like the motion of dust particles seen in a beam of sunlight through a window; a lot of activity is evident, but it is fundamentally without direction. Unfortunately, the scientific pun went over the heads of the assembled audience, and the joke fell flat. "I think it was a good analogy, but the people in the audience didn't know what the hell Brownian motion was. After that talk Nixon used to call me 'Professor Beckman.'"

Arnold Beckman has not returned to the campaign platform, but Nixon's defeat in that election did prompt him to refocus his political activities—toward raising funds. The defeat proved for "Professor Beckman" that the then-current system of political fund-raising was woefully inadequate for ensuring the success of candidates whom he found to be overwhelmingly superior. "When I saw how money was raised and controlled, I said, 'This is a horrible way. We as businessmen ought to be able to do a better job of spending our money effectively.'"

Never one to shirk difficulties, Arnold Beckman promptly organized the Lincoln Club of Orange County to mesh the interaction of principles, politicians, businesspeople, money, and campaigns. The club brought together prominent Orange County businesspeople who wanted to use their financial support for political causes more effectively.

The goal of the Lincoln Club is to identify candidates worthy of support for public office, from the local government of Orange County through the state government, governor, and congressional representatives—all the way to the presidency of the nation. At Beckman's urging the club looked for individuals that it thought would promote the ideals of good government embodied by the man after whom the organization is named. While the club's bylaws make clear that it is an independent entity, without formal affiliation with the Republican or Democratic parties, the Lincoln Club almost exclusively supports Republican candidates. Once the club has decided upon a candidate, the members organize their financial backing for the campaign in a coordinated fashion.

Beckman served as chairman of the Lincoln Club from its founding through the mid-1970s. During his tenure the influence of the club in Republican politics grew steadily in California and beyond. One underlying principle of the club was to support the kind of free-market system that had allowed many of the first members to rise from humble beginnings to prominence. Besides Arnold Beckman, the blacksmith's son, the club counted among its early members Walter Knott, who had started in business by selling boysenberries at his Orange County farm stand. Later, he added pies and chicken dinners to his offerings and the stand became a restaurant, which eventually evolved into one of the county's leading tourist attractions—Knott's Berry Farm.

The Lincoln Club operated where Beckman felt it could have the greatest collective impact: behind the scenes. This low-key choice, combined with a strong preference for privacy, has earned the club a growing mystique. Significant sums of money coming from a highly private group could not but trigger speculation. But for Arnold Beckman on the inside, the club's program was straightforward: "When we found a good candidate, we put money behind his campaign." Being a member was not an all-consuming affair; over the years the club took up little of his time. "The board of directors met once a month on Saturday, so that killed half a Saturday every month for me. My job at the Lincoln Club really was to be a presiding officer. As chairman, my job was to run a board of directors meeting. Others were involved in digging up candidates, and I never did a lot of hard work. My job was to run a smooth meeting." Nonetheless, Beckman's ability to run a smooth meeting translated before long into prominent political successes for the Lincoln Club's candidates. In 1966 the club backed Ronald Reagan's successful California gubernatorial bid.

Much more prominently, the club helped Richard Nixon become president of

Arnold Beckman and Ronald Reagan, 1978.
Courtesy Beckman Coulter, Inc.

the United States in 1968. Quoted in the *New York Times* about the results of the campaign, Arnold Beckman was as succinct as he was proud: "We elected Richard Nixon president of the United States," he declared. "Without California, Dick Nixon could not have won the election. And it was Orange County, with some help from San Diego County, that provided the plurality for him to win California." In the early days of his administration President Nixon sent a letter of thanks to Dr. Beckman. "I am deeply grateful," the president wrote, "not only for your campaign efforts but also for the faith that those efforts represented. I shall do everything I possibly can in the months and years ahead to merit that faith and to make these years a time of which America as a nation and we as Americans can be truly proud." The Lincoln Club continues to play an important role in both California and national politics. Well into the 1990s political candidates from across the nation still clamored to meet with the club so as to convince its members that helping these candidates get elected would usher in good government.

In the 1960s, then, Beckman increasingly operated in the public as well as the private sphere. Organizations like Caltech, the Los Angeles Chamber of Commerce, and his Lincoln Club courted him for his abilities as a problem solver and a facilitator, his ability to confront the most difficult issues affecting an institution's vision for the future, and his commitment to overcoming obstacles in the way of realizing that vision. Corporations also sought Beckman for their boards. They looked to him for guidance in steering their firms toward the kinds of undaunted expansion and success enjoyed by Beckman Instruments. Beckman turned away many more offers than he accepted, taking up only those that promised a truly difficult, and therefore fascinating, problem to solve. And all along he continued to serve Beckman Instruments as ambassador, trusted senior counselor, board chair, and (always a background reality) largest single shareholder.

Disneyland's 1969 Community Service Awards Committee, chaired by Arnold Beckman. *Courtesy Institute Archives, California Institute of Technology.*

William Ballhaus and Arnold Beckman, 1967. *Courtesy Beckman Coulter, Inc.*

New Realities at Beckman Instruments

In 1965 Arnold Beckman turned over the presidency of Beckman Instruments to William Ballhaus. Ballhaus had graduated from Caltech in 1947 with a doctorate in aerodynamics and mathematics. He joined the Northrop Corporation, a major American defense contractor and aerospace manufacturer, soon after earning his Ph.D. By 1957 Ballhaus had become the vice president for an entire division of Northrop devoted to advanced research and development in electronics and avionics. His skillful management of technical and scientific challenges, along with the vagaries of government contracts, brought promotion to executive vice president of Northrop as a whole in 1961.

Ballhaus and Beckman became acquainted after that promotion, when both men served on a committee established by the governor of California. These two executives of major scientific and technological enterprises impressed one another. They both had Caltech doctorates, they both had a flair for advancing the cutting edge of science and technology, and they were both businessmen of long-term vision. As their acquaintance deepened, Beckman came to see Ballhaus as the right person to lead Beckman Instruments into the future. Ballhaus was a solver of technical problems, a decisive thinker, a Caltech product, and an industrial executive of proven skill in guiding large and complex programs to success. Ballhaus became the president of Beckman Instruments in 1965, when Beckman traded in that title for that of chairman of the board.

As Ballhaus and his advisers surveyed the directions and the future of Beckman Instruments in the mid-1960s, the numbers conveyed unmistakable messages: The systems area was weak, instruments remained a bread-and-butter staple of the corporation, and the biomedical field offered yet-unimagined frontiers. Someone made the observation, quickly developed into a mantra by the entire organization, that for every thousand research labs in the United States, there are ten thousand clinical labs, all sending out daily purchase orders. The Ballhaus team was not long in making changes.

From 1965 to 1971 Ballhaus concentrated on realigning the Beckman Instruments business portfolio. In contrast to Arnold Beckman's thirty-year push for ever-growing volume in a myriad of areas, sales under William Ballhaus were relatively stagnant, going from $104 million in 1965 to $136 million in 1971. And profits were equally lackluster, moving from $4.6 million to $3.9 million. On occasion the changes tried the patience of both Beckman and Wall Street, for very different reasons. By 1971, however, under Beckman's "benign neglect" and Ballhaus's careful scrutiny, the firm's managers had repositioned the company. Instruments, especially for medical research, and a major thrust toward diagnostics were now to be the goals. Government business and electronics were on the way out. Over the next decade sales, profits, and—belatedly—the stock price of Beckman Instruments ascended at a steady pace. The rigorous managerial and financial restructuring of Beckman Instruments transformed the company, even as its reinvigorated stock enhanced Arnold Beckman's options as philanthropist and civic leader.

William Ballhaus accepts an award on behalf of Beckman Instruments from President Johnson.
Courtesy Beckman Coulter, Inc.

Beckman Instruments had failed to develop a market for computerized process control and analysis in the chemical industries, yet its computer systems found something of a substitute market in defense and aerospace. But whereas no one could doubt that the space program had glamour, the price of that romantic allure was a program that offered few and very expensive projects, all based on brutally competitive bidding.

The vagaries of bidding aggravated the uncertainties of government funding. If the contractor brought a job in late and over budget, the firm had to absorb these extra costs. But if the firm instead filled the contract faster and cheaper than anticipated, the government reserved the right to alter the terms of the original contract retrospectively and reduce the amount of profit. Thus, for many grappling with government contracts, the situation often looked to be "lose-lose." Yet government contracts (or subcontracting jobs for larger contractors) were the only game in town for the advanced computer systems business in the 1960s.

Making matters even more difficult was that competing firms often operated in a way foreign to long-held traditions at Beckman Instruments. Beckman had instilled in his company his own commitment to honesty and straightforward dealings. While the company was quite willing to make forceful, tough bids for computer contracts, his Systems Division managers always kept their offers real-

Chuck Kayser, a Beckman project engineer, holds electroencephalograph electrodes and a signal conditioner used aboard the Gemini spacecraft to monitor brainwaves of the astronauts. *Courtesy Beckman Coulter, Inc.*

Bob Gafford, a project manager in space engineering, holds a cardiovascular reflex conditioning system that was used in the Gemini missions.
Courtesy Beckman Coulter, Inc.

The collector head of the Viking I's surface sampler. Martian soil was analyzed by an on-board Beckman gas chromatograph.
Courtesy Jet Propulsion Laboratory, NASA.

istic. As Richard Nesbit, the head of Systems in the late 1960s, explained, many of Beckman Instruments' competitors sacrificed realism to success in bidding. "Incompetent competition," in Nesbit's phrase, seems an odd problem for a business, but Beckman Instruments was sometimes closed out of markets by the consistent underbidding of other companies.

Nesbit, who went on to become vice president for research and development, explained the situation thus:

> As an example, Lockheed was going to buy a big [computer] simulator for the Poseidon launch vehicle. We responded to Lockheed's request for a quote with a system price tagged at $4 million at a delivery time of some number of months. One of our competitors quoted the same job for $3 million and something like ninety-day delivery. At $3 million we didn't even want the job. We thought, "Gee, our product must be poorly designed." Well, it turned out that the other company did not deliver on time, did not deliver until the full 10-percent [lateness] penalty was in place. Eventually that company filed Chapter Eleven (under bankruptcy law), lost $18 million in one year, and went out of business.

But in the meantime, Beckman Instruments lost the contract.

Coming as he did from one of the nation's leading aerospace defense contractors, Ballhaus was all too familiar with the economic difficulties that government business entailed. Such work could clearly be important and rewarding, in both fiscal and technological senses. Yet playing on such a field entailed accepting all the changes, compromises, and disappointments that came with the territory. Ballhaus looked at computers and systems the way Beckman himself had once looked at infrared: Would the company have a leading role in the field or was it better to get out altogether? Beckman went ahead with infrared, but Ballhaus organized a retreat from systems and computers, phasing Beckman Instruments out of these areas. "Dr. Beckman probably didn't like us getting out of the government systems business, although he went along with it. He said, 'Doesn't that show that we don't know how to manage?' And I said, 'No, not when your competitors are willing to go broke. That's the kind of business you don't want to be in.'"

Beckman's Components Division had remained an area of steady success for the company since its beginnings with the Helipot. The number and the sophistication of the electronic components the division produced increased throughout the 1960s and the 1970s. The technological success of these components did not engender the public attention and wide appreciation that Beckman successes in instrumentation and in the biomedical field brought. In part the virtual invisibility and ubiquity of these components explains this quieter profile. Precision potentiometers (like the Helipot), trimming potentiometers (often using cermet materials), miniature resistor networks, and hybrid microcircuits found their way into every corner of the exploding bestiary of electronic products from television to the latest in military avionics.

In the 1970s the Components Division offered one highly visible achievement, as Beckman Instruments became the global leader in the production of liquid-crystal displays. Beckman tells the story in this way:

> We decided we wanted a liquid-crystal display with our battery-operated pH meters because liquid crystals use virtually no current, and a battery would last for a couple of years or more [even if] left on continuously. We developed production techniques that were good. We got some good patents. Electric-crystal displays were also of interest to wristwatch makers. We became the world's largest manufacturer of liquid-crystal wristwatch dials. Now, this is completely foreign to our analytical instrument field, but that's one of these fallouts. We developed a technique that was useful in applications other than the one we had. That's been the history of our company in many ways.

Beckman Instruments soon dropped the liquid-crystal business, as it became a commodity business in which production costs exceeded retail prices. However, it was precisely this openness to new developments that kept the company vital and growing through the 1970s.

In Beckman's own tradition, Ballhaus sought to position the company on the sharpest cutting edge. In the late 1960s that was biotechnology and biomedicine. Scientists working with basic cellular components (amino acids, nucleic acids) made discoveries that led to the new field of biotechnology, as the elucidation of the structure of DNA by Watson and Crick opened new fields of genetic research. The Ballhaus team pushed the corporation further into the biomedical fields

Left: Evolution of the Spinco centrifuge.

Right: Manufacturing line for liquid-crystal displays.
Both courtesy Beckman Coulter, Inc.

first launched under Beckman's own leadership. Beckman catalogs already offered the major biomedical labs pH meters, spectrophotometers, and oxygen analyzers; Ballhaus would now add more wonders: new instruments to open new frontiers.

By the late 1970s Beckman Instruments was offering four instruments needed for cutting-edge work. The ultracentrifuge and the amino acid analyzer had been developed earlier but now found new applications. Two other tools were developed in response to the corporation's new emphasis on biomedicine: the protein sequencer (1969) and the protein-peptide synthesizer (1971).

The clinical side of biomedicine offered a different kind of promise, with more immediate financial returns. Beckman's instruments had been familiar in clinical settings from the earliest days of the pH meter and oxygen analyzers. What was new on Ballhaus's watch was the reality—and the recognition of the reality—that the growing clinical field was really two markets. Enterprising corporations could offer sophisticated instruments, but each was a one-time sale. Offering the special chemicals and test kits that went with those instruments promised repeat sales to captive buyers. This was the business thinking that Ballhaus provided, in natural complement and contrast to Beckman's instinctive search for science-based inventions.

Two early results were revolutionary: the glucose analyzer (1969) and the blood urea nitrogen analyzer (1971), both aimed at the health care market. The glucose analyzer (designed by James Sternberg, Beckman's director of applied research and advanced methods development) used a protein, the enzyme glucose oxidase, in a novel rate-sensing system that gave an accurate reading of blood sugar levels within fifteen seconds. No longer would doctors wait for long stretches while laboratory chemists performed time-consuming tests on a patient's blood samples. Doctors could have their vital information quickly and order numerous tests to monitor their patients' conditions much more closely.

The blood urea nitrogen analyzer performed similarly, reading urea nitrogen levels instead. Both instruments are vital in determining whether the stability of body functions has been disrupted. Used in emergency rooms, these analyzers can indicate within a minute whether a patient is undergoing kidney or pancreas distress or failure. Both analyzers used Beckman Instruments' core technology, electrochemistry.

Following its proven technique of earlier decades, the firm combined the glucose and blood urea nitrogen analyzers as part of a new package, the STAT Lab. STAT is an emergency-room term derived from the Latin root word *statim*, meaning "immediately." Dubbing this diagnostic machine the STAT Lab highlighted its suitability for emergency treatment decisions conducted under extreme time pressure. As Beckman described the system in a lecture to the Newcomen Society in 1976, "Typical STAT Labs have automated equipment that measures concentrations of glucose, urea, calcium, and other blood electrolytes such as potassium and sodium. . . . The concept of the STAT Lab is gaining acceptance under constant public pressure for improved health care. Moreover, the term *STAT* is attaining public recognition; you hear it used with appropriate dramatic emphasis on some of the popular medical shows on television these days."

The STAT Lab system, put on the market in the early 1970s, has evolved over the years. In 1985 Beckman predicted that the nature of medical diagnosis was going to change as the instruments used in running tests increasingly came to rely on chemical identification of substances that induce or indicate disease. "We are going to have instruments that will not only measure [such things as hormones or neurotransmitters], but will measure several of them. They'll have computers in there that will tell what the significance is and come up with a diagnosis, with a therapy. All this is going to be done by unskilled people, technicians, it's going to revolutionize the field of medicine." Beckman's vision of the stat lab has largely been realized: Emergency diagnostic machines all have computer components and have become quicker and more efficient in making determinations.

The STAT system was a great success, but it was Beckman's third entry into the medical analytic systems market. Its first entry was the disappointing discrete sample analyzer (DSA), an automated system for conducting a broad range of clinical, chemical analyses. The DSA's basic downfall was reliability. It was not robust enough for the clinical labs in which it had to operate, and its reliability suffered accordingly. A key but troublesome feature was one by which the DSA sought to

Clockwise: An ad for the blood urea nitrogen analyzer; a traveling exhibit of Beckman's biomedical instrument lines; James Sternberg, who designed the glucose analyzer; the first engineering prototype of the glucose analyzer, in 1969. *All courtesy Beckman Coulter, Inc.*

remedy the problems to which its original competitor, the "Technicon," was subject: contamination of the samples to be analyzed.

Even so, the DSA experience built know-how and determination in both management and the R&D staff. They agreed it was worth translating the work put into the DSA into a new project. Howard Teeter, Ballhaus's executive vice president, told the lead engineer that "the corporation was strong and we had money and wanted to go back [into automated clinical chemistry systems], regardless, and . . . if we failed again I wanted to go back a third time. . . . You don't have to prove a thing in the world to me because I know you're the best there is. The corporation needs this medical business; we must have it to grow, and I want you to help us succeed."

Beckman scientists and engineers did just what Teeter urged and transformed the best in technology from the DSA into their new clinical laboratory analysis system, the automated stat routine analyzer (ASTRA). Arnold Beckman had long cherished occasional failures as necessary proof that boundaries were being pushed: If designers and marketers never failed, they were not working hard enough or on the right problems. Experience with the DSA and with the other electrochemical measurements—of glucose and electrolytes—helped greatly. When it came, the ASTRA was a phenomenal success, thanks to the innovative thinking that set Beckman Instruments apart. In the words of Richard Nesbit, "[The glucose analyzer is] a combination of some electronics and some chemistry. After we had [this combination] well established, we put together a system that essentially repackaged [the analytic machines] into one instrument and had the whole thing managed with a microcomputer and a cathode-ray tube and an automatic sample table. That's the story of how a big success developed out of an earlier failure."

Hal Madsen, Lou Rosso, and Hal Pepper, attending a sales meeting in the 1970s. *Courtesy Beckman Coulter, Inc.*

The ASTRA system could run chemical analyses on multiple human secretions simultaneously and had a computer memory of 128 kilobytes to store patient data and operator instructions. A memory of that size was phenomenal at the time. Before the instrument went commercial, sixty machines were built as test systems and run through a three-month battery of tests simulating a laboratory environment. Anticipation for these machines was so great that the sales department had an order for one hundred before the testing period was over. Boasting about the reputation of the company, Nesbit said, "The customers are so convinced that Beckman is going to do the job right that they ordered the fifty-thousand-dollar instruments before any had been delivered." By 1981 the ASTRA analyzers were bringing in over $20 million a month because of their voracious thirst for Beckman's reagent chemicals.

The company continued to flourish during the 1970s under Ballhaus's daily direction. As it built new plants in the United States and opened new sales offices around the globe, Beckman Instruments became a company on the rise. It already operated offices in Germany, Scotland, and England. It now added operations in Ireland, Switzerland, Japan, the Netherlands, Italy, and Spain. With the construction of new plants and new offices came ever-widening sales of Beckman products

Between 1965 and 1974 the stock price of Beckman Instruments stagnated, as the company focused on internal restructuring—a narrowing of its range of fields—and the globalization of its markets. The rewards came in the years from 1974 to 1981, as the market recognized the extraordinary value of the firm that Arnold Beckman had created. In 1965, the year he stepped down as chairman, the company's shares traded at prices from a high of 50½ to a low of 43½. In 1974 the high was 40 and the low 16. Then the stock took off owing to the success of the rapidly growing clinical diagnostics business. In 1976 the high was 57¼, and by the start of 1982 it was 92. The stock had doubled between 1965 and 1982, while the Dow Jones average had risen only 8 percent. Arnold Beckman, as the largest single shareholder in Beckman Instruments, was being rewarded with a currency of increasing value at just the time when he and Mabel were experimenting with the new role of philanthropist.

In 1981 Arnold Beckman made the further momentous decision to part from his company entirely. This was not the same "parting" that had occurred sixteen years earlier, in 1965, when he turned the presidency over to William Ballhaus. This transformation was to be much more profound: Beckman Instruments would merge with the SmithKline Corporation, a Philadelphia-based pharmaceutical company. Although he was already into his eighties, it was not easy for Beckman to let go of the firm that he had nurtured for almost forty years. Now that it was a very large international company, he could no longer boast that he knew all his employees, but he remained very much a symbol of Beckman Instruments' humble beginnings, good fortune, and eye for the future.

The SmithKline Corporation's beginnings date back one hundred years earlier than Beckman Instruments'. In 1830 John K. Smith, a Pennsylvanian of German descent, opened a small apothecary shop in the Northern Liberties section of Philadelphia.

His brother George joined him a few years later, and the Smiths' shop, already well known for its pure products, was soon operating as a wholesale drug supplier. Mahlon N. Kline joined Smith in 1875. An aggressive businessman as well as a pharmacist, Kline brought in many new accounts and spread Smith & Kline's reputation as a trustworthy company. When the company incorporated as Smith & Kline in 1888, it was manufacturing a host of drugs. The research department of the company was founded in 1925, by the chemist Fred P. Nabenhauer.

Employees at the Cherry Street laboratory of Smith, Kline & Company in Philadelphia.
Courtesy SmithKline Beecham.

SmithKline continued to expand as its discoveries were transformed into familiar household products. In 1952 it pioneered the time-release drug capsules known as "spansules," a delivery system used with Dexedrine, a popular wake-up drug. The spansule time-release system and mass advertising created a national rush by cold sufferers to Contac shortly after it was introduced in 1960. It was the first twenty-four-hour cold medicine. But it was Tagamet (cimetidine), introduced in 1976, that gave SmithKline the financial flexibility that made mergers attractive to its board. Tagamet, developed in SmithKline's facilities outside of London, England, was the first successful drug for the treatment and prevention of peptic ulcers and other diseases of the gastrointestinal tract. It was also the world's first "billion-dollar drug."

SmithKline underwent rapid expansion during the 1970s, especially in its international facilities. The firm explored various means of diversification, including acquiring companies that manufactured important clinical, research, and diagnostic instruments. At the time of the proposed merger with Beckman Instruments the Smith-Kline Corporation was among the top twelve ethical pharmaceutical companies in the world, the leader in clinical laboratory services, and top of the world in industrial ultrasonics. It also had four times the research budget of Beckman Instruments. ∾

A longtime friend of Beckman's, Gavin Herbert, suggested that there might be a good fit between Beckman Instruments and SmithKline. Herbert's company, Allergan, had merged with SmithKline in 1980, and he thought that a merger might serve to strengthen common areas and inject new funds into Beckman Instruments' research-and-development program. Riding high on the success of its ulcer treatment drug, Tagamet, SmithKline had sales close to $2 billion and was looking for new investments.

Arnold Beckman flew to Philadelphia in the fall of 1981 to meet with the chairman of SmithKline's board, Robert Dee. The two discussed the advantages a merger could bring to both their companies. Despite nagging feelings of depression about selling his company, Beckman was impressed and brought in Ballhaus to meet with Henry Wendt, SmithKline's president.

The two presidents and the two board chairmen met a few more times during the fall of 1981. Beckman was still of two minds:

Our major obligation was to the shareholders; we were their representatives. Personally I'd have preferred not to sell. After all I had my whole life tied up in the company. I was still the boss and liked being the boss, with all the independence that it carried. But the merger with SmithKline would have advantages for our shareholders. For the employees there would be new opportunities in being associated with SmithKline. We were developing products such as peptides for which we had no adequate sales force in place. SmithKline did. Also we could see that being associated closely with a health-oriented company would help us in our development of instruments for the health care industry. We had research projects we'd like to develop but couldn't because we were spending about as much on research as we could carry—about $60 million that year. Being associated with SmithKline would enable us to get on with some of the research that otherwise might never be done or at least be subject to a long delay. And being part of a larger company would open up advancement possibilities for our employees.

On the evening of 23 November 1981 Beckman and Ballhaus shook hands with Dee and Wendt on the agreement for a merger between the SmithKline Corporation of Philadelphia and Beckman Instruments, Inc., of Fullerton. SmithKline agreed to pay the remarkable sum of over $1 billion for Beckman Instruments, instantly doubling Arnold Beckman's own financial resources.

Not everyone was happy about the merger. When Arnold broke the news to Mabel, she burst into tears. Beckman Instruments represented her husband's career, his hard work, and many sacrifices, and she hated the idea that it would be sub-

The Beckman Instruments board of directors approved the merger with SmithKline. From left, William R. Gould; E. H. Clark, Jr.; Arnold Beckman; William Ballhaus; R. J. Munzer; Lowell Stanley; and H. Russell Smith. *Courtesy Beckman Coulter, Inc.*

sumed by an unfamiliar company on the East Coast. Beckman was upset by his wife's distress, and unable to sleep that night, he lay thinking about what bothered him about the deal. "I finally figured out what it was," he said later. "It was the loss of the Beckman name in the marketplace. That was our corporate identity." The next morning, he called SmithKline and negotiated the addition of "Beckman" to the company's name.

Opinions in the financial world were mixed, but the SmithKline Beckman merger went ahead; on 4 March 1982 shareholders of both companies approved the merger by a margin of over 98 percent. The name "Beckman" joined Smith-Kline on everything from the company stationery to the glass doors at the corporate headquarters.

Beckman himself was now on the SmithKline Beckman board of directors. He was even the board's vice chairman from 1982 to 1986. This was a frustrating connection, for it was his name but no longer his company. He had hoped the various divisions that constituted Beckman Instruments would stay together, but in 1983 the SmithKline Beckman board voted to sell the process instruments and controls and the electronic components divisions to Emerson Electric Company, which thus gained a subsidiary of its own with vestiges of the Beckman name, BI Technologies. With that sale went the Helipot, which Arnold Beckman had invented himself, and the symbiosis that the parts of a broad company offered to each other. SmithKline's idea was to focus its Beckman Division on laboratory instruments for the life sciences and diagnostic fields, in complement to its own pharmaceutical and clinical testing businesses.

Even more changes were to come. By 1988, the top management of Smith-Kline Beckman had decided that while the merger had been productive for both organizations, firms engaged in pharmaceuticals needed to concentrate on this area alone. Seven years after absorbing Beckman Instruments, SmithKline established it again as an independent corporation in 1989, after a partial spin-off in 1988. Led by Lou Rosso, a longtime Beckman employee, Beckman Instruments, Incorporated, was once more a proud, independent name in instrumentation, though the process instruments and electronic components were gone. Throughout the 1990s Beckman Instruments became an enterprise devoted to the "Chemistry of Life," focused on introducing new tools required to expand the investigation of life processes—in sites ranging from the basic research laboratory to the clinic.

In 1997 Beckman Instruments found a new partner when it acquired the Coulter Corporation of Miami, Florida, another leader in innovative instrumentation for biomedical research and clinical application. Today, the new firm, Beckman Coulter, has a portfolio of technologies, enjoys $1.8 billion in sales, employs over ten thousand people, and is led by John Wareham. Wareham joined Beckman in 1984 as the vice president of Diagnostic Systems. Under his leadership, the diagnostics business grew to a position of world leadership and notable profitability. He became president and chief operating officer of Beckman Instruments in 1993. In 1998 he became chief executive office of the newly merged Beckman Coulter.

Arnold Beckman watches and cheers, and he brings tears to the eyes of loyal employees as he visits factories and company events. But just as he had left Caltech in 1939 to go full-time into his new business career, so he retired from Beckman Instruments in 1981 only to throw his creative powers into a third career as philanthropist and head of the Arnold and Mabel Beckman Foundation.

From Chairman to Philanthropist

As he returned to California one evening in December 1981, only two weeks after agreeing to sell his company, Beckman made some notes on the airplane. "Will it really be good for Beckman? Should we have driven a harder bargain? Will the Beckman name we have spent forty-six years in building up be submerged and lost in the shuffle? Will I regret giving up my role as boss? What role will I play after the merger? At age eighty-one shouldn't I retire and spend the rest of my days in leisure, or at least doing only the things I want to do? In view of the newspaper headlines and stories, what do my friends, especially Beckman employees, think of me?" These were searching questions, but he surely knew where he was headed. He had doubts—and still talks about them—when he left Caltech. He still had doubts about the merger, yet with a comfortable modicum of guilt, at age eighty-one he could see the creative excitement of a new project. He had transformed himself from academic to businessman in the 1940s. Now he was leaving business completely behind to devote his efforts full-time to philanthropy. It was with renewed vigor that he took up the engagement with basic science and education, inventing for himself a personal identity of a new kind. He had once approached the cutting edge as an instrument maker. Now that his and Mabel's financial resources had doubled overnight, they would approach the cutting edge as philanthropists for science, devoted as always to excellence, innovation, and the sweet spot of opportunity.

Beckman in his final year as chairman of Caltech's board of trustees, 1974. *Courtesy Beckman family.*

Arnold Beckman and Henry Kissinger, May 1981.
Courtesy Institute Archives, California Institute of Technology.

respected adviser than strategic planner. At the same time he retired from leadership of the Lincoln Club, over a dozen years after founding it. Perhaps it was only coincidental that his retirement from the club coincided with the resignation of its candidate, Richard Nixon, from the presidency of the United States in the wake of the Watergate scandal.

Although Dr. Beckman had "retired" from active, direct leadership roles, his stature in his many communities remained unchanged. L. Donald Shields, president of the California State University, Fullerton, in this era, found Arnold Beckman to be the preeminent figure in Orange County civic and business circles: "There was no one who had the stature of Arnold." Shields often sought out Beckman's counsel for the development and guidance of the university, each time finding his advice "extremely well considered. . . . [Arnold] cut through the matters of concern to get to the substantive issues." Dr. Beckman continued to be highly respected not only in Orange County but also in far wider worlds.

Before we explore Dr. Beckman's life as a philanthropist, we need to record how his retirement also saw his involvement in two major international ventures, one considerably more appealing than the other.

Never a Dull Moment

In the late 1970s Dr. Beckman had a hand in reestablishing academic connections with China. The Cultural Revolution had brought a decade of chaos, sending the economy, along with cultural and political institutions, into a tailspin. China had largely been closed off from the free market. However, with the death of Mao Tse-tung in 1976 and the subsequent implosion of the radical movement, the Cultural Revolution came to an end, and China started to recover. Relations between China and the United States had eased after President Nixon's visit in 1972, but the late 1970s brought real opportunities. Arnold Beckman read that Chou Pei-yuan, president of Beijing University, had been put in charge of reforming China's national education system, one of the early casualties of the Cultural Revolution. And Chou was not just any Chinese academic—he was a physicist who had received his Ph.D. from the California Institute of Technology in 1928.

Beckman wrote Chou a letter on Caltech letterhead suggesting that their two universities reestablish the scholarly exchange program in place before the Cultural Revolution: "Because of my continuing interest in higher education, I am writing to inquire whether there is anything I might do to help re-establish the tradition of graduate training at Caltech for Chinese students. Mrs. Beckman and I have applied for visas to visit the People's Republic of China. We hope that a visit in late spring or early fall [1978] might be arranged."

Chou liked the idea and arranged for Beckman and a handful of his colleagues from Caltech to visit China. When the formal invitation arrived, Beckman was unsure that he would be allowed to enter China. Some years earlier he had been

Arnold Beckman visits Shanghai. *Courtesy Beckman family.*

asked by then-President Gerald Ford to attend the funeral of the Chinese Nationalist leader Chiang Kai-shek. He went and somehow found himself listed in the official roster of funeral goers as Chiang's personal physician. That designation should have made Beckman persona non grata in Communist China, unable to visit the mainland again, but the incriminating record seems to have been lost, for the Chinese government admitted both Arnold and Mabel Beckman with nary a word.

"Once we got inside China, we couldn't pay for anything," Beckman later recalled. "Our hotels, our travel expenses, even our laundry costs were picked up by our hosts. I don't remember any restrictions on our travel; we could go where we liked. When we wanted to see the archaeological ruins recently discovered at Sian, it was a little embarrassing—they took some Chinese passengers off the plane so we could go." Dr. Beckman's guides considered him elderly at seventy-eight and treated him with great respect, even insisting on taking his hand whenever he was confronted with a set of stairs to climb. The agile septuagenarian shocked everyone when he left his party behind to scale the Great Wall unassisted. In the same year a group of Chinese scientists and scientific administrators visited Beckman Instruments in Fullerton, and by 1981 the company had opened a sales branch in Beijing.

Another, far-less-pleasant international experience came out of Beckman Instruments' expansion into El Salvador, where the company had a small subsidiary, called Aplar, with a manufacturing plant. El Salvador had originally appeared both economically and politically stable, but in 1979 it was teetering on the brink of civil war. Under the dictatorship of General Carlos Humberto Romero, El Salvadorans experienced both economic upheaval and the denial of many human rights, as several separatist guerrilla organizations coalesced to undermine the government.

On 21 September 1979 a van arrived at Aplar to pick up Dennis McDonald, the plant's general manager, and Fausto Bucheli, a Beckman engineer visiting the site. The two Beckman employees and the driver set off, only to be stopped suddenly when the van was rammed between two mysterious cars. McDonald and Bucheli were horrified as terrorists leaped from the cars and murdered the driver. The gunmen then took McDonald and Bucheli hostage and contacted Beckman Instruments to begin what proved to be a horrendous negotiating process.

The kidnappers informed the firm's legal counsel that if it contacted the El Salvadoran government or law-enforcement agents, the hostages would be killed immediately. Beckman Instruments sent two negotiators to El Salvador. Before the terrorists would even discuss ransom terms, they demanded that Beckman Instruments publish a radical manifesto in more than thirty newspapers in Central and South America, Europe, and the United Kingdom. One of Beckman's negotiators was given what amounted to a treasure map directing him to that manifesto, taped to the underside of a table in a San Salvador restaurant.

Backs to the wall, the Beckman legal team, headed by Robert Steinmeyer,

The Beckman hostages, released by the El Salvadoran terrorists, arrive home. Fausto Bucheli is at front; Dennis McDonald is behind. *Courtesy Beckman Coulter, Inc.*

rushed to get the manifesto into paid advertisements in various newspapers. Once it was published to their satisfaction, the terrorists agreed to begin discussions. Photographs of the hostages holding dated newspapers established that the captives were at least still alive. New problems loomed during these secret ransom negotiations as El Salvadoran dictator General Romero was ousted from power, plunging the country into civil war. The airport was seized and chaos erupted, making negotiations with the terrorists none the easier for the Beckman team.

When asked about this terrible turn of events some years later, Arnold Beckman replied, "I am strongly opposed to paying ransom, as a matter of principle. For years I had been taught: Before making any decision, lay down your principles. Then make sure that any subsequent actions are fully in accord with the principles. Our principle was clear—no ransom. Do we adhere to it in this case, or do we violate it to save the lives of our two employees?" Knowing that the ransom money would undoubtedly finance more terrorism and violence in El Salvador, yet believing that only the payment of the ransom could save the lives of McDonald and Bucheli, Arnold Beckman and William Ballhaus met with the Beckman board and decided to pay off the kidnappers. In a decision where principles were pitted against human life, it was difficult to justify abandoning life for principles.

Fortunately, the terrorist group released the two hostages on receipt of the ransom money after holding them captive for forty-seven days. Dennis McDonald and Fausto Bucheli had joyful reunions with their families, then were sent to the Loma Linda hospital for physical and psychiatric evaluations. Dr. Beckman has never revealed how much was paid to the kidnappers, but a huge amount of cash was stuffed into an unremarkable suitcase, flown to San Salvador, and handed over on a deserted street late one night.

Philanthropy 101

Arnold and Mabel Beckman's continuing involvement with Beckman Instruments and Caltech remained one of stewardship. Fortunately, most issues on which their counsel and wisdom were needed were less life threatening if not less important than the El Salvador affair. The Beckmans were passionate about both Caltech and Beckman Instruments, concerned about a future for which they felt personal responsibility. Their evolving vision for science-oriented philanthropy eventually grew to link the Beckman name to Caltech in ways that would far outlast Arnold's and Mabel's lives, even as it necessitated a steady and total retreat from identification with the company that also bore their name.

By 1976 the Beckmans had come to the remarkable and very private decision that together they were going to dedicate their energies to philanthropy over the coming years. They wished to make major commitments to the causes and institutions they valued. In that year of the bicentennial, Dr. Beckman revealed their plan to a confidant, Jerry Gallwas, a leader in the instrument end of the Beckman firm. As he and Gallwas chatted on a plane journey, Beckman not only outlined his and Mabel's decision to steadily part with much of their wealth, and thus with some of their stock in Beckman Instruments, but added that they were already finding it "more difficult to give money away than it was to make."

The Beckmans moved their planning to a new level by incorporating the Arnold and Mabel Beckman Foundation in September 1977. They would now focus on support of basic scientific research, with a special emphasis on chemistry, biochemistry, and medicine. Incorporated without public fanfare or announcement, their foundation was a private affair, an instrument for gifts the couple would decide together. There was no staff and no public office.

For the next four years the Beckmans made numerous gifts to support science, medicine, and education, some of the donations quite large—measured in millions of dollars—others quite modest, in the low thousands. This was generous giving in a common, traditional mode of philanthropy, more in keeping with distributing the income of the foundation's investments than in giving away any significant part of its capital. For the Beckmans this was a first stage in their career as serious philanthropists, exploring the difficulties and rewards of trying to invest their wealth responsibly and meaningfully in the future of science.

In the first full year of its existence, the Beckmans' new foundation made a $1 million grant to the Scripps Clinic and Research Foundation, in La Jolla, California. Founded in 1924 with an endowment from Ellen Browning Scripps, the clinic focused in its first years on the treatment of diabetes. With the example

Arnold Beckman, accompanied by Mike Morphy on the guitar, in 1975. *Courtesy Institute Archives, California Institute of Technology.*

of Rockefeller University as inspiration, the clinic was remodeled in 1955 as a center for both clinical medicine and research, and the name was changed to the Scripps Clinic and Research Foundation. Arnold Beckman served on its board in the 1970s, a vantage point that kept him impressed with the advances in immunology and biochemistry coming out of Scripps.

The second of the Beckmans' early, substantial gifts came the following year and grew from older, stronger connections. When federal funding was cut back during the late 1960s, many universities suffered from dwindling resources and found it harder to support all their researchers, programs, and groups. A fundraiser from Illinois had approached Dr. Beckman in the early 1970s for $250,000 to underwrite chemistry research. He did not respond to that request, in part because he strongly believed that departmental research support in a public university should be provided by the state itself. He remembers that it was "unreasonable, outrageous to think that I could provide that amount of money. It [was] only later on that I realized it wasn't so outrageous after all."

This realization came as he began to think about the kind of research that states do not have the resources to support: that of graduate students and young faculty members who have potential but not the prominence to attract grants. What if he were to establish a research fund for young scholars at the University of Illinois, where he himself was once a young scholar? Beckman was well aware that the university's Research Board, composed of eight faculty members and the dean of the Graduate College, was responsible for allocating funds for research projects that merited pursuit. But the available money had become woefully inadequate, drastically curtailing grants from the Research Board.

In 1978 Theodore Brown, a distinguished professor in the university's chemistry department, was a member of the Research Board. Brown had never met the Beckmans and did not know that the university had approached them earlier for a substantial contribution. Chosen now to entertain the Beckmans at a dinner reception on one of their return visits to Illinois, Ted and his wife, Audrey, enjoyed the event until they received a phone call informing them that their youngest son had been taken to the emergency room with a broken arm. Audrey Brown left the reception, while the rest of the party went to dinner. Ted Brown, reflecting on this first meeting, said, "In spite of that bad news [his son's broken arm], we had a pleasant evening. I was of course impressed by the Beckmans and very much taken with their warmth and interest in many things."

The following morning he was surprised to find that Beckman had stopped in at the department to ask after the Browns' injured son. "Dr. Beckman had a full schedule that day. . . . That he took the time to make an inquiry about my son, though we had just recently met, told me a lot about him." Professor Brown and the Research Board made an equally favorable impression on Arnold and Mabel Beckman. They decided to contribute $5 million to the university's capital cam-

Arnold and Mabel Beckman at the 1976 Beckman Instruments Anniversary Dinner. *Courtesy Beckman Coulter, Inc.*

paign, on the condition that the university match that amount and earmark all the money as an endowment for the Research Board. This was no small challenge.

While Mabel Beckman was an active partner with her husband in their new career as philanthropists, Arnold took the lead when it came to the conditions and stipulations of gifts to ensure maximum impact. The decision to make the Illinois gift conditional upon the success of a challenge was his first use of this device for his major giving. It was a tried-and-true technique of traditional philanthropy that he was testing, hoping to transfer his knack for leveraging his investments during his industrial career to his philanthropic endeavors. The university met the challenge, raising $5 million from other sources, with full disclosure that the funds would be restricted to endowing basic scientific research. The Beckmans' gift came in two parts. One was a large tract of farmland near Cullom, Illinois, with an esti-mated value of $3 million; it had been left to the Beckmans by Arnold's uncle, Charlie Jewkes. The remaining $2 million came in the form of stock in Beckman Instruments. The gift injected a rejuvenating sum into research at the university.

One of the Research Board's first responses was to create a Beckman Fellows program at Illinois's Center for Advanced Study, to give exceptional young faculty members a semester to pursue their research uninterrupted. The board also cre-ated Beckman Research Awards, to recognize outstanding research proposals in the sciences. Though the Beckmans' gift was an endowment, Beckman stressed its open-endedness. "I don't attempt to say what will be important twenty years from now. The Research Board twenty years from now will be on top of that. I was thinking of putting the money in the fields of biology and medicine and chemistry; those are my major fields. Then I thought that would be restrictive, and nobody's got the foresight to know what conditions will be in the future. So I've left it open, relying on the judgment of this Research Board." The Beckman endowment also funds an annual Arnold O. Beckman Lecture in Research and Innovation. Not sur-prisingly, Arnold O. Beckman himself gave the inaugural lecture.

Following their challenge-based investment in scientific research at Illinois, the Beckmans continued to make numerous smaller donations to a host of scientific, cultural, educational, and civic organizations over the next three or four years. While some of these gifts were substantial, at the level of a hundred thousand dollars, most of them were in the ten-thousand-dollar range. There were gifts to Chapman University, the American Academy of Arts and Sciences, and the American Association of Clinical Chemistry, among others. In 1982 Caltech received a $100,000 donation, refreshing and continuing the couples' relationship with the school. Several larger donations went to clinical medicine. The Irvine Medical Center benefited from a $50,000 gift, and the Mennonite Hospital of Bloomington-Normal, Illinois, received a $250,000 donation from the couple.

Smaller grantees reflected other interests. Harkening back to his days as an air-raid warden during World War II, Arnold Beckman gave $25,000 to KCET for

Dr. Beckman in his home office. *Courtesy Beckman Coulter, Inc.*

emergency broadcasting, the 1982 equivalent of the air-raid siren. He also gave several thousand dollars for science and technology museums, reflecting how seriously he took his own boyhood awakening to the wonders and challenges of science. These gifts were all straightforward donations, in contrast to the major commitment the Beckmans had made at Illinois, where they used a challenge grant to leverage their investment in scientific research. The truth was that they were taking a pause in the development of their philanthropy, assessing their comfort with the size and style of the gift to Illinois.

At this stage of their philanthropic careers the Beckmans attempted to handle all aspects of giving themselves. As word of their generosity spread, they were gradually inundated with pleas, ideas, and inquiries. Dr. Beckman's desk strained under the weight of scores of lengthy proposals awaiting his and Mabel's attention. Jerry Gallwas recalls that "Mabel kept pressing him to make decisions, but he was still finding his way with where to give and how much to give. There were no criteria [for their giving] other than what the two of them discussed at the breakfast table."

Also at this time Arnold Beckman was experimenting vigorously with a very different philanthropic mode, in an arena far outside of his and Mabel's personal wealth. In fact, the Beckmans slowed the innovations in their own philanthropy, as Arnold Beckman returned again to a "laboratory" of sorts. For, in the early 1980s, he was head of another philanthropic foundation, one grappling with ways to invest huge sums of money most effectively. He and Mabel were learning from his experiments in this new laboratory of philanthropy, so that they might craft their own giving in light of that experience.

Arnold Beckman's Philanthropic Laboratory

Dr. Beckman's retirement from the presidency of Beckman Instruments left him all the more time for the several other boards that had commissioned his services. One board chairmanship that was particularly instructive was that of the System Development Corporation.

In the early 1950s the RAND Corporation, a Southern California not-for-profit organization created by the government as a think tank for the military, contracted to handle software development for the computer systems used by the Department of Defense. Within the Department of Defense, the U.S. Air Force was the biggest customer for these software systems, and its demands were growing exponentially. In a very short time the software and systems development operation of RAND began to overrun its other programs, prompting RAND to spin off this sector as the System Development Corporation (SDC).

Newly independent in 1957, SDC was, like its parent, a not-for-profit corporation. Its mission was to produce software and systems for the U.S. Air Force. Arnold Beckman became a member of SDC's board of trustees just two years after its formation, in 1959, when he was deep in his career as a creator of advanced computing systems for the military and aerospace markets. From 1961 through 1966 his importance to SDC was reflected in his service as the board's vice chairman. Under his watchful eye the corporation grew healthily, until in the mid-1960s companies financed by venture capital began to spring up in competition with SDC and to lure its employees away with promises of stock options and higher salaries.

In 1966 Dr. Beckman became chairman of the board of SDC. Almost immediately, he faced the challenge of a complete reorganization. The managers within the corporation had begun to look into transforming their organization from a not-for-profit, federally funded research-and-development corporation (FFRDC), to a for-profit corporation in the private sector. As an FFRDC, the corporation, though dependent on the federal government for contracts, was run by a board of directors and staffed by employees who were not civil servants. This arrangement allowed a lot of flexibility but not enough for a changing world. Demand in the private sector for software and systems was on the upswing, and there were newly tempting contracts available to corporations not hampered by quasi-governmental status. In addition, employees at private companies could be motivated by stock options.

Dr. Beckman proposed an inventive solution to SDC's problems, and the air force agreed. "We decided that to preserve the viability of SDC, it had to go on a profit-making basis, so we could have the same practices for the employees. We formed the System Development Foundation (which was a nonprofit foundation) as the stockholder, and so we preserved that relationship." After disbursing about one-third of the SDC stock to the company for the incentive programs needed to

Arnold Beckman assumed the chairmanship of the System Development Corporation board in 1966, as announced in its *Bulletin* (7)14. *Courtesy Burroughs Collection, Charles Babbage Institute for the History of Information Processing, University of Minnesota.*

retain the best and the brightest among its employees, the System Development Foundation existed as a holding entity for the rest of the SDC stock, an organization to look after the investment that the American public had made in SDC through its earlier creation to serve the air force.

In 1980 the rationale of the System Development Foundation abruptly changed. Beckman and his colleagues learned that the Burroughs Corporation was interested in acquiring SDC. Burroughs was prepared to buy all the SDC stock, 1.42 million shares, for sixty-nine dollars per share. This was twice the value that the System Development Foundation's financial advisers had placed on the stock. Beckman and his fellow directors felt that they were bound to accept the offer, both because the foundation was nonprofit and because the offer promised a windfall gain for the stockholder-employees of SDC. As a result the foundation found itself the possessor of some $65 million in cash.

It was by no means obvious what to do next. Beckman and his colleagues had joined the SDC board because of their knowledge of defense needs, systems development, and government contracting. The foundation had been a legal device, a means to keep SDC on track in a changing world. It was never meant to be a philanthropy, still less a philanthropic foundation in perpetuity. Here, once again, was a situation in which chance might favor a prepared mind. By now Beckman knew that responsible philanthropy was a serious, draining endeavor. Neither he nor his colleagues saw the foundation as a permanent commitment, now that its role in relation to SDC had vanished. And $65 million was on the table.

Arnold Beckman once again saw opportunity in a radical move. The foundation would spend itself out of existence, quickly. Under Beckman's leadership the board of the System Development Foundation agreed to distribute all its assets over an eight-year period. The foundation would seek to have a major impact on a specific area of science through "megagifts." In keeping with its origins, the board focused on computer science and closely allied fields, especially in areas of frontier research. The megagifts would provide the board with a learning laboratory, even as those gifts fulfilled its decision to disburse the foundation's assets for the public good. By 1988 the board had succeeded in that mammoth task.

The foundation quickly gave $10 million to the RAND Corporation, in recognition of RAND's role in the creation of the SDC in the 1950s. Then came over $20 million to create the Center for the Study of Language and Information, a cooperative, interdisciplinary academic center for researchers from Stanford University, SRI International, and Xerox's Palo Alto Research Center. Other large grants went to MIT's Artificial Intelligence Laboratory and to other educational institutions for projects in the fields of computer science, artificial intelligence, linguistics, robotics, and associated subjects. Once again Arnold Beckman had engineered a mutually beneficial connection between industry and education.

The experience with the System Development Foundation was Dr. Beckman's real education in philanthropic giving on a grand scale. When asked whether his leadership of the foundation was crucial to his education in philanthropy, he replied: "Well, of giving substantial amounts, yes. I'd already had what I think was a reasonable program, but when you give away large amounts, that was new.... [Y]ou have different criteria than you do when you take care of the United Way [with a yearly check]." The experience of making decisions about these huge sums of money allowed Arnold Beckman to think more deeply about his and Mabel's philanthropic options.

The early 1980s were dramatic years for the Beckmans as philanthropists for another reason. Even as Dr. Beckman was organizing major benefactions for the System Development Foundation, his own situation changed greatly, for he and

Howard Teeter, a Beckman Instruments executive, Arnold Beckman, and Mabel Beckman at a picnic in the early 1980s.
Courtesy Beckman Coulter, Inc.

William Ballhaus were talking with the SmithKline leadership about the merger between Beckman Instruments and that firm.

In February 1982 Arnold Beckman and the System Development Foundation officially awarded its $10 million gift to RAND. The next month the stockholders of both Beckman Instruments and SmithKline approved the merger of their firms, and SmithKline Beckman became a reality. With this merger came exchanges of stock, as shares in both Beckman Instruments and SmithKline were converted into shares of the new SmithKline Beckman. The conversion rates for these exchanges reflected the worth that Arnold Beckman had negotiated for Beckman Instruments in the merger, that is, over $1 billion. In March 1982, after the exchange, Arnold and Mabel Beckman found themselves the possessors of a personal fortune that had suddenly doubled.

The Beckmans could only be moved by the conjunction of events. They had been seriously thinking about their personal philanthropy for several years, exploring ways to invest in the future of science and the causes they held dear. And just as Dr. Beckman found a mode of philanthropy that he thought was truly innovative, he and his wife found themselves with vastly expanded personal resources. Arnold and Mabel had again found that sweet spot of opportunity, and they set to work together on a fresh plan to take advantage of these two major occurrences.

Philanthropy in a New Mode

The Beckmans decided to shift the orientation of their philanthropy to incorporate the new techniques of giving that Dr. Beckman was exploring with the System Development Foundation. The new mode would match the greater size of their wealth. They began to transfer major amounts of SmithKline Beckman stock to their Arnold and Mabel Beckman Foundation.

The SmithKline Beckman directors, Irvine, California, 1983. *Courtesy Beckman Coulter, Inc.*

The foundation remained the private operation of the Beckmans, now with assistance from Arnold's long-time secretary Jane Guilarte. Proposals continued to pour in for the Beckmans' consideration, adding to an already considerable backlog. Jerry Gallwas remembers of this juncture that "by the time of the SmithKline Beckman merger in the spring of 1982, [Dr. Beckman] was frantic with trying to manage the demand. . . . But Mabel kept pushing and would say, 'Arnie, what are you waiting for? We can afford it.' "

Working with Jerry Gallwas, Arnold Beckman developed, sharpened, and articulated the criteria that would guide his and Mabel's philanthropy. The foundation would support basic scientific research, with an emphasis on the forward looking in chemistry, biochemistry, medicine, and instrumentation. What would be different was the new goal of the Beckmans' foundation. They would use it to give away not only income from, but the whole capital base of, their fortune during their lifetimes, investing their wealth in ways they determined best. They intended to have their whole fortune disbursed and their foundation disbanded by the end of their lives. By the beginning of 1983 they were ready to make a first move.

City of Hope

Mabel Beckman's brush with tuberculosis in the 1930s was a traumatic time for the young family, a time that shaped her concerns for health and nutrition in the decades that followed. She had been treated for the dread disease in Pottenger's Sanatorium in Monrovia, California. Dr. Pottenger was a leading American clinician fighting tuberculosis, and his clinic attracted movie stars, foreign diplomats, and the spouses of Caltech faculty as its patients. Directly adjacent to Monrovia, in Duarte, California, a very different tuberculosis sanatorium was operating while Mabel Beckman was at Pottenger's. In a fitting tribute to her harrowing experience with tuberculosis, the Beckmans awarded the first of their new, large-scale gifts to the institution that grew out of this other sanatorium: the City of Hope National Medical Center.

In 1912 the garment district of Los Angeles was a poor section of the city, teeming and crowded. Tuberculosis was rampant in the closely packed tenements, and many garment workers were infected. One day in 1912 a young immigrant, recently arrived in Los Angeles and in despair as tuberculosis slowly drained his life, shot himself in the street. This suicide, and the depressing persistence of the disease in the district, prompted the community to begin fund-raising to construct a free tuberculosis sanatorium. Ten acres of open land were purchased in Duarte, which, like Monrovia, is twenty-five miles east of downtown Los Angeles, and two tents were erected. Thus began the Los Angeles Sanatorium, which in 1914 hired its first doctor, a woman named Clara Stone. The tent city evolved into a cluster of clapboard buildings. Only in 1930 did the Los Angeles Sanatorium receive its first solid building—a two-story clinic donated by the Warner brothers of movie studio fame.

The Beckman Foundation's first megagift established the Beckman Research Institute of the City of Hope in Duarte, California. *Courtesy Beckman Foundation.*

The advent of antitubercular drugs, beginning with streptomycin in 1943, eroded the need for a tuberculosis sanatorium. Faced with extinction, the administration voted to change the sanatorium's name to City of Hope and focus its healing attentions on other serious diseases, including cancer and heart and lung ailments. The City of Hope became a national medical center in 1946.

The mid-1940s saw the City of Hope develop a Medical Research Institute, divided into seven departments: biochemistry, cytology and genetics, internal medicine, microbiology, pathology, radiology, and surgical research. Clinical material, equipment, and supplies were shared across departmental boundaries—an early example of interdisciplinary work. Of the seven departments, biochemistry and cytology and genetics were committed to basic research. Out of these departments came a number of important scientific innovations. In 1978 Art Riggs and Keichi Itakura developed the first genetically engineered products to be approved by the Food and Drug Administration. This work led to the creation of synthetic human insulin, a major step in the treatment of diabetes.

In the early 1980s City of Hope's hard work on both the clinical and research fronts won it the National Cancer Institute's designation as a Comprehensive Cancer Research Institute. Around the same time Charlie Todd, the chairman of the newer department of immunology, formed in the mid-1960s, was busy talking up the institute to his colleague Arnold Beckman, for whom he was a consultant.

Todd was enthusiastic about the cutting-edge work being done at the City of Hope and was certain it could benefit from Beckman support. Mabel was sympathetic. Todd did a good job convincing the Beckmans, and in 1983 Arnold and Mabel made a major challenge grant to the City of Hope. They would give the then-huge sum of $10 million for buildings, equipment, and endowment, if that total could be matched from other sources. Megagifts might be the new Beckman mode, but that did not mean that Arnold and Mabel had abandoned their frugal instincts or the desire to leverage their dollars.

The hospital quickly met the challenge, and the Beckman Research Institute of the City of Hope opened its doors in 1983. Its mission is "innovative and creative research in the biological sciences"; more specifically it focuses on the molecules and processes of life, "including those processes important to the causes, prevention, and cure of human disease."

The Beckman endowment enabled basic research to be kept separate from the workings of the hospital: The only stipulation is that the income of the endowment not be spent on any type of patient care but rather on research. Dr. Beckman was clear that "just providing for people's comfort when they become ill, that's not advancing, that's not preventing them from becoming ill in the first place." He also noted that "[patient care is] the sort of thing that appeals to many other people. The general public can support that, where they would not give money for some research project with some strange name that [they] wouldn't understand."

John S. Kovach, director of the Beckman Research Institute at the City of Hope, practices just the kind of prevention-oriented research that Arnold Beckman finds to be true "advancement." In his research in molecular epidemiology, Kovach uses genetic maps and environmental data to identify women at risk for breast and other types of cancer. His work is part of a large, interdisciplinary effort that aims at not only controlling breast cancer but also preventing it by attacking its causes. In accord with Beckman's own interests, Kovach bridges forward-looking research and clinical application, as he also seeks to shape City of Hope's work on viral and nonviral gene delivery vectors, monoclonal antibodies, and genetically engineered blood cells.

The Big Five

With this first very large donation, Arnold and Mabel Beckman also created their first "Beckman Institute," at the City of Hope. The Beckmans began to focus their central efforts toward defining and developing a very small number of such megagifts. No other strategy would disburse funds fast enough or have as large an impact on scientific endeavor. These megagifts, eventually five in number, were surrounded by a larger number of significant donations, gifts to unique scientific ventures close to Dr. Beckman's heart. An outer penumbra of more personal and idiosyncratic grants would complete the portfolio of the Beckman philanthropic team.

Arnold and Mabel Beckman approached philanthropy as a couple, with Arnold providing the intellectual vision and Mabel participating substantively by reviewing proposals, visiting sites, and attending meetings. Together they interviewed, traveled, and probed. As one author of this biography can testify personally, an application to the Beckman Foundation in the mid-1980s was a rigorous, demanding, exhilarating process, if one made it past Guilarte's "watchdog" scrutiny into the ongoing seminar with Dr. and Mrs. Beckman that comprised two to three years of "proposal review" before a grant was made.

As Harry Gray, Arnold O. Beckman Professor of Chemistry at Caltech, expressed it, "Dr. Beckman was more thoughtful and more intellectually demanding than many other philanthropists." This was in part because he saw himself as an "upstart academic . . . still looking in his philanthropy for the innovation, creativity, and application of science to the betterment of mankind" that he had glimpsed as an assistant professor and practiced during his career as a scientific entrepreneur. The choices made out of that thoughtful probing had a commensurately powerful effect. Stanley Ikenberry, president of the American Council on Education and former president of the University of Illinois, calls the Beckman Institute created at Illinois by the Beckmans' philanthropy the "most significant academic event at the University of Illinois in the last half of the twentieth century." The Illinois Institute has become instrumental in attracting other funds and support and top faculty and thus has a "massive impact on intellectual life at the university."

The sequence of events by which Arnold and Mabel Beckman together made five megagifts between 1983 and 1989 involved both logic and happenstance. As the decade progressed and word spread of their remarkable reinvigoration of the pre–World War II tradition of private philanthropy for science, a steady stream of hopeful supplicants found their way to Dr. Beckman's door. What the five successful institutions had in common was academic excellence, considerable persistence, and strong ties to Beckman's earlier life. In the case of one, physical propinquity to their "retirement" world of home in Corona del Mar and the office in Irvine where he housed his assistant in a now-demolished plant at the Scientific Instruments Division of Beckman was also a factor.

Beckman Laser Institute

About the time that the City of Hope's Beckman Research Institute was founded, Dr. Beckman became interested in work under way at the newest school in the University of California system. University of California, Irvine, opened in 1965, and seven years later a young Cornell-trained professor of biology named Michael Berns took up a position in Irvine's biology department. In due course Berns applied for a National Institutes of Health biotechnology grant to fund an instrumentation center. Lasers were still a relatively new technology in the early 1980s; the first successful laser was constructed only in 1960, by the physicist Theodore

Maiman. Berns proposed establishing a facility dedicated to using laser microscopy to manipulate intracellular components.

Michael Berns was awarded the grant and built his center. He then held an open house to which he invited all the CEOs of major technology companies in Southern California. He wanted to "educate the corporations in Orange County as to what was going on in our resource center." The day of the open house turned out rainy, and very few CEOs showed up. One who did brave the rain, though, was Arnold Beckman. On a tour through the lab he expressed a great deal of interest in the scientific possibilities presented by lasers, and he watched Berns's laser demonstrations closely.

A short while later Michael Berns was approached by a surgeon who asked whether lasers could be used to activate certain drugs that bind to cancerous tumors. This method of treatment, called photodynamic therapy, was a new field, and the use of lasers to treat various diseases, including cancer, seemed very promising. Berns kept Dr. Beckman apprised of these new developments and a short while later sent him a proposal for yet another innovative facility: an institute filled with both basic research scientists and clinicians working together on developing instrumentation and drug-based systems that could be applied in a clinical setting.

Dr. Beckman was excited by the connection between basic research and clinical application. Though in his eighties, he was as keenly interested in innovation as

The Beckman Laser Institute at the University of California, Irvine.
Courtesy Beckman Foundation.

ever. Berns's proposal offered an interesting variant on the medical research at the City of Hope; the Irvine campus was on Beckman's doorstep, young and growing in reputation; and Berns was brilliant, charming, and persistent. The combination proved irresistible. The Beckman Laser Institute and Medical Center was duly established on the Irvine campus as a nonprofit corporation independent of the university. Dr. Beckman did not want to give money directly to the school because he felt, as a taxpayer in the state of California, that his money was already going to support the University of California system. Berns and Beckman worked out an agreement with Irvine such that the university would provide the space and management for the Laser Institute, although it would be in a private building on campus. That the Beckman Laser Institute (BLI) is private and not for profit has

Arnold Beckman cuts the ribbon with a laser at the opening of the Beckman Laser Institute at the University of California, Irvine. Michael Berns, the director of the Laser Institute, holds the ribbon. *Courtesy Institute Archives, California Institute of Technology.*

opened doors, again leveraging Beckman dollars by attracting other donors. (David Packard, cofounder of Hewlett-Packard, gave BLI $2 million and served for a time on its board.) In the bylaws of the BLI, Arnold Beckman and Michael Berns are listed as cofounders and have permanent board membership.

A pamphlet printed after the Laser Institute opened in 1986 predicted that lasers would be used in a myriad of clinical applications, including new forms of surgery, genetic engineering, and cancer diagnosis and treatment. Today many of the predictions are commonplace practices, among them orthoscopy, genetically engineered crops, and advanced disease therapies that use light-sensitive dyes and drugs to bind to harmful elements and destroy them using laser beams. "The laser is emerging rapidly as a powerful new tool for medical research and clinical use . . . with the potential for revolutionary advances in the practice of medicine," wrote Dr. Beckman at the beginning of the 1986 pamphlet. With typical foresight, he has proved astute in judging the future of scientific research.

The University of Illinois

Even as Michael Berns and Arnold Beckman were busy laying the groundwork for the Laser Institute at Irvine, a group of administrators at the University of Illinois, including Ted Brown, were discussing possible new initiatives to attract private donors. A new facility with an interdisciplinary focus and cutting-edge research could be attractive, it was decided. Two committees were convened and charged

The Beckman Institute at the University of Illinois, Urbana-Champaign.
Courtesy Beckman Foundation.

with developing potential programs. The proposed center would have three aims: to establish the University of Illinois as a world leader in the intellectual territory it covered; to focus on areas of growth potential for which substantial federal funding was available; and to draw upon diverse expertise and interests encompassing more than one department. Ted Brown remembers that he asked the two committees, to "think about the ways in which the University of Illinois at Urbana-Champaign might strengthen its already strong science and engineering efforts through the development of interdisciplinary programs [and think about] both organizational structures and new physical facilities that would promote the growth and development of interdisciplinary efforts." The first of the two committees drew up a program ranging across engineering, the physical sciences, and information sciences. The second formulated a program across neuroscience, cognitive science, biomolecular science, and artificial intelligence.

The two committee reports were polished and refined into a proposal for an interdisciplinary research center spanning the physical and biological sciences. In the summer of 1984 the president of the university, Stanley Ikenberry, presented the proposal to Dr. Beckman. That fall the Illinois football team had an excellent season that landed them at the Rose Bowl in Pasadena on 1 January 1985. The Beckmans, now being actively courted by the Illinois administration, were invited to join the Illinois party attending the big game. As Brown tells the story, "The game itself was a disaster for [Illinois]. There was little to cheer about . . . [I]n the midst of the game, the scoreboard suddenly changed to read 'Caltech 128, MIT 0'! The bogus display stayed on for some time until perplexed officials could figure out how to get it back to normal." Arnold Beckman, Brown recalls, was both amused and proud that "his Caltech kids" had once again disrupted a Rose Bowl game in time-honored tradition.

While Beckman was not particularly interested in football, he certainly was interested in the potential of interdisciplinary research. In July 1985, after discussions with Mabel, he requested a more detailed proposal from Illinois. Brown prepared a twenty-five-page supplement, reemphasizing how Illinois fostered, and excelled at, interdisciplinary research. In the absence of private funding, the university would be at a growing disadvantage, owing to its inadequate instrumental resources and research facilities. Wrote Brown, "Our proposal for the Arnold O. and Mabel M. Beckman Institute, however, is far more than simply a request for bricks and mortar. It is based on a vision of an organizational structure and an operating philosophy that we believe will enhance, even transform, the individual research efforts of the faculty. This vision involves an emphasis on individual excellence and on intense interaction among faculty members who are at the forefront of a broad spectrum of different disciplines. It is built upon an understanding of the rapidly developing interdependence of key, but often disparate, research frontiers."

Shortly after drafting this supplemental proposal, Brown went on vacation. Returning to Urbana, he was greeted by the news that the Beckmans were planning a gift of $40 million toward the establishment of the proposed facility. "It would be too mild a term to say I was surprised," says Brown, "astonished is more like it." The proposal had requested $40 million, the upper limit needed to realize all facets of the research facility. "We had expected that we would more likely be receiving half of that, and that we would need to make some tough choices." Arnold's affection for his undergraduate school, along with Mabel's support and their emerging strategy of making a few megagifts, combined to surprise the folks at Illinois.

The agreement between the Beckmans and the university stipulated that the

Beckman gift be preceded by an immediate $10 million from the state of Illinois toward the actual construction of the "Arnold and Mabel Beckman Institute for Advanced Science and Technology." The exciting news was announced at the fall 1985 homecoming meeting of the University of Illinois Foundation. The Beckmans found themselves attending yet another football game hosted by the Browns. This time Illinois was playing Ohio State in a very close game. In the last quarter the game was tied, and the Illinois players were making their way toward a goal. In the midst of this excitement Arnold Beckman stood up, put his coat on, and said to his wife, "Come on, Mabel. If we leave now, we can beat the crowd." Brown remembers that Mabel looked at her husband in amazement and said "Arnie, are you nuts? Illinois is about to try a field goal!" Thus chastised, Beckman sat down and watched the Illinois victory.

Ground was broken in the fall of 1986, and over the course of the next two years the Beckmans visited frequently, thoroughly excited and pleased by the building they saw taking shape. Despite their advanced ages, both delighted in exploring the site, crowned in hard hats and dodging piles of rubble. The Illinois Beckman Institute was dedicated in April 1989. A five-story building, it houses two hundred offices, specialized laboratories for diverse scientific fields, and numerous formal and informal meeting areas. As Dr. Beckman noted, "a central atrium, with, at each corner, a little place to sit around, with seats, and chat . . . [T]hose small,

Arnold and Mabel Beckman with Ted and Audrey Brown at the April 1989 dedication of the Beckman Institute at the University of Illinois.
Courtesy Ted Brown.

Arnold Beckman at the University of Illinois's Beckman Institute.
Courtesy Beckman Institute, University of Illinois, Urbana-Champaign.

informal conversation groups are where a lot of the progress is made in science." Arnold and Mabel Beckman with their children and grandchildren attended the dedication ceremonies. Although Mabel had been in the hospital earlier and was advised by her doctor to stay at home, she insisted that she could get along as well in Illinois as she could in California. Fighting cancer, she arrived in Urbana looking tired and small, huddled in a wheelchair. However, it was clear to everyone that she was very happy to be there. In Brown's words, "The Beckman Institute at Illinois, as doubtless with all their philanthropic activities to that point, was very much the product of their joint decision making."

Ikenberry had much the same impression as Brown. The full extent of Mabel Beckman's partnership in the couple's career in philanthropy was driven home for Ikenberry one evening during discussion about Illinois's proposed Beckman Institute. Ikenberry and the Beckmans had just finished dinner, and he was feeling the strain of keeping pace with Dr. Beckman's serious questioning and testing of the Illinois proposal. In fact, Ikenberry was experiencing a moment of despair, wondering if the grand project would ever come to fruition. He knew the best and the brightest in science from around the world were pressing the Beckmans with rival plans and suggestions. As they stood to leave the dinner, Mabel noticed the evident strain in Ikenberry's expression. She took him aside for a private word, telling him not to worry, that Illinois was one of her "favorites" and one of her

Ted Brown and Arnold Beckman. *Courtesy Beckman Institute, University of Illinois, Urbana-Champaign.*

husband's as well. Mabel was unambiguous. She was a full partner in the decision, and she was favorably inclined. Ikenberry left much relieved.

The Beckman Institute at the University of Illinois includes basic research in engineering and in the physical, life, and behavioral sciences. The original vision for the center called for a revolutionary bridging of the physical and life sciences under the heading "intelligence," and today its research programs run the gamut from artificial intelligence to molecular biophysics, and cognitive neuroscience to engineering networks. Projects are grouped within three major areas of the Beckman Institute: biological intelligence, human-computer interaction, and nanostructures. Under the auspices of the institute more than five hundred professors and students from two dozen or more departments now conduct interdisciplinary and multidisciplinary research.

Crucial to the realization of the institute, Ted Brown was appointed its first director and served until his retirement in 1993. He recalls his years working with the Beckmans as "the most stimulating and productive decade of my life." Jiri Jonas, a colleague from the chemistry department replaced Brown as director. "Thanks to Jiri's vigorous leadership," writes Brown, "the Arnold and Mabel Beckman Institute for Advanced Research and Technology at the University of Illinois is, by any standard, a world-class facility. The institute has lived up to the most optimistic expectations."

The Beckman Center at Stanford University's Medical School. *Courtesy Beckman Foundation.*

Stanford

The laboratories of Stanford University's Medical School have long been centers of research, turning out significant discoveries. The school traces its roots to 1858, when Samuel Elias Cooper founded California's first medical school in San Francisco. The Cooper Medical College merged with Stanford University in 1908, but only in 1959 did the medical school move from San Francisco to Palo Alto. Designed by Edward Durell Stone (the architect who would later design the Beckman Auditorium at Caltech), the new Medical Center at Stanford was dedicated in September 1959. It was in this year also that future Nobel laureate Paul Berg joined the faculty, in the Department of Biochemistry.

Berg was a pioneer in molecular biology, and by the mid-1970s he was convinced that medicine would become a genetic and molecular science and that treatment would take account of the molecular basis of disease. Berg and his colleagues in the biochemistry department began looking for funding to explore these frontiers in medical research at Stanford. A new entity was needed, they claimed, one that would be "an interface of bench and bedside," central to a research program that would launch the fields of molecular and genetic medicine. Developmental biology was another program with more ideas than space to accommodate them—likewise physiology, which was evolving toward molecular and cellular physiology. Planning began to focus on a new building for the thirty members in these departments.

The developmental biology department aimed to "explore the mechanisms underlying developmental decisions in the cell and determine how those decisions can best be influenced to prevent or alleviate certain diseases and disorders that compromise the human condition." A new molecular and cellular physiology department would complement it, through the investigation of the "mechanisms by which the cells in important physiological systems communicate with one another to coordinate their behavior and functions." Such study held the promise of new methods and systems to treat and prevent a spectrum of pulmonary, endocrine, coronary, and neurological diseases.

This approach to medicine was right up Dr. Beckman's alley, as it explicitly focused on the scientific basis of disease.

Plans beget grant applications in the world of scientific medicine. Soon the Howard Hughes Foundation, a major force in that world, awarded Stanford $20 million toward the project. The Hughes Foundation's promised gift led to architectural plans for a six-story building. However, the grand design stalled, as the dean who had pushed the project left Stanford, few of the key players were happy with the design, and no other funds were forthcoming. As the university sought ways forward, President Donald Kennedy held a conference at his house on cooperation between universities and major corporations. Attending that day in the early 1980s were Stephen Jobs of Apple Computer; Alejandro Zaffaroni, head of Alza; and Arnold Beckman.

While the Beckmans had no direct personal connection to Stanford, they did possess a strong indirect connection. Rudy Munzer, a longtime friend of Arnold Beckman and a director of Beckman Instruments, was also a trustee of Stanford. He alerted Stanford's president and officers that the Beckmans were conducting their philanthropy for science in the new mode of truly large-scale gifts and planned ultimately to give away the whole of their foundation's assets. Beckman's previous associations with Palo Alto were mixed at best. It was the site of the very successful Spinco Division, yet it had been home to the disastrous Shockley Semiconductor. Stanford University itself was new to him, though the conference was

Arnold Beckman at Stanford University, May 1985. Paul Berg and Donald Kennedy, Stanford president, stand to Beckman's right.
Courtesy Institute Archives, California Institute of Technology.

an introduction. And Beckman's interests and previous gifts gave him a natural curiosity about the research planned for the new medical center. He had developed a great taste for cutting-edge biomedical investigations at world-renowned institutions.

Berg and his colleagues invited Arnold and Mabel Beckman to come see what Stanford had planned and to hear about their vision of a "new medicine." Beckman seemed impressed, but he went away without making any commitment. Like many who had applied, Berg and his colleagues waited and waited, hearing nothing by phone or mail for over a year. As presidents will, Donald Kennedy told Berg that the next initiative was his. Either he had to find funding and become the project's director, or the venture was doomed. Faced with such a challenge, Berg was not one to back down. He was in a position to make a strong case, since he had won the Nobel Prize in 1980 for his work on the fundamental biochemistry of recombinant DNA, work that had opened up the technologies of genetic engineering. He was also quick to reshape the concept of the center. It would now include one more department, biochemistry.

Rather than wait by the mailbox, Berg called Beckman and said, "I want to come see you." Beckman agreed to an appointment. Berg arrived with Stanford's President Kennedy and their colleague Arthur Kornberg, also a Nobel laureate. Quite directly, they told Beckman how important the project was and how critical his support could be. They were not subtle. Could he give them $12.5 million? A week later they got a call: The Arnold and Mabel Beckman Foundation would give them just what they had asked for over a period of five years. Suddenly there was new hope for the project.

Some time later they made another presentation to him, and Dr. Beckman, now in the roll of cocreator of the center, pledged another $3.5 million for an X-ray crystallography facility. But there was more. Beckman himself now sat on the board of SmithKline Beckman. At a SmithKline Beckman board meeting he lamented that most corporations offered little help in academic alliances. By the time he was done, SmithKline Beckman had committed almost $8 million toward the project. And Munzer, the link between the Beckmans and Stanford, got personally interested in the project as well and pledged $1 million. From all his sources Beckman thus produced almost $25 million for Stanford, and the new institute appropriately became the Arnold and Mabel Beckman Center for Molecular and Genetic Medicine.

The center officially opened on 24 May 1989. Its purpose, Dean David Korn said, was "to make it easy for scientifically astute physicians to rub shoulders with clinically astute basic scientists and thus encourage a collision of ideas between the research laboratory and the clinical setting." The Beckman Center at Stanford houses the biochemistry, developmental biology, and molecular and cellular physiology departments as well as the Howard Hughes Institute for Molecular and Genetic Medicine.

Paul Berg, the first director of the Beckman Center at Stanford, underscores its interdisciplinary focus:

> Many of the biological problems that lie before us are extremely complex, perhaps too complex to be managed by a single investigator's research group. Often they require experience, skills, techniques, and specialized facilities that are not available in a single investigator's research group or even in a single department. I see interdepartmental interactions, sharing information and reagents freely, with collaborations as a more effective way of doing today's science. And if we are going to make an impact in medicine, it will be important to engage both basic and clinical people, particularly those whose interests bridge both domains, to work towards common goals.

Caltech

Beckman's connections with Caltech remained deep. He had marked his retirement as board chair with the gift of the Mabel and Arnold Beckman Laboratories of Behavioral Biology. As he moved his foundation to a new mode, Caltech kept his attention.

In the early 1980s Dr. Beckman was a member of the visiting committee for the chemistry division, whose chairman was a leading chemist, Harry Gray. Confident of the academic, intellectual, and scientific quality of Caltech, Beckman and the committee nonetheless worried that Caltech might lose a generation of

The Beckman Institute at Caltech. *Courtesy Beckman Foundation.*

promising young scientists to schools with better laboratory facilities. Gray, who would later become director of the Caltech Beckman Institute, remembers how positively Dr. Beckman responded to the proposition that he refurbish the school's chemistry resources.

By 1984 Arnold and Mabel Beckman had enthusiastically agreed to fund improvements for the chemistry division. Parts of the Church and Crellin chemistry laboratories would now be joined together, allowing for substantial renovations of aging spaces. Newly connected and refurbished, the laboratories would be known by a single new name: the Arnold and Mabel Beckman Laboratory of Chemical Synthesis. New spaces would do little to maintain the competitive advantage of Caltech if they were not filled with the latest and best in scientific instrumentation and equipment. To meet this need, the Beckmans also set up a substantial equipment fund for the new laboratory, to be matched with funds from other sources, ensuring the finest new instruments, computing resources, and technical personnel. In all, the Beckmans made a $15 million investment in the future of Caltech chemistry.

Soon Arnold Beckman began to drop hints around Caltech that more was in store. His interest fired up by the recent Beckman Institute at Illinois, he wanted a similar cutting-edge, interdisciplinary institute at Caltech.

At Illinois, at the Laser Institute, at the City of Hope, and later at Stanford, four "big Beckman Centers" were born out of previously existing hopes and plans, which Arnold Beckman shaped and reshaped in his fertile seminar. Caltech was different, for here a faculty group led by Harry Gray, Eric Davidson, Peter Dervan, and Leroy Hood worked from the start with Beckman himself, planning a major center. By now, Beckman's experience was such that he could surely have qualified as a professor of philanthropy, if any such existed. The questions he raised were correspondingly tough, and the discussion vigorous.

By May 1986 enough questions had been answered to Dr. Beckman's satisfaction for him to give the go-ahead for an announcement at commencement: Arnold and Mabel Beckman would give $50 million for Caltech's own Beckman Institute.

The mission of the institute would be to foster new efforts in chemistry, biology, and related fields, with a special interest in promoting research generally considered too far afield for conventional funding sources. The institute would also promote the invention of methods, instrumentation, and materials that could potentially open entirely new areas of research in the chemical and biological sciences. Caltech's magazine *Engineering and Science* had its own metaphorical take on this bold program: "The institute will be supporting potential home-run hitters whose research could cause far-reaching changes if it doesn't strike out." These research projects were to be long-term, requiring multiyear commitments from the research teams. The institute would also focus on establishing and maintaining

Harry Gray holds up a Model G pH meter in a clear case for Arnold Beckman's inspection at his eightieth birthday party. *Courtesy Institute Archives, California Institute of Technology.*

Mabel Beckman with
Jean Tang, commence-
ment day June 1986. Tang
was the first recipient of
the Mabel Beckman
Prize, given annually to
the most outstanding
female upperclassman at
Caltech. *Courtesy Institute
Archives, California Institute
of Technology.*

superior instrumentation facilities. While these facilities would be available first and foremost for Beckman Institute projects, the entire Caltech community would have access to them as need warranted. In keeping with the aim to fund nontraditional research, seed money for small-scale, exploratory programs would be available. After almost two years of debate and discussion, the charter for the Beckman Institute was adopted by the Caltech faculty board at the end of 1987.

The Beckman Institute at the University of Illinois and the Beckman Institute at Caltech differ in architectural style as much as they do in composition. While the Illinois institute is vertically oriented, with high ceilings, large windows, and a six-story tower, the Caltech institute is a lower, Spanish-style building. Designed in the Southern California idiom by A. C. Martin, a sailing friend of Arnold Beckman's who is also an architect, the institute is built around a courtyard and topped with a ceramic tile roof. A reflecting pool graces the front entrance, and the San Gabriel Mountains rise in the distance, creating an impressive vista.

The Beckman Institute at Caltech was dedicated on 26 October 1989. Dr. Beckman was subdued at the time. He simply said, "My passport says I'm an executive. I looked 'executive' up in the dictionary to see what it means, and I learned it means someone who delegates responsibilities to others. So I'm delegating responsibility for speaking to others here." Harry Gray presided over the ceremony, with comments from Leroy Hood, who spoke about his research on molecular biotechnology, and Carver Mead, who described efforts to use the neural structure of a

Breaking ground for the Beckman Institute at Caltech, 11 April 1988. Caltech president Thomas Everhart is third from left, Arnold and Mabel Beckman are at center, and Harry Gray is at the far right. *Courtesy Institute Archives, California Institute of Technology.*

flatworm (nematode) as a model for a new computer chip. George Deukmejian, the governor of California, also spoke. He was followed by Ruben Mettler, chair of the Caltech board, and Arnold Beckman's old friend, David Packard, the chairman of Hewlett-Packard—altogether an auspicious start.

The Beckman Institute is divided into nine resource centers, each focusing on a specific area of research. Six facilities provide technical support and instrumentation necessary to a broad spectrum of research across the chemical and biological sciences. Harry Gray, the director of the Beckman Institute at Caltech since its conception, describes it thus: "The main operating unit in the Beckman Institute is the resource center . . . a unit in which we have professionals, experts in certain technologies and certain instruments." These people are doing front-line research, "but one component of their activity entails making their instrumentation available to the community." They also are directed to develop new methods and new instruments that push the state of the art ahead. Following Dr. Beckman's commitment to education, the institute is active in involving Caltech students—postdoctoral, graduate, and undergraduate—in the research undertaken there.

The National Academies of Sciences and Engineering

One other, quite different beneficence sprang from the planning of this final "Big Five" institute. During the negotiations between the Beckmans and Caltech on the scope and mission of its proposed Beckman Institute, Dr. Beckman had entertained

An aerial view of the Beckman Center of the National Academies of Sciences and Engineering, which also houses the Beckman Foundation (Irvine, California).
Courtesy Beckman Foundation.

the idea of putting the new institute in Irvine, but still under Caltech's auspices. The aim proposed for "Caltech at Irvine" reflects his own earlier interests and frustrations: The institute was to bridge the gap between basic research in science and its quick commercialization. Knowing that academic scientists often lack the moral and financial support necessary to transform a brilliant idea into a process or product for the social good, he wanted to establish a center to handle follow-through on work by academics that might be patentable. "Universities," he noted, "by and large do not have the interest or structure to speedily develop basic discoveries and quickly convert them to everyday needs." An institute in Irvine devoted to these ends would be close to a growing number of high-technology firms (and, not incidentally, to the Beckmans' home). Marvin Goldberger, the president of Caltech at the time, vetoed the plan—arguing that Caltech could not effectively manage a center in Irvine, fifty miles away.

Undaunted, Arnold Beckman returned to the drawing board with Harold Brown, Goldberger's predecessor at Caltech. Together they reconfigured the idea. Rather than a single institute, two separate institutions would be built. One center, the Beckman Institute, would be located on Caltech's campus and would bring to five the number of "big Beckman Centers," focused on academic research. The other, in Irvine, would be a conference center bringing together industrialists and academics to encourage the application of science and technology. Gradually, as Beckman and Brown consulted together and with other interested parties, the concept of this second center shifted. The application of science and the needs of Orange County's high-tech industries receded. The need to recognize the national prominence of the West Coast's basic researchers came to the fore.

Aside from his stint at Bell Labs, Arnold Beckman's whole adult life and career had been spent west of the Mississippi. He was acutely aware that accidents of history had placed most of the national organizations of science on the East Coast. Now was the time to redress the balance by giving western scientists a place of their own, which could also serve to draw visitors from the East.

Acting as go-between and Washington insider, Harold Brown (who had served as Secretary of the Air Force before coming to Caltech and Secretary of Defense immediately after leaving) persuaded the presidents of the National Academies of Sciences and Engineering of the merits of the plan. A $20 million grant from the Beckman Foundation and a donation by Donald Bren (developer of the Irvine Ranch) of seven acres on the crest of a hill adjacent to the University of California, Irvine, campus were soon forthcoming. The Arnold and Mabel Beckman Center of the National Academies of Sciences and Engineering opened its doors in April 1988, with a gala celebration.

Beckman had little involvement with the physical design of this center. He requested only two design features: a covered carport for himself and a covered front entrance. Unfortunately, the building did not turn out quite as he had hoped. "They built this thing," he said, "and there was no front entrance; you couldn't tell where the entrance was. I told them it looked like the back of a supermarket." Unhappy with the results, Beckman "refused to pay the last of the money until they corrected that. I was disappointed." He did concede, however, that "functionally, the building is pretty good." It is a long, low structure that manages a secluded, retreat-like atmosphere despite its location in the heart of Orange County. Covering 48,000 square feet, it houses not only an auditorium, numerous meeting rooms, and private working offices but also the headquarters of the Arnold and Mabel Beckman Foundation.

Investments in Excellence

Beyond those major gifts, the Beckmans also made numerous smaller bequests over the course of the 1980s, ranging from two thousand to a few million dollars. These smaller gifts illustrate other enduring interests of the Beckmans. Among their recipients were what has become the Chemical Heritage Foundation and Illinois Wesleyan University.

Individual studies for historical researchers at CHF's Beckman Center for the History of Chemistry, Philadelphia. *Both Chemical Heritage Foundation.*

Established through an initiative of the American Chemical Society in 1982, the Chemical Heritage Foundation (CHF) seeks to make known the contributions of the chemical and molecular sciences and industries to society. The American Institute of Chemical Engineers became the second sponsor in 1984. The impetus for much of the development of the foundation during the late 1980s and the 1990s came from the philanthropy and the vision of Arnold Beckman. Beckman's "early bird" challenge grant in 1986 and his practiced entrepreneurial advice catalyzed the growth of CHF.

Arnold Beckman did two things for CHF. First, he pushed for a wide view of its mission, beginning the process that took CHF from its original two to twenty-seven affiliated organizations by 2000. To Dr. Beckman it was barely worth discussion that CHF's Arnold and Mabel Beckman Center for the History of Chemistry, the guardian of his science, chemistry, should define the chemical heritage broadly, as running from biotechnology to materials science and petrochemicals. He felt instinctively that academic, professional, and trade organizations from all these sectors must be encouraged to participate. Second, and equally important, was the power of his name and example. The interest of Arnold and Mabel Beckman signaled that the Chemical Heritage Foundation had promise, that it should be taken seriously. Just how seriously became apparent when the Beckmans' early-money gift of $2 million was matched and overmatched by another remarkable chemical engineer and academic emulating "that instrument fella." Donald Othmer of Brooklyn Polytechnic had been present in 1986 when the Beckmans' challenge was announced. That announcement stimulated Donald and Mildred Topp Othmer to endow gifts for CHF's library that, by 2000, amounted to $125 million. Dr. Beckman had once again been first to sense a new trend and to leverage his opportunity.

The $500,000 gift to Illinois Wesleyan was of an even more personal nature for Arnold Beckman. He had gone to the University of Illinois, but his brother Fred and his sister, Wilma, stayed in Bloomington to attend Illinois Wesleyan. Wilma graduated in 1926 and went on to Cornell, where she had pursued a Ph.D. in nutrition before she married. She died in 1984. Fred graduated from Illinois Wesleyan's law school in 1922. His wife and their children were also alumni of the college. Fred died in 1931, and Arnold Beckman named a science auditorium at Illinois Wesleyan in memory of the brother who had helped him with his first patent.

Other, more peripheral gifts were dispensed to centers for vision and hearing. These gifts, while definitely of a scientific tenor, represented an immediate, personal concern of Dr. Beckman's: For a number of years both his vision and his hearing had been deteriorating. The Beckmans supported the Doheny Eye Institute at the University of Southern California, and they invested $3.5 million to create the Beckman Vision Center at the University of California, San Francisco. Like the Doheny, the Beckman Vision Center is a comprehensive organization that promotes cutting-edge research and close collaboration with clinicians. In keeping

The Center for Natural Science Learning and Research at Illinois Wesleyan University houses the Frederick P. Beckman Lecture Room.
Courtesy Illinois Wesleyan University.

with these investments in vision care, the Beckmans also established the Leopold Chair in Ophthalmology at the University of California, Irvine. The Beckmans also gave over $5 million to support basic research and new technologies related to hearing. In particular, they invested in the work of Caltech's Carver Mead, who was exploring hearing at the intersection of computation and neural science.

The Beckmans gave other gifts to more traditional recipients of philanthropic gestures: cultural institutions and hospitals. Forty thousand dollars went to rejuvenate the Cullom Memorial Library in Dr. Beckman's boyhood hometown; $2 million went to the Patty and George Hoag Cancer Center in Orange County; $1.25 million went to the Sloan-Kettering Cancer Center in New York City. In a related investment the Beckmans endowed the Arnold O. Beckman Conference in Clinical Chemistry with $500,000. Initiated to bridge the gap between laboratory scientists and those involved in direct patient care, this topic-oriented conference presents noted lecturers who address issues from the perspectives of both the laboratory and clinic. Through the Beckman Foundation the Beckmans also endowed a number of professorial chairs at a variety of institutions. These professorships, like the Beckman centers, reflect Dr. Beckman's interests. At Rockefeller University there is a Beckman Professorship in the Laboratory of Biochemistry and Molecular Biology, and at the University of California, Irvine, a Beckman Chair in Biomedicine. Dr. Beckman gave almost $500,000 to Caltech toward the Harold Brown Professorship.

The Beckmans also supported science and education at a variety of other institutions of higher learning. Harvey Mudd College received an Arnold and Mabel Beckman Research Fund of $1 million, and Pepperdine University received a sub-

Clockwise: Cold Spring Harbor Laboratory, New York; another view of the Cold Spring Harbor Laboratory; Arnold Beckman and James Watson. *All courtesy Beckman Foundation.*

stantial gift for the creation of a Beckman Management Center. The microbiology department of the University of California, Irvine, received a $100,000 gift, and a similar donation went to the university to establish a summer science institute. Stanford accepted $3.5 million for an Arnold O. Beckman Fund for Structural Studies, and Rockefeller University received a $6 million endowment to fund basic research. Nor were the Beckmans finished with creating new facilities for centers of scientific and educational excellence. For instance, they gave $8 million to fund the Beckman Neuroscience Center at the Cold Spring Harbor Laboratory, led by James D. Watson.

Mabel Beckman at the Beckmans' Corona del Mar home. *Photography by Antony di Gesù. Courtesy Beckman family.*

A Major Blow: The Loss of Mabel

By the end of the 1980s Arnold and Mabel had overseen the establishment of five big Beckman institutes, a range of other Beckman centers, and a host of more personal gifts. Then a major blow struck. At 3:15 A.M. on 1 June 1989, Mabel, Arnold Beckman's partner and companion of sixty-four years, passed away. It was just nine days before their wedding anniversary. It was a terrible shock to lose Mabel. Arnold had discussed every major life and career decision with her, traveled around the world with her, depended uniquely on her advice and counsel. Absolutely devoted to him, Mabel had left her family in New York six decades earlier to come with her husband to California, where they remained for the rest of their lives together. One little vignette displays how close they were. Throughout his career he went home to have lunch with Mabel whenever possible. In 1985, when invited to a lunch whose guests were, according to the *Register*, "Southern California's movers and shakers," Arnold chose to eat at home with Mabel instead.

Mabel Beckman's funeral was private, for just the family and the closest of friends. Fittingly, a much larger memorial service was held at Caltech, the institution to which she had given so much herself in many ways. The service took place in the late afternoon of 10 July 1989 in Caltech's Beckman Auditorium.

Mabel had always served as Arnold Beckman's sounding board. She was an excellent judge of character; as one friend said, "She could spot a phony a block away." Intensely private, she did not allow any business entertaining to take place in her home but was an unfailingly gracious companion at events around the globe. That she did not have any formal scientific training made her all the more valuable as a confidante and consultant for her husband. He could count on her for opinions representing what those without his specialized and highly trained background might feel about his decisions or plans. Those who knew her had the strong impression that Mabel had Arnold Beckman's ear in all fields and on all subjects. They made decisions together, and she had a great deal of input—more than she has been given credit for—in National Technical Laboratories and Beckman Instruments. Mabel Beckman was an unfailing supporter of her husband in all his capacities.

Seemingly unaffected by their accumulating fortune, Mabel remained in charge of their household even after they could well have afforded a host of domestic help. She did all the cooking and the bulk of the housekeeping, save a few particularly laborious jobs, such as window washing. Out of commission only for the months she had tuberculosis, Mabel was very independent and took a great deal of pride in and satisfaction from keeping house. Her first daughter-in-law, Ellyn Seaquist, remembered, "I think I learned everything about entertaining through [Mabel]—everything. Mabel taught me how to [be a] gourmet cook. She

Left: Mabel with her grandsons, Arne (right) and Kurt, 1967.

Right: The path leading from Mabel Beckman's beloved house to the Pacific Ocean below. *Both courtesy Beckman family.*

encouraged me in that. She encouraged me to set a nice table. . . . Those are things that had not even occurred to me. . . . I had a lot of mentoring on home life from Mabel. That's where she excelled, too, entertaining and making people feel comfortable in her home." Always conscientious about food and nutrition, Mabel, as Seaquist recalled, was a big fan of angel food cake and would often prepare it topped with fresh strawberries.

While she was an early partisan of vitamins and healthy diet, Mabel Beckman was also very much a member of her generation. She valued good manners and always took care to dress nicely. Today the vision of a woman vacuuming or doing laundry in a dress, formal shoes, and stockings might seem anachronistic and out of place, but for Mabel this was simply the appropriate way to conduct oneself. In addition to her flair for cooking and her vigilant housekeeping, she had artistic inclinations and was talented at needlework and painting. She sewed Christmas ornaments adorned with sequins and felt, and she made needlework pictures of circus animals. Her grandson, Arnold William Beckman, has one of her oil paintings. Mabel also had an eye for beautiful, tasteful jewelry and was generous in making presents of it to the younger women of her family.

When asked to find the adjectives to describe Mabel, her family and friends have supplied such words as *warm, comfortable, generous, private,* and perhaps above all, *selfless.* This selflessness extended to the last months of her life, when she refused to let friends know how sick she was, sparing them the painful details of her fight with cancer. In the weeks before her death Arnold noticed a change come over his wife. "She would never discuss death or funeral arrangements or anything like that dur-

President George Bush presents Arnold Beckman with a National Medal of Science in 1989. Ronald Reagan awarded the National Medal of Technology to Dr. Beckman in 1988. *Courtesy Beckman Coulter, Inc.*

Top left: Dr. Beckman with Sandy and Jerry Gallwas in 1998. *Courtesy Beckman Foundation.*

Top right: Michael Berns, director of the Beckman Laser Institute, presents Arnold Beckman with a card commemorating his ninetieth birthday, while Gavin Herbert, later a Beckman Foundation board member, looks on. *Courtesy Beckman Coulter, Inc.*

Right: Arnold Beckman entertains guests at his ninetieth birthday party. *Courtesy Beckman Coulter, Inc.*

ing our whole sixty-four years together," he remembered. "But about two weeks before the end she talked openly and freely about wanting me to burn all her letters and about her views of giving her personal things to this person or that person. She had a smile on her face that I'd never seen before; she'd come to peace with death."

A New Agenda for the Foundation

Dr. and Mrs. Beckman had together given away almost $200 million in the course of the 1980s—a sum equal to their wealth at the start of the decade. Ironically, Arnold Beckman still possessed much that same amount, thanks to the growing value of SmithKline Beckman. However, he no longer had Mabel as his companion-in-arms in the adventure of philanthropy. And as he approached his ninetieth birthday, even Arnold Beckman admitted that it was time to trim his sails.

Dr. Beckman reflected long and hard. He and Mabel had failed in their plan to give away their funds during their time together. As the Beckman Foundation bank account continued to grow, the task of disbursing it all in ways that would meet his austere standards became ever more daunting. In the months that followed Mabel's death, he wrestled with what to do with the philanthropy that was his and Mabel's intensely personal legacy to the world. He struggled as well with his grief over Mabel's loss, and in late 1989 he was faced with a grave challenge to his personal health. He fell, seriously fracturing his hip. His recovery required extended hospitalization and treatment.

Arnold Beckman's ninetieth birthday card. It is remarkable in having five consecutive presidents' signatures on it. *Courtesy Beckman Coulter, Inc.*

Gradually recovering from his injury and from his grief, Beckman's thoughts as to how to refashion his and Mabel's philanthropic legacy began to crystallize. Soon after the celebrations attending his ninetieth birthday, he decided that the foundation should be recast as a foundation in perpetuity, spending only its income. This was a profound shift from what he and Mabel had earlier set out to accomplish. Jerry Gallwas remembers: "The pain was very real. Mabel was gone, he was ninety years old and making a decision different from what he and Mabel had agreed on."

Nevertheless, Beckman knew that he had to move forward with his solution. To place his reformulated foundation on solid ground, he made an arrangement with Caltech for the financial management of the foundation's assets. More significantly, he drafted a "Philosophy Statement" that clarified the purpose of the really permanent foundation, revealed a creative plan for the disbursement of its income, and detailed unique, innovative aspects of the foundation's organization.

Dr. Beckman supplied a very specific idea of how his foundation would focus on imaginative work of the sort Beckman Instruments had made possible for decades—breakthrough work in biochemistry, chemistry, and medicine. The foundation's mission was laid out in clear terms: to "support leading-edge research in the fields of chemistry and life sciences, broadly interpreted, and particularly to foster the invention of methods, instruments, and material that open up new avenues of research and application in these disciplines and related sciences." Beckman directed the application of this new philosophy personally until his final "retirement" in 1993.

By the time the status of the Beckman Foundation changed from fixed-term to permanent, Arnold and Mabel Beckman had already overseen the establishment of five major Beckman institutes. These institutes represented the bulk of Beckman philanthropy during the 1980s, and all were grand in scheme, centers for the advancement of science through interdisciplinary research and cooperation. As part of his rethinking, to create the framework of the perpetual foundation, Dr. Beckman developed a guideline that a part of the available funds each year might be designated for the five Beckman institutes, with a formula determining the relative amounts to each.

The other use of the income would be to foster innovative projects, with the advice of a Grants Advisory Council. This council was to be composed of the directors of the five big Beckman centers and of the chief scientific officer of Beckman Instruments—who better to serve as advisers? As Dr. Beckman wrote, "This group of individuals has been chosen for two reasons: (1) They, by their positions and accomplishments, should be knowledgeable concerning leading-edge research in the scientific fields of interest, and (2) they should be well informed and competent judges of research carried on at many other institutions." Within this modest statement lies another of Arnold Beckman's inventions of excellence: the guarantee of expert advice, in perpetuity.

In the course of the 1980s, through their megagifts, he and Mabel had created five centers that stood on leading campuses. Their heads were individuals of extraordinary accomplishment, knowledge, and talent. They knew science and the cutting-edge needs of interdisciplinary research in chemistry-related domains. Necessarily, they were deeply committed to the fair name of their own Beckman centers and thus of the Beckman Foundation. Though all busy, burdened, and multiply committed, they could not but take with the utmost seriousness their new role as advisers on Dr. Beckman's philanthropy. And while they, and he, would pass from the scene, the Beckman centers themselves—possessing the immortality of institutions—would provide an ever-renewing cadre of equally talented directors to whom the board of the Arnold and Mabel Beckman Foundation could turn.

The words concerning the Grants Advisory Council and its functioning were hammered out in the first half of the 1990s. Deceptively simple, they provide one means of focusing the foundation on the sweet spots of scientific opportunity—on the cutting edge of interdisciplinary endeavor. To make assurance doubly sure, Dr. Beckman added one further thought: "My preference is to favor young investigators, new ideas, and a variety of projects rather than fund large, established ones of long duration."

Education and Science

In the first full decade of the "new" Arnold and Mabel Beckman Foundation, funding centered on advanced scientific work at the professional or senior faculty level. Dr. Beckman continued to pursue investments of the kind that he and Mabel had devised in the 1980s. In 1991 he made another large pledge to Caltech, for the

Arnold Beckman, July 1992. *Courtesy Beckman Coulter, Inc.*

Trustee Fund, promising $10 million payable over the next decade. In 1992 he promised $5 million toward the construction of the Arnold and Mabel Beckman Center for Chemical Sciences at the Scripps Research Institute. This was another state-of-the-art research facility at the meeting point of chemistry and biology: molecular design, chemical synthesis, and bio-organic chemistry. But a growing concern with science education awakened new interests in Dr. Beckman. He worried about young scientists who would not necessarily be as attractive to traditional sources of funding as older, established professors.

The Beckman Center for the Chemical Sciences at the Scripps Research Institute. *Courtesy Beckman Foundation.*

A Professorial Research Study funded by the Beckman Foundation at the Salk Institute for Biological Studies. *Courtesy Beckman Foundation.*

ARNOLD AND MABEL BECKMAN
Professorial Research Study

The Beckman Young Investigators program was inaugurated in 1991 and provides grants for junior researchers in the chemical and life sciences. Grants at the $200,000 level, paid over three years, are given for projects that are explicitly "innovative departures" from established lines of research. Dr. Beckman wishes to encourage the brightest young faculty members to undertake risky, forward-looking projects that hold the promise of revolutionizing scientific disciplines and society at large. By 2000, this program had provided $25 million to 128 investigators. One Beckman Young Investigator, Ronald Breaker, a Yale University professor, was awarded his Beckman grant in 1996 to develop the novel method called "combinatorial testing," for example. Breaker uses his method to sort through trillions of different molecules and find the rare types that are the subject of his investigations. He examines DNA and RNA molecules that act as enzymes, opening up new knowledge of the role these molecules play in the biochemical processes of life. Besides enlarging the understanding of fundamental biology, Breaker's DNA and RNA enzymes have potential application as sensitive probes for environmental toxins, as antiviral agents, and as a means for gene therapy.

**Arnold Beckman peruses
his company's Web site.**
Courtesy Beckman Coulter, Inc.

Two 1995 Beckman Young Investigators have produced remarkable results as well. Nikola P. Pavletich's Beckman grant supported his X-ray crystallographic studies of a protein, p53, that repairs DNA, thereby preventing cancer and tumor formation. Pavletich's studies of p53 may lead to effective new anticancer drugs. Michael J. Mahan used his Beckman grant to support an investigation of disease-causing microbes. Mahan has created techniques to make such microbes particularly vulnerable to the human immune system, and his work may lead to powerful new vaccines and antibiotics.

The Beckman Young Investigators are the new generation of scientists, individuals that Dr. Beckman foresees as future leaders of the Beckman Institutes—hence his support of their research early on.

Retirement

Dr. Beckman, in characteristic fashion, kept working, driving, having lunch at the Pacific Club, and going on tours to such places as Germany. Even so, by 1993 he was talking of retirement, or at least a vacation, after four years of almost single-handed administration of the foundation. When asked where he would go if he were to take that vacation, he said, "Antarctica." Why? He had never been there. Most ninety-something-year-olds do not have the choice between a trip to Antarctica or heading up a multimillion-dollar foundation.

Any visitor to his office in that era remembers his gracious manners, perceptive mind, and crowded aisles, as dozens of proposals filled his office. At one point he reported there were two hundred pending proposals, many of which came with framed drawings of a coveted Beckman Hall. He was still driving—getting fewer tickets—but tiring. Another retirement sounded good. He decided to cease day-to-day leadership of his foundation. He would continue as chairman emeritus with considerable influence. But there would be a new chair of the board.

Into the Future

The Beckman Foundation's board of directors was expanded as part of the change. Beckman's grandson, Arnold W. Beckman, became a director, as did Gary Hunt and L. Donald Shields. Harold Brown, former president of Caltech, became chairman of the board. George Argyros, a prominent Orange County entrepreneur and philanthropist, was appointed vice chairman. Ted Brown of the University of Illinois became a director in 1994, as did Harry Gray of Caltech. In 1995 Jerry Gallwas from Beckman Instruments was added as well. These additions stabilized the reorganized philanthropy and populated the board with directors who represented and personally knew the many sides of Dr. Beckman, his interests, and his beliefs.

After his "retirement" from this, the third of his life's careers, Arnold Beckman continues to be engaged with the foundation's programs, mission, and stewardship. In 1995, at the age of ninety-five, he expressed strong opinions about further changes and directions for his foundation in a letter to George Argyros, who had become chairman of the foundation that same year. He had decided that there was an urgent, immediate need for a professional, permanent staff: "An experienced executive director with appropriate administrative support would go a long way in getting us started along the road to independence. . . . The foundation should be served by an independent, strong, lean, professional administrative staff function."

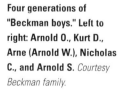

Four generations of "Beckman boys." Left to right: Arnold O., Kurt D., Arne (Arnold W.), Nicholas C., and Arnold S. *Courtesy Beckman family.*

Jerry Gallwas, Pat Beckman, and Arnold Beckman, 1996. *Courtesy Beckman Foundation.*

Beckman Hall at Chapman University in Orange, California. *Courtesy Beckman Foundation.*

He also let it be known that he desired a diverse board of directors, "qualified by a variety of experiences and interests." When he had become chairman emeritus of the foundation in 1993, he thought that the chairman should continue to be a scientist and that the board of directors should have a majority of "scientists of distinction." After two years of reflection, he had changed and broadened his perspective.

The foundation had been operating without a professional staff but with attendant difficulties, especially given the expansion of the board over this period. Besides continuing to fund the five big Beckman centers and the Beckman Young Investigators program, the foundation contributed another $500,000 to the equipment fund of Caltech's Laboratory of Chemical Synthesis, pledged over $1 million toward a new astroscience laboratory at Caltech, donated $300,000 to Chapman University for laboratory modernization, endowed a professorship at Harvey Mudd College in honor of Donald Strauss (a longtime executive at Beckman Instruments and a director of the foundation until his death in 1995), invested $1 million in the Discovery Science Center in Santa Ana, California, and granted $500,000 to the plankton laboratory at the Monterey Bay Aquarium.

That the Beckman Foundation could manage to review proposals and make these gifts without the help of a professional staff was quite an accomplishment. But the lack of that seasoned staff was a drag on the philanthropic innovation Dr. Beckman wanted to see pursued. Jacqueline Dorrance joined the foundation in the early spring of 1996 as its first professional, permanent executive director. She came

to the foundation with a strong background in executive administration in the corporate sector. Under her direction the Beckman Foundation has taken on far more structure. Its bylaws and minutes were organized and reviewed, and its procedures have been codified. In short, she managed the foundation's successful transition from a temporary, personal instrument of the Beckmans to a permanent organization with a businesslike, professional structure.

As the bylaws were solidified under the careful guidance of George Argyros and Jacqueline Dorrance, the foundation's board of directors was expanded to ten. Dr. Beckman's daughter, Pat Beckman, joined the board in 1996. Gavin Herbert of Allergan, Inc., joined in 1998. With an expanded, more diverse board and a professional administrative staff, the Arnold and Mabel Beckman Foundation is now well equipped to pursue the course that Dr. Beckman has set: innovative philanthropy for science and education.

The foundation has initiated a strategic planning process, assessing the logic of its activities and crafting new, innovative extensions. It is supporting some of the most creative and important senior researchers through Beckman institutes and centers. It is investing in and providing incentives for researchers at the postdoctoral and junior faculty level to conduct innovative, forward-looking projects through the Beckman Young Investigators Program. In essence, the Beckman Foundation is investing in the careers of highly promising scientists, helping to create "future Arnold Beckmans." It was only natural to consider extending this investment in future Arnold Beckmans to an even earlier point in their educations.

The Beckman Foundation's board of directors in 1997. From left: George Argyros, Harry Gray, Jerry Gallwas, Pat Beckman, Donald Shields, Jacqueline Dorrance, Ted Brown, Arnold W. Beckman, Gary Wescomb, Paul Berg, and Jim Moore. Dr. Beckman is seated in front. *Courtesy Beckman Foundation.*

The foundation received encouragement for this extension of the philanthropy's activity in 1997, in the form of a letter from none other than Arnold Beckman to George Argyros, the chairman. "Education was not specifically mentioned in my philosophy statement," wrote Beckman. "This was an oversight. I have always been strongly interested in education. I am especially interested in the education of teachers and children." In making this statement, Beckman's commitment to science had come full circle, concurring with an earlier statement he made: "I'd like to get young kids interested in science. . . . The young mind is inquisitive enough that you don't have to worry about scaring up enthusiasm; you simply need to keep them interested and excited about science."

The foundation initiated the Beckman Scholars Program in 1998. In this program some sixty or so top undergraduate students are selected each year to receive support for one academic year and two summers of scientific study and research. The foundation invites leading schools to participate and to nominate their most extraordinary undergraduates. The foundation's generous support allows each student to engage in scientific research in the chemical, biochemical, biological, and medical sciences (or a combination thereof) under the guidance of a prominent faculty mentor. By 2000, the Beckman Scholars Program had disbursed $2.5 million to 134 students at thirty-six universities.

In 1998 the foundation also announced a $14.5 million, five-year effort directed at the elementary school students of Orange County. "Beckman@Science" is designed to reform elementary education by making the study of science an integral focus from kindergarten to sixth grade. Administered by the California

State University, Fullerton, this multifaceted initiative includes programs for training school district administrators in science education reform, grants for teacher training, creation of a cadre of leading science teachers to promote and disseminate reforms, the production and free distribution of "Beckman Discovery Boxes" to bring new materials and activities into the classroom, and an informational campaign to build community support for science education reform. The overall goal is systematic change in American science education to develop the natural curiosity of children, to give them "hands-on and minds-on" experiences in the classroom. In announcing the program, George Argyros stressed how this magnificent gift reflected "the guiding principle of Dr. Beckman and his beloved late wife, Mabel, both lifelong partners in the belief that knowledge can make all things possible. On the cusp of beginning his second century of curiosity and learning, Dr. Beckman has helped many thousands of Orange County students and their teachers embark on their own educational journey."

From 1995 to 1999 Dr. Beckman's permanent foundation gave over $64 million, all told, to science and education. At the start of the new millennium the foundation continues to seek ways to build upon the decisions and the spirit of Arnold and Mabel Beckman. In a Research Technology Initiative, for instance, two grants of $2.5 million each have been awarded to promote the creation of new technologies for research, tools for opening up promising avenues of exploration at the forefront of the leading fields of science. At the University of Minnesota a grant from the foundation's Research Technology Initiative supports the development of "Sleeping Beauty," a novel gene-transfer system. Eventually this system may

Arnold Beckman with Judie and George Argyros, 1998. *Courtesy Beckman Foundation.*

The terrace of the Beckmans' house in Corona del Mar, overlooking the ocean.
Courtesy Beckman Foundation.

produce powerful technologies for identifying the functions of genes and for identifying genes associated with cancer. The second Research Technology Initiative grant underwrites the development of new chemical and biological sensors at the University of Texas at Austin. The sensors are microfabricated chips designed to detect various chemical compounds and elements, DNA, RNA, antibodies, enzymes, and pH levels. The blacksmith's son has through the years taken great pride and satisfaction in the ways that his instruments, his innovative research technologies, his new tools for science have opened up research vistas and transformed the nature and the pace of the creation of knowledge. His foundation, through the Research Technology Initiative, seeks to promote the same kinds of achievements for future Arnold Beckmans.

Dr. Beckman Today

Arnold Beckman today looks with satisfaction on the results of his third career, as a philanthropist, where he has once more made inventions of excellence. The scale of his investments has been substantial. His creation of the five big Beckman centers, his plan for the permanent foundation, and his programs for supporting science education and careers at all levels from kindergartners through Nobel laureates are all dramatic, substantial, and creative innovations.

Through his example Dr. Beckman has become a role model for a rising generation of philanthropists. He has particularly influenced George Argyros, himself a leading Orange County entrepreneur, civic statesman, and philanthropist. Argyros is the chairman and CEO of Arnel & Affiliates and a member of Caltech's board of trustees as well as chairman of the Arnold and Mabel Beckman Foundation. He regards Arnold Beckman as his hero and his role model in how to move from humble beginnings to business success, civic vision, and social responsibility: "You have impacted my life in so many wonderful ways. Your personal courage, pioneering spirit, and fortitude have always been an inspiration to me and a motivating force in my life. I thank you for your mentoring and for modeling genuine compassion, discernment, and foresight. Arnold, you have made a big difference in the lives of so many, and I can think of no greater calling than this. Your significant business and personal contributions, vast generosity, and ever humble spirit have made our world a better place. You represent the best of the American system!"

Gavin Herbert also marvels at "Arnold Beckman's integrity in all aspects of life." Herbert, a distinguished pharmaceutical entrepreneur and civic leader, sees Beckman as "having an highly ethical approach to business, civic activity, and private life." Herbert knows how much the reputation of Dr. Beckman means to leaders on the local, state, and national levels. "Dr. Beckman's endorsement of an individual or an initiative has become a powerful stamp of approval, a certification of excellence."

Today Arnold Beckman continues to live at home in Corona del Mar, in the house that so captivated Mabel Beckman, which he has transformed and improved with his own craftsmanship. With him as his constant companion is his daughter, Pat. His son, Arnold S., maintains a home nearby. Also living a short distance away are his grandchildren, Arne Beckman and Kurt Beckman, so Dr. Beckman is able to enjoy seeing his great-grandchildren, Nicholas, Arne's son, and Kurt's son, James.

Beckman goes to great lengths to enable her father's engagement with the scientific community, through meetings and trips across the nation, even as the trials and tribulations of an aging body compete with the activities that keep him vital, engaged, and happy. Arnold S. is similarly committed to helping his father continue his life of learning, of new experiences; he recently took his father for his first ride on a Harley-Davidson motorcycle to celebrate his birthday.

Many of Dr. Beckman and Pat's travels in the late 1990s have been to celebrations for the awards that he continues to receive. In the 1990s alone he received the Bower Award for Business Leadership from the Franklin Institute in Philadelphia, the Achievement Award for Excellence from the Center for Excellence in Washington, D.C., and the Order of Lincoln from the State of Illinois. In April 1999 he

John Kirk, president of the National Inventors Hall of Fame, welcomes Arnold Beckman into the hall.
Courtesy Beckman Coulter, Inc.

traveled to Washington, D.C., to accept the Public Welfare Medal from the National Academy of Sciences. This is the prestigious academy's highest honor, and it was conferred on Dr. Beckman for "his leadership in developing analytical instrumentation and for his deep and abiding concern for the vitality of the nation's scientific enterprise."

When asked which of his many achievements has given him the most pleasure, Beckman quipped, "Well, the fact that I survived into my nineties." With characteristic modesty he went on to say, "I've been the recipient of unmerited awards. I've never published many scientific papers; I've been given far more credit than I deserve as a scientist. As an instrument maker, a toolmaker, fine. I get credit as a businessman, and I don't consider myself a businessman. When I was confronted with a situation, I learned enough to do the immediate jobs, but I never became an expert in them. I won't say all of them; I still think I was a damn good teacher. I think 'jack-of-all trades and master of none' is the best label I could put on myself."

Such modesty notwithstanding, in each career he has chosen to pursue—from professor to entrepreneur to philanthropist—Arnold O. Beckman has made extraordinary contributions. He has truly lived the rule that there is no satisfactory substitute for excellence.

Arnold Beckman with schoolchildren participating in the Beckman@Science program. *Courtesy Beckman Foundation.*

Selected Honors and Awards of Arnold O. Beckman

Honorary Degrees and Memberships

Arnold O. Beckman has received many honorary degrees in recognition of his scientific and technical achievements, his civic leadership, and his philanthropic activities, among them the following:

Doctor of Science degrees from the University of Illinois, Chapman University, Whittier College, Clarkson University, Illinois Wesleyan University, and Rockefeller University;

Doctor of Humane Letters degrees from California State University and Illinois State University, Normal; and

Doctor of Laws degrees from the University of California, Riverside; Loyola University of Los Angeles; and Pepperdine University.

Dr. Beckman is also a member of the National Academy of Engineering, a fellow of the American Association for the Advancement of Science, a fellow of the Association of Clinical Scientists, an honorary fellow of the American Academy of Arts and Sciences and the American Institute of Chemists, a Benjamin Franklin Fellow of the Royal Society of Arts, Great Britain, an honorary trustee of the California Museum Foundation, and an honorary member of the American Association of Clinical Chemistry.

Awards

Arnold O. Beckman Award, established by the Instrument Society of America, 1960
"Illini" Achievement Award, University of Illinois, 1960
Business Statesman Award, Harvard Business School of Southern California, 1966
California Industrialist of the Year Award, California Museum of Science and Industry, 1971
SAMA Award, Scientific Apparatus Makers Association, 1974
Private Enterprise Award, Pepperdine University, 1979
Life Achievement Award, Instrument Society of America, 1981
Hoover Medal, American Association of Engineering Societies, 1981
Diploma of Honor, Association of Clinical Scientists, 1982
Man of Science Award, Achievement Rewards for College Scientists Foundation, 1982
Golden Plate Award, American Academy of Achievement, 1982
Rock of Free Enterprise Award, Economic Development Corporation of Orange County, 1983
Distinguished Alumni Award, California Institute of Technology, 1984
Outstanding Philanthropist Award, National Society of Fund Raising Executives, 1984
Robert A. Millikan Medal, California Institute of Technology, 1985
Vermilye Medal, Franklin Institute, 1987
National Inventors Hall of Fame, 1987
National Medal of Technology, 1988
Presidential Citizens Medal, 1989
National Medal of Science, 1989
Henry Townley Heald Award, Illinois Institute of Technology, 1989
Charles Lathrop Parsons Award, American Chemical Society, 1989
Good Scout Award, Orange County Council, Boy Scouts of America, 1990
Order of Lincoln, Lincoln Academy, State of Illinois, 1991
Bower Award for Business Leadership, Franklin Institute, 1992
Excellence in Entrepreneurship Hall of Fame Award, Chapman University, 1998
Public Welfare Medal, National Academy of Sciences, 1999
Othmer Gold Medal, Chemical Heritage Foundation, 2000

The Patents of Arnold O. Beckman

The following are all U.S. patents.

No. 1,684,659:   Arnold O. Beckman. "Signaling Device." Filed 7 May 1927; issued 18 September 1928.

No. 2,038,706:   Arnold O. Beckman. "Inking Reel." Filed 8 May 1934; issued 28 April 1936; assigned to National Technical Laboratories.

No. 2,041,740:   Arnold O. Beckman. "Inking Device." Filed 8 June 1934; issued 26 May 1936; assigned to National Technical Laboratories.

No. 2,058,761:   Arnold O. Beckman; Henry E. Fracker. "Apparatus for Testing Acidity." Filed 12 October 1934; issued 27 October 1936; assigned to National Technical Laboratories.

No. 2,277,287:   Arnold O. Beckman; William A. Bush; Harry Rubin. "Manufacture of Coated Materials and Product." Filed 4 February 1939; issued 24 March 1942.

No. 2,302,097:   Arnold O. Beckman. "Swing Spout Device for Dispensing Liquids." Filed 13 December 1941; issued 17 November 1942; assigned to National Technical Laboratories.

No. 2,348,103:   Arnold O. Beckman. "Method of Soil Analysis for Location of Oil Deposits." Filed 31 January 1940; issued 2 May 1944; assigned to American Geochemical Corporation.

No. 2,351,579:   Arnold O. Beckman. "Method and Apparatus for Proportioning." Filed 22 November 1941; issued 20 June 1944; assigned to National Technical Laboratories.

No. 2,351,580:   Arnold O. Beckman. "Method and Apparatus for Proportioning." Filed 22 November 1941; issued 20 June 1944; assigned to National Technical Laboratories.

No. 2,454,986:   Arnold O. Beckman. "Variable Resistance Device." Filed 22 October 1945; issued 30 November 1948; assigned to National Technical Laboratories.

No. 2,473,048:   Arnold O. Beckman. "Variable Resistance Unit." Filed 22 October 1945; issued 14 June 1949; assigned to National Technical Laboratories.

No. 2,613,126:   Arnold O. Beckman; James D. McCullough. "Recording Apparatus for Recording Gas Concentrations in the Atmosphere." Filed 18 February 1946; issued 7 October 1952; assigned by James McCullough to Arnold O. Beckman.

No. 2,755,243:   Arnold O. Beckman; Edwin P. Arthur. "Electrochemical Electrode Structure." Filed 13 May 1952; issued 17 July 1956; assigned to Beckman Instruments, Incorporated.

No. 3,234,540:   Arnold O. Beckman. "Meter Pointer Position Monitor Means Utilizing Heat Absorbing Vane and Thermistors." Filed 6 December 1963; issued 8 February 1966; assigned to Beckman Instruments, Incorporated.

Selected Scientific Publications of Arnold O. Beckman

Arthur A. Noyes; Arnold O. Beckman. "A Periodic Table of the Structure of Atoms and Its Relation to Ion Formation and Valence." *Proceedings of the National Academy of Sciences* 13:11 (15 November 1927), 737–743.

Arnold O. Beckman. "An Improved Quartz Fiber Manometer." *Journal of the Optical Society of America* 16 (April 1928), 276–277.

Arthur A. Noyes; Arnold O. Beckman. "The Structure of Atoms as a Periodic Property and Its Relation to Valence and Ion-Formation." *Chemical Reviews* 5:2 (1928), 85–107.

Arnold O. Beckman; Roscoe G. Dickinson. "The Products of the Photochemical Decomposition of Hydrogen Azide." *Journal of the American Chemical Society* 50 (1928), 1870–1875.

Arnold O. Beckman; Roscoe G. Dickinson. "The Quantum Yield in the Photochemical Decomposition of Hydrogen Azide." *Journal of the American Chemical Society* 52 (1930), 124–132.

L. Reed Brantley; Arnold O. Beckman. "The High Temperature Equilibrium of Titanium Dioxide and Carbon with Titanium Carbide and Carbon Monoxide." *Journal of the American Chemical Society* 52 (1930), 3956–3962.

Ralph R. Wenner; Arnold O. Beckman. "The Quantum Yield in the Photochemical Decomposition of Gaseous Hydrazine." *Journal of the American Chemical Society* 54 (1932), 2787–2797.

Albert R. Myers; Arnold O. Beckman. "The Mercury-Sensitized Decomposition of Hydrogen Azide." *Journal of the American Chemical Society* 57 (1935), 89–96.

Norwood L. Simmons; Arnold O. Beckman. "The Mercury-Photosensitized Decomposition of Arsine." *Journal of the American Chemical Society* 58 (1936), 454–459.

Henry J. Welge; Arnold O. Beckman. "The Photodecomposition of Ammonia." *Journal of the American Chemical Society* 58 (1936), 2462–2467.

Howard H. Cary; Arnold O. Beckman. "A Quartz Photoelectric Spectrophotometer." *Journal of the Optical Society of America* 31 (1941), 682–689.

Arnold O. Beckman; William S. Gallaway; Wilbur I. Kaye; William F. Ulrich. "History of Spectrophotometry at Beckman Instruments, Inc." *Analytical Chemistry* 49:3 (March 1977), 280A–300A.

Note on Sources and Suggestions for Further Reading

To tell the story of Arnold Beckman's life, we have drawn on a range of source materials, including scientific articles, the historical literature, corporate documents, unpublished papers and letters, oral histories, interviews, and photographs. Some of the published sources are listed below.

Documents relating to the course of Dr. Beckman's life and career were provided by the Beckman family; to his business career, by the Heritage Center of Beckman Coulter, Inc.; to his philanthropic career, by the Arnold and Mabel Beckman Foundation; and to the history of Caltech and of Arnold Beckman's part in it, by the Institute Archives of the California Institute of Technology.

Many reference works, scientific journals, technological monographs, instrumentation catalogs, and historical studies were readily available to us, as to any researcher, in the Donald F. and Mildred Topp Othmer Library of Chemical History at the Chemical Heritage Foundation. The Sheean Library of Illinois Wesleyan University also provided services and resources, as did the Van Pelt Library of the University of Pennsylvania and the library of Penn's Department of Chemistry.

Our biography relied heavily on unpublished manuscripts, oral histories, and interviews. Primary among the oral histories were four conducted with Dr. Beckman in the 1980s as part of the Chemical Heritage Foundation's Oral History Program. Other resources were the American Chemical Society's Eminent Chemists oral histories program, oral histories in the Institute Archives of the California Institute of Technology, and a sequence of oral histories conducted with Dr. Beckman's family and close associates as part of a Beckman family history project of the California State University, Fullerton. Besides the documentary sources listed above, we had access to unpublished manuscripts by Clayton Rasmussen and by Harrison Stephens, who also supplied us with many hours of audiotaped interviews. Numerous taped interviews were also conducted by Arnold Thackray, Minor Myers, jr., and David C. Brock during the course of research for this book.

Robert Bates. *Electrometric pH Determinations.* New York: John Wiley & Sons, 1954.

Claude Baum. *The System Builders: The Story of SDC.* Santa Monica: System Development Corporation, 1981.

Arnold O. Beckman. *Beckman Instruments, Inc.* New York: Newcomen Society in North America, 1976.

Arnold O. Beckman; William S. Gallaway; Wilbur Kaye; William F. Ulrich. "History of Spectrophotometry at Beckman Instruments, Inc." *Analytical Chemistry* 49:3 (March 1977), 280A–296A.

Jeremy Bernstein. *Three Degrees above Zero: Bell Labs in the Information Age.* New York: Scribners, 1984.

Robert Bud; Deborah Jean Warner. *Instruments of Science: An Historical Encyclopedia.* New York: Garland Press, 1998.

Robert Buderi. *The Invention That Changed the World: How a Small Group of Radar Pioneers Won the Second World War and Launched a Technological Revolution.* New York: Simon & Schuster, 1996.

Ted Goertzel; Ben Goertzel. *Linus Pauling: A Life in Science and Politics.* New York: Basic Books, 1995.

Judith Goodstein. *Millikan's School: A History of the California Institute of Technology.* New York: W. W. Norton, 1991.

Julius Grant. *The Measurement of Hydrogen Ion Concentration.* London: Longmans, Green, 1930.

Clayton R. Koppes. *JPL and the American Space Program: A History of the Jet Propulsion Laboratory.* New Haven, Conn.: Yale University Press, 1982.

Keith J. Laidler. *The World of Physical Chemistry.* New York: Oxford University Press, 1993.

Roger W. Lotchin. *Fortress California 1910–1961: From Warfare to Welfare.* New York: Oxford University Press, 1992.

Carol L. Moberg, editor. *The Beckman Symposium on Biomedical Instrumentation.* New York: Rockefeller University/Fullerton, Calif: Beckman Instruments, 1986.

Michel Morange. *A History of Molecular Biology.* Translated by Matthew Cobb. Cambridge, Mass.: Harvard University Press, 1998.

Peter J. T. Morris. *The American Synthetic Rubber Research Program.* Philadelphia: University of Pennsylvania Press for the Chemical Heritage Foundation, 1989.

Richard Rhodes. *The Making of the Atomic Bomb.* New York: Simon & Schuster, 1986.

Michael Riordan; Lillian Hoddeson. *Crystal Fire: The Birth of the Information Age.* New York: W. W. Norton, 1997.

John W. Servos. *Physical Chemistry from Ostwald to Pauling: The Making of a Science in America.* Princeton, N.J.: Princeton University Press, 1990.

Herman Skolnik; Kenneth M. Reese, editors. *A Century of Chemistry: The Role of Chemists and the American Chemical Society.* Washington, D.C.: American Chemical Society, 1976.

Harrison Stephens. *Golden Past, Golden Future: The First Fifty Years of Beckman Instruments, Incorporated.* Claremont, Calif.: Claremont University, 1985.

Note on the CD-ROM

A video in CD-ROM format is attached to the page facing the inside back cover of this volume.

This video portrait allows the reader to see and hear Arnold O. Beckman talk about his early life as the son of a blacksmith, his sixty-four-year partnership with his wife Mabel, and his philosophies of research, invention, education, and philanthropy. The video is narrated by Dr. Beckman's grandson Arne Beckman, who invites you to add the senses of sight and sound to your enjoyment of *Arnold O. Beckman: One Hundred Years of Excellence.*

This state-of-the-art technology is a fitting addition to the biography of Arnold O. Beckman, noted for his application of technology to aid human endeavor.

Source materials for the video have been reproduced with permission from the following:

The Arnold and Mabel Beckman Foundation
The Arnold O. Beckman Family
Beckman Coulter, Inc.
Bell Labs of Lucent Technologies
BellSouth Intellectual Property Corporation
California Institute of Technology, Institute Archives
California Institute of Technology, Office of Public Relations
Chemical Heritage Foundation
Cullom Memorial Library
KOCE-TV, Huntington Beach, California
MIT Museum
National Aeronautics and Space Administration
National Archives and Records Administration
National Inventors Hall of Fame
"Success Story," produced by the Richfield Oil Company
University of Illinois Archives

The CD-ROM was produced by Metro Video Productions, Williamsburg, Virginia. Jeffrey I. Seeman, executive producer.

Index

Page reference for photos are in italic type.
Because of their number, pictures of Arnold O.
Beckman and Mabel Beckman are not indexed.

A

acidimeter, *See* pH meter, creation of
Adams, Howard, 19–21, 26
Adams, Roger, 46, 49, 118, *48*
air pollution. *See* Smog
Air Pollution Committee, Los Angeles
    Chamber of Commerce, 226
Air Pollution Control District, Los Angeles
    (APCD), 219, 226–227, *218*
Air Pollution Foundation, 225
air raid wardens, *187*
Alger, Horatio, 9, 16, 27, 32, 204
Amacher, Johnnie, 12
American Association for the
    Advancement of Science, 86
American Chemical Society, 48, 78, 159,
    200, 229, 346
    Beckman's presentations to, 133–134
amino acid analyzer, 267, 301
Anders, Paul, 50
Anson, Fred, *342*
Aplar, 315
Appel, Lewis, 14
Arga, 270
Argyros, George, 359, 362, 363, 365, *361,*
    362, 363
Argyros, Judie, *363*
Aries (family boat), 204, 285–286
Arnold and Mabel Beckman Center,
    Institute, *etc. See under* Beckman
    Center, Institute *etc.*
Arnold O. Beckman, Incorporated, 178,
    183, 205, *181*
Arthur H. Thomas catalog, 134–136,
    271–273
Ashton, Idaho, 37, 44–46, 74, 109, *37*
atomic bomb test, 178–179, *176, 179*
automated stat routine analyzer (ASTRA),
    304–305
Avery, Oswald, 262

B

Baer, William, 124, 126
Ball, John, *247*
Ballhaus, William, 276, 316
    as president of Beckman Instruments,
    296–297, 299–301, 305, *296, 297*

SmithKline Corporation merger and,
    305, 307–308, 324, *308*
Baltimore, David, 288
Bardeen, John, 162, 242, *238, 239*
Barger, Thomas, 19
Barnes, R. Bowling, 162, 165, 207
Barton, Robert C., 95, 123, 131, 137
Bates, Stuart J., *71*
Bausch and Lomb, 151–152
Baxter, Donald E., 291
Baxter, Warren, 155
Beckman, Arnold Orville
    Ashton, Idaho, and, 37, 44–46, 74, 109
    business enterprises of. *See individual*
    companies and divisions
    careers and occupations of, early: at Bell
      Labs, 60–61, 64–67; as chemical
      analyst, 13, 15, 21–22, 23, 26–27, 43–
      44; in childhood, 13–15; as consultant
      and expert witness, 113–119, *114,*
      117; as marine, 31–36; as professor,
      90–92, 95–98, 143. *See also* Beckman,
      Arnold O., piano playing of
    chemistry and, in childhood, 9–10, 12,
      13, 15–22. *See also* Beckman, Arnold
      O., education of
    childhood of: in Cullom, 6–10, 12–15;
      in Normal, 15–17; in Bloomington,
      18, 28
    children, adoption of, 103–104. *See also*
      Beckman, Arnold Stone; Beckman,
      Patricia
    as driver, 72–74, 87–88, 216, 220
    education of: at Caltech, 57–60, 80,
      83–87, 89–90; in Cullom, 14–15; at
      University High School, 16, 18–22,
      26–27; at University of Illinois, 38,
      40–44, 46–56
    family life of (after marriage), 80, 83,
      102–104, 106–107, 109–110, 197,
      202–205, 216, 273–275, 350–353,
      365–366
    instruments invented by. *See names of*
      individual instruments
    Meinzer (Beckman), Mabel, and: cross-
      country trip with, 72–75; engagement
      to, 56–57; marriage to, 67–69;
      meeting and dating, 33–34, 35–36. *See*
      also Beckman, Arnold O., family life
      of; Beckman, Mabel Meinzer
    mentors of, 14, 19–21, 26, 40, 41. *See*

also Beckman, Arnold O., education of
    piano playing of, 7–8, 12, 15, 19, 24–25,
      26, 36, 37–38, 44, 132
    philanthropy of. *See* philanthropy of the
      Beckmans
    philosophy of: business, 213, 255, 259,
      266, 300; instrument-making, 59,
      129–130; 153–156; 205–213,
      266–267; management, 198–200,
      232–233, 241, 246–248; political,
      292. *See also* philanthropy of the
      Beckmans
    retirements of, 296, 305, 310, 358–359
Beckman, Arnold Stone, 274, 365, *202,*
    275
    early childhood of, 104, 106–107,
      109–110, *104–111 passim, 188*
    recollection of parents by, 202–204, 275
Beckman, Arnold W. (Arne), 365, *275,*
    351, 359
Beckman, Elizabeth Ellen Jewkes, 5, 6–7,
    12, *8*
Beckman, Frederick (Fred), 8, 15, 17, 18,
    20, 22, 27, 31, 87, 347, *5, 6, 8, 19, 31*
Beckman, George W., 4–5, 6, 9, 12, 13,15–
    16, 17–18, 27, *5, 19*
Beckman, Kurt, 365, *351, 359*
Beckman, Mabel Meinzer
    and Arnold Beckman: cross-country trip
      with, 72–75; engagement to, 56–57;
      marriage to, 67–69; meeting and
      dating, 33–34, 36
    cancer of, 334
    children of, adopting, 103–104
    Corona del Mar house and, 274–275,
      274, 275, 364
    death of, 350–353
    death of mother of, 108–109
    as homemaker, 106–110, 202–234
    philanthropy of. *See* philanthropy of the
      Beckmans
    reaction to SmithKline Corporation
      merger, 309
    as trusted adviser, supporter, and confi-
      dante, 107, 197–198, 204, 318, 320,
      328, 334–335
    tuberculosis of, 105–109, 325
Beckman, (Gloria) Patricia (Pat), 196, 274,
    365, *202, 205, 233, 275, 360, 361*
    early childhood of, 104, 106–107,
      109–110, *104–111 passim, 188*

recollection of parents by, 202, 203, 204

Beckman, Roland, 17, 27, 31, 136, *5, 6, 8, 19*

Beckman, Wilma Blanche, 6, 17, 347, *5, 8, 19*

Beckman Auditorium, at Caltech, 286, 287, 289–291, 351, *278, 289*

Beckman Center for the Chemical Sciences, at the Scripps Research Institute, 356, *357*

Beckman Center for the History of Chemistry, at CHF, 346, *346*

Beckman Center for Molecular and Genetic Medicine, at Stanford University, 339, *336*

Beckman Center of the National Academies of Sciences and Engineering, at University of California, Irvine, 343–345, *344*

Beckman Coulter, Inc., 234, 309

Beckman Fellows program, at University of Illinois, 319

Beckman Foundation, 317, 324–325, 328
  Beckman's retirement from, 359–364
  redirection of after Mabel's death, 353–356

Beckman Hall, at the Lost Valley Scout Reservation, *348*

Beckman Institute, at Caltech, 339–343, 344, 345, *340, 343*

Beckman Institute for Advanced Science and Technology, at University of Illinois, 331–335, 342, *331*

Beckman Instruments, Inc., *201, 226, 234, 235, 251, 252, 253, 303*. See *also* Ballhaus, William; Beckman, Arnold O., philosophy of, business, instrument-making, *and* management; catalogs, instrument dealers'; marketing, strategies and problems; National Technical Laboratories (NTL); *and names of individual instruments*
  acquisitions and divisions of: Liston-Becker Instrument Company, 208; Statham Laboratories, 253–254; Systems Division, 253–259; Watts Manufacturing Company, 265–266. *See also* Arnold O. Beckman, Inc.; Berkeley Scientific Corporation; Helipot Corporation (Components Division); Shockley Semiconductor

Laboratories; Spinco (Specialized Instruments Corporation) Division
  financial information on, 193–194, 197, 242, 244, 269–271, 276, 297, 305, *194, 196*
  globalization and foreign subsidiaries of, 212, 232–233, 305, 315, *233*
  government contracts (projects) and, 213–214, 255–259, 298–300
  name changes of, 194–196, 234, 309
  SmithKline Corporation merger with, 305, 307–310, 324

Beckman Laboratories of Behavioral Biology, at Caltech, 287, 291, 339

Beckman Laboratory of Chemical Synthesis, at Caltech, 339–343

Beckman Laser Institute at University of California, Irvine, 328–331, *329*

Beckman Neuroscience Center, at the Cold Spring Harbor Laboratory, 349, *349*

Beckman Orchestra, 25, 132, *24, 26*

Beckman Research Awards at University of Illinois, 319

Beckman Research Institute at the City of Hope, 327. *See also* City of Hope

Beckman Scholars Program, 362

Beckman Vision Center at University of California, San Francisco, 347

Beckman Young Investigators, 357–358, 361

Beckman@Science Web site project, 358, 362–363

Beckmann, Agte Wildte, 3

Beckmann, Rolf C., 3

Bell, Alexander Graham, 62

Bell, James E., 92, *71, 87*

Bell Labs, 60–67, 68, *62. See also* Shewhart, Walter Andrew; Western Electric
  Shockley, William, and, 237, 238

Berg, Paul, 336–337, 338, 339, *338, 361*

Berkeley Scientific Corporation (Division), 197, 209, 250, 252–253, *209*

Berns, Michael, 328, 329, 330, 331, *330, 353*

BI Technologies, 175, 309

biology, and new instruments, 143, 259–260, 262–263, 265–266

biomedicine, instruments for, 266–269, 301, 305

Bishop, Jack, 214, 215, 244, 250, 255, 270, *215*

Black, Harold, 63

Blank, Julius, 242

blood urea nitrogen analyzer, 301–302, *303*

Bloomington, Illinois, *18, 21*
  Irvin Theatre in, 24–25, *23*
  move to, 17–18

Bloomington Research Laboratories, 21–22, 23, 132

Boyer, Wakefield "Fat," 36–37

Brattain, Robert, 162, 163, 164

Brattain, Walter H., 162, 242, *238, 239*

Breaker, Ronald, 357

Bregman, Michael, *196*

Bren, Donald, 345

Brode, Wallace Reed, 56

Brooklyn Navy Yard, 32 36

Brown, Audrey, 318, 333

Brown, Edmund, 292–293

Brown, Harold, 282–283, 286, 287, 344, 345, 359

Brown, Pat, 276, 288

Brown, Theodore, 318, 331, 332, 333, 335, 359, *333, 335, 361*

Bryant, Joel, 25

Bucheli, Fausto, 315, 316, *316*

Burke, Harry, 25

Burke, Paul, 25

Bush, George, *352*

Bush, Vannevar, 169, 175, *175*

C

California Chamber of Commerce, 228

California Institute of Technology (Caltech)
  Beckmans' philanthropy to, 286, 287–288, 289–291, 339–343, *278, 285*
  Arnold O. Beckman's trusteeship of, 275–276, 279, 282–287, 313–314
  history of: "DuBridge era," 280–282; early: 76–79, *75, 77*; "Millikan years": 75, 80–99, 279–280; World War II, 280. *See also* California Institute of Technology, Arnold O. Beckman's trusteeship of

Caltech. *See* California Institute of Technology

Campbell, George, 62

Carnegie, Andrew, 78

Carothers, Wallace, 49, 56, *42*

Cary, Howard H., 140, 200
    DU spectrophotometer and, 151, 152–
        153, 154, 155, 164
catalogs, instrument dealers', 10, 134–135,
    136, 271–273, *125, 134*
Center for the Study of Language and
    Information, 323
centrifuges. *See* ultracentrifuge
cermet components, 211–212, 240
Chance, Britton, 192, *167*
Chemical Heritage Foundation (CHF),
    345–347, *346*
chemistry, importance of, 38–39, 54. *See
    also* names of individual chemists
Cherniss, Ed, *269*
Chiang Kai-shek, funeral of, 315
China, exchange program with, 314–315
Chou, Pei-yuan, 314
Christensen, "Hacksaw Tom," 44, 45
chromatography, 263–266
Chrysler Corporation, 88
Church, Norman W., 119
City of Hope, 325–327, 328, 330, *326*
Clark, E. H., Jr., 308
Clevite Transistor Company, 249
Clifford, F., Jr., *247*
Coleman Instruments Corporation, 149,
    149
Compton, Arthur H., 175
computer automation, 250–258, 260
Conant, James B., 175, *175*
Conant, Karl T., *175*
control charts, 65–66
Cooper, Samuel Elias, 336
Cotton, Charles, 195
Coulter Corporation, 309
Cox, James E., 115–119
Crick, Francis, 262, 263, 300
Cullom, Illinois, 3, 5–6, 16, *4, 7, 14*
    Beckman's life in, 6–10, 12–15

D

Darrow, Karl, 63
data processing system, Model III, *199*
Davidson, Eric, 341
Davisson, Clinton, 63
Dee, Robert, 307, 308
De Forest, Lee, 62, 100, 101–102, 113,
    238, *102, 240*
De Forest, Marie Mosquini, 102, *102, 240*

Delta Upsilon Fraternity, 55, *55*
Deming, W. Edwards, 61
Dervan, Peter, 341, *342*
Deukmejian, George, 343
Dickinson, Roscoe Gilkey, 59, 82–84, 85,
    86, 89, 91, 93–94, 95, 99, *71, 82, 91*
Dietrichson, Gerhard, 52
discrete sample analyzer (DSA), 302–304
Dodge, Harold F., 66
Dornaus, Arthur (dance band leader), 25
Dorrance, Jacqueline, 360–361, *361*
dosimeter, 177–178, 186
Dozier, Richard, *269*
DU spectrophotometer, 148, 151–159,
    160, 161, 186, *152, 157, 192*
    innovations due to use of, 156–159
    as model for other instruments, 163–164
    models of: early, 152–155; Model B
        (1949), 207–208, *206*
Dubbs, Carbon Petroleum, 115
DuBridge, Doris, *283*
DuBridge, Lee, 169, 225, 280–281, 282,
    286, 291, *167, 283*
Duncan, Donald, *198, 208*
Duryea, Leslie, 249
du Vigneaud, Vincent, 56
Dyson, Freeman, 113

E

Earl, O. K., 102
EASE analog computer, 252, 256, *252*
Edison, Thomas, 61
Edman, Pehr, 267–268
Ehrman, Frederick L., 197, *196*
Einstein, Albert, 59, 81, *60*
El Salvador, 315–317
Elder, Albert, 56
electrochemistry, 52, 53, *53*
electrolysis, ionic theory, and pH, 53
electrophoresis, 262, *263*
electronics, *212. See also* Bell Labs; Helipot
Ellis, James H., *71*
EPUT (events per unit time) technology,
    209
Everhart, Thomas, *343*

F

Fairchild, Sherman, 313
Fairchild Semiconductor, 248–249, 250
Federal Air Quality Board, 228
film-coating machine, 100, 101, *100, 101*

Fletcher, Taylor, *215*
Ford, Gerald, 315
Fourteen Weeks in Chemistry (by Joel
    Dorman Steele), 9–12, 40, 150, *11,
    150*
Fracker, Henry, 88, 123, 124, 131, 137
Frary, Francis C., 51
Frederick P. Beckman Lecture Room, 347
Funk, Eugene D., Jr., 25
Funston, Keith, *196*

G

Gafford, Bob, *299*
Gallman, Herb, 270
Gallwas, Jerry, 317, 320, 325, 353, 355, 359,
    353, 360, 361
Gallwas, Sandy, *353*
galvanometers, 126, 128, 129
gas chromatography, 263–266, *265*
Gates Laboratory, 75, 79, 80, 84, 96
Gemini project, 256–257, *258, 298*
Germer, Lester, 63
glassblowing, 50, 51, 85, 96–98, 183–184,
    51, 97
    course by Beckman in, 96–98
glucose analyzer, 301–302, 304, *303*
Goforth, George (dance band leader), 25
Goldberger, Marvin, 344
Goodstein, Judith, 280
Gould, William R., *308*
Gray, Harry, 328, 339, 340, 341, 342, 343,
    359, *343, 361*
Grey, Bill, *263*
Grinch, Victor, 242
Groves, Leslie, 175
Guilarte, Jane, 325, 328

H

Haagen-Smit, Arie J., 222, 223–224, 225
Hale, George Ellery, 75, 77, 79, 80, 90,
    151, *80*
Hanafin, Maurice, 247, 259, 260
Harrison, H. G., 63
Hawes, Roland, 200
Helipot (potentiometer), 171–175, 186,
    208, 210–212, 256, 300, *146, 171,
    172, 173*
Helipot Corporation (Components
    Division), 174–175, 208, 211–213,
    256, 300, *208, 210, 211*
Henson, Fred, 97, 123, 131, 132

Herald, Earl, *260*

Herbert, Gavin, 307, 361, *353*

Hertz, Heinrich, 168–169

Hewlett, William, 243, *243*

Hincke, Bill, 58, *58, 68*

Hill, Dora, *208*

Hoerni, Jean, 242

Homberger, Alfred W., 41, *41*

Hood, Leroy, 341, 342

Huff, Willard, 195

Hunt, Gary, 359

hydrazine, 83–84, 94

hydrogen azide, 84, 85, 93–94

I

Ikenberry, Stanley, 328, 332, 334–335

Illinois Chemist, 54–57, 124, *54*

Illinois Wesleyan University, 345, 347, *347*

infrared spectrophotometry, 159–166, 186
 NTL IR spectrophotometers, 163–166,
 166

Instrument Society of America, 253

inventions, Arnold O. Beckman's early:
 inking, 120–122, *113, 120, 121;*
 manometer, 85, 96, *85;* proposed, 89–
 90, 143, *88*

ion-exchange chromatography, 262

Irvin Theatre, 23, 24–25

Itakura, Keichi, 326

Ives, Herbert, 63

J

James, A. T., 264

Jergins Oil, 122, 132, 197

Jewell, Hector W., 121

Jewett, Frank Baldwin, 63, 71, 79, *63*

Jewkes, Charles, 14, 15, 72, 319

Jewkes, Elizabeth Ellen (Beckman,
 Elizabeth Ellen Jewkes), 5, 6–7, 12, *8*

Jewkes, John, *5*

Jewkes, Mary, *5*

Jobs, Stephen, 337

Johnson, Lyndon Baines, *297*

Johnson, Seeley, 55

Jonas, Jiri, 335

Joseph, Glen, 54, 124–126, 128, 129, 134,
 147, 160, 211

Journal of the American Chemical Society, 85,
 94

Journal of the Optical Society of America, 85

K

Kayser, Chuck, *298*

Kennedy, Donald, 337, 338, *338*

Keystone Steel and Iron Company, 26–27

Khrushchev, Nikita, 230, 231, 232, *231*

Kingdon, Erve, 12

Kingdon, George, 12

Kingdon, Gertrude, 12

Kirk, John, *366*

Kissinger, Henry, *314*

Kleiner, Gene, 242

Kline, Mahlon H., 306

Knight, Goodwin J., 225

Knott, Walter, 294

Korn, Dean David, 339

Kornberg, Arthur, 338

Kovach, John S., 327

L

labor relations, 198–200, 232–233

Lacy, William, 98, 101

Lady Pat (boat), 204, 239, *205*

Lange, Hattie, 12

Last, Jay, 242

Lavoisier, Antoine, 155

Lawrence, Ernest O., 169, *175*

Leiserwitzes' general store, 13

Lewis, Gilbert N., 49, *87*

Lewis, Joseph, 183, 218, 246, 272, 285,
 286, *269*

Lincoln Club, 279, 288, 292–295, 314

liquid-crystal displays, 300, *301*

Liston, Max, 208

Liston-Becker Instrument Company, 208,
 271, *207*

Loomis, Alfred, *175*

Los Angeles Chamber of Commerce, 225,
 227, 229–232. *See also* smog

Lucas, Howard, *71*

lunar surface analyzer, 256

Lyon, Leonard, 114, 115–116, 117, 122

Lyons, I. H. "Buzz," 119

M

Mabel and Arnold Beckman Laboratories
 of Behavioral Biology, 287, 291, 339

Madsen, Hal, *304*

Mahan, Michael J., 358

Maiman, Theodore, 328–329

Manhattan Project, 175–179

Manning, Jerry, 44–45, 74–75

Manning, Togo, 44–45, 74–75, *45*

manometer, 85, 96, *85*

Marines, U.S., 31–36

marketing, strategies and problems,
 134–135, 165, 192, 260, 262, 271–
 273, *273. See also* Beckman, Arnold
 O., philosophy of, business

Martin, A. C., 342

Martin, Archer J. P., 264

Marvel, Carl (Speed), 40–44, 46, 49, *42*

mass spectrometers, 214–215

Massachusetts Institute of Technology, 55,
 57, 78, 166–167, 169, 176, 280, 323

Maxfield, J. P., 63

Maxwell, James Clerk, 168

McCabe, Louis C., 220–221, 222

McCarthy, Joseph, 282

McDonald, Dennis, 315, 316, *316*

McWilliams, Carey, 217

Mead, Carver, 342, 348

Meinzer, Alice Stone, 36, 72, 108–109,
 110, *57*

Meinzer, Charles, 35, *68*

Meinzer, Mabel. *See* Beckman, Mabel
 Meinzer

Meinzer, Walter, 35, *68*

Merrifield, Bruce, 155

metallography, 20–22, 23, 26

Mettler, Ruben, 343

Meyers, Albert E., 92

Michelson, Albert A., 63, 79

micro-microammeter, 175, 176–177, *177*

Millikan, Robert Andrews, *60, 197*
 Caltech and, 58–59, 71, 75, 79, 80, 90,
 279–280
 connections to outside agencies of, 63,
 100–101, 113, 130

Millikin, Trent, 25

Minneapolis-Honeywell Regulator
 Company, 195–196

MIT. *See* Massachusetts Institute of
 Technology

mobile air quality laboratory, *218, 221*

Moore, Gordon, 242, 246, 249

Moore, Jim, *361*

Moore, Stanford, 266, 267, *266*

Moore-Stein amino acid analyzer, 262

Morisette, Guy, 12

Morphy, Mike, *317*

Mosquini, Marie. *See* De Forest, Marie Mosquini
Munzer, R. J., 337, 339, *308*
Murdock, John J., 123, 132, 195, 196
Murphy, Steve, 164

N

Nabenhauer, Fred P., 306
NASA. *See* Gemini project
National Bureau of Standards, 156
National Defense Research Committee (NDRC), 169, 180
National Inking Appliance Company, 122–123, 131–132, *123*
National Postal Meter, 119–124, 132
National Technical Laboratories (NTL), 131–144, 163, 165, *140, 143, 144, 148. See also* DU spectrophotometer, infrared spectrophotometer, micro-microammeter
  birth of, 131–132
  board of directors' attitude to war demands, 172–173; 182–183
  buildings for, 135–136, 147–148, 191, *136*
  expansion of, 191–194
  control of by Beckman, 195–197
  name changes, 131–132, 196
Nesbit, Richard, 255, 256, 299, 304, 305, *256*
new biology and new instruments, 259–260, 262–263, 265–266
Newcomen Society, 302
Newport Harbor Yacht Club, 204
Nies, Todd, 60–61
Nixon, Richard M., 228, 230, 231, 232, 288, 292–295, 314, *231, 293*
Normal, Illinois, 15–17, *15*
  University High School in, 16, 18–20, 25, 26, 27, *16*
Norman Bridge Laboratory, 75, 80
Noyce, Robert, 242, 249
Noyes, Arthur Amos, 71, 78–79, 81, 82, 83, 91, *79, 87*
  Caltech chemistry department and, 98, 100, 101
  as member of triumvirate, 75, 79, 80, 90
Noyes, William Albert, 46, 48–49, *46*
NTL. *See* National Technical Laboratories

O

Office of Rubber Reserve, 161–163, 166

Office of Scientific Research and Development (OSRD), 175
Oppenheimer, Robert J., 282
Ostwald, Wilhelm, 78
Othmer, Donald, 346–347
oxidant recorders, 224
oxygen analyzers, 180–186, *183, 185*

P

Packard, David, 243, 330, 343, *243*
Parr, Samuel W., 46, 47, 49, 54
Parr calorimeter, 46, 47, *47*
Partenheimer, Frances, *68*
Pasadena, brief history of, 76, *75, 76. See also* California Institute of Technology
Patterson, Ed., Jr., 134–135, 136, 137, 154, 273
Pauling, Linus, 82, 99, 101, 180, 181, 282, 283, *91, 99*
Pauling oxygen analyzer, 180–184, *180, 182*
Pavleitch, Nikola P., 358
Peck's Bad Boy, 9, 204, *9*
penicillin, 157–158, 159, *158, 159*
Pepper, Hal, *304*
periodic table, 86–87, *86*
pH, measuring, 124–131, 140–141. *See also* pH meter
pH meter, 147, 154, 174, 182, 272, 300, *137, 138, 139, 191, 193, 206, 341*
  core technology at NTL/Beckman Instruments, 186, 191, 218, 259, 266–267, 301
  creation of, 126, 129–131, *127, 130, 133*
  DU spectrophotometer, used in, 151, 153
  as model for or source of other instruments, 138–139, 153, 163–164, 176–177, 205, 208, 211, 213, 265
  name of, 131, 136
  parts used elsewhere, 141, 166, 170–172, 265. *See also* Helipot
  producing, 135–136, 137–141
Phelps, Gray, 204
philanthropy of the Beckmans, 313–367. *See also* Beckman Foundation
  Beckman Auditorium, at Caltech, 278, 286, 287, 289–291, 351
  Beckman Center for Molecular and Genetic Medicine, at Stanford, 339
  Beckman Center of the National

Academies of Sciences and Engineering, at Irvine, 343–345
  Beckman Institute, at Caltech, 339–343
  Beckman Institute for Advanced Science and Technology, at University of Illinois, 331–335, 342
  Beckman Laser Institute, at Irvine, 328–331
  City of Hope, 325–327, 328, 330
  smaller gifts, 319–320, 345–349, 356–364
  strategies and models for, 286–287, 317–320, 321–323, 327–328, 353–355
photochemistry, 82, 83–84, 91, 92–95, *83, 93, 94*
Pickels, Edward, 259, 260, 267, *260*
potentiometers, 138. *See also* Helipot
Pottenger, Francis, Jr., 106
Pottenger, Francis Marion, 106, 325
Pottenger Sanatorium, 105–106, 109, 325
Poulson, C. Norris, 229
Pringle, Ralph, 19
process control systems, *254*
protein-peptide synthesizer, 268, 301
protein sequencer, 268, 301
Pupin, Michael, 62

Q

quality control, at Bell Labs, 61, 64–66

R

Rabi, I. I., 169, 178, *167*
radar development, 168–169, *168, 169, 170*
Radiation Laboratory at MIT, 166–167, 169–170, 172, 175, *167*
Rains, Arnold, 270
Ramsey, Dwight, 25
RAND Corporation, 321, 323, 324
Rasmussen, Clayton, 163, 198–199, *198, 199*
Rassweiler, Clifford N., 56
Reagan, Ronald, 294, *295*
Remsen, Ira, 46
Research Technology Initiative, 363–364
RF gas analyzer, 215–216, 217, *217*
Riggs, Art, 326
Roberts, Sheldon, 242, 245
Rodebush, Worth Huff, 49–50, *48*
Romero, Carlos Humberto, 315, 316
Roosevelt, Franklin Delano, 161
Rosenberg, Paul, 166–167, 170, 171, 172

Rosenberry, W. K., 209
Rosso, Lou, 304, 309
rubber, synthetic, 160–163, *160, 161, 162.*
    See also infrared spectrophotometry
Ruckelshaus, William D., *281*

S

Salk, Jonas, 260
Sargents, Herb, 184
Scripps, Ellen Browning, 317
Scripps Clinic and Research Foundation,
    317–318
Seaquist, Ellyn, 351–352, *275*
Sharp Laboratories, 268
Shepard, Alan, *258*
Shewhart, Walter Andrew, 61, 64–66, 156,
    61
Shields, Donald, 314, 359, *361*
Shockley, William, 100, 162, 237–242, 259,
    261, 271, *237, 239, 244*
    problems with, 244–250
Shockley Semiconductor Laboratories,
    241–242, 244–250, 259, 270, *248*
Silicon Valley, 242, 248, 249, 250
Smith, David, F., 87
Smith, G. Frederick, 50, 134, *50*
Smith, George, 306
Smith, John K., 306
Smith, Russell, *308*
SmithKline Corporation, 305, 306, 307–
    310, 324, *306, 307, 324*
smog, 217–219, 220–228
Sommerfeld, Arnold, 59
Sorensen, Royal, 176
Sørensen, Søren P. L., 125
Soviet Union (U.S.S.R.), 229, 230–232
Spackman, Darrel, 267
Special Committee on Air Pollution,
    California, 225
spectrometer, mass, 214–215, *215*
spectrophotometer, 149–150, *154, 192,*
    206. See also DU spectrophotometer;
    infrared spectrophotometer
Spinco (Specialized Instruments
    Corporation) Division, 242, 247, 259,
    260, 262, 266, 267, 301, *262, 301*
Sprechel, Max, *269*
Stanford Industrial Park, 242, 243, 246. *See*
    also Silicon Valley
Stanford University, 241, 242, 243, 323,
    336–339

Stanley, Lowell, *308*
STAT Lab (instrument), 302
Statham Laboratories, 253–254
Steele, Joel Dorman, 11
Stein, Herman, 104
Stein, Lettie, 104
Stein, William H., 267, *266*
Steinmeyer, Robert, 315–316, *316*
Sternberg, James, 301–302, *303*
Stevens, Frederica, 4
Stevenson, Adlai, 231
Stone, Clara, 325
Stone, Edward Durrell, 290–291, 336
strain gauge recorder, two-hundred-
    channel, 255
Strauss, Donald, 360
Stravinsky, Igor, 291
Sturdivant, Holmes, 180
Svedberg, Theodor, 261
Swanstrum, Fred, 37–38
Swift, Ernest, 135
Synge, Richard L.M., 264
System Development Corporation (SDC),
    321–323, *321, 322*
System Development Foundation,
    321–324

T

Tang, Jean, *342*
Teeter, Howard, 303–304, *323*
Terman, Frederick, 242, 243, *243, 247*
thermocouples, 94
thermodynamics, 50, 52
Thomas, Lou, 25
Throop, Amos Gager, 76, *76*
Throop Institute. *See* California Institute
    of Technology
Todd, Charlie, 326–327
Tolman, Richard Chace, 57, 59, 80, 81, 83,
    90, 91, *81*
transistorized data processor, Model 210,
    257
Tretolite Company, 114
triumvirate (Caltech), 75, 79, 80, 90, *79*
Trudeau, Edward, 105

U

ultracentrifuge, 259–263, 264, 266, 268,
    261, 263
ultraviolet spectrophotometer. *See* DU
    spectrophotometer
Union Gas and Electric, 21, 22

unions, 232–233
University High School, 16, 18–20, 25, 26,
    27, *16*
University of Illinois, 20–21, 38, 56, *38, 56.*
    See also Beckman, A. O., education of
    Beckman philanthropy to, 318–319,
    331–335, 342, *331*
U.S. News, 228–229
U.S.S.R. (Soviet Union), 229, 230–232

V

vacuum-tube amplifier, 126, 128–129, *128*
Van Alstyne, Toby, 25, 28
Vidler, Jayce, *270*
Viking project, *299*
Volwiler, Ernest, 49

W

Walrath, Florence Dahl, 103
Warren, Earl, 117, 118, 119, 219, *118*
Watson, James D., 262, 263, 300, 349
Watt, Robert Alexander Watson, 169
Watts Manufacturing Company, 265, 266
Wendt, Henry, 308, *307*
Wenner, Ralph R., 91–92, 94
Wescomb, Gary, *361*
Western Electric, 60–61, 62–63, 79. *See*
    also Bell Laboratories
Westoff, Lucky, 25
White, Frank, 12, 13, 14, 50
White, T. A., 50, 52, 53, 55
Willard, Hobart, 134
Wolf, Joe, 139
Wright, Norman, 159–161

X

Xerox, 323
X-ray crystallography, 80, 82
X-ray diffraction, 99

Z

Zaffaroni, Alejandro, 337
Zarem, Abe, 223